Westward Bound

PATRONS OF THE OSGOODE SOCIETY

Blake, Cassels & Graydon LLP
Gowlings
Lax O'Sullivan Scott Lisus LLP
McCarthy Tétrault LLP
Osler, Hoskin & Harcourt LLP
Paliare Roland Rosenberg Rothstein LLP
Torkin Manes LLP
Torys LLP
WeirFoulds LLP

The Osgoode Society is supported by a grant from
The Law Foundation of Ontario.

THE LAW
FOUNDATION
OF ONTARIO

The Society also thanks the Law Society of Upper Canada
for its continuing support.

LAW AND SOCIETY SERIES
W. Wesley Pue, General Editor

LAW AND
SOCIETY

The Law and Society Series explores law as a socially embedded
phenomenon. It is premised on the understanding that the
conventional division of law from society creates false dichotomies
in thinking, scholarship, educational practice, and social life.
Books in the series treat law and society as mutually constitutive
and seek to bridge scholarship emerging from interdisciplinary
engagement of law with disciplines such as politics, social theory,
history, political economy, and gender studies.

A list of titles in the series appears at the end of the book.

Westward Bound

Sex, Violence, the Law, and the Making of a Settler Society

LESLEY ERICKSON

PUBLISHED BY UBC PRESS FOR
THE OSGOODE SOCIETY
FOR CANADIAN LEGAL HISTORY

UBC Press • Vancouver • Toronto

20 19 18 17 16 15 14 13 12 11   5 4 3 2 1

Printed in Canada on paper that is processed chlorine- and acid-free, with vegetable-based inks.

Library and Archives Canada Cataloguing in Publication

Erickson, Lesley, 1971-
    Westward bound : sex, violence, the law, and the making of a settler society / Lesley Erickson.

(Law & society series, 1496-4953)
Includes bibliographical references and index.
Also issued in electronic format.
ISBN 978-0-7748-1858-2

    1. Criminal justice, Administration of – Canada, Western – History. 2. Sex discrimination in criminal justice administration – Canada, Western – History. 3. Women – Crimes against – Canada, Western – History. 4. Female offenders – Canada, Western – History. 5. Criminal law – Social aspects – Canada, Western. I. Title. II. Series: Law and society series (Vancouver, B.C.)

| HV9960.C2E75 2011 | 364.082'09712 | C2011-903598-7 |

Canadä

UBC Press gratefully acknowledges the financial support for our publishing program of the Government of Canada (through the Canada Book Fund), the Canada Council for the Arts, and the British Columbia Arts Council.

This book has been published with the help of a grant from the Canadian Federation for the Humanities and Social Sciences, through the Aid to Scholarly Publications Program, using funds provided by the Social Sciences and Humanities Research Council of Canada.

Printed and bound in Canada by Friesens
Set in Garamond by Artegraphica Design Co. Ltd.
Copy editor: Audrey McClellan
Proofreader: Jenna Newman
Indexer: Patricia Buchanan

UBC Press
The University of British Columbia
2029 West Mall
Vancouver, BC V6T 1Z2
www.ubcpress.ca

HISTORIANS
ARE THE QUINTESSENTIAL VOYEURS,
NOSES PRESSED
TO TIME'S GLASS WINDOW.

– Margaret Atwood, *The Robber Bride*

Contents

Contents

viii   Contents

Figures and Tables

Tables

Foreword

The Osgoode Society for Canadian Legal History

The history of crime and punishment is one of the principal lenses through which historians of the law investigate the relationship between the law in the books and the law in action, and the uses of law to regulate relations among social groups. Lesley Erickson's account of the operation of the criminal law in the prairie West in the late nineteenth and first half of the twentieth centuries performs both tasks admirably. Using local court records and a rich variety of other sources, Erickson examines the use of the law on reserves, in the cities, and in the countryside, from high-profile cases to day-to-day policing and punishment practices. This is an invaluable addition to the Osgoode Society's socio-legal history collection by a young historian who we hope to publish again in the future.

The purpose of the Osgoode Society for Canadian Legal History is to encourage research and writing in the history of Canadian law. The Society, which was incorporated in 1979 and is registered as a charity, was founded at the initiative of the Honourable R. Roy McMurtry, formerly attorney general for Ontario and chief justice of the province, and officials of the Law Society of Upper Canada. The Society seeks to stimulate the study of legal history in Canada by supporting researchers, collecting oral histories, and publishing volumes that contribute to legal-historical scholarship in Canada. It has published 84 books on the courts, the judiciary, and the legal profession, as well as on the history of crime and punishment, women and law, law and economy, the legal treatment of ethnic minorities, and famous cases and significant trials in all areas of the law.

Current directors of the Osgoode Society for Canadian Legal History
are Robert Armstrong, Christopher Bentley, Kenneth Binks, Patrick Brode,
Brian Bucknall, David Chernos, Kirby Chown, J. Douglas Ewart, Martin
Friedland, John Honsberger, Horace Krever, C. Ian Kyer, Virginia MacLean,
Patricia McMahon, Roy McMurtry, Laurie Pawlitza, Jim Phillips, Paul
Reinhardt, Joel Richler, William Ross, Paul Schabas, Robert Sharpe, James
Spence, Richard Tinsley, and Michael Tulloch.

The annual report and information about membership may be obtained
by writing to the Osgoode Society for Canadian Legal History, Osgoode
Hall, 130 Queen Street West, Toronto, Ontario, M5H 2N6. Telephone:
416-947-3321. E-mail: mmacfarl@lsuc.on.ca. Website: http://www.osgoode
society.ca.

R. Roy McMurtry
President

Jim Phillips
Editor-in-Chief

Acknowledgments

Researching and writing a book is often a long and, by necessity, lonely process. Yet many institutions and people come together to produce the final product. This book began in the mid-1990s as a study of women and crime in western Canada, and it took on new layers of meaning as time passed. I have many people to thank for that. Louis Knafla, Sarah Carter, and Constance Backhouse have been an inspiration, not only in the encouragement they have shown for this book and my work in general but also in the care and enthusiasm they bring to their own scholarship and writing. Special thanks are also due to Warren Elofson, Chris Levy, Veronica Strong-Boag, Erin Van Brunschott, Kerry Abel, and the anonymous peer reviewers for their thoughtful comments and suggestions.

In addition to receiving financial assistance and support from the Department of History at the University of Calgary, I was fortunate to receive doctoral and postdoctoral grants from the Social Sciences and Humanities Research Council of Canada that allowed me to concentrate on research and writing at the University of Calgary and at McMaster University. I'd like to thank John Weaver and David Wright for making my time in Hamilton truly enjoyable. The research for this book also owes much to the expertise of the knowledgeable staffs at Library and Archives Canada, the Glenbow Archives, and the Provincial Archives of Manitoba, Saskatchewan, and Alberta, who responded to my requests for information sometimes with puzzlement but always with enthusiasm.

Throughout the publishing process, I have had the good fortune to work with an excellent group of editors. Randy Schmidt at UBC Press was instrumental in shepherding the manuscript through the peer review process and finding a home for it in the Law and Society series and with the Osgoode Society for Canadian Legal History. I am also indebted to Wes Pue and Jim Phillips, editors of each series, for their support, and to Ann Macklem, project editor, for her expert editorial suggestions and eagle eye. Ann brought together a crack team to produce the best book possible. Thanks to Audrey McClellan, copy editor, for her careful eye and for pointing out infelicities in logic or language in the kindest way possible; Mauve Page, for designing the cover; Eric Leinberger for producing the maps; Irma Rodriguez, for typesetting; Jenna Newman, for proofreading; and Patricia Buchanan, for preparing the index.

Finally, this book would not have been possible without friends and family. My grandmother, Anna Kristina Erickson, drove home the importance of getting an education and fostered in me a true love of learning – perhaps I took the lessons a little too much to heart. My parents, Lynne and Gary Erickson, and my brother, Neil, have always encouraged my long-term interest in Canadian and legal history, while my partner, Roland Longpré, has provided invaluable moral support, taking the time over the years to read manuscripts, attend conferences, and listen to papers and lectures – tasks truly not in the job description. I dedicate this book to him.

Introduction

In 1997, investigations into the murder of Pamela George, a Saulteaux
woman of the Sakimay Reserve in southern Saskatchewan, culminated
in a trial before the Regina Court of Queen's Bench that provoked
debates about the nature of violence in the prairie West and the function
of law and legal institutions in Canada. The controversy began on 30
January, when Justice Ted Malone sentenced two university students,
Steven Tyler Kummerfield and Alexander Dennis Ternowesky, to six and
a half years in prison for a killing he described as cruel, cowardly, and
despicable.[1] On the evening of 18 April 1995, the two men – journalists
called them white, middle-class southenders – had cruised the inner-city
streets of Regina in search of a prostitute. After repeated rejections,
Ternowesky hid in the trunk, and Kummerfield persuaded George to get
into the car. The next morning a motorist discovered George's battered
body lying facedown in a ditch near the airport on the city's western
margins. According to the Crown's forensic pathologist, George died from
a blow from a blunt instrument. During the trial, which lasted for six
weeks, the accused claimed that George had performed oral sex on
Kummerfield and was in the process of doing the same to Ternowesky
when something went wrong. Kummerfield pulled George from the car
and began to beat her. Ternowesky joined in. The accused claimed that
George was screaming, but alive, when they drove away. The pair never
explained why they beat George, but Crown prosecutor Matt Miazga offered the victim's race, gender, and occupation as motivating factors. In
his opinion, George's death constituted first-degree murder because the

defendants had sexually assaulted and forcibly confined the victim. Justice Malone galvanized public controversy, however, when he charged the jury to remember that George was indeed a prostitute as they deliberated on the issue of murder.[2] The jury found Kummerfield and Ternowesky guilty only of manslaughter on the grounds that the defendants' drunkenness mitigated their intent.

The Pamela George case provoked discussions about inequalities in prairie society and exposés on discrimination in Canada's criminal justice system. Kripa Sekhar, Saskatchewan's representative to the National Action Committee on the Status of Women, argued that Malone's charge dehumanized women who worked the streets and trivialized the murder. Aboriginal people, supported by the Saskatchewan Coalition against Racism, denounced the case as a miscarriage of justice and charged that there were two systems of law in prairie Canada: one for whites and another for Aboriginal people. Academic Ron Bourgeault argued that the case reflected disparities and discrimination that lurked beneath the surface of prairie communities, while sociologist Sherene Razack argued that the trial outcome showed how violence and justice systems have helped to build and reproduce social boundaries and hierarchies of difference in settler societies.[3] Within the local community, people debated the case, took sides, and tried to determine what it said about them.

Pamela George's body was found on a field near where I used to live, where the neighbourhood kids and I used to play. I was drawn to the case because of my connection to the place and because of my long-term interest in the history of women in the Canadian and American Wests, particularly the idea – developed by Peggy Pascoe, an advocate of the new Western history – that a more inclusive history of the North American West, one that surmounted the colonialist and paternalistic assumptions that underlay the idea of the frontier, could be written if we focused on women who stood at its cultural crossroads.[4] In other words, the Pamela George case gave me the original premise or inspiration for this book. It suggested the fruitfulness of focusing on criminal cases that involved women – as either victims or perpetrators – to open a door into the lives of women who lacked the time, desire, or ability to leave behind written accounts of their thoughts, experiences, and dreams. Although the history of the American West continues to evoke images of prostitutes, saloons, and gunslingers, the settlement of the Canadian Prairies is dominated by the equally sensational story of the Mountie and the mild West he allegedly produced. But surely the arrival and accommodation of over 1.5 million European and American immigrants had been accompanied by conflict and strife, by social dislocation and crime? Surely the criminal courts of the past – which served as local centres of law and government but also as cultural hubs and social gathering places – had been the scene for sensational trials such as the Pamela George case, cases that constitute what Natalie Zemon Davis, a pioneer in the use of non-traditional sources such as legal records to explore the past, calls telling events that speak beyond themselves?[5] What could these cases, if their records still existed, tell me about the lives of women in the past; their treatment by police, judges, and juries; and how race, class, and gender shaped their treatment by the courts?

Historians at that time, in the mid- to late 1990s, in Canada and abroad, were approaching the history of women, crime, and the law either from the perspective of women who had been accused of crime – for instance, prostitution, theft, abortion, infanticide, or murder – or from the perspective of women and girls who had been the victims of rape, assault and domestic violence, or what was then known as the crime of seduction. Some focused on sensational trials; others documented day-to-day interactions between women and the courts. Regardless of the approach, the stories that emerged from the courts' archives illuminated aspects of the past, such as power relationships in the family or among groups, that had previously eluded the grasp of historians. These studies traced how legislators, judges, and all-male juries had held men and women to different sexual standards and punished victims of rape or seduction for transgressing prohibitions of female desire. They showed how some women offenders, in turn, had manipulated notions of a passive, submissive womanhood in their favour to avoid punishment. The lenient treatment these women received, however, was often no more than paternalism in disguise. And historians demonstrated that battered wives' appeals for justice belied the ideal of companionate marriage that had begun to take shape in Western society in the early twentieth century and that early historians had taken for granted.[6] Although they varied in approach, these studies offered important insights into the present-day treatment of women in the criminal justice system and a fresh perspective on issues such as abortion.

Given the fruitfulness of these approaches – qualitative case studies or quantitative case file analyses; focusing on victims or focusing on perpetrators – I wanted to harness them to explore prairie women's engagements with the criminal justice system not only during the settlement period but also during the interwar years, an under-examined period in history. I was particularly intrigued that the accounts of abused prairie women in historian Terry Chapman's pioneering studies of wife battery and sex crimes contradicted popular or frontier-inspired depictions of prairie Canada (or, as its boosters had raved, "the Last, Best West") as an environment that had offered single gentlewomen a flannel shirt and liberty, prostitutes a happy hunting ground, and married women a pioneering partnership with men. A spirit of frontier egalitarianism, some proponents of this view argued, had produced a society open to innovations such as votes for women and the first female magistrates in the British Empire.[7] No doubt some women experienced new freedoms after immigrating to the New World. But Canada's prairie West – what would become the provinces of Manitoba, Saskatchewan, and Alberta – was settled during a period of rapid and profound economic, social, and political change. Between 1886 and 1940, the outside dates of this study, Aboriginal women encountered European and Canadian settlers and their institutions, including the law, in a sustained way; immigrant women built farms and homes alongside their husbands and children; middle-class women fought a successful suffrage campaign; and women of all ages, races, classes, and ethnic backgrounds experienced urbanization, the First World War, and the Depression. I wanted to develop a criminal case file sample that would capture how women in all of their diversity experienced these changes.

Doug Owram, a prominent Canadian intellectual historian, has commented that the case file method poses particular challenges because historians must make choices to deal with too many rather than too few sources.[8] This was particularly true given that I wanted to explore more than five decades of women's engagement with the law, at all levels of the criminal justice system, via a case file sample that would also reflect the region's geographical, economic, and cultural diversity. I discovered that cases involving women as victims or perpetrators accounted for approximately 10 percent of the courts' caseloads in the region during these decades. Murder or child murder cases that resulted in conviction and the death penalty posed no problem because those that involved women as either victims or perpetrators were fairly uncommon: they happened approximately once a year throughout the region as a whole, for a total of fifty-one cases.[9] The extensive yet erratic nature of the provincial archives' collections made it more difficult to create a representative sample of indictable and summary offences, however. The superior court records for the three prairie provinces (formerly Manitoba and the North-West Territories) are filed according to judicial district, the names and boundaries of which were subject to change over time. I decided to focus on five districts (see Figures 1 and 2). Because criminal case files for all judicial

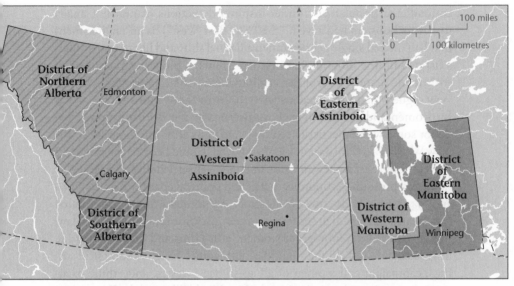

FigURE 1 Judicial districts: Manitoba and North-West Territories, 1889-1907. |
Map of judicial districts, Department of the Interior, RG 15, Series D-11-1, vol. 549, Reel T-13803,
f. 161696, Library and Archives Canada; H7 614.2, fb 1884, Provincial Archives of Manitoba.

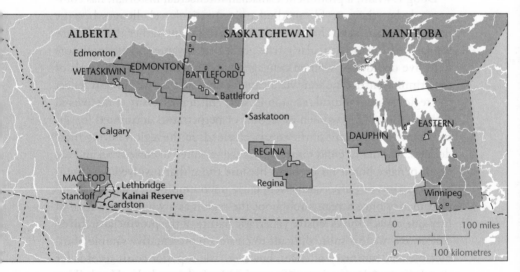

FigURE 2 Selected judicial districts: Manitoba, Saskatchewan, and Alberta, 1917. |
Department of the Interior, Map of Land Registration and Judicial Districts, 1917, Glenbow
Archives.

districts in Manitoba and Alberta have been processed, I chose the judicial districts of Winnipeg (formerly Eastern Manitoba); Dauphin, Manitoba; Macleod (formerly Southern Alberta); and Edmonton-Wetaskiwin (formerly Northern Alberta) because they encompass certain urban, rural, immigrant, and Aboriginal populations.[10] In addition, these judicial districts included regional economies – wheat- and mixed-farming districts in the plains and parkland, and ranching and mining communities in southern Alberta – that might have influenced local attitudes toward crime. In Saskatchewan, I limited the analysis to the records of the Regina Judicial District (formerly Western Assiniboia) because they remain the only processed series of criminal case files in the province's collection. The remainder of the criminal court records are accessible to researchers, but a flood damaged or destroyed many series. In some cases, I consulted the criminal registers for these judicial districts to engage in comparative analysis.

Judges and juries in the superior courts of the selected districts in this period heard 202 cases with women offenders and 624 cases with women victims. Many of the cases that involved women were not heard in the superior courts, however, but in the intermediary (county or district) and summary courts. To overcome a potential bias in favour of certain types of cases and offenders, I also consulted records from these lower courts if they were available, but I learned that the lower the court's position in the legal hierarchy, the less likely its records had been preserved. Fortunately, the Provincial Archives of Manitoba's collections for the Winnipeg Judicial District include the registers and case files of the county criminal court and the record books of Winnipeg's Police Court. Unfortunately, the district court records for all judicial districts in Alberta were destroyed. But because of an unusual filing system, cases heard by Edmonton's Police Court and appeals of decisions in the superior courts have been preserved and are filed chronologically among the records of the superior court for the Northern Alberta–Edmonton Judicial District. In Saskatchewan, the records of the Regina Police Court are not open to researchers, but Regina's district criminal court records survive for the brief period between 1932 and 1940. The records for many of these courts are incomplete, but they are among the only existing sources we have for exploring magistrates' and judges' responses to domestic violence in marginalized working-class, immigrant, and Aboriginal communities. And these record series also include offences related to prostitution and vagrancy that are absent when superior court records are relied on exclusively.

Finally, to explore the impact that British Canadian systems of law had on Aboriginal reserve communities, I drew on the records of the Department of Indian Affairs and the North West Mounted Police (NWMP), particularly for the Kainai (Blood) Agency in the Macleod Judicial District. Available at Library and Archives Canada and at the Glenbow Archives, these record series include legal documents and correspondence regarding NWMP investigations of complaints and summary offences tried by Indian agents between 1899 and 1910 and from 1929 to 1941.

Over a number of years, I gathered information on well over a thousand cases that, centred as they were on diverse women offenders and victims, crossed race and class boundaries and were unique to no particular geographical area or cultural community. As other social and cultural historians discovered before me, however, there are other issues involved with using case file collections as a foundation to examine interactions between ordinary people, institutions, and the state. When historians Franca Iacovetta and Wendy Mitchinson published the edited volume *On the Case: Explorations in Social History* in 1998, for instance, the book led to debate about the nature of historical evidence and its production, the possibility of arriving at a historical truth, and the issues of relevance and representation.[11] The editors defined case files as fragmentary records generated by state officials or administrators in other institutions to categorize and assess a given population. The goal, they argued, was to supervise, treat, punish, or reform individuals or groups deemed in some way deviant.[12] In her critique of the book, however, criminologist Mariana Valverde pointed out that not all records designated as case files by historians and commentators fit the bill. The term *case file*, Valverde argued, was being used inaccurately in their work as an umbrella term for three different types of information format: the register, the clinically oriented case file, and records produced in and for the legal process.[13] Only the latter two categories deserve to be called case files.

The importance of these distinctions was apparent as I sifted through countless registers and legal documents that, depending on the court and the nature of the criminal process documented, generated different types of knowledge about cases and the individuals and groups involved. The Winnipeg Police Court record books and the criminal registers and docket books for the superior courts are registers in the sense that they were produced to document the court's business. As a result, they tell us nothing about the feelings of victims or defendants or why magistrates, judges, or juries made the decisions they did. Arranged chronologically, registers include the date of the trial, the name of the accused, the charge or indictment, the verdict, and the sentence. Recorders for Manitoba's Court of King's Bench also included the accused's age, occupation, marital status, level of education, religion, race or ethnicity, and sex. Registers allowed me to know individuals only in a generic sense or in aggregate terms.[14] Because magistrates in Winnipeg's police court heard thousands of cases each year, I decided to restrict my analysis of the court's record books to eight-year intervals, beginning in 1886. When I discovered that the court's business boomed in the interwar years because of population increases, an expanding police force, and the prosecution of municipal bylaws, I was forced, for the sake of expediency, to limit my analysis for the years 1918, 1926, and 1934 to alternate months, beginning with January.

The capital case files and superior and intermediate court records I consulted likewise contained information that had been generated in a specific context, for a specific purpose. Criminal case files were not produced to gather clinical knowledge about individuals, their feelings, or their actions but rather to provide textual documentation for the purpose of legally resolving a case.[15] Clerks produced and gathered superior court records to help public prosecutors decide whether a high probability of guilt had been established at the preliminary hearing. These records are highly formatted documents that contain a copy of the information (the formal criminal charge lodged by the prosecutor), depositions of witnesses, the indictment, and the trial outcome and sentence. The case file may or may not include a Statistics Canada form that details the accused's personal information. (Because hearings and trials were matters of public record played out in the courtroom, the media, and the local community, I chose not to disguise the identity of the parties involved.) Depositions were taken down in the accused's presence during the preliminary hearing. Unless the accused called witnesses to establish direct evidence of his or her innocence (or to explain away circumstances cited in evidence by the prosecution), depositions usually include only the testimony of witnesses for the prosecution. In certain instances – particularly when the accused was unrepresented by counsel – the case file may also contain a written statement by the accused. I discovered that in rural areas and most jurisdictions before 1905, depositions were short and often written in the witness's own hand. If the witness was illiterate or spoke no English, a court official, with the assistance of a translator, took down his or her statement. After the First World War, when the accused was more likely to be represented by defence counsel, a stenographer recorded the examinations of witnesses. Superior court case files do not contain trial transcripts. To offset this limitation, I consulted newspaper accounts of trials to gather clues about defence strategies, trial outcomes, and the public's response to each case.

As Annalee Lepp, a historian who has used legal records to study family violence, notes, criminal case files from all levels of the criminal trial process are incomplete and riddled with frustrating gaps and silences. Lepp observes that it is difficult (and sometimes impossible) to get at the truth behind allegations, the accused's response to them, or how the jury rationalized its decision. When individuals enter a court of law – regardless of whether they are the victim, the accused, an attorney, or a witness – they tend to use repetitive rhetorical strategies shaped by the evidentiary requirements of the case and the formal structure of the legal process. Depositions and trial testimonies, therefore, often blur the line between truth and narrative.[16] This limitation could be considered an inherent weakness of case file research, but determining which rhetorical strategies held the most weight in the courtroom and whether they reflected common assumptions about individuals or groups proved to be one of the most fruitful, and telling, aspects of this study.

This was particularly true of capital case files and the legal records generated by or for the Department of Indian Affairs (DIA). Unlike superior court records, federal agencies produced these two series of documents to collect information on accused individuals, convicted offenders, and certain cases or behaviours. In all circumstances, government officials wanted information on the current state of public opinion to help them arrive at and justify decisions. The DIA's records include correspondence between Indian agents and their superiors regarding the handling of specific cases or categories of offences, newspaper items that criticize department policy, NWMP arrest and investigation reports, and trial summaries. Read alongside criminal registers and case files for the superior courts, these records allowed me to trace, almost literally, the movements of a few Aboriginal men and women over an extended period of time. The records are riddled with negative stereotypes that might have shaped Indian agents' and police officers' treatment of Aboriginal offenders and victims. But they contain few clues that indicate how Aboriginal communities felt about particular cases or their treatment by the police or the courts.

By contrast, capital case files, which were gathered after a jury decided to convict and a judge sentenced the accused to hang, include extensive information on the various meanings that were attached to a given case. Murder and child murder cases that ended in guilty verdicts often triggered public debate, outrage, and clemency campaigns on behalf of the convicted offender. The final prerogative of mercy, however, resided with the federal government. Following a conviction, the trial judge forwarded to the

secretary of state a copy of the trial transcript, the jury's recommendation
of mercy, and a personal assessment of the case. The secretary of state
would then transfer all papers, including any petitions for mercy received
from the public, to the Department of Justice. The minister of justice
briefed cabinet members, and cabinet members reported their final recommendation to the governor general, who officially decided whether
the accused would live or die. Each capital case file includes all of this information alongside transcripts of retrials or appeals of decisions, police
investigation reports, newspaper accounts of trials, editorials, prison reports, and pleas made on the convicted offender's behalf to the Remission
Branch, the department responsible for receiving and arranging the documents. The chief remissions officer wrote a summary report of the case
and appended documents such as medical or psychiatric assessments.
The judge's report and the summary report from the remissions officer
were among the most influential documents in clemency decisions.[17]

Just as the Pamela George case had suggested, capital case files offered
a rich and rare documentary source to probe the multiple layers of meanings that were attached to crime and the criminal justice system by law
officials, social reformers, neighbours, family members, and the convicted
offender. Legal historian Carolyn Strange argues that capital case files
should be approached as textual artifacts of competing truths that, when
analyzed, result in new narratives of invention that are unsettlingly in-
conclusive.[18] Yet official government decisions – commutations of death
sentences, for example – followed capital cases, and capital case files reveal
which truth claims resonated the most with government officials and which
official decisions ran against the grain of public opinion. As historian Karen
Dubinsky has argued, the biases of the legal process often work to our
advantage because case files suggest whether discrimination shaped the
victim's or perpetrator's reception in the courtroom, local community, or
government bureaucracy.[19] Although the very existence of a case file implies
the intrusive and coercive power of the state over people's lives, capital
case files include unsolicited opinions and narratives that give voice to the
thoughts and experiences of those who lived in communities far from the
centres of power.[20]

Taken together, these various sources yielded both quantitative and
qualitative evidence of trends. Registers and record books are imprinted
with traces of prosecution and sentencing patterns that suggest deep-seated
prejudices among judges and juries. I also used these sources to render
collective portraits of victims and perpetrators within a long-term chronological framework, and I chose representative cases that illustrate how the

accused and the victim constructed or manipulated their account of events
– either to meet the evidentiary and procedural requirements of the court
or to play upon popular prejudice. To offer a fuller account of the possible
meanings and implications of individual cases or trends, I also drew on
demographic data, social surveys, commissions of inquiry, popular imagery and novels, law and procedure manuals, and federal criminal law
legislation.

Finally, I decided to include sensational cases that were not representative but were telling events, much like the Pamela George case. As a number
of historians have revealed, accounts of sensational murders or acts of
violence – whether those accounts originate from members of the public,
the judiciary, the police, or the media – often contain oblique references
to popular assumptions about crime and violence that are only rarely articulated in official forums or documents.[21] Because they centre on extreme
acts of violence, public reactions to sensational trials often contain verbal-
izations of widely held beliefs regarding what constitutes normal or acceptable behaviour – for instance, justifiable homicide or child beating.
As Sander Gilman, a leading cultural historian, has argued, the way that
people in the past conceived the normal is reflected in their treatment of
the Other – in other words, marginalized individuals or groups.[22]
Depending upon the race, class, or ethnicity of the accused, the judge's,
jury's, or public's response could vary from empathy to condemnation.
Natalie Zemon Davis and other advocates of microhistory and anthropo-
logical approaches to the past, such as Carlo Ginzburg and Edward Muir,
argue that historians can use uniquely revealing documents, interrogations,
or individual case files to recapture interactions between elite and popular
cultures.[23]

Historians often compare the criminal trial to the stage. When I began
this study, I planned to focus the spotlight on women, and my research
did produce the expected stock of female characters – abused wives and
victims of sexual assault, prostitutes and murderesses, unwed mothers and
seduced daughters. But the male members of the cast – pimps, johns,
and procurers; seducers and abortionists; social reformers and police officials; wife abusers and rapists; and murdered husbands or victims of theft
– kept creeping into the limelight. Cases involving women introduced me
to Aboriginal women, urban domestic servants and housewives, unwed
mothers, farm wives, and farm daughters whose experiences with prostitution, abortion and infanticide, and domestic and sexual violence opened
a window to explore not only the relationship between the law and the
status of women but also the role that criminal courts and trials played in

the construction of femininity – or, rather, femininities – in prairie Canada. But these same cases also proved to be an entry point into the lives of Aboriginal men, farmers, urban professionals, and labourers. Historian Garthine Walker has observed that although we know a lot about the history of women and crime, we have scarcely begun to address how criminality and violence were related to masculinity.[24]

By pulling together a sample of diverse cases, similarities in the treatment of different groups and the strategies of different offenders became more apparent, as did the underlying logic, or assumptions, of the criminal law. For example, except in a few high-profile cases, victims of rape and sexual assault from marginalized communities were less likely to convince the courts of their veracity. But farm labourers, men who failed to meet the masculine ideal, who were accused of sexually assaulting or seducing farmers' wives or daughters, faced a similar problem. Prairie women accused of violent crimes such as husband or child murder tried to manipulate trials in their favour by conforming to the script for a passive and submissive womanhood. But Aboriginal men accused of violent crimes against women likewise played to settlers' idea of a weak, ignorant, and infantile indigenous masculinity to evade punishment. The criminal courts – which sat at the intersection of law and society – reflected and helped to shape perceptions of Aboriginal people, white settlers, immigrants, and the working class relative to one another.[25] Because they stood at the cultural crossroads, criminal cases that involved women served as a stage upon which larger developments and conflicts – between Native and newcomer, men and women, capital and labour, and adults and youths – played out.

The explicit, and often inexplicable, narratives of sex and violence that I discovered in criminal case files sat uncomfortably with mythic images of Canada's prairie West as a land of opportunity, a place of fruitful land and happy homes, a settlement frontier where law and order, embodied by the North West Mounted Police, preceded settlement. As Peggy Pascoe had predicted, by focusing on cases that would make it possible to reimagine the so-called frontier as a cultural crossroads or intercultural dialogue rather than as a geographical freeway, a more nuanced image of the region emerged, one in which it was possible to explore how complex variables such as class, race, ethnicity, age, and gender influenced power relationships in the region.[26] By focusing on cases that stood at the cultural crossroads, the traditional narrative of the Canadian Prairies – and the false dichotomy of the mild versus the wild West on which it rested – gave way to narratives of intercultural exchange that were sometimes defined by cooperation and sometimes by conflict. The traditional narrative of western exceptionalism gave way to narratives that drew the region's past not only into the larger story of nation building in Canadian and North American history but also into the history of the British Empire and the creation of settler societies such as Australia and New Zealand (the subject of Chapter 1).

As I read the burgeoning literature on these larger developments – particularly works that addressed the role of the law and the role of the intimate in colonialism and nation building – I realized that the cases I had gathered offered a unique opportunity to explore how the criminal courts reflected and reinforced the social boundaries and discourses of difference that underpinned the construction of a settler society and a liberal economic order on Canada's settlement frontier. One of the central projects of colonialism – a practice of domination that involves the subjugation of one people to another and the transfer of a population to a new territory – was defining the cultural boundary between colonized and colonizer.[27] As Stuart Hall, a prominent cultural theorist and sociologist, has argued, discourses of difference – beliefs and practices that define who does not belong to a given community – were central to colonialism, and they were fundamental to the construction of national identities.[28] Criminal case files are replete with sensational stories of men and women who defied these beliefs and practices and the erection of cultural boundaries and hierarchies. Aboriginal men and women resisted attempts to restrict their movement and behaviour. Agricultural labourers defied their employers' attempts to limit access to their daughters. Farmers' daughters defied their parents' and the authorities' attempts to regulate their sexuality. Wives refused to be locked into the role of submissive helpmates. And victims of rape refused to be cast as the promiscuous woman undeserving of the courts' protection. The intimate frontiers that these ordinary people inhabited were as much a part of the region's history as the triumphant march of the NWMP, the building of the railroad, and the construction of a vast agricultural settlement frontier. As places in which redemption and punishment were offered in equal measure, criminal courts were arbiters of belonging in the colonial and nation-building projects.

The alternative narrative of the prairie West that I pieced together from the courts' records took shape in a thematic rather than a chronological manner as I sought explanations for particular classes of cases or prosecutorial trends: the treatment of Aboriginal victims and accused (Chapter 2); the relationship between prostitutes, social reform, and police courts

(Chapter 3); the overrepresentation of farm labourers in rural sex crime and seduction cases (Chapter 4); cases of sexual violence, drug possession, abortion, and seduction that highlighted the girl in the city in the Roaring Twenties and the Dirty Thirties (Chapter 5); judges' and juries' responses to incest, wife beating, and wife murder in the domestic sphere (Chapter 6); and the treatment of violent female offenders and the capital punishment debate (Chapter 7). The chapters describe developments that occurred simultaneously in discrete settings in both the public and private spheres. In each of the four social settings examined – the reserve, the city, the countryside, and the home – I move the locus of regulatory power from the pronouncements of federal policy makers and legislation to the proceedings of local courts, where federal power was only one of many factors involved in the attempt to regulate people's lives. Brad Asher, a scholar of Native American history, has argued that local courts are a critical, if under-examined, element of colonialism and nation building.[29] In *Westward Bound* I examine their contribution to this process during decades when dreams of nation and empire came to reside on Canada's settlement frontier.

At the turn of the twenty-first century, criminal cases such as the Pamela George murder provoke social criticism and debate among competing interest groups in Canadian society. At the turn of the twentieth century, however, criminal cases involving women often played themselves out within a cultural milieu that desired a single truth or narrative, in an era when dominant groups and interests believed that the challenges of modernity – labour movements, colonial unrest, and the woman's suffrage movement – were blurring boundaries between the classes, races, and sexes.[30] Constructed visions of the Prairies as the last, best West served this narrative function in Canada. Canadian government officials and propagandists and British travel writers promised potential immigrants that life in the region would be free from the hierarchies and constraints that typified life in the Old World, and western judges and juries maintained an invested interest in ensuring that this vision remained uncontested. Although millions of immigrants were westward bound in search of land and opportunity, their interactions and confrontations with Aboriginal peoples and the criminal courts reveal that they helped to create, and encountered, old hierarchies and new constraints. Testimonies by witnesses, victims, and defendants belie mythic visions of the Prairies as a region built upon the foundations of law, order, and pioneering partnerships between men and women, capital and labour, and Native and newcomer. Although the testimonies they contain were often disguised, suppressed, or manipulated, criminal case files give a voice to men, women, and youths who lived life in the margins but who nonetheless contributed to the creation of a distinct legal and socio-economic culture that continues to influence attitudes toward sexuality, gender, crime, violence, and law and order in postcolonial societies.

I

Fruitful Land, Happy Homes, Manly Titans

Settlement Frontiers, Law, and the Intimate in Colonialism and Nation Building

In 1889, the city of Calgary in Canada's North-West Territories was the scene of a murder and trial that cast doubt on the quality of justice on the Prairies. On 1 March 1889, a journalist with the *Herald* reported that the police had discovered the "mutilated body of a murdered squaw" in William "Jumbo" Fisk's living quarters above the Turf Club restaurant. The case went to trial in April, and an all-male, white jury brought in a verdict of not guilty. The verdict flew in the face of Crown evidence that Fisk, an avowed aficionado of the Jack the Ripper murders that had terrified Londoners in 1888, had admitted to taking a woman known as Rosalie, an alleged prostitute, up to his rooms. George Kelsy testified that he had heard strange noises coming from his friend's room on the evening of 28 February. Upon investigation, he found Jumbo in the room and a bloodstained woman lying on the bed. Kelsy claimed that Rosalie was still alive when the two men went to dinner. A North West Mounted Police (NWMP) detective testified that the murderer had ripped apart the victim's abdomen with his bare hands and that investigators had found a bloody handprint that matched Fisk's on the wall. Given this evidence, Justice Charles B. Rouleau emphasized the need for inter-racial equity in his charge to the jury and demanded a retrial following the verdict. During the second murder trial, which occurred in July, Justice Rouleau asked the jury to "forget the woman's race and consider only the evidence at hand," and he declared, "It made no difference whether Rosalie was white or black, an Indian or a negro. In the eyes of the law, every British subject is equal."[1] Despite Rouleau's admonition, the jury found Fisk guilty only of manslaughter, and the judge sentenced him to fourteen years of hard labour at Stony Mountain Penitentiary.

William Fisk did not conform to Calgarians' image of the rapist and murderer. He hailed from a well-established eastern Canadian family and had migrated to the West in 1882. He had worked on a Canadian Pacific Railway construction crew and served during the 1885 Northwest Rebellion. One of his uncles was a doctor in Ontario, and another had found a vocation as a clergyman in Quebec. Buckboard Williams, the famous reporter for the Toronto *Globe,* was also his uncle. After coming home from the Rebellion, Fisk became part owner of the Turf Club. Although Justice Rouleau pushed for a life sentence for murder, petitions by members of Parliament and members of the Calgary elite warned him that such an outcome would be ill-advised because Calgarians' sympathies lay with the accused. As far as white Calgarians were concerned, Rosalie conformed to popular perceptions of a dangerous and dissolute Aboriginal womanhood, while Fisk embodied the British Canadian, middle-class ideal of frontier masculinity. The lesson learned from the case was that it was best to "keep the Indians out of town."[2]

Was Justice Rouleau's emphasis and insistence on the rule of law and inter-racial equality typical, or did it run against the grain of judicial practice in the British Empire and Canada? Was Fisk's social status and Rosalie's sex as important to the trial outcome as his or her race? In the jury members' opinion, did Fisk's ethnicity or masculinity weigh more in his favour than Rosalie's class? What was more damaging, the victim's race or her alleged profession? The multiple layers of interpretation and meaning that can be attached to this single case suggest how criminal cases both reflected and contributed to local, national, and global developments that were transforming prairie Canada from a place where a common or middle ground between Aboriginal peoples and newcomers was still possible into an established white settler society in a vast colonial empire and liberal economic order.[3]

FROM REGION TO EMPIRE: WIDENING THE LENS

Settled by Europeans whose descendants remain politically dominant over the indigenous peoples they dispossessed, settler societies such as Canada, Australia, the United States, Aotearoa New Zealand, and South Africa once loomed large in the imagination of imperialists, novelists, and historians. Following the Second World War, however, historians lost interest in exploring common developments and connections among settler colonies and their settlement frontiers and instead wrote historical narratives of their home and native land. Within the nation, the practice of history writing fragmented further as historians focused on the so-called limited identities of race, gender, class, and region. In the past twenty years, however, globalization, decolonization, transnational immigration, and the growth of multinational corporations have compelled us to step back to broaden our view of region, nation, and empire and the role these limited identities played in their creation.[4] This new perspective has reignited interest in tracing how imperial and national administrators tried to build an extension, or replica, of British society overseas.[5] This new scholarship has encouraged historians to once again place the history of Canada between Confederation and the 1950s within the larger context of the British world. Even though Canada became a self-governing colony in 1867 (and a dominion after 1907), most members of the English Canadian majority, those who held economic and political power, wanted Canada to remain with the Empire and continued to self-consciously define their country as a British nation until the 1950s. The Dominion of Canada was essentially a "larger British colony with imperial ambitions of its own – in particular, to spread across the continent before the Americans beat them to it."[6] The settlement of the prairie West, preferably with Canadian or British citizens, was a cornerstone of Canada's own colonial and nation-building project.[7]

A renewed interest in colonial and nation-building projects has also produced a growing body of scholarship that highlights how both the law and gender – the cultural construction of masculinities and femininities – produced the boundaries and hierarchies of difference upon which white settler societies were built.[8] As the Rosalie trials illustrate, criminal case files involving women provide an exceptional vehicle to examine these larger processes because they reveal how the law constituted race, class, and gender in colonial settings and how, in turn, these tensions and divisions shaped trial outcomes. Throughout the British Empire, judges such as Rouleau used the charge to the jury as an opportunity to assert the superiority of English justice and the legitimacy of British rule and middle-class dominance over what were deemed the primitive and the pauper.[9] To borrow a phrase from legal historian Martin Chanock, the law served as colonialism's cutting edge and, in white settler societies such as Canada, national governments wielded it to maintain social order in the face of resistance from indigenous peoples and to contain conflicts between Native peoples and newcomers, capital and labour, and men and women. Because the criminal courts were connected intimately to the institutional apparatus of the empire or nation-state, they served as the law's leading edge: imperial agents and government officials harnessed their ability to define crime and control systems of punishment to their larger project – to order the political and moral allegiance of indigenous and immigrant groups and to communicate new notions of sovereignty.[10]

Anthropologist John Comaroff argues, however, that the law's function was complicated by the ontological contradiction at the core of nineteenth-century colonialism: colonialists rationalized dispossession in the name of a humane, enlightened universalism, and they legitimated it by promising to usher non-Europeans into the citizenship of the modern word.[11] The divergence between white Calgarians' and Justice Rouleau's response to the Rosalie trial suggests that this inherent contradiction complicated the law's function in colonial settings. Rouleau's insistence on the rule of law and inter-racial equity illustrates how, in one instance, imperialists and nationalists in Britain and Canada sought to dispossess and regulate by "inclusion and domestication rather than by confrontation."[12] The criminal courts, consequently, served not only as sites for dominant groups to impose their vision of society, law, and morality, they also provided a forum for subordinates to resist those visions or propose alternatives.[13] In prairie Canada, white Calgarians understood that the stability of their settler society – in other words, the settler construct – depended on the applica-tion of a system of law that was both discretionary and discriminatory. Fisk's sexual relationship with an Aboriginal woman and Rosalie's presence off the Indian reserve and outside the bounds of the patriarchal family flew in the face of policies that were being put in place to manage domestic and sexual relationships to maintain the social categories and hierarchies upon which colonial and national rule depended. As cultural and post-colonial historians have demonstrated, discouraging and prohibiting sexual relations between colonized and colonizer was integral to colonial and nation-building projects, and the British, more so than the French or the Spanish, attempted to impose their system of monogamous heterosexuality and patriarchal household governance on so-called problem indigenous, working-class, and immigrant populations.[14]

FRUITFUL LAND: DREAMS OF NATION AND EMPIRE

Rosalie's death and the trials that followed reflected tensions of empire and nation and the challenges of modernity as they were beginning to play

out on Canada's settlement frontier. The Canadian government opened
the Prairies to white settlement during the first crisis of modernity in the
history of the empire and nation.[15] The Canadian government's military
victory over Louis Riel, his Metis followers, and a handful of Indian rebels
during the 1885 Northwest Rebellion reconfirmed the region's status as a
colony of the Canadian federal government and as a colonial outpost of
an empire that advocates of the New Imperialism were doing their best to
refashion in the face of mounting challenges to traditional authority.
Imperialists such as British prime minister Benjamin Disraeli began to
perceive the colonies as bulwarks against German, Italian, and American
threats to England's colonial markets. Challenges to empire came also from
within: working-class radicals were demanding an honest wage for honest
work; suffragists were campaigning for political and social equality; and
social Darwinists and the pseudo-science of eugenics were giving birth to
fears of race suicide and national degeneracy. In response, and to counter
their political opponents, New Imperialists advocated a spirit of defensive
aggressiveness against external threats and internal decay. Proclaiming the
superiority of the Anglo-Saxon race, Rudyard Kipling, for instance, declared it the white man's burden to civilize the unfortunate races of Asia,
Africa, Australia, and Canada. By the mid-1880s, many of those who held
positions of power and authority believed that the future vitality and
strength of the British Empire would come from the colonial frontier.[16]

Dreams of nation also settled on the Canadian Prairies. The Northwest
Rebellion coincided with the completion of the Canadian Pacific Railway,
an accomplishment that (at least symbolically) consolidated Canada as a
country from sea to shining sea. The elements of Prime Minister Sir John
A. Macdonald's national policy to broaden the base of Canada's economy
and restore faith in the country's development were falling into place. All
that remained was to ensure that the Prairies were safe for white settlers.

Although most Aboriginal peoples had remained loyal to the Crown
during the Rebellion, Macdonald's Conservative government manipulated
the idea of a general Indian uprising to rationalize and reinforce its policy
to dismantle the tribal system and place Aboriginal peoples more thorough-
ly under the authority of the Department of Indian Affairs and the North
West Mounted Police.[17] The new era opened with the trial and execution
of Louis Riel and with the hanging of eight Indian men who stood trial
for murder before Charles Rouleau and a white jury at North Battleford.
The trials and the executions served a performative function. Their purpose
was to demonstrate to Aboriginal people, in the most effective way possible, the consequences of disloyalty to the Crown.[18] Government officials

forced students of the Battleford Industrial School to witness the executions. The events of 1885 proved to be a turning point for the people of
prairie Canada, for they "put to rest any hopes or possibilities for a progressive partnership, a shared common world" between Native peoples
and newcomers.[19] Prime Minister Macdonald remarked that "the execution
of the Indians ... ought to convince the Red man that the White man
governs."[20]

The Rosalie trials also occurred at a moment when British and Canadian
government officials, journalists, social gospellers, and travel writers were
selling the prairie West to potential immigrants as a land of equal opportunity and as a woman's paradise. Throughout the 1880s it became increasingly apparent that the region's population imbalance in favour of bachelors
was a problem. In 1888, Scottish author and journalist Jessie Saxby tried
to coax unmarried British women to the region by promising them a
landscape where "the men treat the women with a chivalry and tenderness
which cannot fail to bind the feebler sex in willing chains": "It is refreshing
to eyes accustomed to the tired, anxious faces, and listless or stilted gait
of the average Briton, to look on the manly Titans of the west. They are
Britons, yes, but Britons of larger body and larger heart than those at
home. There is a freedom of gait, a heartiness of manner, a hopefulness of
expression, a frank courtesy, a liberal-mindedness which impresses me
profoundly. You feel that here is a race of men who must be winners in
life's battle, and who can keep what they win 'by the might of a good
strong hand.'"[21] Two years after the Rosalie trials, Nicholas Flood Davin,
a Conservative member of Parliament and publisher, wrote *Homes for
Millions*, which ignored the presence of indigenous peoples in the West
and likewise promised potential male immigrants, particularly farmers
and farm labourers, a landscape "where they can have fruitful land for
nothing; happy homes; independence."[22]

Davin's emphasis on fruitful land and freedom reflected the new utopian
vision of the prairie West held by Canadian expansionists and British
imperialists who viewed "frontiers" as potential places for settlement and
economic development. What were once considered wastelands were
transformed in the imaginations of their promoters as gardens of the Lord
that begged for British Canadian appropriation, rationalized freehold land
tenure, crop production and export, and resource exploitation.[23] Images
of the Prairies changed from 1850 onward as policy makers and imperialists tried to extend a liberal economic order – the political form of modernity that remained hegemonic through to the 1940s – across the North
American continent. Turning dream into reality required that liberal

nationalists extend across time and space a belief in the primacy of the category "individual." Davin's emphasis on independence, consequently, reflected nineteenth-century liberal conceptions of the law as a system that did not place limits upon the individual (whose freedom should be constrained only by obligations to others or to God) but instead protected his right to self-preservation and the pursuit of property. As my use of the masculine pronoun suggests, liberals envisaged the rights-bearing individual as the rational male: in opposition, they constructed women, indigenous peoples, and the unpropertied as deficient individuals. If Canadian history is reconceived as a project of rule, as historian Ian McKay suggests it should be, it is the historian's task to map not only the grids of power (the application of federal criminal law, for instance) that constructed a given hegemonic social order but also the forces of resistance that threatened or changed the larger project.[24] The colonization and settlement of the West from the 1880s onward, McKay contends, is a key chapter in this story because the liberalization of the Prairies and British Columbia was a highly contentious and endangered program.

Happy Homes: Family, Nation, Empire

Davin emphasized the West as a place that would foster happy homes because colonialism and nation building were also about making families. The late Ann Leger-Anderson, a historian of prairie women, wrote that the "sod hut or tar paper shack – a sort of pioneer icon – is also a symbol, or signifier, of imperialism as much as the machine-gun or the braided uniforms of proconsuls or generals."[25] As her observation suggests, imperialists and nationalists incorporated images of domestic life into an ideology of domination: white women served as harbingers of civilization, and colonies served as stages for a reinvented, or reinvigorated, patriarchy (see Figure 3).[26]

The Prairies were settled during an era when the ideal of companionate marriage was emerging as a cornerstone of modernity and liberalism in Western industrializing nations. The early- and mid-nineteenth-century middle-class ideal of the chaste and diligent wife who focused on being a loving mother with few needs and rights of her own was giving way to the ideal of the modern woman as a partner in a new model of marriage based on greater moral and spiritual equality. The change partly reflected the decline of kinship ties and economic considerations in the choice of spouse, and it partly reflected the influence of liberal and democratic ideologies

FIGURE 3   Images of domestic life were incorporated into an ideology of colonial and national domination as illustrated by M. Leone Bracker's "Pioneer Settlers," created for a Canadian Pacific Railway fiftieth anniversary menu cover in 1931. | Canadian Pacific Archives, BR 183.

in the United States and England. As feminist historians have pointed out, however, the ideal of companionate marriage softened patriarchy but did not eliminate it. The ideal wife was still portrayed as a helpmate because, in nineteenth-century liberalism, moral and spiritual equality was not the same as social equality. The companionate ideal did not eliminate hierarchy – but it did lead to rising expectations for marriage, and it did contribute to new standards for acceptable masculine behaviour.[27] (The discrepancy between expectation and reality sometimes led to conflicts between husbands and wives, and the acts of violence that ensued often found their way into the criminal courts.)

Although the ideal of companionate marriage led to a new willingness to reconsider and reform married women's property law in other parts of North America, Britain, and colonies such as Australia and New Zealand, on the Canadian Prairies, to simplify land transfers and remove possible encumbrances to title, federal and provincial legislators designated the region's land – and therefore wealth – as an almost exclusively male preserve. The Dominion Lands Act of 1872 precluded all but widows and divorced or deserted wives with dependent children from taking up eligible homesteads. Provincial legislators in Manitoba abolished dower – the widow's life-interest in one-third of her husband's freehold property – completely in 1885, and federal legislators followed suit with the Territories' Real Property Act of 1886. Although the prairie farm wife could own property separate from her husband, she had no right to the matrimonial home, which was held in her husband's name, or to property or income acquired by the couple's joint labour. She also did not have the right to be consulted about the disposition of the family farm by sale, mortgage, or gift. Women who moved to the Prairies from other parts of the common law world did not have the same dower rights in their husband's new homestead as they would have had back home.[28] Property law for married women in prairie Canada belied the ideal of companionate marriage that was taking hold in other Western industrializing nations; it made, from the outset, a true pioneering partnership between husbands and wives difficult, if not impossible.

As it was imagined, however, the liberal economic order presumed separate, ostensibly equal, spheres for men and women. Although civil society (the public world of men) rested on the tenets of freedom, equality, reason, contract, impartial law, and property for individuals, the domestic domain (the private world of women, children, and unwaged work) was associated with particularity, subjection, blood, emotion, love, and sex. The development of a distinct domestic domain was a corollary of industrial capitalism and central to bourgeois ideology. Nineteenth-century liberal theorists, however, represented the family as an "apolitical, altruistic haven from the heartless capitalistic world of rational self-interest."[29] In truth, marriage and family stood at the threshold between the private world of the household and the public world of the state. Family was the foundation of freedom in the liberal order, the core from which radiated outward all other civil rights, with the husband and father serving as intermediary. In the eyes of policy makers, marriage was "a civilizing force and a measure of civilization."[30]

Policy makers passed legislation that restricted married women's access to property in prairie Canada because they recognized that the domestic domain was a "hot zone where the new liberal order was created or contested."[31] Legislators, who likely had one eye on developments in the American West, believed that shoring up the patriarchal family on the Prairies would tame the acquisitive individualism that would accompany the progress of liberal capitalism in the region. Constructing the domestic domain was imperative in a region that had a large Aboriginal population with fluid notions of marriage, family, and gender and, in the first decades of settlement, a rural male-to-female ratio that was as high as 202 to 100 in some non-Aboriginal communities. Liberals, reformers, and legislators viewed the arrival of marriageable white women, the maintenance of strict boundaries between colonized and colonizer, and the formation of families on middle-class models as panaceas for unregulated male desire, which posed dangers to the social structure.[32] Maintaining and imposing a strict division between public and private was therefore a key factor in colonialism and nation building: the autonomy of liberalism's free man rested not only on the subordination of women but also on the domination and exploitation of indigenous peoples and the working class.[33] Maintaining these lines or boundaries was also, in the eyes of imperialists who feared that British men were becoming devitalized, necessary for the future of the British race.

MANLY TITANS: REINVIGORATED MASCULINITY ON THE SETTLEMENT FRONTIER

Jessie Saxby, whose writings on prairie Canada were sparked by a trip to visit two sons homesteading in the Qu'Appelle Valley, emphasized the physical fitness, health, and vitality of the region's manly titans because Canadian expansionists and imperialists envisaged colonialism and nation building as more than the Canadian Pacific Railway, staples export, and industrialization. Their goal was to recruit male heads of households who would produce a morally and physically healthy citizenry based on love for and loyalty to Canada and the Empire.[34] The colonial frontier was more than a space for the creation of a liberal economic order and white Christian settlement; it was also imagined as an environment that would foster a reinvigorated masculinity: "British manhood would bring civilization to the hinterlands of the world; in turn, the hinterlands of the world would save British manhood for civilization." For Canadian nationalists, the making of the man would likewise be the making of the nation.[35] Late-nineteenth- and early-twentieth-century posters not only promised potential immigrants land for nothing but also promised "the right land for the right man" (see Figure 4).

Settlers flooded the Prairies during a renaissance of manliness, and William "Jumbo" Fisk embodied the new, hegemonic ideal of white, middle-class masculinity as it was evolving in North America and throughout the British Empire. In the late nineteenth century, middle-class men became preoccupied (some would argue obsessed) with manhood and with men's right to wield power. Discourses on freedom and the frontier as a space for a reinvigorated masculinity reflected this obsession.[36] Between 1880 and the First World War, the middle class increasingly adopted the term *masculinity* over *manliness* in a spirited defence against the demands of modernity – against the threat that labour unrest, feminism, and colonial rebellion posed to their authority and the threat that city living and industrialization posed to men's vitality. Victorian manliness – which was distinguished by honour, high-mindedness, respectability, domesticity, and strength from self-mastery – faltered as middle-class men began to fear that they were losing control of nation and empire. In response, a reinvented, muscular form of imperial masculinity emerged to fend off the anxiety and lassitude triggered by the perceived paradoxes of modernity and overcivilization.[37]

Hegemonic, imperial masculinity varied from nation to nation. As defined by the new men's historians, hegemonic masculinity is the configuration of gender practices that legitimates patriarchy. It ensures that men have superior control over goods and property, over the state and the military, and over women's bodies. Masculinity, however, is also about differentiation between men, and historians, the new men's historians argue, must trace how notions of race and class constructed subordinate masculinities in distinct historical contexts.[38] By the late nineteenth century, for instance, the normative middle-class Englishman exuded muscular

FIGURE 4 Canadian immigration posters not only promised land for nothing but also promised "The Right Land for the Right Man." | Glenbow Archives, Poster-13.

FIGURE 5   Graphic images and art on Canadian Pacific Railway posters, like this
one, c. 1920, featured visions of muscular, Anglo-Saxon men taming the wilderness. |
Courtesy Canadian Pacific Archives, A.6199.

Christianity, while his American counterpart, typified by Teddy Roosevelt, represented a racialized, imperial masculinity: he was an adventurous, but civilized man who tamed or defeated savage men of colour.[39] On the Canadian Prairies, popular authors such as Ralph Connor (a pseudonym for the Reverend Dr. Charles William Gordon) and Robert J.C. Stead fashioned a Protestant masculinity of work that they felt was suited to civilizing the West. In Connor's fiction, the West was a place that assimilated foreign cultural identities, thereby creating a new breed of Anglo-Saxon man who tempered his rugged strength and forceful courage with hard work.[40] Graphic images of muscular, Anglo-Saxon men taming the wilderness were featured in the artwork on Canadian railway posters (see Figures 4 and 5).

The British Canadian preference for law, order, and authority over brasher American claims to freedom and liberty also moderated imperial masculinity on the Prairies. In his novel *Corporal Cameron* (1912), Ralph Connor tells the story of an agricultural labourer who travels west with the NWMP to do great work and make the dominion a great empire. As Connor's choice of hero suggests, the Mountie, and legal officials in general, epitomized normative British Canadian masculinity (see Figure 6). In non-fiction narratives, novels, and journalism, authors portrayed the Mountie as a white, middle-class, masculine hero who vanquished the enemies of modernity: the savage, working-class, or foreign criminal (see Figure 7).[41]

ON THE CHARACTER OF CRIME AND VIOLENCE

Just as normative masculinity underwent transformation in the late nineteenth and early twentieth centuries, so too did representations of the criminal. Whereas people in the early Victorian period tended to view the criminal as a product of triumphant individualism, those late Victorians and early Edwardians who accepted the ideas of Darwinian evolution and biological determinism began to fear that repressive control of the self-will, or excessive civilization, was creating devitalized individuals or social wreckage. Cesare Lombroso's *L'Uomo delinquente* (Criminal Man), which was published in 1876, refashioned the criminal in the image of primitive man (or woman) by drawing upon recapitulation theory in evolutionary anthropology. Henri Julien, who accompanied the NWMP on their march west, played upon prevailing stereotypes of the criminal in his illustration

SITTING BULL ON DOMINION TERRITORY.

U. S. SOLDIER :—Send him over to our side of the line and we'll take care of him.

N. W. MOUNTED POLICE OFFICER :—So long as he behaves himself, the British right
of asylum is as sacred for this poor Indian as for any royal refugee.

FIGURE 6   As Henri Julien's cartoon "Sitting Bull on Dominion Territory" suggests,
normative British Canadian masculinity (epitomized by the NWMP) was built by constructing Aboriginal masculinity, in opposition, as inferior. The cartoon appeared in the
Canadian Illustrated News of 22 September 1877. | Library and Archives Canada, C66055.

"The Criminals' Millennium," which depicts a gallery of rogues – a tramp,
an Irishman, an African American, a remittance man, a Metis, and a prostitute – taking refuge on the American side of the border (see Figure 8).[42]

The mass hanging of Aboriginal men that followed the Northwest
Rebellion, and the death of Rosalie and the trials that followed, however,

FIGURE 7   The Mountie epitomized normative, British Canadian masculinity on the Prairies, exemplified by the illustration "Turning Out Prisoners for Work," which appeared in the *Illustrated Sporting and Dramatic News* of 28 November 1883. | Glenbow Archives, NA-2275-3.

expose the degree to which the exceptional story of the mythic, masculine Mountie and the mild West has obscured the dark side of the settlement process. Historians often interpret violence against women and indigenous people as indicative of a crisis in masculinity, but historian Toby Ditz asks the following: could it have simply been one of the sanctioned methods that some men used to maintain gender, race, and class privileges over women and other men?[43] Physical and sexual violence fit uneasily into Canada's classic narrative of western expansion. As the story goes, Prime Minister Sir John A. Macdonald created the NWMP in 1873 to save the Prairies west of Manitoba from American annexation and to protect Aboriginal peoples from unscrupulous whiskey traders and intertribal warfare. On the completion of the march west in 1874, the Mounties had an immediate, transformative impact: they handily put American whiskey traders out of business, they established Canadian sovereignty north of the forty-ninth parallel, and they persuaded warring factions of Indians to adhere to British Canadian systems of law and to sign treaties with the Crown. Unlike their American counterparts, the NWMP established the rule of law in the West without recourse to violence and by administering justice irrespective of social class or skin colour.[44]

THE CRIMINALS' MILLENNIUM.

FIGURE 8   Henri Julien, who accompanied the NWMP on their march west, plays upon prevailing stereotypes in "The Criminals' Millennium," which appeared in the *Canadian Illustrated News* of 26 August 1876. Julien depicts a gallery of rogues taking refuge on the American side of the border: a tramp, a Metis, an Irishman, an African American, a remittance man, and a prostitute. | Library and Archives Canada, C4515.

Although historians have since demystified dime-novel depictions of the Mountie, he continues to grip the popular and academic imagination as a moral icon. With the exception of Terry Chapman's pioneer study of sex crimes and domestic violence in Alberta, only a few historians of prairie Canada have chosen to systematically explore the law's function in society beyond the early settlement period.[45] And many remain preoccupied with exploring the issue of crime and violence within a comparative framework.

Their research has exposed the mild versus wild West paradigm as a false dichotomy that draws attention away from the law's contributions to imperial and national projects on both sides of the Canadian-American border. However, by focusing on homicide, range wars, and cattle and horse theft, this research continues to conceptualize the issue of frontier crime and violence in exclusively masculine terms.[46] *Westward Bound* moves beyond the NWMP to examine the criminal courts they served and gender as a category of historical analysis during decades when indigenous peoples' and immigrants' acceptance of the rule of law and the white settler construct that the Mountie represented was far from certain.

CRIMINAL COURTS FOR A SETTLER SOCIETY

In the aftermath of the 1869-70 Riel Resistance and the 1885 Rebellion, Canadian legislators officially extended British Canadian law across the Prairies by creating a regular system of judicial districts and criminal courts for the province of Manitoba and for the North-West Territories (which became the provinces of Alberta and Saskatchewan in 1905).[47] Although many historians have drawn attention to the boundary survey, the arrival of white women, and the Mountie as symbols of cultural or national sovereignty, few have noted the symbolic importance of this legislation. Much like the act of mapping land that was described by Europeans as unknown territory, the creation of a judicial district and the erection of a courthouse (which dominated the landscape of prairie towns and cities) signalled for many white pioneers the arrival of civilization and British Canadian law in their community (see Figure 9). Myron Noonkester argues that the implantation of counties (see Figures 1 and 2 for a map of judicial districts) was crucial to an English conquest of global proportions: "The spatial notion of shire was readily translated into a mental universe populated by officials possessing a socially ordained right to rule."[48]

When Canadian legislators created an official court system for Manitoba in 1872 and for the North-West Territories in 1886, they borrowed from English common law tradition but adapted it to regional circumstance. The Manitoba Court of Queen's Bench and the Supreme Court of the North-West Territories consisted of a chief justice and *puisne* judges appointed by the Crown. The judges had complete original and appellate jurisdiction until the provinces created higher courts of appeal for Manitoba in 1906 and for Saskatchewan and Alberta one year later. At that time, the superior courts in Alberta and Saskatchewan became the

Court House, Winnipeg, Man.

FIGURE 9   As was the case in other colonial and national contexts, courthouses served as moral architecture. Proclaiming the majesty and scope of British Canadian law, they loomed over main streets and dominated the geography of town and city centres. This photo shows the Law Courts on Kennedy Street in Winnipeg, c. 1910. | Provincial Archives of Manitoba, Still Images, no. 8.

Supreme Courts of Alberta and Saskatchewan, and the Supreme Court of Saskatchewan became the Saskatchewan Court of King's Bench in 1917. Judges conducted most of their business on circuit, using the English institution of commissions of gaol delivery. Each judge held quarterly sessions of the court in the various judicial districts and, increasingly with jury, passed judgment on defendants accused of indictable offences as defined by federal legislation and, after 1892, the Criminal Code.[49]

Below the superior courts, the judges of the intermediate courts – Manitoba's county criminal courts and Alberta's and Saskatchewan's district courts – could, if the accused consented or pleaded guilty, conduct speedy trials of specific indictable offences without a jury. District and county criminal court judges also conducted summary trials of indictable offences such as aggravated assault, petty theft, and keeping or being an inmate of a disorderly house, which were specified by federal criminal law provisions. Punishment and fines in these cases, however, could not exceed $100 or a six-month prison term, with or without hard labour. Judges in the county criminal and district courts also heard appeals of decisions from the magistrates' courts. As was the case with the superior courts, the federal government appointed county and district court judges, but the judges were required to reside permanently in their county or district.[50]

At the lowest level of the court system, summary offences were heard by one or two justices of the peace (JPs), by members of the NWMP acting as stipendiary magistrates, by magistrates in urban police courts, or by Indian agents on reserves. Appointed by the lieutenant governor in council, JPs were most often prominent members of the local community who had no official legal training. In addition to judging summary offences, JPs and magistrates conducted preliminary hearings for the superior courts, in which they determined if there was a probable case of guilt in an alleged indictable offence. Magistrates and JPs heard complaints and accusations, took depositions, and issued warrants of arrest, summons, and commitment.[51]

The patriarchal assumptions that underpinned the Prairies' newly imposed system of property law extended to the criminal justice system. Although a few women, such as Emily Murphy and Alice Jamieson, would grace the halls and benches of police stations and criminal courts after the First World War, the region's legal establishment remained almost monolithically white, British Canadian, middle class, and male until the 1960s. In 1890, for instance, the North-West Territories and Manitoba limited jury service to male British subjects. Although provincial legislation permitted women in Alberta to serve on civil trial juries after 1921, they were not obliged to do so. Legislation also prohibited women from judging criminal cases until "the parliament of Canada enacts that it shall not be necessary to keep the jury together during the adjournment of a trial of an indictable offence."[52] Canadian officials did not pass official legislation to protect individuals from disqualification or exemption on the grounds of gender until 1972. The criminal courts' day-to-day operation, therefore, occurred within a legal and professional culture bound by the masculine values of fraternity, hierarchy, and conformity. A significant majority of the judges and lawyers who settled on the Prairies – or were born, raised, and educated in the region – hailed originally from the British Isles, Ontario, or the Maritimes. Many – such as Nicholas Flood Davin, Arthur L. Sifton, and Frederick William Haultain – pursued distinguished political careers and were among the West's most avid promoters and propagandists. While professional lawyers in Manitoba and the North-West Territories made their living by acting as businessmen – for instance, drawing contracts for railways, banks, insurance companies, and real estate – those in Alberta acted as lenders of the first resort, agents for financial institutions, and organizers of credit networks. As part of their cultural baggage, they, like Justice Charles Rouleau, believed implicitly in the superiority of British and Canadian cultural values and in the pre-eminence of the English common law tradition.[53]

CIVILIZING THE PRIMITIVE AND THE PAUPER

Courthouses loomed over townscapes, and judges such as Rouleau intervened in the trial process because Canadian officials and legislators understood that settling the Prairies would pose particular challenges to the liberalization of Canada. In addition to contending with threats of the West's annexation by the United States, policy makers had to deal with developments that were, in their minds, equally problematical: the region's Aboriginal peoples and cultures did not disappear after the 1885 Rebellion, and the immigrants who answered Davin's call were more ethnically diverse than expected and, like the region's Aboriginal peoples, held disparate views on marriage and family. The white, British Canadian settler agenda required the mediation of relations between Native peoples and newcomers, the transformation and assimilation of Aboriginal peoples and cultures, and the regulation of incoming immigrants' behaviour. Indian Commissioner Hayter Reed, the architect of Canada's Indian policy after 1885, viewed Aboriginal peoples as a foreign element that needed to be broken up, disbanded, and assimilated. Under his guidance, federal government officials tried to use the Indian Act as a framework for coercive assimilation.[54] The 1876 Indian Act consolidated earlier colonial legislation and created a set of rules, regulations, and directions that sought to manage Aboriginal people's lives, create patriarchal (and therefore lawabiding) families, and maintain spatial and racial boundaries between Native peoples and white settlers. The Indian Act constituted a comprehensive program for naming, defining, and surveying Aboriginal people. By designating Indians as a special class of persons dependent legally on the Crown, legislators consigned them to what one historian has called a legal never-never land.[55] The act defined Indians as British subjects but made them wards of the state – a status they shared with children, felons, and the insane. Disqualified from voting, Indians required the permission of the Indian agent to live on the reserve and to buy or sell land and agricultural produce. By blurring the line between Indians and criminals, the state pathologized Aboriginal peoples. The Indian Act, for instance, criminalized behaviour (such as drinking or selling alcohol) that white settlers carried out routinely. In addition, the Indian agent was designated a justice of the peace for offences under the act and presided over summary trials in special courts. These courts created a top-down and autocratic legal order on reserves, which had the potential to undermine family- and community-based systems of dispute resolution and law. The Indian Act's regulatory power had the same force as the Criminal Code and served as a constitution for those people who came under its purview.[56]

Following the Rebellion, Reed, who was then assistant commissioner of the Department of Indian Affairs (DIA), drafted a "Memorandum on the Future Management of Indians" in which he laid out a plan to dismantle the tribal system and promote individualism through the policy of the Bible and the plough. The plan was approved by Edgar Dewdney, commissioner of Indian affairs, and by Prime Minister Macdonald, who was also the superintendent-general of Indian affairs. Missionary-run residential and industrial schools would promote aggressive civilization by severing the ties that bound children to the culture of their parents, while a ban on religious and cultural ceremonies such as the potlatch and the Sundance would destroy "communist" perceptions of property and pave the way for liberal ones. Reed believed that the allotment of reserve land in severalty would likewise destroy communal farming practices by creating subsistence farmers and patriarchal heads of households who were property owning and, he assumed, law abiding.[57]

To assimilate, or de-Indianize, Aboriginal peoples, federal officials applied diverse techniques – such as education, missionization, or military force – that varied over time and from region to region. Regardless of the scheme, all efforts were informed and reinforced by attempts to surveil reserve residents.[58] After the Rebellion, officials increased the number of NWMP personnel and Indian agents, subdivided reserve lands into forty-acre plots, and issued nominal certificates of ownership to male heads of Aboriginal households. Hoping to undermine aspects of Aboriginal culture that were anathema to the liberal economic order – including communal notions of property, polygamy and divorce, and matrilineal or bilateral rules of descent and inheritance – legislators instigated a system of statutory subordination for Aboriginal women by determining Indian status through the male line. Canadian legislation enfranchised Aboriginal men and awarded them private property if they proved themselves to be debt-free, literate, and of good moral character. By contrast, legislation prohibited Aboriginal women from partaking in band business, and it stripped

Aboriginal women who married non-Indian men, and any children from the union, of their status. If an Indian woman married a Status Indian from another band, the DIA automatically transferred her to her husband's band. The legislation sought to refashion Indians in the image of the English common law, to transform wives into the virtual property of their husbands. As was the case throughout the British Empire, imperial and colonial enterprises on the Prairies took shape through the bourgeois, Victorian cult of marriage and domesticity.[59]

British Canadians likewise perceived newly arrived immigrants to the Prairies as a threat to empire and to Canada's central place within it. Between 1901 and 1931, the region's population increased sixfold, from slightly more than 0.4 to 2.4 million people; Saskatchewan became, overnight, the third-largest province in Canada, and Manitoba and Alberta followed in fourth and fifth place. Although the Canadian government designed aggressive recruiting schemes and campaigns to draw central Canadian and British women and farmers westward, the labour needs of an unprecedented wave of agricultural and industrial expansion made it necessary to recruit settlers whom many British Canadians deemed less than ideal. Between 1897 and 1905, for instance, Clifford Sifton, minister of the interior in Wilfrid Laurier's Liberal government, actively promoted the immigration of Canadian, British, and European farmers but rigorously opposed the recruitment of Britain's urban working class. His policy resulted in the arrival of thousands of eastern European peasant farmers with their families, many of whom took up homesteads in bloc settlements. Canadian immigration policy changed again when Frank Oliver replaced Sifton in 1905. Whereas Sifton had focused on the occupation of potential immigrants, Oliver deemed immigrants desirable based on their ethnicity or race. A series of revisions to the Immigration Act between 1906 and 1910 closed Canada's doors to criminals, radicals, and the medically and morally unfit and actively encouraged immigrants from England. Oliver said that settling the West was not "merely a question of filling that country with people who will produce wheat and buy manufactured goods" but also of "building up ... a Canadian nationality so that our children may form one of the great civilized nations of the world."[60] He worried that immigration could "deteriorate rather than elevate the conditions of our people." Although more Britons came, by the time of the First World War, British Canadians accounted for less than 50 percent of prairie residents, and half the region's population had been born in another country: eastern Europeans (Ukrainians, Austro-Hungarians, Poles, and Russians) and western Europeans (German, Dutch, and French) each constituted 20 percent of the total population.[61]

To the dismay of Canadian government officials and British Canadian westerners, changing immigration policy also coincided with manpower shortages on the Prairies, a high unemployment rate in English cities, and imperialistic rhetoric that encouraged Britons to remain under the flag. Britain's working class sought a new life on the Prairies, while British farmers remained at home. By the outbreak of the First World War, 20 percent of all male immigrants to the Prairies entered not as heads of farm households, but as itinerant agricultural labourers and potential farmers. Unfortunately, homestead entries peaked in 1911, and the scarcity of good, cheap farmland forced many of these men to find their fortunes in rapidly expanding urban centres and resource towns. Between 1911 and the beginning of the war, 65 percent of immigrants did not take up land but instead became either full- or part-time industrial workers. As itinerant labourers, they migrated throughout the region in pursuit of a variety of seasonal or temporary jobs in railway construction, mining, lumbering, or farming. In Winnipeg, the region's largest urban centre, foreign-born immigrants and itinerant labours increasingly lived or roomed in the city's North End: in 1913, it housed 87 percent of the city's Jews, 83 percent of its Slavs, and 22 percent of Manitoba's urban-dwelling Germans.[62] By 1914, advocates of social and moral reform, such as Methodist minister James S. Woodsworth, viewed the immigrant, working-class slums of rapidly growing cities such as Calgary, Edmonton, and Regina as cesspools of vice and violence, as site and symbol of the ills of modernity.[63]

As was the case in all Western, liberalizing states of the late nineteenth and early twentieth centuries, advocates of social reform and moral purity (for example, the Social Gospel, prohibition, and women's suffrage) and their interwar pseudo-scientific successors (for example, social and mental hygiene) saw new immigrants as a threat to the creation of a homogenous society – or "the social" – based on Protestantism and British liberal institutions.[64] Canadian sociologist Mariana Valverde argues that the term *nativism*, which refers to overt hostility to ethnic groups, was in fact a fantastical construct that invented a native British Canadian people and naturalized British ideas about law, the state, and society.[65] From the 1880s onward, many reformers in Canada advocated medical testing, deportation, and eugenics as panaceas for degeneracy. They also sparked a proliferation of new laws and the reform of existing ones to criminalize, by 1914, all sexual relations outside of marriage. Their underlying goal was coercive liberalism, which would shore up the white life for two as a foundation for nation building and as a bulwark against the secularization of society and race suicide. Regulating sexuality and enforcing compulsory heterosexuality and monogamy were implicit components of the reform agenda.[66]

CRIMINAL COURTS AS CONTACT ZONES

As the outcome of and responses to the Rosalie trials indicate, when women became involved in the criminal trial process as either victims or accused, the court became a stage where the various tensions of empire and nation played out. Courthouses were places where representatives of settler society such as officials, reform advocates, judges, magistrates, and juries came into contact and conflict with the primitive and the pauper and confronted their fears about nation and empire. They were also places where marginalized Aboriginal peoples, women, children, immigrants, and labourers aired their grievances, complaints, and conflicts as they faced the challenges and upheavals of modernity. Court records make it possible to explore how the criminal law was critical to the making of fruitful land, happy homes, and manly titans in rural, agricultural communities and in urban settings. This book traces the complicated process by which policy makers, social reform advocates, judges, juries, and average men and women turned to the criminal courts to create, protect, or challenge the idea that the prairie West should become an extension of the liberal economic order.

Contrary to constructed visions that represented the West as a place that would provide immigrants with freedom from the hierarchies and constraints that typified life in the Old World, the Prairies were settled during decades when the tensions of empire and nation building were at their height. In a social setting in which people were frequently on the move, unfamiliar with their neighbours, or socially isolated, diverse groups turned to the criminal law and the criminal courts to resolve their competing visions of law, society, family, sexuality, and morality. The criminal courts, consequently, served as contact zones between Aboriginal peoples and newcomers, capital and labour, British Canadians and new Canadians, and men and women.[67] In *Local Knowledge: Further Essays in Interpretive Anthropology*, cultural anthropologist Clifford Geertz argues that law is local knowledge – it does not simply reflect social life; it helps to construct it. Understood in this way, criminal justice is more than an instrument of power in the hands of an elite. It is also a process or struggle that reveals "contested states of governance, mind, and being" peculiar to any given culture at any given time.[68] How did criminal cases such as the Rosalie trials, for instance, reflect and reproduce social boundaries and hierarchies of difference as white settler societies emerged in prairie Canada? How did the law's function in prairie Canada compare to what was occurring in other developing settler societies and frontiers?

To answer these questions, I view the law as a site for the performance of hegemony and resistance.[69] Theorists throughout the disciplines have increasingly emphasized hegemony's role in the negotiation of power. Whereas ideology is a system of beliefs, meanings, and values articulated by a social group (with the dominant group's ideology reigning ascendant), hegemony is that part of ideology that appears so natural it is invisible.[70] To reconcile the concept of hegemony with the realities of resistance, Jean and John Comaroff argue that movement along the continuum between ideology and hegemony is marked by consciousness. Hegemony, consequently, is subject to negotiation and transformation. The law is simultaneously a maker of hegemony and a means of resistance. In developing settler societies, criminal courts functioned as sites for the performance of hegemony and resistance by serving as classrooms where litigants and the public alike were taught (through the performances demanded by the court and newspaper coverage) to distinguish between acceptable and deviant behaviours – as defined by dominant groups – and to accept culturally constructed categories as natural. Although the cultural turn has been debated vociferously by historians over the past decade, if we view the criminal courts and law in this way, political economy and culture are recognized as fundamental to the domains of power: the law's constitutive impact in colonial and national settings was both instrumental and cultural.[71]

In the next three chapters, I examine the criminal courts as contact zones – as sites for conflict resolution and identity construction – in three distinct social settings: Aboriginal reserve communities and places represented as the fringes of civilization; red-light districts; and rural, agricultural communities. In these three places, the criminal courts functioned as contact zones for competing masculinities and femininities and as forums through which deficient individuals (Aboriginal men and women, prostitutes, farm women and their daughters, and the unpropertied hired hand) were taught the repercussions of failing to live up to middle-class standards of domesticity, masculinity, and sexual morality. They also learned the consequences of failing to maintain the race and class boundaries fundamental to white settler societies and the prairie family farm. In Chapter 2, I trace how high-profile cases such as the Rosalie trials helped to establish the hegemony of British Canadian law in Aboriginal communities and how the day-to-day business of the police and courts contributed to the construction of Aboriginal masculinities and femininities. In Chapter 3, I examine the cultural, symbolic, and discursive meanings that were attached to female criminality in late-nineteenth-century discourses and to prostitutes and indigent women discovered in the streets and red-light districts of Winnipeg and, to a lesser extent, Edmonton. I use police records, social surveys, and social reform rhetoric to trace how early-twentieth-century contestations between police authorities, social reform advocates, and prostitutes disrupted the traditional separation of the private and public spheres but, ultimately, gendered the city male, setting the conditions for increased regulation of the private lives of working-class women and girls in the interwar years.[72] In Chapter 4, by contrast, I explore how the differential treatment of farmers and hired hands in rape, sexual assault, and seduction cases constructed normative white, British Canadian, and middle-class masculinity and hastened the emergence of class boundaries in rural, agricultural communities following the First World War. I trace how a more fully capitalist economy shaped and reshaped the contest between labourers and farmers over the appropriation of power, which was symbolized by sexual control of and access to women's bodies through marriage. As was the case in other Western industrializing regions and nations, dominant groups constructed the bachelor or disorderly man in the Canadian Prairies as being only one rung above the Aboriginal male on the evolutionary ladder.[73]

In Chapter 5, I switch the focus once more to the city during the progressive era and interwar years, when dislocations associated with the rise of the New Woman, rapid urbanization, and the emergence of a distinct adolescent youth culture once again appeared to threaten the lines between the private and the public spheres. During these decades, the bourgeois obsession with masculinity shifted to a preoccupation with the sexual behaviour of women and girls; in response, discourses on working-class women's deviant sexuality became metaphors for the malaise of empire and nation. The subsequent criminalization of all sexual practices outside of marriage by the First World War problematized the private female body in the public sphere, drawing marriage, motherhood, and female sexuality increasingly into the ambit of state and voluntary social reform.[74] The chapter highlights how abortion, drug, and rape prosecutions in the 1920s and 1930s shored up the family by regulating women's and girls' sexuality. It also traces how the urban criminal courts became settings for judicial authorities to hold husbands and lovers to their responsibilities and to pass judgment on male sexual practices and behaviours deemed an affront to middle-class masculinity.

Criminal case files not only allow me to trace how the private invaded the public and how the law responded, they also allow me to explore how the public, through the law, invaded the private. In the final two chapters, I narrow the focus to the domestic domain during an era when reformers, policy makers, and legal officials increasingly invaded the private to sustain the public-private dichotomy that was so integral to the liberal economic order. During the first three decades of the twentieth century, a confluence of social, cultural, and political forces drew public attention to sexual and physical violence in the private sphere. As many historians have observed, the strains and tensions of the new liberal society were often worked out in the homes of the nation through both violence and regulation. In these chapters, I examine cases of wife abuse, the sexual assault of female children, and spousal murder to explore the question of what role violence, and the law's response to it, played in the creation of a reinvigorated masculinity and reinstituted patriarchy on the Prairies. Did the law, the state, and social agencies, as some historians argue, construct the normative family by sanctioning a certain amount of deviance and violence among its members? In Chapter 6, I seek answers to these questions by exploring the meanings that were attached to incest and domestic violence in rural and urban settings. In Chapter 7, I examine the multiple meanings that were attached to women's most overt challenge to patriarchal authority: child and husband murder. Both chapters address the conditions under which some types of violence were deemed acceptable and, by doing so, they contribute to a small, but growing, literature that examines how the law and violence constructed gender identity – masculinities and femininities – among newly arrived white immigrants in settler societies.[75] Taken together, the chapters trace how a combination of federal legislation, high-profile cases, day-to-day policing, and punishment practices helped to re-create hierarchies of difference in a region that was, ostensibly, to be a land of opportunity, a very garden of the Lord.

2

They Know No Better

Maintaining Race and Managing Domestic Space at the Fringes of Civilization

One year after a white jury in Calgary found William "Jumbo" Fisk guilty only of manslaughter in the violent death of an Aboriginal woman, an editorial in the *Regina Leader* commended Hugh Richardson, chief justice of the Supreme Court of the North-West Territories, for his masterful handling of a similar case. In this instance, Justice Richardson had passed a harsh sentence on George Evanse when a jury found the German settler guilty of attempting to rape Harriet Thorne, an Aboriginal woman. Echoing Rouleau's admonition to jurors in the Rosalie trials, Richardson stated in his charge to the jury, "So long as a woman – be she White or black, Negro, Indian, or Circassian – conducted herself properly she was as much entitled to protection as the highest lady in the land."[1] Showing little sympathy for the accused, who pleaded drunkenness in his own defence, Richardson urged the jury to bring a guilty verdict, and he sentenced Evanse to serve three years at Manitoba Penitentiary.

Sexual or gendered violence, when it occurred in colonial settings or in emerging settler societies, was implicated more deeply in power relations than it was in the metropole.[2] Today, Aboriginal people's accounts of sexual or physical abuse at the hands of residential school instructors, missionaries, and settlers have provided some of the most forceful condemnations of Canada's past treatment of Aboriginal people.[3] In the past, by contrast, imperial agents were prone to link the abuse of indigenous women to the larger conquest of land: the physical conquest of indigenous women's bodies reinforced the bonds between heterosexual violence and the larger colonial project.[4] In the mid-nineteenth century in Rupert's Land and British Columbia, for example, judges and magistrates often dismissed Aboriginal women's complaints of sexual assault at the hands of white men because colonial discourses on sexually available Aboriginal women coloured their response to individual cases.[5] In addition, the fabric of the nineteenth-century British world was interwoven with periodic rape scares in which white women were represented as frail harbingers of civilization subject to the lascivious, rapacious interest of indigenous men.[6] The sexual assault of Metis women during the 1885 Northwest Rebellion, for instance, received virtually no public attention, whereas journalists and officials manipulated the relatively good experiences of two white women held captive by Cree chief Big Bear's band to promote mass hysteria and provide the Canadian government with a rationalization for its Indian policy.[7] As Hugh Richardson's charge to the jury in *R. v. Evanse* suggests, however, the situation on the post-Rebellion Prairies was more complicated. Judges and juries did not always turn a blind eye to Aboriginal people's complaints and allegations.

Although Aboriginal people today are more likely to become the victims of physical violence and crime than non-Aboriginal people and account for 50 percent of prison populations in the prairie provinces, they have not always been overrepresented in the region's criminal justice system.[8] With the exception of livestock theft, it has been estimated that the crime rate for Aboriginal people in the North-West Territories from 1878 to 1885 was less than 20 percent that of white settlers. Although judges, lawmen, journalists, and white settlers in this era spoke constantly of restraining the lawless savages, Canadian authorities tended to apply Canadian criminal law only to disputes between nations or bands or to disputes between Aboriginal people and white settlers. Depending on the circumstance, Aboriginal men and women could choose between Canadian law or their own systems of law and dispute resolution. Political, demographic, and economic changes after 1885, however, diminished Aboriginal people's bargaining power. And the reserve environment and the civilizing efforts of missionaries and government agents gradually eroded Aboriginal institutions and law over the next five decades.[9]

This chapter examines two discrete but related series of cases that began to trickle into the courts in these decades: sensational rape, incest, and murder trials that involved Aboriginal victims or defendants, and more routine cases of trespass, the sale and consumption of alcohol, and domestic and sexual violence that came to the attention of police and Indian agents in southern Alberta. Judges' pronouncements during the Rosalie trials and the Evanse trial suggest that the rhetoric of restraint that characterized the late 1870s and early 1880s was giving way to the rhetoric of benevolence that came to be an integral component of Canadian identity and Indian policy.[10] How typical were the Rosalie trials and *Evanse*? Did Aboriginal victims of physical or sexual violence who turned to the Canadian courts for protection always convince officials and juries of the truth of their claims? What role did considerations such as class and ethnicity play in the resolution of cases? What happened when the tables were turned and Aboriginal men or women were accused of being aggressors or perpetrators? Did magistrates, judges, and juries base their decisions on the facts of the case alone, or did larger concerns come into play? In other words, what was the reality behind the rhetoric? What function did criminal cases in the contact zone serve when the eyes of the nation and empire were turned elsewhere?

ABORIGINALITY IN THE CONTACT ZONE: HIGH-PROFILE RAPE, INCEST, AND MURDER TRIALS

Harriet Thorne's allegations of rape against a white settler came at a time when Canada's prairie Indian policy was the subject of debate and some derision. In April 1886, Liberal MP Malcolm Cameron alleged that law and government officials on the Prairies – men he described as dishonest, unscrupulous, and tyrannical – were defiling Aboriginal women and starving their children by withholding food rations. Cameron's allegations joined those of Samuel Trivett, a Protestant minister who claimed that parents at the Kainai (Blood) Reserve were being forced to sell young female children into slavery. White men, Trivett claimed, came onto the reserve, bought the girls, and turned them out onto the streets of Fort Macleod as prostitutes when they grew tired of them.[11] The federal government responded to the allegations by publishing *The Facts Respecting Indian Administration in the North-West* (1886), which drew upon evolutionary anthropology to depict reserve residents as alcoholics and lazy beggars and blamed Aboriginal people themselves for the poor reserve conditions forcing women into prostitution.[12] Cameron's allegations also enhanced the federal government's determination to present a sterling image to the public. After the incident, Department of Indian Affairs (DIA) officials deliberately edited negative developments from annual reports and correspondence and emphasized positive developments such as Aboriginal people's involvement in fairs and exhibitions.[13]

Enhanced policing and extra-legal measures following the Rebellion also shored up the DIA's and North West Mounted Police's ability to regulate and survey Aboriginal people's movement and behaviour on and off the reserve. The federal government doubled the number of North West Mounted Police (NWMP) from five hundred to one thousand. Prime Minister Sir John A. Macdonald also hoped to foster more intimate ties between the DIA and the NWMP by appointing Lawrence Herchmer, a well-connected DIA official, commissioner of the force in 1886. Macdonald's initiatives were presented as part of a larger strategy to police the Canadian-American international border and protect Aboriginal peoples from the potentially corrupting influence of white settlers.[14] The pass system, which had been devised as a temporary measure to control and monitor Aboriginal people's activities during the Rebellion, became a regular feature of reserve life in this period. The system required Indians to have a letter of recommendation from a farm instructor or Indian agent before they could leave the reserve, thereby making it more difficult for reserve residents to perform in or attend religious ceremonies or to visit family members and children who lived off the reserve, across the border, or at residential or industrial schools. Although members of the NWMP were opposed to the pass system because it had no legal justification, and Aboriginal people resisted and defied its application at every turn, certain Indian agents and police tried to use it to control so-called difficult individuals and reserve populations.[15] Department officials justified the policy by blanketing it with the rhetoric of protection: the pass system, they argued, would protect Aboriginal women from the perils of prostitution; it would limit Aboriginal peoples' access to alcohol; and it would enhance the enjoyment of life in rural, agricultural communities.[16] When Commissioner Hayter Reed of the DIA wrote Commissioner Herchmer in 1891 to say that he had received reports of Indians from the Siksika (Blackfoot) Reserve taking adolescent girls to Lethbridge for immoral purposes, he stated that he wanted the local NWMP detachment to keep "a sharp look out ... at all times for loitering Indians and to see that Indians without a pass be sent back to the reserve."[17]

The trial and imprisonment of George Evanse for the attempted rape of an Aboriginal woman was one of three cases that judges and juries of the Supreme Court of the North-West Territories heard between 1889 and 1898. Like the Rosalie trials in Calgary, the *Evanse, Motow,* and *Bourassa* cases stirred up fear and anxiety among white settlers in Regina, the territorial capital and heart of the Western Assiniboia Judicial District.[18] The incidents occurred in the Fort Qu'Appelle and File Hills regions, where

Cree, Assiniboine, and Saulteaux bands had negotiated Treaty 4 with the Canadian government in 1874 and then settled on the Pasquah, Piapot, Muscowpetung, and Standing Buffalo reserves near Fort Qu'Appelle and on the Peepeekisis, Okanese, Star Blanket, and Little Black Bear agencies in the File Hills region. Few immigrants had settled in the region following the treaty, but the arrival of the Canadian Pacific Railway precipitated a land rush in 1882 and 1883. The influx of white settlers coincided with drought, disease, and starvation on reserves, and by the late 1880s the Qu'Appelle area had become contested terrain between Aboriginal peoples and the emerging settler society.

The Canadian government exacerbated the situation in 1888 when it began to allot reserve land in severalty and introduced the peasant farming scheme to the area. By forcing reserve farmers to make and use outdated implements and farming methods, the policy limited the scope and success of Aboriginal farming and paved the way for further settlement. Both policies brought the federal government into direct confrontation with those Cree, Saulteaux, and Asssiniboine reserve residents who refused to relocate to the surveyed plots.[19] The *Motow, Evanse,* and *Bourassa* cases, therefore, occurred during a period of heightened tension between Aboriginal peoples, white settlers, and government officials. With memories of the Riel and Rebellion trials still fresh in the minds of Aboriginal and white observers alike, and with Cameron's and Trivett's allegations fresh in the minds of government officials, Supreme Court judges such as Charles B. Rouleau and Hugh Richardson proceeded with caution and shaped their charges to the jury and their sentences to maintain – and in some cases re-establish – faith in the rule of law.[20]

On 3 July 1889, in the same month that Calgarian William "Jumbo" Fisk faced Justice Rouleau and a second jury on charges of murder, a Cree man called Gopher Tom (Motow) stood accused in Regina before Justice Richardson and a jury for attempting to rape Bertha Noseda, a fifteen-year-old white girl. Like Rouleau, Richardson had presided over the post-Rebellion trials of Louis Riel, Poundmaker, Big Bear, and One Arrow at Regina. Although Richardson's handling of the Riel trial is today a matter of debate, the judge enjoyed a reputation for impartiality in the view of white settlers, Metis, and churchmen. Born in London in 1826, Richardson immigrated to Canada with his parents when he was five years old. He was admitted to the Upper Canadian Bar in 1847 and, after practising law, joined the civil service at Ottawa as chief clerk in the Department of Justice. Four years later, Richardson headed west to Fort Battleford, where he became the third stipendiary magistrate of the North-West Territories.

FIGURE 10   The First Supreme Court Judiciary of the North-West Territories, c. 1890, was made up of *(from left to right)* Sheriff James H. Benson, Justice E.L. Wetmore, Colonel James F. Macleod, Hugh Richardson (chief), Charles B. Rouleau, T.H. McGuire, and "Dixie" Watson, clerk of the court. | Glenbow Archives, NB-16-239.

In 1887, the federal government appointed him to the Supreme Court in the Western Assiniboia Judicial District (see Figure 10). By the time Richardson heard Motow's case, he had had thirteen years of experience working as a judge in the West.[21]

The *Gopher Tom* case came to the authorities' attention when Bertha Noseda, the daughter of the carpentry instructor at the Qu'Appelle Industrial School, accused Motow, a member of the Peepeekisis band of the File Hills region, of attempted rape. At the preliminary hearing, held before Frederick Proctor in mid-June that same year, Noseda deposed that on the afternoon of 10 June she had been gathering flowers on the trail between Fort Qu'Appelle and the industrial school when the accused jumped her, tried to stuff a rag into her mouth, and hit her on the face. Noseda claimed that at one point during the struggle, Motow tried to raise her skirt. When a rig driven by white settlers approached, however, the assailant ran away. In his defence, Motow claimed that he had received a pass from the Indian agent to visit his children at school. Following the visit, the accused maintained that he went straight home without encountering Noseda. Indian Agent Henry L. Reynolds disputed Motow's testimony and claimed that the accused had never applied for a pass and did not "bear a good reputation. He has the nature of assaulting women. He has got that nature and character."[22]

Five years earlier, Motow had stood trial for larceny and argued in his defence that hunger and desperation had driven him to theft. Drawing public attention to the inadequacies of Indian policy prior to the Rebellion and the federal government's treatment of reserve residents, Motow argued that he had committed the crime because he had been starving at the File Hills Reserve.[23] The trial occurred on the same day that Yellow Calf and his followers, who had taken up arms to protest rationing policies at the Crooked Lake reserves, also stood trial for larceny. Although the attorney general dismissed the charges against Yellow Calf, the other accused, including Motow, pleaded guilty. Although the accused's actions stood as a scathing indictment of the federal government's Indian policy, Reed attributed the outbreak to Indian dancing, which he believed had worked the Indians into a frenzy.[24]

When Motow came up for trial on charges of attempted rape, indecent assault, and common assault in July 1889, Richardson took measures to ensure that neither white settlers nor Aboriginal people could find fault with the legal process or accuse him of judicial bias. Eight – rather than the typical six – jurors heard the case. (They were, of course, all propertied British Canadians.) Richardson also had Justice of the Peace H. Le Jeune sit as an associate on the bench, while Amédée Forget, assistant Indian commissioner, represented the interests of the DIA. The jury found Motow guilty of indecent assault, and Richardson, rather than sentencing the accused to the maximum penalty of two years in prison with a whipping, sentenced him to three months in the North West Mounted Police (NWMP) guardroom with hard labour and twelve lashes.[25] The lenient sentence – and Richardson's paternalistic treatment of the accused – drew attention away from the fact that the jury had based its verdict solely on the accused's general reputation, as disclosed by the Indian agent, and the complainant's testimony that she thought the accused might be the same Indian who had attacked her.

Richardson's lenient treatment of Motow stood in direct contrast to his handling of *R. v. Evanse,* which came to trial one year later. The case first came to the authorities' attention when Harriet Thorne, a Metis woman married to a Status Indian, complained that she and another woman had been driving a cart near Fort Qu'Appelle on 5 October 1890 when the accused ran down a hill, "showed us his privates, and shook it."[26] According to Thorne, Evanse then pulled her from the cart and tried to rape her. At the trial, which was heard in mid-October, Richardson again chose to preside with a JP as associate on the bench. Evanse – perhaps assuming that the victim's race would ensure an acquittal – refused counsel and pleaded drunkenness as a mitigating circumstance in his defence. On Richardson's prompting, however, the jury found Evanse guilty of attempted rape. Editorials in the *Regina Leader* commended Richardson's decision to punish Evanse with a three-year term at Manitoba Penitentiary, and the authors interpreted the case as a notice to the public that the courts would not countenance sexual violence against women, irrespective of skin colour.[27] During sentencing, however, Richardson emphasized the complainant's race as a factor in his decision to punish the accused harshly: "This was one of the first cases of its kind to come before me in these parts of the Territories and it was necessary to award exemplary punishment."[28]

Two years later, Justice Richardson again presided over a potentially scandalous rape case that occurred in Regina and that also involved an Aboriginal woman. On 31 May 1892, Adelaide Trottier, a thirteen-year-old former student of the Qu'Appelle Industrial School, complained that a "half-breed," Pierre Bourassa, had raped her while she made her way home following church services. Trottier was working in Regina as part of the outing system, which had been devised by missionaries as a solution to the region's domestic servant shortage. In 1891, the principal of the industrial school, Father Joseph Hugonnard, OMI, pressed more than twenty female students into service as maids, nannies, and household assistants. Hugonnard arranged the terms of service and payment, retained the majority of the students' wages, and provided their parents with only a small stipend. Hugonnard and federal officials believed that girls such as Trottier could better prepare for arranged Christian marriages if they had the opportunity to practise English and adopt British Canadian habits and ways in isolation from their families and reserve communities. The girls' parents, however, resisted the practice, and religious and political authorities expressed anxiety over its potential for scandal.[29]

Bourassa's trial took place on 8 July before Justice Richardson and twelve jurors.[30] Trottier testified that she had been working in Regina for six weeks before she and two friends met the accused near the railway station. Claiming to be a friend of a friend, Bourassa followed the girls to Mrs. McCusher's home, where one of the girls worked. Bourassa then allegedly attacked Trottier on the open prairie when she continued home alone. Although the Cree interpreter, Peter Houri, had some problems translating the complainant's testimony, Trottier met the evidentiary requirements of nineteenth-century Canadian rape law: she established that she had been previously chaste; she reported the rape immediately to a secondary party;

and she established that the sexual assault had been accompanied by force. Richardson made sure that the accused heard Trottier's accusations in Cree, and he allowed the accused to question the witness in the same language. In his defence, Bourassa attempted to harness stereotypes of Aboriginal women as sexually available in his favour: Trottier, he contended, had not only consented to sex; she had initiated it, pulling him to the ground when he proved hesitant.[31]

Fulfilling his earlier promise that Aboriginal women – so long as they conducted themselves properly – were as entitled to the courts' protection as the "highest lady in the land," Richardson explained the inappropriate-ness of Bourassa's defence to the jury. Consent, he argued, was not at issue because Father Hugonnard had established that Trottier had been only thirteen years old at the time of the incident. The alleged crime therefore fell under unlawful carnal knowledge, for which the maximum sentence was life imprisonment and a whipping.[32] The jury deliberated for forty-five minutes and brought in a guilty verdict, but it made a strong recommen-dation for mercy on the grounds that the accused, because he was a mixed-blood, was unfamiliar with British Canadian law. Richardson endorsed the jury's recommendation and, by doing so, cultivated the judiciary's image as a protector of Aboriginal people's interests. When Richardson lectured the accused at sentencing, however, he perpetuated and enhanced white settlers' tendency to view Aboriginal women through a lens darkened by colonial discourses that sexualized their behaviour: "The schools like the Industrial School, where she had been for the purpose of elevating these girls and putting them in a position where they would become perfectly civilized and of removing any distinction between, as we may say, their colour and that of whites and if ever there was a duty incumbent upon a young man even if she had on that night asked you to cross the prairies with her it was your duty above all to have avoided anything wrong even if she had proposed it herself."[33] Offering the victim's and the accused's race as mitigating circumstances in the commission of the crime, Richardson reduced Bourassa's sentence from life imprisonment to five years at Manitoba Penitentiary, with twenty strokes of the cat-o'-nine-tails. The *Leader* made no comment on Richardson's sentence and, significantly, chose not to mention Trottier's connection to Qu'Appelle Industrial School.[34]

As in other Canadian regions and settler societies, the desire to maintain the integrity of colonial categories and national boundaries informed judges' responses to high-profile cases of sexual violence that involved Aboriginal people. Judges had one eye on the trial over which they presided and the other on developments in the nation and empire. The trials became sensational instances for judges to establish the law's hegemony among Aboriginal peoples and to reinforce British Canadian identity and sovereignty north of the forty-ninth parallel by demonstrating Canada's fair and equal treatment of the colonized and the superiority of British Canadian law.[35] If the defendant's ethnicity or class placed him outside the bounds of dominant British Canadian, middle-class notions of morality and masculinity – as was the case in the *Evanse* trial – establishing the law's legitimacy was that much easier. Judges such as Richardson could afford to be generous because cases such as Harriet Thorne's rarely came before the superior courts. The relatively lenient treatment of Motow and Bourassa, by contrast, suggests that in prairie Canada, as in British Columbia, jury members' attitudes toward Aboriginal men were shaped by negative stereotypes of Aboriginal people.[36] As Bourassa's defence strategy suggests, Aboriginal men, in turn, could respond by manipulating the performative aspects of the trial process to their advantage. They could harness negative stereotypes of Aboriginal women in their favour or offer culture – for instance, ignorance of law, customary law, or alcohol abuse – as mitigating circumstances in their defence to avoid punishment from a system they feared and distrusted.[37] Historian Tina Loo, who has examined Aboriginal defence strategies and discretionary justice in capital murder trials in British Columbia, argues that this trend saved a few men at the expense of many.[38]

Evidence from the Prairies indicates that high-profile incest and murder trials that involved Aboriginal men, much like rape trials, likewise shored up white settler society – not only by reinforcing negative stereotypes about Aboriginal women but also by refashioning Aboriginal men as infantile, uncivilized, and immoral, and Aboriginal people in general as doomed to extinction.[39] Justice Richardson used judicial discretion in the Bourassa rape trial to mitigate the law's severity and re-establish Aboriginal people's faith in the rule of law only five years before *R. v. Machekequonabe* (1897) established a precedent throughout the British Empire that colonial law applied universally – even in cases where indigenous men or women had never been exposed to English common law.[40] In that year, Machekequonabe, an Anishinabe male who shot a man he believed to be a Wendigo or cannibal spirit, was tried for murder but found guilty only of manslaughter because the prosecution could not prove intent. Despite the precedent, Aboriginal men accused of committing incest continued to put forward ignorance of law or culture as mitigating circumstances to justify their behaviour and avoid harsh punishments well into the twentieth century.[41] In 1902, for instance, Jean Baptiste Laferty, a Metis employee of the Hudson's Bay Company at Fort Vermilion in northern Alberta, faced charges of having an incestuous relationship with his underage sister. At the conclusion of the preliminary hearing, which was held in the North, the presiding JP wrote Justice Thomas McGuire of the Supreme Court of Alberta to inform him that Laferty was an honest and willing employee. He warned: "In my opinion the moral effect on the Aboriginal population by the fact of the NWMP coming in and taking him out of the northern country to be punished for his crime, will be as great with a light sentence as with a heavy one." At the trial, Laferty pleaded guilty to attempted incest and received a suspended sentence. He and his sister, Antoinette, both testified that they had consented to the sexual relationship and did not consider it a crime.[42]

Aboriginal men were still harnessing the cultural defence in their favour and receiving lenient sentences thirty years later. In March 1932, for instance, John Baptiste Lafournaise stood before Justice A.K. Dysart of the Manitoba Court of King's Bench and a jury on charges of committing incest with a half-sister. The illegitimate son of his sister's mother, Lafournaise was also a married man who had separated from his wife and five children. As was the case in *Laferty,* the Crown did not prosecute the female party. But the sister, like the brother, did testify that the sexual relationship had been consensual. Although incest carried a maximum penalty of fourteen years and a whipping, Dysart sentenced Lafournaise to only one year with hard labour at Manitoba Penitentiary.[43] In both *Laferty* and *Lafournaise,* the demands of an imposed system of law required the defendant to manipulate stereotypes of Aboriginal women's sexuality and the colonizer's idea of custom and culture to negotiate a more lenient sentence for himself. Although judges and juries on the Prairies tended to treat incest charges among the non-Aboriginal population seriously (see Chapter 6), Aboriginal men in general evaded punishment. One exception, however, reveals that the effectiveness of the cultural defence in incest cases did have limits. In 1910, an Aboriginal man was accused of having sexual intercourse with his daughter at their home near Crowley in the Porcupine Hills. As in the other cases, the accused did not deny the charge. He did, however, ask the arresting officer to call witnesses to testify to his daughter's reputation for sexual promiscuity. Although the accused tried to employ negative stereotypes of Aboriginal women in his favour – and, by doing so, reinforced them – the jury convicted, and the judge sentenced the defendant to serve five years in Alberta Penitentiary.[44]

Just as incest trials reinforced negative stereotypes of Aboriginal men as ignorant and infantile, so too did high-profile murder trials, which likewise became sites for the production and maintenance of race and gender identities. In 1899, for instance, three years after the *Machekequonabe* judgment, the Supreme Court of the North-West Territories in the Edmonton district became the setting for a murder trial that involved a Dene man, Sabourin, accused of murdering his sister-in-law, Josephine Landry, near Great Slave Lake, which at that time was part of the judicial district. In this case, the jury brought in a verdict of guilty and the judge sentenced the defendant to hang. In his defence, Sabourin argued that he had acted according to Aboriginal law. When it became apparent that his sister-in-law had been possessed by a Wendigo, he shot her in the back of the head. Sabourin's sentence was eventually commuted. Records not only reveal the attitudes of local and federal authorities but also suggest the degree to which political pragmatism and prejudice shaped the outcome. James Smart, deputy superintendent-general of the DIA, for instance, advised the minister of justice that by extending the prerogative of mercy to Sabourin – by commuting Sabourin's sentence to life in prison – the government would hasten Aboriginal peoples' acceptance of Canadian law and governance in the Northwest.[45] Similar objectives informed Oblate missionary Father Albert Lacombe's pleas on Sabourin's behalf. Writing to the minister of justice, Lacombe argued, "As a member of the royal commission of last summer among these Indians, I ask for the commutation, on account of the fair way the said commission have [sic] been received ... The kindness and liberality of your government will have the effect to well dispose them more and more."[46] To enhance his plea for mercy, Lacombe argued that Sabourin, who suffered from "ignorance and poor health," would likely die in the penitentiary anyway. Lacombe's observation was prescient: Sabourin contracted and died of tuberculosis in Stony Mountain Penitentiary in November 1902.

When Aboriginal men were involved in sensational, high-profile murder cases that involved white women, medical and colonial discourses on women's mental health, the perils of miscegenation, and Aboriginal masculinity and sexuality likewise coloured government officials' and legal authorities' responses to the case. When the Alberta Provincial Police dragged the body of Hugh Jackson, a white farmer who had been reported missing since Christmas, from a lake near Swan River in northern Alberta on 2 June 1920, for instance, they set in motion an investigation and trial that turned received notions about sexual violence, gender, and race on their heads. Foul play was apparent. Police discovered Jackson's body bound in a horse blanket and weighted down with a rock. The victim's wife, Sadie or Sarah Jackson, immediately confessed to the murder and implicated two Northern Cree men, Zerma Coutereille and Jo Sounds, as accessories after the fact. Jackson's trial took place on 28 and 29 September before Justice William Walsh of the Supreme Court of Alberta and a jury. Perhaps swayed by expert medical testimony, the jury convicted with a strong recommendation for mercy.[47] Dr. Henry Derton Loggie, a neurologist whose examination of the accused was confined to trial adjournments, concluded that the accused "was a woman of low moral type and a distinctly animal nature and of uncontrollable passions and of a sexual nature and one who in stress of circumstances such as preceded the crime might have been governed by an unreasoning fear of an animal kind."[48] Loggie based his assessment of Jackson's mental health solely on the accused's admission that she had engaged in a long-term sexual relationship with an Aboriginal man.

Jackson's married daughter, Dora Beatrice Stevenson, however, contradicted her mother's plea for mercy on the grounds of insanity. During her testimony, which lasted for four hours, Stevenson explained that Jackson, the mother of five children, had been intimate with Coutereille in the summer of 1919 when Stevenson's father was away from the homestead. Stevenson herself admitted to having a fondness for the Indian Jo Sounds. She continued her testimony by describing how Jackson, following a quarrel with her husband, had planned to kill him by bashing his skull in with a hammer. Her mother later decided to use a gun because she did not think that she could hit her husband hard enough to kill him. Stevenson then testified that Jackson woke her up on Christmas Eve and said, "I shot him, he is dead." Mother and daughter burned the victim's clothes, placed the body on a toboggan, and hauled it out to the barn. After spending the remainder of the evening cleaning up the scene of the crime, Stevenson and Jackson made it known among their neighbours that Hugh Jackson had left the district on business. The following Friday the two women asked Zerma Coutereille to help them hide the body in a nearby slough. As a witness for the prosecution, Coutereille admitted that, come spring breakup, Jackson's body had moved nearly a quarter of a mile. After he and Sounds dragged the body to the shore, Sadie Jackson helped the two men hide it in Posie's slough. When asked to explain her and her mother's behaviour, Stevenson testified that she and her mother had killed Hugh Jackson because they wanted to live freely and openly with Sounds and Coutereille.[49]

In his address to the jury, Crown Prosecutor E.B. Cogswell stated, "If this act is to be justified, there is no justification anywhere."[50] However, a neighbourhood petition organized by defence counsel H.H. Robertson suggests that white settlers in the Swan River area justified Jackson's behaviour by drawing on prevailing discourses on race and gender at the fringes of civilization. Members of the local community did not truly believe that Jackson was insane, Robertson argued. They did, however, believe that she suffered from shattered nerves, which caused her to be open to the influence of Indians.[51] H.C. Reynolds, a resident of Camrose, Alberta, wrote the minister of justice,

> This woman being always clean and progressive fell a victim to a certain man, the latter died in defence of his country in France, sometime afterward she remarried Hugh Jackson whom I believe was immoral which was unknown to her, he Jackson moved into the wilds with her where he no doubt led a reckless and immoral life ... Leaving her alone surrounded by Halfbreeds without the necessities of life her mental condition deteriorated and she no doubt became the helpless prey to any person ... Here she was surrounded by men of low moral type, in the Wilds of the West, far from civilization, threatened by an immoral husband.[52]

These arguments, the accused's status as a wife and mother, and the jury's recommendation of mercy resonated with federal government officials, for they reduced Jackson's sentence to life in prison on 9 December 1920 (see Chapter 7 for details of the clemency campaign on her behalf).

Negative stereotypes of Aboriginal men likewise turned in Coutereille's and Sounds's favour when they too stood trial in late September that year. Both men pleaded guilty to being accessories after the fact to murder and became liable for a life term in prison.[53] Journalists' treatment of the trial emphasized Coutereille's status as a full-blooded treaty Indian, and problems with translation and miscommunication drew the jury's and judge's attention to the defendants' race throughout the trial.[54] Claiming that he was sensitive to the issue of the accused's youth and race, Justice Walsh chose not to bring the full force of the law to bear against them and sentenced both to two years less a day at Fort Saskatchewan Penitentiary. The *Edmonton Journal*, which covered the Coutereille trial, then presented for the pleasure of its white audience a portrait of a wise, learned, and paternalistic judge dispensing justice to an ignorant, infantile example of Aboriginal masculinity: "His lordship, in simple language, which the aboriginal could understand, told Coutereille that what he had done was very wrong and that he could be sent to the penitentiary for life. Experience in the past had shown that where Indians are sent to the penitentiary they quickly contract tuberculosis and die soon after admission."[55]

The rhetoric of benevolence and discourses of Aboriginal men and women as dissolute, infantile, and undisciplined were likewise reinforced and played a determining role in the trial of Round Nose, a resident of the Kainai Reserve, who was accused of murdering his wife during the Depression. At the preliminary hearing, the prosecution established that the accused had been released from prison in September 1939 after serving a sentence for wife beating. The accused's wife had left him and was living with her closest male relative, Spear Chief. She had recently taken a temperance pledge. Although the full sequence of events that culminated in murder was not established at the hearing, members of the Royal Canadian Mounted Police (RCMP) did report that they had received a search warrant from Indian Agent John E. Pugh to investigate an assault case at the reserve. The RCMP found Round Nose's wife near death from a severe blow to the head. They also discovered evidence of recent alcohol consumption by both the accused and the victim. Round Nose's brother-in-law produced a butcher knife that Mrs. Round Nose had allegedly used to stab her husband. Round Nose claimed that the conflict with his wife had been started by Spear Chief, who had demanded fifty dollars to turn his sister over to her husband's care.[56]

Round Nose faced a jury composed of white settlers, but members of the Kainai community spoke on his behalf and filled the courtroom. Mike Mountain Horse, RCMP scout and interpreter, testified that Round Nose had admitted to him that he had given his wife "a licking out of the ordinary, a little more severe." In response, Round Nose's attorney, Max Moscovitch, maintained that his client had acted in self-defence after his wife tried to stab him. Because Round Nose had been intoxicated at the time, Moscovitch concluded that the accused could not be deemed responsible for his actions. Round Nose was "but a poor simple Indian that could not understand one word of the Court proceedings" and "did not know better."[57] Chief Justice Thomas Mitchell Tweedie advised the jury that a murder verdict was out of the question because Round Nose had acted in self-defence. Manslaughter, he reasoned, was the only possible verdict.[58] Rather than focusing on the issue of domestic violence in the Kainai community or the legal issues involved in the case, newspaper accounts of the trial emphasized that Round Nose and his wife had been drinking rubbing alcohol prior to the offence. Reporters also noted that the trial proceedings had been observed by the Reverend Canon Middleton, principal of St. Paul's Residential School, and Robert Nathanial Wilson, former policeman and agent. The latter assured the public that Round Nose had received a fair trial and that his wife's interests had been protected to the best of the court's abilities. Mike Mountain Horse's interpretations of the proceedings, Wilson argued, had been exacting.[59] In his charge, Justice Tweedie told the jury to bear in mind that there were no witnesses to the assault, he discounted the intoxication defence, and he pushed for a manslaughter verdict.[60] The jury, however, after one hour of deliberation, acquitted Round Nose on all charges.

Although rare, high-profile rape, incest, and murder trials such as *Round Nose* – cases that involved Aboriginal people and had a gendered component – helped to maintain the boundaries of race that were so essential to the development of settler societies. On the one hand, judges' charges to the jury and journalistic treatments signalled to the reading public and observers alike that justice was being served, by benevolent officials, irrespective of skin colour. On the other hand, Aboriginal defendants were not held to the same standard as white settlers. Whereas Justice Richardson and a jury refused to accept drunkenness as a mitigating circumstance in *Evanse,* the defence was used, despite the judge's charge, to good effect in *Round Nose.* Ignorance of law as an effective defence likewise belied the rhetoric of impartiality that had blanketed proceedings since the 1880s and 1890s. Although the discrepancy between rhetoric and prosecution patterns in high-profile trials would have been apparent to discerning observers, with a few exceptions it largely went unnoticed at the local level in the realm of everyday law enforcement and decision making.

MANAGING THE MARGINALIZED:
REGULATING WOMEN AND GIRLS IN SOUTHERN ALBERTA

In 1933, RCMP officers stationed at Lethbridge, Alberta, reported to the Indian agent that they had received a complaint about Bertha Thomas trespassing on the Kainai Reserve. Two years earlier, the police had arrested, and an Indian agent had convicted, Thomas for residing in the home of her relative Big Sorrel Horse without the department's permission.[61] In this new case, the investigating officer discovered that the trespasser was Thomas' daughter, Sarah, who had received permission to be on the reserve from Indian Agent John E. Pugh.[62] In late November, Pugh advised the DIA that it was in everyone's best interests to keep the woman off the reserve. Bertha Thomas, he argued, had been enfranchised on her own application in 1927, and she was the daughter of the notorious murderer Charcoal. Sarah, he continued, was the product of Thomas' marriage to a white man; consequently, according to the Indian Act, she had never been a Status Indian.[63] Pugh alleged that Sarah Thomas' cousin Big Sorrel Horse had arranged for the nineteen-year-old girl to marry a reserve resident who was already married by Aboriginal law to a woman who lived at the Blood Reserve in Montana. Pugh concluded his report with an assessment of Sarah Thomas' character: "This girl is most undesirable, in all ways, and not a fit person to have on the reserve. Both the girl and her brother have been charged for liquor contravention, and I felt therefore that she is undesirable."[64]

John E. Pugh, who was Indian agent at the Kainai Reserve from 1926 through to the Second World War, was the sole representative of the DIA on a reserve that stretched hundreds of miles across Alberta between the St. Mary and Belly rivers south of Fort Macleod (see Figure 11). The reserve was home to Kainai – part of the Blackfoot Nation of the northern Great Plains, which also included Siksika and Piikani – whose traditional territory stretched south across the forty-ninth parallel into Montana. Kainai comprised several bands, or extended families, headed by a chief. Although Kainai numbered 2,058 when they negotiated Treaty 7 in 1877, poverty, hunger, and disease had reduced that number to 1,111 by 1920. Christian missionaries, residential schools, and the peasant farming scheme had also created divisions among reserve residents. While some families lived in teepees and off the proceeds of itinerant labour in the ranching and farming industries, families headed by residential school graduates lived in frame houses, operated small farms and ranches, and maintained close ties with Anglican and Catholic missionaries.[65]

Bertha and Sarah Thomas, by virtue of their status as defined by the Indian Act and the Indian agent, were forcibly excluded from the Kainai community. Their experiences and lives, of which only telling fragments remain in legal and governmental records, suggest the degree to which state regulation and the normalizing power of state policy fell heavily on Aboriginal women. But these same records simultaneously reveal the strategies that Aboriginal women employed to resist or circumvent the state's efforts to control their lives or define their identity.[66] The Thomas women shared a long history of entanglements and run-ins with the criminal justice system and the DIA, which had their origins in their blood relationship to Charcoal – a Kainai warrior who gained notoriety in 1886 when he killed his wife's lover and an NWMP officer – and in

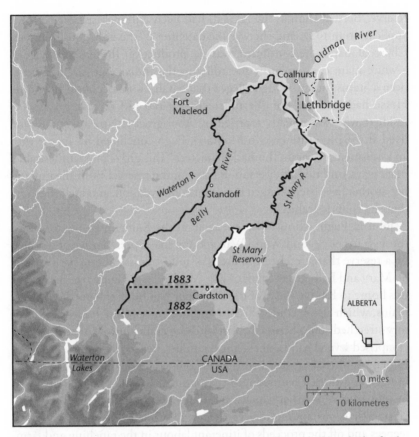

FIGURE 11 The Kainai Reserve in southern Alberta, which stretched hundreds of miles across Alberta between the St. Mary and Belly rivers south of Fort Macleod, was one of the most heavily policed Aboriginal communities in Canada after the Northwest Rebellion. | Adapted from "Blood Indian Reserve Alleged Claim Area," Indian and Northern Affairs Canada.

Bertha Thomas' decision to marry a non-Aboriginal man. Section 3 of the Indian Act denied status to any Indian woman who married a white man, and the act stated that "no half-breed ... shall, unless under very special circumstances to be determined by the Superintendent-General or his agent, be accounted an Indian."[67] Unless they were accepted by band officials, illegitimate children and the children of enfranchised Indian women could be excluded from the mother's band membership; however, the decision had to be sanctioned by the superintendent-general of the DIA.[68] The legislation also gave each Indian agent the power to issue a warrant to local police authorities, or "any literate person willing to act," to have

Non-Status Indians removed from the reserve or committed to jail for up to thirty days.[69]

The authorities' reaction to Sarah Thomas' case reflected British Canadian fears that mixed-race men and women posed a threat to colonial rule: determining who was Indian and who was white was central to the nation-building project. Unlike lawmakers in other parts of the British Empire and parts of the United States, Canadian legislators never defined white by law, and they did not criminalize marriage between white settlers and indigenous peoples. Defining who was an Indian therefore became a central facet of federal Indian policy because status determined access to rights, citizenship, and land. The Indian Act linked blood ties with real property and citizenship by basing selection criteria on an individual's relationship with an Aboriginal man, and the legislation assumed a patrilineal definition of *blood* that was anathema to many Aboriginal nations. By constructing the category of the half-breed, Canadian legislators placed many Aboriginal people who identified as Indian outside of the reserve space, and they created divisions between and within Aboriginal communities. The legislation did, however, create a problem for colonial authorities because they could not legally regulate mixed-race people in the same way as Indians. Indian agents and the NWMP used the trespassing and liquor provisions of the Criminal Code and Indian Act to control the movement and behaviour of enfranchised women and their mixed-blood daughters who resisted their authority. By doing so, they constructed an image of mixed-blood men and women as bad characters who exhibited the worst features of both races – sexual immorality, criminality, and habitual drunkenness.[70]

When it came to policing the behaviour and sexuality of Status Indian women, evidence suggests that police and Indian agents often had to rely on liquor and trespassing laws because they encountered problems applying laws against prostitution and enforcing the pass system. Just as the Indian Act rendered alcohol consumption a crime only if the accused was Aboriginal, it also designated prostitution-related offences involving Aboriginal men and women as a special category of crime. Amendments to the Indian Act in the early 1880s also prohibited white settlers from allowing Indian women or prostitutes on their property or in tents and wigwams. Following Trivett's accusations, it became illegal in 1886 for any Indian to keep, frequent, or be found in a disorderly house, tent, or wigwam. By contrast, prosecutors had to prove that a white man caught in the same situation was a habitual frequenter. The 1892 Criminal Code reaffirmed the legislation but restricted it to women who were Status Indians, and it categorized Aboriginal prostitution as an offence against morality. By contrast, keeping a common bawdy house (the category under which non-Aboriginal prostitutes were commonly prosecuted) was subsumed within the vagrancy provisions of the Code. Whereas Aboriginal prostitution was an indictable offence, vagrancy was a summary offence that fell under the rubric of "common nuisances."[71]

Laws against Aboriginal prostitution reflected fears about miscegenation and a desire to preserve racial boundaries. The legislation also reinforced stereotypes of Aboriginal women as dangerous and dissolute and did much to link prostitution and Aboriginal women in the minds of white settlers. As government officials struggled to apply the law, they revealed not only problems of enforcement and Aboriginal people's resistance but also deepseated assumptions about Aboriginal women and the underlying rationale for the legislation. Deputy Superintendent-General Lawrence Vankoughnet of the DIA, for instance, wrote to the Department of Justice in 1886 and asked if Indian agents could have Indian women who worked as prostitutes committed to jail. The case in question involved an Indian woman who lived alone and allegedly worked as a prostitute at the Maniwaki Reserve in Quebec. In response, representatives of the Department of Justice quoted prostitution and vagrancy laws then in effect and noted that they did apply to Aboriginal women. Because they interpreted prostitution and vagrancy laws narrowly, however, they concluded that the law could not be applied to the case in question because the woman did not keep, frequent, or reside in a disorderly house, nor did she wander the fields, public streets, or highways.[72] Similar problems plagued the prosecution of prostitution in Alberta. No Aboriginal women were among those convicted for prostitution-related offences between 1878 and 1885, and between 1886 and 1940, within the five selected judicial districts, Indian women stood accused in fewer than 10 of the 279 indictable cases involving female accused. Only one of these women was accused of being an inmate of a house of ill fame. Similarly, the record books of the Winnipeg Police Court for the two sample years 1886 and 1894 list only five Indian women out of a total 376 female offenders: police arrested all five for public drunkenness.[73]

Superintendent Richard Burton Deane's correspondence with NWMP commissioner Herchmer in the 1880s and 1890s illuminates the difficulties the police encountered when they tried to regulate prostitution among Aboriginal women in Alberta and suggests why the NWMP turned increasingly to liquor provisions to govern reserve residents' lives. Deane reported from Lethbridge in 1888 that there were "far too many Indians roaming this section of the country. Some of them come here to prostitute their women about the time of the miner's payday – vis. the 15th of each month." Deane advised his superior that his men typically made the women return to the reserve, "but I have now told them to let it be known that I will lock the women up if they come again for any such purpose." Six months later, Deane reported that although a few Indian women had exchanged sexual favours for money with white men, the NWMP had charged only one of them with a criminal offence: drunkenness.[74] When the police discovered six Indian women in the same river bottom selling sexual services to miners in November 1889, Deane reported that he "sent them back to the reserve with a note to the agent asking him to impress upon them that they would be locked up under the Vagrancy Act." Given that the police were under intense public scrutiny following Cameron's and Trivett's allegations, Deane complained one week later that it was "extremely incriminate" having a number of "dirty and diseased Indian women" in the NWMP guardroom.[75] In 1891, when white settlers again claimed that young Kainai girls were being sold into prostitution at Lethbridge, Deane reported to Commissioner Herchmer, "I do try to send Indians back with no pass but since we have no right it behoves one careful [sic] so as not to have to take 'back-water.'"[76] Superintendent Samuel B. Steele likewise reported from Macleod that it was difficult to enforce the pass system because "few of our men can speak sufficient Blackfoot to make themselves understood and the Indians when it suits their purpose can be very obtuse; they are aware too that we have no legal right to turn them back."[77] Despite these difficulties, Deane concluded that Indians in southern Alberta were beginning to understand that they could not leave the reserve without a pass: "A gentle but persistent pressure will teach them that the Reserve is the best place for them."[78]

Liquor prohibitions, at both the federal and provincial levels, stood at the heart of colonial attempts to maintain race by creating spatial boundaries between Aboriginal peoples and white settlers. The Indian Act's liquor provisions created a special category of offence for Aboriginal peoples by using race to determine who could sell or drink alcohol and where he or she could drink it. In the 1880s the Indian Act was amended so that any Indian found in a state of drunkenness could be liable to thirty days in prison or a $30 fine. By the 1890s, any person found guilty of selling liquor to Indians faced fines between $50 and $300, or, in default of payment, could serve a prison term. To enhance the provision's effectiveness, informants received half of the proceeds from the fine.[79] Any judge, Indian agent, justice of the peace, or police or stipendiary magistrate could arrest intoxicated Indians without a warrant and have them confined until they were either sober or their case came up for trial.[80] Despite the law's severity, Deane reported to Herchmer in 1888 that "the Indians are becoming very cunning about the liquor question and vary their stories so that conviction is almost out of the question." He advised Herchmer that an undercover Indian scout would be the best way to catch and convict offenders.[81] In 1891, Robert Nathanial Wilson, Indian agent at the Piikani Reserve, wrote Herchmer to complain that Indians could purchase as much liquor as they wanted from "vagabonds, Cree half-breeds, and white vagrants" at Macleod because the police were not doing all they could to secure convictions. Between 1889 and 1893, Deane responded to this charge and others by reporting that he had arrested some Indian women in Lethbridge for drunkenness and dismissed them with a warning but had also arrested and fined others: "The Guard Room has been overfull or I would not have given them the option of a fine."[82] Within a decade the NWMP could report that they had initiated 86 liquor-related proceedings in 1901 and 141 proceedings the following year.[83]

Homi Bhabha has argued that the ambivalence of colonial discourse left space for dissent, difference, and ambiguity. This argument was borne out on the Prairies when a number of white settlers began to question the manner in which certain law enforcement officials and Indian agents were applying the liquor laws to Aboriginal people in southern Alberta.[84] In 1895, the Reverend Harry William Gibbon-Stocken, an Anglican missionary stationed at the Tsuu T'ina (Sarcee) Reserve, wrote to Hayter Reed to let him know that informants in cases of selling liquor to Indians tended to be destitute Indians who risked conviction for drunkenness to receive the informant's share of the fine, which was far greater than that paid for drunkenness. Gibbon-Stocken also felt that it was unfair that there was no provision for the acquittal of Indian prisoners under conviction for drunkenness.[85]

Ten years later, an anonymous correspondent to the *Macleod Gazette* criticized the manner in which the Indian agent at the Kainai Reserve was applying the law to Aboriginal women. The writer disclosed that Indian Agent Robert Nathanial Wilson, a former member of the North West Mounted Police and member of the Free Masons Lodge, had recently sentenced a woman with a two-month-old child at her breast to either pay a fine of $450 or serve a nine-month jail sentence. The accused had allegedly sold a bottle or more of whiskey to Indians. According to the writer, Wilson did not give the woman the opportunity or time to appeal the conviction to the Supreme Court before committing her to prison. Wilson, he accused, had known that the woman, who was the sole provider for three or four children, could not pay the exorbitant fine: "The question of her guilt or not is immaterial for the purpose of these remarks which is regarding the punishment imposed and which is out of all proportion to the offence and out of the bounds of reason and against the dictates of Christianity and civilization and illustrates the danger of permitting unqualified and irresponsible persons exercising and abusing judicial power."[86] The author noted that the same agent had also sentenced another woman, found guilty of committing the same offence, to serve nine months in Calgary Jail without the option of a fine. The sentence, he alleged, had resulted in the death of her child, "under the most revolting, heinous, and shameful circumstance." Two years earlier, the superintendent in command of the Macleod District had written the commissioner of the NWMP to inform him that a white lawyer and a deputation of Piikani Indians had come to the detachment to lay a complaint against Wilson. Wilson, they claimed, was cutting their rations as discipline for criminal conduct. In response, Commissioner Aylesworth Perry and Frank Pedley, deputy superintendent-general of the DIA, advised the NWMP that officers of the force were never to hold interviews with reserve residents: all communications with the force were to be made through the Indian agent.[87]

Department of Indian Affairs and police reports to the Indian agent are replete with references to the fining or imprisonment of Indian and mixed-blood women for liquor infractions, and as early as February 1901, Indian Commissioner David Laird commended Wilson for his treatment of offenders: "I approve of your action ... not giving the Indians the option of a fine but sending them to jail. This will prevent them from squandering their money and give them time to think over the evils of intemperance."[88] Letters from Matron Fahey of Kingston Penitentiary, which detailed the effect of prison on Maggie Two Flags, did not, however, bear out the commissioner's prediction. The police had arrested Two Flags in January 1905, and she was convicted for perjury because she allegedly lied during a police investigation of liquor infractions at the Kainai Reserve. The judge sentenced her to serve three years in the federal penitentiary. Fahey wrote Wilson that Two Flags had been ill since her arrival and that the prisoner was "dying to hear some news from home or some of her own people." The matron disclosed that there was only one woman in prison who somewhat knew Two Flags's language. In general, however, the prisoner was unable to communicate with anyone.[89]

Department of Indian Affairs officials and legal authorities tried to use infractions of the liquor laws to maintain rigid boundaries between white settlers and reserve residents, boundaries that were threatened by the movement and behaviour of people such as Two Flags and the Thomas women. Sarah Thomas' alleged sexual immorality and her willingness to enter into a polygamous union with a reserve resident were likely perceived by Indian agents, police, and some reserve residents as threats to the civilizing process. Their treatment of her case and others like it suggest that government officials and legal authorities believed they had not only a right but also a duty to use any means at their disposal to isolate Aboriginal women they deemed immoral from reserve residents and settlers alike. In the Thomas case, Pugh and the police knew that Sarah Thomas had been a complainant in a case of unlawful carnal knowledge against two Asian Canadian men in 1927. Coerced by the police to make a complaint and testify, Thomas admitted to RCMP detectives that she had frequently engaged in sexual intercourse with Mah Hong and Quong How, owners of a Macleod laundry. Although Bertha Thomas refused to support her daughter's accusation and claimed at the hearing that her daughter was lying, a local physician testified to Sarah's unchaste state. Defence counsel played upon Sarah Thomas' blood connection to Charcoal and insinuated that, despite her age, the complainant's willingness to engage in sex with multiple partners rendered her unworthy of the court's protection. He also manipulated the fact that Bertha Thomas' husband had deserted her sixteen years earlier (leaving her and her daughter with no financial income) to suggest that Sarah Thomas was little more than a common prostitute.[90] A Supreme Court of Alberta judge dismissed the case against Hong, but a jury found How guilty of indecent assault and fined him fifty dollars.

The RCMP likewise cited the alleged sexual promiscuity of another woman, Lucy Under Mouse of the Blackfoot Reserve in Browning, Montana, as justification for her removal from the Kainai Agency. On 12 June 1929, Sergeant Howard of the Lethbridge Division reported to Pugh that Under Mouse, a "woman of undesirable character," had been living with Joe Snake Person at the Kainai Reserve. Under Mouse, Howard continued, had been convicted previously for vagrancy and had left her husband in Montana to live with Snake Person. When Under Mouse pleaded guilty to the charge, the Indian agent made her pay a fine of five dollars and the costs of the court, and he ordered her to "go back to the Reserve where she belonged."[91]

MODERNIZING THE MARGINALIZED:
LAW AND FAMILY IN SOUTHERN ALBERTA

As the Under Mouse case suggests, the regulation and policing of Indian and mixed-blood women and youths not only maintained and legitimated boundaries between Aboriginal peoples and white settlers, it also shored up the federal government's policy of reshaping Aboriginal sexuality and family structures to fit the Christian, patriarchal, and monogamous mould. Although the 1867 case *Connolly v. Woolrich* had recognized the validity of marriages entered into according to Aboriginal law, the Indian Act and unofficial DIA policies encouraged Indian agents to police and discourage practices that fell outside of monogamy and lifelong union.[92] Revisions to the Indian Act in the 1890s empowered the superintendent-general of the DIA to stop distribution of annuities, interest money, or band properties to any Indian man who separated (by choice or imprisonment) from his wife or children. To make annuity payments, all agents were required to monitor and record legitimate marriages and births. Policy circulars likewise counselled agents to discourage marital separations by cutting off offenders' treaty payments and rations.[93]

Criminal cases heard by the superior courts in the same decades reveal that the government's and judiciary's acceptance of Aboriginal marriage law had limits. In 1899, Chief Justice Charles Rouleau convicted Bear's Shin Bone of polygamy – polygyny, the practice of one man having many wives, was common among Plains Indians in the nineteenth century – by interpreting the accused's first marriage as a form of common law contract that could not be broken. Bear's Shin Bone was released on a suspended sentence on the understanding that he would give up his second wife. Officials with the DIA viewed *Bear's Shin Bone* as a test case, one that they hoped would encourage Aboriginal people to obey the law. Clearly, judges and federal officials did not embrace all aspects of Aboriginal law pertaining to marriage. Divorce, which was also accepted among Plains people, was also forbidden by the Indian Act.[94]

Because Aboriginal laws were fluid and process-oriented rather than concentrated on rules or rights, there are problems with trying to pin down Aboriginal law pertaining to marriage and sexual misconduct.[95] Yet oral and written sources reveal fundamental differences between Kainai and Euro-Canadian approaches to marriage and marital dispute resolution. In *My People the Bloods* and *The Ways of My Grandmothers,* Mike Mountain Horse and Beverly Hungry Wolf depict Kainai marriages at the turn of the twentieth century as systems of reciprocal obligation controlled by community elders. A family would advise a young man that he was ready for marriage and then cast about for his better half. Parents rarely consulted the wishes of the bride-to-be. (Given that divorce was relatively easy, however, it was difficult to force young men and women to marry if they did not want to. In these cases, another match would be pursued.) The young man's parents typically set up a teepee for the couple and provided their son with horses as a bride price. The bride then presented the groom's parents with moccasins and moved into the teepee. Once the groom moved in, the marriage had taken place. The newly wedded couple would then pay a visit to the bride's parents, and each of her male relatives would receive a pony – the gifts were symbolic acts that, again, sanctioned the union.[96] Although marriages typically involved a man and one or more women, most Plains Indian societies sanctioned same-sex unions because they were not wedded to a fixed, or binary, idea of gender roles or marriage.[97]

Although non-Aboriginal observers promoted the idea that an Aboriginal woman could divorce her husband by simply placing his belongings outside the teepee, this was not the case. Women usually considered incompatibility, physical abuse, or failure to provide as grounds for divorce. But family and clan elders typically tried to reconcile differences and disputes between husbands and wives. If reconciliation failed, or if the wife's kin did not approve of the husband's behaviour, the wife could leave her husband to live in her brother's or father's lodge. To obtain forgiveness, pardon, and his wife's return, an abandoned husband relied on his senior kin, who negotiated on his behalf with his wife's senior blood relatives (perhaps this was the cause of the dispute between Round Nose and his brother-in-law).[98] If the couple had children, divorce was less common. If divorce did occur, however, children could go with either parent but typically lived with the mother.[99]

Husbands usually considered laziness or adultery on the part of their wives as grounds for divorce. Sanctions against wifely infidelity could be formal and organized, diffuse and moral, religious and ritualistic, or immediate and retaliatory.[100] For instance, a Kainai woman accused of sexual impropriety could be subjected to the chastity tests required of women who participated in the Sun Dance. In the Owns Alone ceremony, a woman over forty publicly declared her steadfastness to her husband. If someone challenged her declaration, he or she would be asked to swear an oath. Once sworn, the community would pelt the adulterer with buffalo chips and run her out of camp. Although other breaches of marriage or residency rules could result in diffuse or retaliatory sanctions such as public shaming or physical mutilation, the family remained the primary regulatory force in instances of marital discord, unfaithfulness, and sexual promiscuity.[101]

The persistence of Aboriginal marriages and marriage law runs as a constant theme in correspondence between Indian agents, the DIA, and the NWMP. For instance, Bear's Shin Bone's case had come to the authorities' attention in 1898 when Indian Agent James Wilson reported to the DIA that six or seven young men had taken second wives in the past year, despite his efforts to prevent polygamy. The department secretary responded, "It is possible that trouble may follow attempts to enforce the law, especially among the Indians of Treaty 7, but with a little firmness I believe with the hearty co-operation of Mounted Police Officers in command at the various posts, it can be accomplished."[102] Two weeks later, in mid-August, Commissioner Amédée Forget advised Wilson to collect all data pertaining to the cases and submit them to the Crown prosecutor. If the state wished to proceed against them, Forget said, Wilson should call a meeting of the chiefs, bring the young men before them to hear an explanation of the law, and assure the older men that no action would be taken against them, "since they commenced the practice before they knew the existence of the law."[103] In November, Wilson also reported that he had held repeated meetings with Red Crow and other chiefs and counselled them that the Indian Act allowed him to refuse treaty payments to women who had deserted their families to live with another man. The admonishments, he argued, had worked – only three polygamy cases remained. In December, Forget urged Wilson to proceed in the three cases. After Bear's Shin Bone was prosecuted successfully for polygamy and released on a suspended sentence, Wilson again asked the other two men to give up their second wives.[104]

In the summer of 1900, the agent at the Siksika Reserve reported to James Wilson that Calf Robe had been living at the agency with another woman, a widow of doubtful morals, even though he had a wife and son at the Kainai Agency. In response, Wilson asked the police to send the "offender" home at once.[105] Two years later, Agent J.A. Markel at the Blackfoot Reserve provided Wilson with more advice on the DIA's Indian policy. Wilson had reported that a Kainai woman who was married according to Indian law to One Soot had taken up with another man. Markel advised Wilson that since the woman was not One Soot's first wife, nothing could be done: "If she is the plural wife it has been the rule with me not to encourage the holding of more than the original wife and if No. 2 at any time wishes to leave the home or her reputed husband, I have not encouraged her to return"; "If it is No. 1," he continued, "I will try to make her go back."[106]

The DIA's policy on marriage was met with confusion, uncertainty, and resistance in Aboriginal communities. Joseph Hicks, a lawyer, wrote to Indian Agent Wilson at the Kainai Reserve in 1905 to let him know that a reserve resident, Brown Weasel, had consulted him regarding his legal right to his daughter. According to Brown Weasel, his wife had left him to live with another man and had sent two Indian scouts to retrieve her daughter. Hicks supported Brown Weasel's desire to have his child returned to him and advised Wilson that "he had no doubt but that the scouts are acting on their own responsibility and a word from you will save a lot of trouble."[107] Four years later, Wilson complained to the secretary of the DIA about the state of marital relations at the Kainai Reserve: "[There are] constant cases of married people separating ... sometimes under mutual agreement but more often against the wishes of one of the parties. In these matters I always endeavour to secure a reconciliation by talking to the young couple and their relations ... only occasionally are such efforts successful."[108] Wilson referred to a case that had come recently to his attention in which a woman had returned to her mother's home after leaving her husband. At the husband's request, Wilson spoke to the wife, but she told him that "she was afraid of him, hated him and would not live with him under any circumstances." Wilson then chose to speak to the wife's brother – whom he referred to as the dominant member of the family – who refused to force his sister to return to her husband. After Wilson's attempt to resolve the dispute, the husband asked for permission to marry again because he was only twenty-five years old and could not remain single. Wilson counselled the DIA that the husband had been married according to Aboriginal law – he had paid a bride price of nineteen horses – and asked for advice as to the best course of action. Frank Pedley, superintendent-general of the DIA, advised Wilson that although the Canadian government had a liberal view of Aboriginal marriage, it did not recognize divorce. Wilson was to punish all bigamists harshly.[109]

The federal government's policy on Indian marriages, and the increasingly intrusive role of the Indian agent in the family life of Kainai men and women, created confusion and uncertainty in Aboriginal communities and fuelled tensions between husbands and wives. In the early twentieth century, reserve residents and Indian agents complained repeatedly to the DIA that its policy and administration of marriage law (i.e., recognizing the validity of Aboriginal marriage law but not recognizing divorce, and applying the law only to first wives) had created a situation that encouraged

Indian men to desert second and third wives. In 1914, Duncan Campbell Scott, who was then deputy superintendent-general of the department, sent yet another circular defining the government's policy and urging agents to prosecute for bigamy under the provisions of the revised Criminal Code if Indian men took a second wife. In May, department officials sought the advice of the Department of Justice regarding the actions that should be taken against Tom Many Feathers at the Kainai Reserve. Many Feathers, the agent had reported, had been married once by the church and three times by "tribal custom." After living briefly with each of the three girls, who were students discharged from residential schools, Many Feathers sent them home. The agent told the DIA that he had made the last wife swear out an information that she had been deserted and required necessities. The attorney general of Alberta and the Crown prosecutor, however, advised the agent that, since an Indian is a ward, she could not be in a condition of necessity; the prosecution would also fail because the woman was not legally Many Feathers' wife. Officials in the Department of Justice responded by outlining the case law pertaining to Aboriginal marriages and reasserting that marriages by tribal custom were valid. If a husband deserted a wife by Aboriginal law, the superintendent-general of Indian Affairs could intervene under section 72 of the Indian Act by stopping the payment of annuity money and interest. Many Feathers could not, however, be prosecuted for bigamy because, according to the Justice Department, his marriages according to Aboriginal law did not constitute a valid marriage as defined by the 1888 Consolidated Orders-in-Council. However, the Justice Department did encourage DIA officials to prosecute Many Feathers for intemperance and profligacy under the Indian Act.[110]

Records that survive from the 1930s indicate that police and Indian agents arrested and charged a number of men for non-support or desertion and sentenced them to one-month prison terms. Interference in these cases likely did more harm than good because the Indian Act required the cessation of all rations and treaty payments to offenders. The police and Indian agents' handling of domestic violence cases did similar damage. Cases of wife beating, which typically arose from conflicts over the legal right to children, separation, or alcohol abuse, were dealt with swiftly and harshly by legal authorities, often against the wife's wishes. Although some women asked the Indian agent to intervene, others feared that the level of physical violence directed against them would increase upon their husband's release from jail. In one case, after the Indian agent sent the RCMP to the home on frequent occasions, the wife reported to a detective, "[My

husband] told me that should I report him, that when he came out of jail
I would get the worst of it."[111]

The Truth of Her Statements Are Not Satisfactory

Although legal authorities and government officials were eager to assert
themselves as arbiters of justice in domestic affairs and marital disputes
among reserve residents and in cases of sexual violence such as *Evanse,*
which crossed racial boundaries, they were less willing to become involved
in cases of sexual violence between Aboriginal men and women. While
we know a lot about the process by which myths concerning white women
as victims of rape were constructed, the important issue of how the colonial
project created conditions that condoned sexual and physical violence
against indigenous women – by white and indigenous men – remains
under-examined.[112] A number of observers have noted that judges and
juries in contemporary Canada often consider Aboriginal complainants
in sexual assault cases as unworthy of the courts' protection because the
classic rape in legal discourse was perpetrated on a white woman. In addition, Aboriginal men accused of assaulting Aboriginal women, physically
or sexually, often offer culture as a mitigating circumstance in their defence
to avoid punishment. Teressa Nahanee, a member of the Skxwúmish First
Nation, interprets the lenient sentences that result from these strategies as
an example of white patriarchs bonding with brown patriarchs in a legal
process that does not use the "reasonable man" standard but instead
confuses culture with race when it relies on the courts' invented or fic-
tionalized Aboriginal man. To confront male violence in contemporary
Aboriginal communities and overcome the dangers of relying upon culture
as a mitigating circumstance, sociologist Sherene Razack argues that we
must examine whether violence in Aboriginal communities is a legacy of
colonialism.[113]

Between the *Bourassa* rape trial in 1892 and the Second World War, JPs,
judges, or juries in the superior courts of the five selected judicial districts
heard only eleven sex crime cases that involved Aboriginal accused and
complainants. As in incest or murder cases, the majority of the cases ended
in dismissal, acquittal, or a prison sentence of only a few months. Aboriginal men received harsh sentences only when the victim was very young,
the accused was a repeat offender, or the Aboriginal community pushed
for a conviction.[114] The extreme rarity of these cases, and their outcomes,

suggests that Aboriginal women either were reluctant to bring their complaints forward or preferred to have them dealt with according to Aboriginal law. Prosecution patterns in the cases that did come to the authorities' attention suggest that Aboriginal women had reason to distrust the system. A case that never made it to trial at the close of the period under discussion offers particularly telling clues about the issues Aboriginal women faced when they tried to establish the truth of their claims.

A Piikani woman accused two youths of rape in 1937. At the preliminary hearing, which was held at Brocket, Alberta, on 2 November 1937, the complainant deposed that two masked men had raped her in the early hours of 24 October. Although the accused wore masks to avoid identification, the complainant contended that the men's identities had been obvious to her since she had known them since they were children. The complainant also deposed that she had immediately reported the assault to Jim Small Legs, a RCMP scout. Small Legs corroborated the complainant's statement by deposing that when she arrived at his home she was in a dishevelled state and had blood on her face. Other witnesses for the prosecution stated that the two accused had been drinking at a Pincher Creek pool hall until the early hours of the morning. During the ride home, the accused discussed how much they liked women and that they had never been to jail. The complainant, furthermore, testified that one of the accused youths had called in at her home on 22 October and asked her why, and for how long, her husband would be away. When she told him that she had separated from her husband, he allegedly threw her on the bed and tried to rape her. The complainant avoided a full assault, however, by fighting back and threatening to report her assailant's behaviour to a scout.[115] Although the complainant presented more than enough evidence to proceed to a jury trial, Justice Harry W. Lunney of the Supreme Court of Alberta dismissed the charge on 21 March 1938 in a courtroom crowded by residents of the Piikani Reserve. Lunney informed the court of the seriousness of the charge and justified the dismissal on the grounds that the complainant had failed to corroborate her claim and had not decidedly provided the scout with the names of her assailants. In addition, he was not "satisfied that [he] could accept as the complete truth any of her statements."[116]

The complainant's veracity had been demolished by legal authorities and the defence during cross-examination at the preliminary hearing. Defence attorney Max E. Moscovitch began his examination by demanding that the complainant cease her crying. He then asked her if she had lived apart from her husband for two weeks. When she replied in the affirmative, Moscovitch proceeded to suggest, through leading questions, that she suffered a poor reputation in the community:

Q: Now, you have a habit, haven't you, of leading men on?
Q: Do you ever attend dances?
Q: Do you get wild at some of these dances?
Q: Have you ever been brought before a police magistrate for misconduct before?

After asking the victim's husband to leave the courtroom, Moscovitch completed the cross-examination by asking the complainant if she had ever had sexual relations with a man other than her husband.[117]

Arrest records and police reports filed with the Indian agent at the Kainai Reserve indicate that the police and Indian agents either ignored, disbelieved, or reduced Aboriginal women's rape complaints to charges of common or indecent assault.[118] In 1934, for instance, a married Kainai woman complained to the RCMP detachment at Cardston that she had been raped by a reserve resident. Upon investigation, Constable R.C.S. Hawkins reported that the complainant, her husband, and the accused had been seen drinking alcohol at the Lethbridge Fair. Following a domestic dispute between husband and wife, the accused drove off with the complainant. Hawkins reported that, upon questioning, the complainant "denied having been drunk or even tasting drink at Lethbridge." In response, he charged her with being intoxicated in a public place. His report concluded, "In view of the statements as above which proves that at least part of this woman's first statement is false, no further action is proposed in regard to this woman's complaint of being raped."[119]

CONCLUSION

Historian Lauren Benton argues that the colonial legal order, by its very nature, was a plural legal order: it created multiple legal authorities through the imposition of colonial law and through the persistence, protection, and invention of indigenous legal practices.[120] Criminal case files for high-profile rape, incest, and murder trials and everyday policing and prosecution of reserve residents in prairie Canada, although fragmented and incomplete, reveal that the extension of British Canadian law in Aboriginal communities – that is, the law as the cutting edge of coercive liberalism – was indeed an uncertain and complex process shaped by the competing agendas of judges, juries, federal government administrators, police, Indian agents, and Aboriginal men and women. High-profile rape, murder, and incest trials, on the one hand, offered the judiciary an opportunity to demonstrate the superiority of British Canadian law and Canada's fair and benevolent treatment of Aboriginal people and to present themselves as models of imperial masculinity. When Aboriginal men entered the docket, however, they entered a contact zone in which white juries viewed them through a lens clouded by stereotypes of Aboriginal men as primitive, devitalized, irrational, and doomed to extinction. They likely faced white settlers seeking evidence of primitive man to contrast with Canadian standards of civilization, orderliness, and moral respectability. Aboriginal defendants, hoping to evade punishment, gave them what they wanted by employing the cultural defence, particularly ignorance of law, and cultural stereotypes such as drunkenness in their favour. This defence strategy, in turn, shored up negative stereotypes that served as a rationale for prohibiting Aboriginal people from consuming alcohol or travelling at will. Negative representations of Aboriginal women as promiscuous and immoral likewise circulated as subtexts in these trials, and they served as an underlying rationale for Canadian legislation that created Aboriginal prostitution as a distinct category of crime.

For police officers and Indian agents who were confronted by Aboriginal women such as Maggie Two Flags or Bertha and Sarah Thomas – women who resisted these men's authority to use the criminal law to define or control their sexuality, behaviour, identity, or relationship with their families – maintaining race and managing domestic space was hard work. Prostitution laws and the pass system were difficult to implement or enforce, and liquor and trespassing laws could be applied only to women who engaged in the liquor trade or were enfranchised Indians. Confrontations and conflicts between the NWMP and reserve residents and between Indian agents and Aboriginal men and women also accompanied government policies to refashion Aboriginal marriages into the Western, Christian model of monogamy and lifelong union. Although Canadian legal authorities recognized the validity of Aboriginal marriages, they did not recognize Aboriginal divorce. Over time, the records suggest that Aboriginal men turned increasingly to the NWMP, Aboriginal scouts, and DIA officials to resolve disputes that would have once ended in divorce, separation, remarriage, or reconciliation. As historian Sarah Carter has shown, the creation of impoverished single mothers in reserve communities was one of the unanticipated outcomes of enforced monogamy, as second and third wives were turned away and abandoned.[121] The diverse records consulted here suggest that the confluence of various trends – particularly the lenient treatment of Aboriginal men found guilty of committing serious acts of violence and the criminalization of Aboriginal women through prostitution, liquor, and trespassing laws – helped to create the conditions by which Aboriginal women's complaints of physical and sexual violence fell, and continue to fall, on deaf ears.

3
The Most Public of Private Women

Prostitutes, Reformers, and Police Courts

On 7 January 1904, the citizens of Winnipeg witnessed an unprecedented spectacle when the police, following a moral panic over the alleged white slave trade, raided the city's unofficial red-light district – the Thomas Street brothels. The event took on the atmosphere of a parade as approximately three thousand men crowded the square on James Street to watch the police bring twelve madams and seventy-two scantily dressed prostitutes to the station by paddy wagon. One reporter described the women, who ranged in age from fifteen to fifty, as "fine feathers, but sad birds"; "the collection of hats could have put to shame the elegance of the most pretentious eastern display." Another described them as haughty Americans who exhibited a "bravado born of their knowledge and their complete abandon."[1] A reporter with the *Winnipeg Tribune,* however, focused on the male spectators, "the collection of degenerates who pursued their unmanly conduct around the front of the building [the courthouse] with the ferocity of a pack of famished wolves."[2]

At the turn of the century, middle-class observers in Western industrializing nations inflated prostitution as the social evil of the Belle Époque, and prostitutes' bodies, much like Aboriginal women's, became sites of inscription upon which competing interest groups – Christian social reformers, physicians, law officials, and feminists – wrote the deep-seated fears and ambitions for authority that accompanied their confrontations with modernity.[3] Depending upon the observer's vantage point, the prostitute's increasingly visible presence in the public spaces of European, British, and American cities raised the spectres of disease and social

78

degeneration; an unregulated, financially independent womanhood; and the collapse of bourgeois morality. Competing discourses on prostitution resonated with diverse middle-class groups in Canada but, as historian Philippa Levine has observed, prostitution and the alleged white slave trade also took on new meanings when the ground shifted from the metropolis to the settlement frontier.[4]

Whether she was one of the Kalifornia Female Kickers in Ralph Connor's *Black Rock: A Tale of the Selkirks* (1898) or Mrs. Vogel in Frederick Phillip Grove's *Settlers of the Marsh* (1925), the prairie prostitute loomed large in the bourgeois imagination because she, alongside the dangerous and dissolute Aboriginal woman, was a female variant of the serpent in the wilderness.[5] In 1903, the Reverend J.B. Silcox of Winnipeg argued, "The Bible is True and History confirms it, in declaring that the fallen woman is the worst foe of human society ... [Prostitution] is a community vice that has sunk cities under the fires of heaven's imagination."[6] As was the case in other liberal, democratic nation-states, discourse on (and the regulation of) prostitution established, both figuratively and literally, zones of degeneracy (and bodies marked as degenerate) into which bourgeois subjects journeyed on their path to respectability.[7] Although the prostitute resided on the margins of society, her presence, both physically and discursively, was central not simply to prairie but also to Canadian identity formation. While the savage, hired hand, and foreigner stood as foils to the stalwart Mountie, the prostitute was the antithesis of the pioneer woman – a moral icon that embodied the values of restraint, self-sacrifice, chastity, godliness, and civilization. The prostitute stood in defiant contradiction to utopian images of the West that depicted it as a paradise for women and girls and as landscape that would foster a reinvigorated imperial masculinity.[8] Because the prostitute personified the dark side of progress predicted by conservative social commentators across Canada, she was a figure to be observed, examined, surveyed, and regulated but never heard.[9] And because historians of the Canadian Prairies have tended to focus on prostitution as it affected civic politics, policing, or the movements for social and moral reform, the prairie prostitute remains one of the most elusive historical characters – the ultimate subaltern subject (see Figure 12).[10]

Prostitutes' experiences are obscure – as the Winnipeg journalist's emphasis on the behaviour of male witnesses to the Thomas Street raid and Silcox's delineation of sexual promiscuity as a community rather than a female vice suggest – because the western Canadian campaign to eradicate prostitution was as much about disciplining unruly working-class and immigrant men as it was about regulating their wayward female

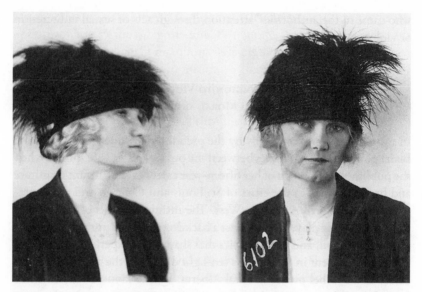

FIGURE 12   Prairie prostitutes, such as the woman represented in this Calgary City
Police identification photo from 1919, remain elusive historical characters. Listed as
Danish from the United States, the woman was identified as Pauline Sylvia Fair and
was arrested for keeping a disorderly house. However, she was later fined for vagrancy
under the name Irene Walker. | Glenbow Archives, NA-625-16.

counterparts. Reformers came to view the prostitute as a public figure that
was both a source of danger and endangered.[11] Drawing upon social reform
tracts, social surveys, criminal registers, and case files, this chapter explores
the nuances of this paradox and the larger story of the drive for progress
and modern governance in Canada that it illuminates.[12] It places the white
slavery scares and socio-economic developments that influenced the treatment and lives of prostitutes on the Prairies in an international context
and then traces the various conflicts and negotiations that ensued as Christian and feminist reformers, the North West Mounted Police (NWMP),
municipal authorities, and prostitutes themselves employed the issue of
prostitution to nurture and foster competing visions of masculinity, femininity, sexuality, the state, and the public sphere in an emerging settlement
society. The new legal and moral regime that emerged from the ashes of
these conflicts and negotiations – a regime that was reflected in prosecution patterns for female offenders and prostitution-related offences between
1886 and 1940 – would influence not only how western Canadian judges
and juries treated *all* women unfortunate enough to stand as the accused
or the victim in a court of law but also working-class and immigrant men

who came to the authorities' attention through acts of sexual indiscretion or violence.

FROM SITES OF CONTAGION TO VICTIMS OF MODERNITY:
THE PROSTITUTE IN MEDICO-MORAL AND LEGAL DISCOURSE, 1835-85

In 1919, a woman known only by the pseudonym Madeleine (Madeleine Blair) pushed the boundaries between the public and private spheres when she published an account of her fifteen-year career as an itinerant prostitute and brothel owner in the cities of St. Louis and Chicago and the boom-towns of the North American West. The intimate details of Madeleine's career in Canada played out against a backdrop of social purity campaigns, police regulation, and moral panics that shaped her experiences, from her first summer spent in Winnipeg's red-light district in the mid-1880s to her career as a brothel owner in rural Alberta. By the 1890s, Madeleine had earned enough money working as a prostitute in Banff to set up her own house outside Edmonton. Contrary to expectation, she discovered that municipal police officials and the district commanding officer of the NWMP welcomed her establishment. The officer had discovered among his men an alarming increase in venereal disease, which he linked to the many "dissolute squaws" and "half-breed" women in the area. The police condoned prostitution by settler women, Madeleine believed, because it protected single, unmarried men from Aboriginal women. As long as Madeleine's girls subjected themselves to regular medical examinations by a physician and paid regular fines, the police turned a blind eye to their business.[13]

Published by Harper and Brothers, *Madeleine: An Autobiography* gained short-lived notoriety as one of the first personal accounts published on prostitution, and it became the subject of high-profile litigation that centred on the issues of obscenity, freedom of speech, and white slavery. Moral reform and social purity advocates took umbrage at the author's defiant shamelessness, and they denounced the publication as one of the worst, most dangerous books of its day. As an unregulated working-class woman who operated outside of traditional family structures and morality, Madeleine was sign and symbol of the ills of modernity, an allegorical threat to nation and empire. In a description of her experiences at Banff, Madeleine boasted, "[I] could go wherever I like and not be subjected to questioning" because she "outwardly conformed" to society's idea of what a respectable woman looked like.[14] Madeleine not only drew public attention to the system of cooperation and graft that had developed between prostitutes and police officials – policies that served the interests of the larger colonial and nation-building project; she also subverted dominant Christian and feminist narratives of prostitution by representing herself as the victim of hypocrisy rather than of pimps, procurers, or white slavers. Madeleine viewed herself, and others like her, as the casualty of a society that left working-class women few viable opportunities outside of marriage, motherhood, or prostitution.

Raised in poverty by a single working mother, a teenaged Madeleine had sought the aid of state- and church-run charitable organizations when she became pregnant out of wedlock. Advised to submit herself to the care of a reform school or a House of the Good Shepherd for fallen women and unwed mothers, Madeleine decided that the punishment did not fit the crime. She chose instead the hazardous, uncertain life of a prostitute. Madeleine acknowledged that prostitution had a dark side that rendered women (including herself) vulnerable to alcohol and drug abuse, violence, and unwanted pregnancy, and she admitted that she had left prostitution to live a "Christian life." The former prostitute, however, had nothing positive to say about rescue efforts led by Christian moral reform and social purity advocates. Madeleine believed that women who sold their bodies for money differed little from so-called respectable women "who sell themselves into unloved and often loathsome marriage."[15] Madeleine urged citizens to consider the possibility that Christian reformers and their feminist allies, people who represented prostitutes either as dangerous threats to the sanctity of marriage or as passive victims of sexual exploitation by pimps and procurers, did little more than create moral panics that caused young, precocious, working-class girls to fear the possibility of independence. Popular representations of prostitution and the alleged white slave trade, she concluded, served only to draw girls' attention to their physical desirability and market value, causing them to avoid all contact with unfamiliar men and opportunities in the public sphere.[16]

Madeleine's outspoken narrative and scathing criticism of social purity and moral reform efforts not only resisted the underpinnings of classic liberalism, which relegated women and discussions of sexuality to the private sphere, but also challenged discourses on prostitution that had evolved since the early nineteenth century. Madeleine worked unabashedly as a prostitute and described her experiences at a time when neo-regulationist and abolitionist movements were at their height in Western industrializing nations. In response to these movements, she constructed herself not as the whore of Babylon depicted by evangelical reformers, nor as the victim of unscrupulous pimps and procurers depicted by muckraking journalists and imperial feminists, but as an ordinary woman who, with the cooperation of the police, dealt with extraordinary circumstances.

Madeleine had been drawn to the red-light districts of the Canadian prairies by a fellow prostitute in Chicago who, after having spent only one summer in the region, returned to the Midwest with a fat bankroll. Suffering from poor health, and responsible for the care of her two-year-old son, Madeleine hoped that temporary relocation to Canada would provide her with enough money and freedom to establish a legitimate business before her child understood what she did for a living. Taking a gamble, she wrote to the most successful madam of the Thomas Street brothels. The madam agreed to meet her at St. Paul, Minnesota, where she would be procuring new women for her business. Madeleine arrived in Winnipeg with four other women and took up residence in "Madam von Levin's" bawdy house, which stood in a short, one-street, red-light district known as the American colony. The district was not located in Winnipeg but in the middle of the prairie two miles from town. Madeleine entered a culture in which it was unwritten law that the bawdy houses remain separate from those owned by respectable citizens and that "no girl should be allowed to remain in Winnipeg who 'made a show of herself' on the streets."[17] The municipal police, she argued, did not subject madams and inmates to graft or fines unless they sold liquor without a licence. Within this unofficial regulatory system, business was good and profits were enormous. Although her experiences in the region differed from Jessie Saxby's (described in Chapter 1), Madeleine shared the Scottish gentlewoman's belief that the prairie environment transformed effete immigrants into men: "Here were no blasé habitués of wine-rooms and bawdy-houses, seeking a new sensation by learning a new perversion. Here were men, fine and strong, courtly gentlemen, such as I have never met anywhere else in the world. Their visits to the houses were part of their playtime; they were not seeking a new sensation, these red-blooded men of the North-west; they brought their sensations with them, and they showed a tenderness and a courtesy toward women which often brought a choking into my heart."[18] English remittance men were the only exception, Madeleine believed, because they exhibited the worst characteristics and tendencies of their class.

Madeleine experienced and described structural changes in the sex trade that were accompanying urban industrialization in nations and their settlement frontiers. Throughout the nineteenth century, new forms of economic exchange and resource extraction propagated gender imbalances in cites as diverse as Moscow, Buenos Aires, Paris, Chicago, and Winnipeg as male peasant migrants congregated from nearby or distant countrysides into urban slums and boarding-house districts. This floating population of single men delayed marriage, and its members availed themselves of prostitutes' services in unprecedented numbers. These same developments and dislocations created a ready supply of migratory, independent, and low-wage-earning women such as Madeleine, who increasingly viewed prostitution as an alternative to poverty. As a result, the sociability – in countries such as Egypt, Greece, or India, one could say sacredness – that characterized relations among prostitutes, mistresses, and their elite or aristocratic clients gave way to commercial, public sexual exchanges structured by the market and the state.[19] The state, however, trumped the market when the middle and upwardly mobile working classes began to turn to federal and local authorities to enforce adherence to their ideal of companionate marriage.

The conflict and tension among prostitutes, police, and reformers described in Madeleine's memoir stemmed from competing discourses on prostitution, sexuality, and the state that began to circulate throughout Europe and England in the early nineteenth century. Alexandre Jean-Baptiste Parent-Duchâtelet, a French physician and sanitary engineer, opened the dialogue when he published *On Prostitution in the City of Paris* in 1835 and proceeded to construct a carceral system for his city organized around the brothel, the hospital, the prison, and the reformatory. Parent-Duchâtelet imagined prostitutes as a subterranean counter-society that symbolized disorder, excess, pleasure, and providence. Because he identified the bodies of prostitutes and working-class women as sites of contagion and the origin of venereal disease, Parent-Duchâtelet viewed prostitution as a serious moral, social, sanitary, and political threat to the nation. Transient prostitutes such as Madeleine, women who managed to reintegrate into respectable society, haunted him. Unlike Madeleine, who viewed prostitutes as normal women caught in unfortunate circumstances, Parent-Duchâtelet placed prostitutes outside the bounds of womanhood altogether when he described them as a seminal drain on society.[20] As a woman who worked outside the family, engaging in public sexual acts for pecuniary gain, the prostitute was – for Parent-Duchâtelet and other physicians and sanitary engineers – one of the most visible and discordant figures in the emerging urban landscape. Parent-Duchâtelet's theories of and approaches to prostitution declined in popularity in Europe in the 1850s. They persisted abroad, however, and became the basis for a continental system of tolerated houses and segregated districts. The middle-class professionals who supported them believed that state surveillance and medical examination of prostitutes by physicians, police, and public officials were necessary to identify and control female sexuality and maintain the boundaries between the private and public spheres.[21]

The unofficial regulatory system Madeleine experienced in Winnipeg emerged as the city's municipal council and police force tried, on the one hand, to contain the proliferation of prostitution by pragmatically adopting aspects of the continental model and, on the other, to appease social purity advocates, imperial feminists, and Canadian legislators steeped in English approaches to prostitution.[22] As was the case on other settlement frontiers, gender imbalances made policing the Prairies' white settler societies difficult. By the outbreak of the First World War, single males outnumbered females 8,550 to 5,920 in Edmonton, 13,616 to 6,020 in Regina, and 43,000 to 32,000 in Winnipeg. The existence of this large, floating, single-male population hastened the formation of a distinct homosocial culture characterized by alcohol abuse, gambling, and prostitution.[23] Fuelled by these men's demands and wages, Winnipeg's red-light district included approximately fifty brothels by 1910, and it was home to from 150 to 250 women who had emigrated from the United States, Mexico, Japan, eastern Canada, and Europe. In 1910, undercover investigators hired by the Moral and Social Reform Council disclosed that 40 percent of the district's population were non-white, while nearly 20 percent were French.[24]

Social and moral reform advocates and feminists, influenced by developments in England, opposed state regulation of these two distinct masculine and feminine subcultures. The campaign to eradicate prostitution in the Anglo-American world had originated as a deregulation movement, led by radical feminists and evangelical reformers, against England's Contagious Diseases Acts. In the mid-nineteenth century, physicians exploited medico-moral discourse on prostitutes' bodies as sites of disease and contagion to secure a position in England's burgeoning state apparatus. In December 1852, *The Lancet,* the journal of the British Medical Association, published a piece that called for the expansion of privately maintained lock hospitals to deal with diseased prostitutes. Over the next decade, the publication of William Acton's *Prostitution, Considered in Its Moral, Social and Sanitary Aspects* and Bracebridge Hemyng's *Prostitution in London* (which was included in the fourth volume of Henry Mayhew's influential text *London Labour and the London Poor*), and the release of reports that revealed that more English men had died of sexually transmitted diseases than injury during the Crimean War, combined to undermine English resistance to state regulation of private matters. Medical practitioners argued forcibly for adoption of the continental system, and legislators responded by passing the first of the Contagious Diseases Acts in 1864, which provided for medical and police inspection of prostitutes in garrison towns and ports. New acts in 1866 and 1869 extended the legislation to common prostitutes and northern cities, and legislation by colonial governments in New Zealand, Australia, Tasmania, India, Hong Kong, the Straits Settlements, and Canada would extend its scope throughout the Empire.[25]

The Contagious Diseases Acts, and the white slavery scares that they precipitated, became contested terrain between radical feminists, labour groups, and evangelical Christian reformers, who viewed the acts' repeal as integral to their campaigns to renegotiate their role in the public sphere, the urban economy, and secular society. In 1871, radical feminist Josephine Butler penned *The Constitution Violated*, which advocated repeal on the grounds that the legislation contravened fundamental civil liberties by extinguishing the rights of one category of woman. Butler and her supporters in the National Ladies Association believed that the legislation was symptomatic of a more general, insidious societal tendency to view women as beings defined by their bodies and sexuality. Butler objected to laws and practices that left women alone responsible for the consequences of consensual sex: babies, childrearing, and sexually transmitted diseases. In 1877 she published *Government by Police*, in which she argued against state regulation of prostitution because she believed it could only result in police despotism on the continental model. Although Butler was inclined to cast working-class women in the role of victims to male-dominated state institutions, she opposed regulation of private moral transgressions and upheld uncoerced self-control as the highest form of citizenship. Police measures to regulate prostitution simply disrupted the work of moral reform and made prostitutes, such as Madeleine, suspicious of reformers, she argued.[26]

Although the anti-regulationist movement gained repeal of the Contagious Diseases Acts in 1886, the movement collapsed under the weight of its success when muckraking journalist William Thomas Stead precipitated a worldwide white slavery panic with the publication of "The Maiden Tribute to Modern Babylon," which appeared in the July 1885 edition of the *Pall Mall Gazette*. Working in concert with Butler and Catherine Booth, wife of William Booth and co-founder of the Salvation Army, Stead treated readers to a week-long account of child prostitution at the heart of the Empire. The description of his efforts to procure an underage virgin in London played upon the familiar scenario of working-class women exploited by aristocratic rakes. Stead allegedly used the services of a reformed procuress recommended by Butler to buy thirteen-year-old Eliza

Armstrong from her mother. He then subjected the girl to a medical examination that re-enacted the outrages of the Contagious Diseases Acts. In a final effort to parallel the actions of alleged white slavers, Stead sent Armstrong to a real-life London brothel, and then on to France, where she was placed in a Salvation Army rescue home for reformation.[27]

Stead's exposé, and the trial for abduction that followed, galvanized new regulationist and abolitionist movements worldwide. Abolitionists were influenced by Butler's anti-regulationist campaign, but they promoted a new sexual order based on social purity – individual responsibility, internalized sexual repression, and self-control – in essence, a single standard of sexual morality for men and women. By contrast, neo-regulationists wanted to regulate prostitution, not for reasons of sexual morality and social order (as had Parent-Duchâtelet), but because they feared the consequences of white slavery, venereal disease, and racial degeneracy. Advocates of social purity, sanitarianism, and hygiene pushed for medical supervision without government intervention, a policy that would guarantee the continued marginalization of prostitutes.[28] In England, the neo-regulationist movement culminated in 1885 with passage of the Criminal Law Amendment Act. Butler had persuaded herself that Stead's investigation, repeal of the Contagious Diseases Acts, and reformation of the criminal law would not enhance state surveillance and regulation of young women and the sexual double standard; instead, these measures would protect girls and liberate them into self-reliant adulthood.[29] This strategy, however, went awry during the Stead trial. To gain male working-class support for criminal law reform, Stead portrayed the white slave as the victim of male aristocratic lust. To shift blame away from himself, the journalist also cast women – mothers and procuresses – as the true villains of the piece. By design or error, the Criminal Law Amendment Act increased the regulatory scope of the criminal law over female sexuality: the legislation raised the age of consent for girls from thirteen to sixteen and gave the police more authority to prosecute streetwalkers and brothel-keepers.[30]

When the white slavery panic swept the Canadian Prairies at the turn of the twentieth century, debates and scandals concerning prostitution at the heart of the Empire had already disrupted the gendered assumptions of the liberal economic order. Prairie police forces and municipal councils found themselves in the same bind as the London Metropolitan Police: they had to operate within the constraints of a system in which official regulation of prostitution was out of the question, but they found themselves increasingly under pressure from social purity and anti-vice groups to regulate working-class homosocial culture and suppress the presence

of women such as Madeleine in the public sphere to make room for respectable women.[31] The renegotiation of the public that emerged from
this conflict set the stage for increased surveillance and regulation of not
only prostitution but also consensual heterosexuality in the war and interwar years.

THE PRAIRIE PROSTITUTE AS CONTESTED TERRAIN:
SOCIAL REFORMERS, FEMINISTS, AND LEGAL AUTHORITIES
DEBATE PROSTITUTION, 1886-1940

Madeleine spent only one summer in the Thomas Street red-light district,
but she returned to the Prairies after spending a decade working sporadic-
ally as a prostitute in the United States, Europe, Asia, and Mexico. For
the next six years, her business in Alberta was constrained by bitter rivalries
between city police and the NWMP over who should regulate the liquor
and sex trades; by graft, which she paid willingly to city officials and failed
to report to the police; and by violence and discord, which stemmed
primarily from excessive alcohol consumption, on her part and that of her
customers and girls. Although Madeleine took pride in her independence,
she conceded that "from Winnipeg to Vancouver and from the American
boundary to the farthermost outpost of transportation, every town and
hamlet was a port of missing women, or the wrecks of women, time-
battered derelicts who had drifted up from the States seeking an undis-
covered harbor."[32] Madeleine refused, however, to give credence to the
allegations of reformers: "But the one girl I never met in all those years
and all those cities I visited was the pure girl who had been trapped and
violated and sold into slavery, and held a prisoner unable to effect her
escape – the so-called white 'slave.'"[33]

The campaign to repeal the Contagious Diseases Acts and the passage
of the Criminal Law Amendment Act ushered in a new carceral regime
for prostitutes and young working-class English women. The repercussions
were felt throughout the Empire in the form of prohibitions against inter-
racial liaisons and efforts to abolish state-regulated prostitution.[34] As was
the case in other white settler societies such as colonial Queensland, Silcox's
subverted narrative of Aboriginal women being sold into slavery to white
men resulted in new, separate modes of regulation for Aboriginal and mixed-
blood women (see Chapter 2).[35] When social purity advocates and their
feminist allies turned their attention to the problem of regulated prostitution in the non-Aboriginal population, their campaign followed British

precedent. Morality campaigns and conflicts with municipal and police officials generated public spectacles, social surveys, and exposés that transformed prostitutes from victims of white slavers to dangerous, dissolute threats to region, nation, and empire.

Winnipeg, the region's largest urban centre and gateway to the West, led the way in setting the contours of public debate when the city became the site for three morality crusades that centred on the white slave trade, which had allegedly infiltrated the Prairies when the Winnipeg Police Force, acting on the recommendation of the Police Commission, created unofficial red-light districts in the city. Constructed as a dangerous and endangered public figure who represented the worst excesses of the Old World, the prairie prostitute became contested terrain between legal and municipal authorities, Protestant clergymen, and first-wave feminists who exploited her image in their parallel, but often competing, campaigns. Legal and municipal authorities hoped to establish the rule of law on the settlement frontier; Protestant clergymen tried to resist the tide of secularization by reasserting Christian ethics; feminists struggled to negotiate a respectable public role for women in a patriarchal society. The results of these social tensions and conflicts took their most public expression during the Thomas Street raid.

Conflict between reform advocates and police officials over the best way to eradicate or regulate prostitution caused the Winnipeg Police Commission to vacillate between unofficial toleration and repression, which resulted in the erection and dismantlement of three distinct red-light districts: Colony Creek (pre-1883), Thomas Street (1883-1904), and Point Douglas (1909-12). The coalition of regional and national social purity advocates that sparked these vacillations included J.B. Silcox, of Winnipeg's Congregationalist Church; Frederic B. Du Val, of Knox Presbyterian Church, also in Winnipeg; and John G. Shearer, Presbyterian minister and secretary of the Moral and Social Reform Council of Canada. As head of the latter, which was an umbrella organization created in 1907, Shearer was national spokesman for various strands of the social purity movement, which included the Temperance, Prohibition, and Moral Reform Department of the Methodist Church and the Presbyterian Board of Moral and Social Reform.[36] All three men were proponents of the Social Gospel who believed that Canada's moral and physical health was in decline, and they sought to turn back the tide of secularization and degeneration through social analysis and community activism.[37] As eastern European immigrants began to outnumber Britons, social purity and expansion as imperial concerns coalesced to make the region's Social Gospel movement an integral component of the Empire's civilizing mission. Men such as Silcox and Du Val hoped to Christianize and Canadianize the primitive and the pauper who congregated in cities and, they believed, threatened the West's imperial destiny. In their view, the fallen city and the fallen woman would lead ultimately to the decline of the Anglo-Saxon race.[38] Appalling conditions and poverty in the city could be alleviated or eradicated, Silcox and Du Val argued, if the authorities would only enforce Sunday-observance laws, prohibitions against liquor consumption, and a single standard of sexual morality for men and women.[39] Silcox, Du Val, and Shearer's efforts to hold back the tide of modernity culminated in Manitoba's Robson Commission on Social Vice, which sat in Winnipeg in 1910, and amendments to the Criminal Code, which widened the regulatory scope of Canada's prostitution laws.

Although Du Val, Shearer, and Silcox collectively represented the interests of a fair portion of the city's middle class through the Winnipeg Ministerial Association and the Citizen's Committee for the Suppression of Vice, as individuals they gave voice to competing and conflicting discourses on the causes and consequences of prostitution that would influence prosecution patterns on the Prairies. They were allied, for instance, with women's organizations such as the Woman's Christian Temperance Union (WCTU), which promoted the interests of Canada's middle-class maternal feminists, and they pushed for the establishment of relief and rescue work by the largely working-class Salvation Army.[40] As Silcox's 1903 sermon on the fallen woman suggests, he and his cohort also adhered to and promulgated medico-moral discourses on prostitution that were simultaneously exerting an influence on the social hygiene movement within the medical and psychological professions. As early as 1883, when Silcox led a coalition of male Protestant ministers to campaign for the relocation of Winnipeg's Colony Creek brothels outside the city limits at Thomas Street, the reformer declared, "We drove the small pox out and we can do the same with the plague."[41] In his 1903 sermon, which fuelled public support for the closure of the Thomas Street brothels, Silcox blamed municipal politicians and law enforcement officials for fostering an atmosphere in which the scarlet sin could multiply: "We quarantine the house where scarlet fever rages. Why not quarantine the house where the scarlet sin runs rampant? If we have the right to protect our families from physical contagion, why not from moral infection?" he asked. Silcox demanded more rigorous enforcement of existing prostitution laws by likening prostitution to a cancerous growth: "For three years the ministerial associations

of this city have been trying, in quiet way[s], to induce the police commissioners to enforce the laws of the land against this plague-spot of
iniquity, this hell-hole of licentiousness, this cess-pool of damnable corruption that with cancerous persistence has fastened itself as an institution
on our fair city."[42]

The following year, Frederic Du Val likewise criticized police policy in
his popular pamphlet *The Problem of Social Vice in Winnipeg*. But Du Val
went one step further than Silcox when he likened prostitutes rather than
prostitution to noxious weeds that "grow under passive permission."[43]
When James Shearer spoke before the Robson Commission in 1910, he
echoed Silcox's and Du Val's sentiments. Shearer referred to prostitutes as
festering sores on the face of the city and disclosed that he had, during a
vice tour of the Point Douglas district, discovered that Japanese and
Chinese men were the principal procurers in the region's white slave trade.[44]
Whereas advocates for the Contagious Diseases Acts had justified their
demands for criminal law reform by linking the spread of venereal disease
to the proliferation of prostitutes in garrison towns, ports, and cities, turn-
of-the-century reform advocates demanded stricter enforcement of prostitution laws by identifying the bodies of sexually impure women as the
sources of not simply venereal disease but also feeble-mindedness and
racial degeneration.[45]

In sermon, lecture, and pamphlet, Silcox, Shearer, and Du Val inundated
Canadians with their vision of the prostitute's body as a site of contagion
and danger in the apocalyptic city. Yet these men's alliances with women's
organizations and labour groups, along with their ideological conflicts
with state authorities, caused them to temper that vision by demanding
an expanded role for the state, not to regulate the sexually impure woman,
but to protect her from corrupt police officials, liquor interests, municipal
governments, and man's "perfidy and lust." While members of the Winnipeg WCTU and its umbrella organization, the National Council of
Women in Canada, often failed to challenge their male counterparts'
negative portrayal of black and Asian men as pimps and procurers, they,
alongside other prairie feminists, did resist the sexual double standard as
part of their larger campaign to achieve woman suffrage. Emily Murphy,
an Edmonton-based writer and activist, declared: "The unjust status of
men and women is directly or indirectly the cause of three quarters of the
social evil."[46] Although maternal feminists in Canada, such as Murphy,
resisted women's unequal political status within the emerging liberal economic order, they embraced the cult of domesticity, which advocated

FIGURE 13   Maternal feminists in Canada embraced the cult of domesticity. This
cartoon, which was titled "The Door Steadily Opens" and appeared in the *Grain Grower's
Guide* on 21 September 1910, illustrates the suffragists' argument that women would
clean up society's ills if they only had a larger role to play in the public world of men.

separate spheres for men and women on the grounds that women's maternal
function fostered in them a natural predilection for piety, purity, submis-
siveness, and domesticity. If women only had a larger role to play in the
making of public policy, first-wave feminists argued, they would literally
clean up society by eradicating political corruption, prostitution, poverty,
and domestic violence (see Figure 13). Murphy and other leaders of the
suffrage campaign traced these social problems, through an intricate causal
web, to the dominance of liquor interests in municipal politics, alcohol
abuse in working-class masculine culture, and the prevalence of the sexual
double standard in law and society.[47]

When the moral panic over white slavery first swept Canada in the late
nineteenth century, the WCTU created a committee dedicated to elim-
inating prostitution and the traffic in women, and the National Council
of Women of Canada created the Committee on the Equal Moral Standard
and Traffic in Women, which stated: "We have constructed this social evil
as a female proposition; and our criminality has been the persecution of
the woman, while permitting the easy escape of the man ... some of us

think the social evil is a masculine proposition."[48] Canadian suffragists hoped to do more than eradicate prostitution: they wanted to reform the entire male population. The purity issue aroused a degree of sex antagonism in feminists that united them in sisterhood against men, and they were outraged when male reformers, legislators, and law enforcement officials cast the prostitute, who often "fell" through hunger or starvation wages, as villain, while her male clients got off with nominal fines. Maternal feminists also challenged the manner in which male social purity advocates used the term *white slaver;* they recognized, particularly following Trivett's allegations, that non-white women were more often exploited than white women in the sex trade. Lillian Beynon Thomas, a prominent Winnipeg journalist and feminist, believed that men should suffer the same mortification as did prostitutes and urged the police to publish the names of men found in the houses of red-light districts in newspapers.[49]

Whereas reformers in Toronto, by 1900, had ceased to think about prostitution in terms of urban villains and innocent maidens (they associated it instead with female factory workers who were enjoying the perils and pleasures of the city), a combination of forces on the Prairies – including the strength of the Social Gospel movement, its alliance with feminists, and a regional economy that offered women and girls few opportunities for urban-industrial employment – created an intellectual milieu in which prostitutes continued to be portrayed as victims until the First World War.[50] Silcox, for instance, echoed arguments made by his feminist allies and moved beyond medico-moral discourse on prostitution when he conceded that industrial capitalism, which depressed wages and offered women few options outside marriage and motherhood, forced working-class girls to either "sin or starve."[51] Silcox was also immensely popular with working-class audiences and adopted aspects of the Left's perspective on prostitution, which represented the white slave trade as an integral part of a capitalist system that not only depressed wages for women but also created a demand for prostitutes by working-class men who could not afford to marry.[52]

Male social reformers' quest for moral and political authority over women and working-class men in the public sphere, however, circumscribed their ability to wholeheartedly embrace the Left's position on prostitution. To protect women, children, and the moral well-being of the family, Silcox, Du Val, and Shearer adopted aspects of the feminist position on prostitution and blamed itinerant labourers and single, working-class men for the proliferation of prairie brothels. In 1883, Silcox's colleague, the Reverend J.E. Starr, postulated, "Young men who are strangers here have no place to visit and thus being removed from the restraints of society, they allow themselves to be led rapidly on the road to ruin." When the moral reform movement gathered momentum across Canada and culmin-ated in the closure of the Thomas Street brothels, male social purity ad-vocates such as Silcox and Du Val also directed sermons and pamphlets at young men in which they argued that prostitution would be eradicated only through a regulatory regime that combined the restraints of law, medicine, and religion to reform working-class masculinity. They saw the eradication of prostitution and strict enforcement of Canada's prostitution laws as the first steps on the path to a single standard of sexual morality. When the Purity League of Winnipeg came into being a few years later, its members passed a bylaw that expressed regret that adultery and licen-tiousness among the unmarried were not yet criminal offences. Du Val concurred and argued in *The Problem of Social Vice* that the police needed to regulate men's sexuality in the same manner they regulated the sexuality of women.[53]

By 1909, women's organizations, religious leaders of the moral reform movement, and the Salvation Army believed unconditionally that pros-titutes and working-class women were the victims of degenerate single men, pimps, and procurers. In that year the WCTU, the Moral and Social Reform Council, and the Salvation Army combined forces to hire two detectives to find evidence of white slavery in the Point Douglas segregated district, which the police and municipal council had created in the heart of the city to solve problems associated with unregulated prostitution fol-lowing the Thomas Street raid. The investigative report appeared in early 1910, the same year that Madeleine published her scathing criticism of social purity advocates and the white slavery scare. Contrary to Madeleine's description of prostitution in Winnipeg's red-light district, the report's authors argued that 55 percent of the district's prostitutes had been coerced into the trade. According to Adjutant McElhany of the Salvation Army, who also testified at the Robson Commission, madams kept their "inmates" – 45 percent of whom came from the sub-marginal homes of Winnipeg's North End – in a state of slavery through a combination of debt and ad-diction.[54] Working-class women, the report concluded, did not voluntarily choose prostitution – they were seduced into it by pimps, procurers, and white slavers.[55]

As in England, the moral panic over white slavery and reform campaigns to eradicate prostitution culminated in new legislation to better protect women and girls. In practice, however, police and magistrates used the legislation to regulate the behaviour and sexuality of women. Two years after the Robson Commission brought out its report, Shearer was selected to head a new subcommittee of the Social Service Council (formerly the Presbyterian Board of Moral and Social Reform), the National Committee for the Suppression of the White Slave Traffic, which lobbied for criminal law amendments against prostitution and procurement. The subcommittee had the backing of the National Council of Women of Canada, and Shearer, as the subcommittee's head, represented Canada in the international movement led by William Thomas Stead. Shearer and his supporters argued that amendments to Canada's prostitution laws would better enable the police and the courts to punish those men and women who profited most from prostitution – pimps, procurers, and madams. Yet because Protestant ministers and first-wave feminists were also wont to view prostitutes as mentally and morally weak examples of their sex, they believed that prostitutes too should experience the full force of the law.[56] They argued that existing legislation in Canada was not adequate to this task, even though it was harsher than England's prostitution laws.

Unlike the situation in England, where a woman had to be both a streetwalker and behaving in public in a riotous or indecent manner to face charges for prostitution, Canadian legislators made the very status of being a streetwalker or prostitute a crime through two categories of law in the 1892 Criminal Code and 1907 amendments. The vagrancy provisions – which included streetwalking and keeping, being an inmate of, or frequenting a common bawdy house – were directed at prostitutes and madams. Any "common prostitute or night walker" found in a public place who did not, when asked, give a good account of herself could be charged with a summary offence and tried in a police court.[57] Although the vagrancy provision "living off the avails of prostitution" was a pimping provision that could apply to men or women, police rarely charged male offenders. Similarly, under the category of indictable nuisance offences, "keeping a common bawdy house" could apply to both women and men, but in 1907, legislators extended the law to include individual prostitutes working out of a residence or room.[58]

Because of pressure from the moral reform lobby and feminists, the Canadian government amended the Criminal Code in 1913 and 1915 to correct the class and gender biases of the existing procuring provisions. The 1892 Criminal Code had made it illegal to procure girls and women, either openly or fraudulently, for service in brothels or as common street prostitutes. The law, however, did not apply to women of known immoral character.[59] Following the Robson Commission, the Borden government enacted stiffer penalties against procurers and created new categories of moral infractions to "protect" women. While the summary offences of "keeping a bawdy house" and "living off the avails of prostitution" were upgraded to indictable offences with harsher penalties, procurers became liable to a whipping on conviction at the judge's discretion. Despite these amendments, criminal law provisions continued to reflect the sexual double standard: while being an inmate of a bawdy house was upgraded to an indictable offence, the new offence of being found in a bawdy house, directed at men, was established only as a crime upon summary conviction.[60] The expanding scope of Canadian criminal law increasingly caught female rather than male offenders in its net. Municipal police forces and magistrates, constrained by evidentiary requirements but forced to respond to public pressure, punished more harshly and more frequently the common prostitute rather than procurers, keepers, or their male customers.[61]

The masculine bias of the legal establishment and the prevalence of the sexual double standard in the West's homosocial culture underlay the discrepancy between the rhetoric of protection and the realities of punishment. Given the West's unbalanced male-to-female ratio, the Winnipeg Police Commission, the chief of police, and magistrates, much like members of the NWMP, tended to look upon prostitution not as a social evil but a necessary one.[62] Police officials maintained a vision of working-class masculinity that did not differ radically from that held by maternal feminists. Their attitude toward the role of the state and prostitution, however, did differ. Police officials argued that segregated red-light districts protected respectable pioneer women and girls from working-class men who could not control themselves. Although they did not favour legalization, most police forces across the Prairies pursued what they felt were pragmatic policies of toleration and segregation. In Winnipeg, for instance, police and magistrates tolerated prostitution as long as the prostitutes adhered to unofficial rules that kept them off the streets and out of the sight of the city's more respectable citizens. Under segregation, prostitutes could work as long as they confined their activities to private dwellings, rode in closed carriages on public thoroughfares, and subjected themselves to police patrols.[63]

During the Robson Commission, Chief John McRae of the Winnipeg Police Force met social reformers' criticisms with the response that "prostitution, like poverty ... will never go away."[64] Thomas Mayne Daly, Winnipeg police magistrate from 1904 to 1909, concurred. Born in Stratford in the United Province of Canada in 1852, Daly was the first lawyer and mayor in Brandon, Manitoba, and sat in Sir John A. Macdonald's cabinet. Although Daly did not accept prostitution as a social necessity (he embraced the underlying goals and motivations of the social purity campaign), he did feel that suppression, rather than segregation, caused prostitution to spread geographically, thereby contributing to greater social ills. Following the suppression of the Thomas Street brothels, for instance, Daly argued that his court had been inundated with prostitutes, "common streetwalkers," who were significantly younger than would have been allowed during the period of unofficial segregation. Daly unabashedly testified at the Robson Commission that, as a member of the Winnipeg Police Commission, he had advocated and supported the commission's decision to allow Chief McRae to create the Point Douglas segregated district in 1909. A segregated red-light district on the continental model, he believed, was the most efficient means to suppress juvenile prostitution and delinquency, arrest the rising rate of illegitimate births, and stop the spread of venereal disease.[65]

As Daly's preoccupation with the spread of venereal disease suggests, medico-moral discourses on prostitution continued to grip the imagination of legal officials, and that grip tightened following the First World War, when the prevalence of venereal disease among Canadian soldiers, and the fragmentation of the first-wave feminist movement, created an opening for social hygiene advocates to obtain a position of dominance in the social and moral reform movement.[66] During the 1920s and 1930s, medico-moral theories of female criminality and sexuality infiltrated the criminal justice system as magistrates familiarized themselves with the most recent literature during training and as social workers, doctors, psychiatrists, and psychologists contributed to an integrated system of socialized justice that regulated the so-called deviant woman in new ways.[67] The degree to which the double standard of sexual morality and medico-moral discourses continued to inform approaches to prostitution became evident when Emily Murphy was appointed the first female magistrate in the British Empire.

Women's organizations had long campaigned for a female presence in Canada's criminal justice system, and in 1916 the National Council of Women in Canada's Committee on Delinquent Women and Girls published a report that advocated the creation of a prison farm for women, the appointment of female juvenile court judges, industrial training for delinquent girls, and female police officers. That same year, Murphy and a group of concerned women tried to attend the trial of Edmonton prostitutes who had been arrested under questionable circumstances. After being ejected from the court on the grounds that the testimony was not fit for mixed company, an outraged Murphy wrote to the attorney general

FIGURE 14   Magistrate Emily Murphy, Edmonton Police Court, 1917. | Glenbow
Archives, NC-6-3152.

of Alberta, C.W. Cross, and argued that it was high time for a women's
court because only women, "with their key role and experiences as guard-
ians and managers of the family," could understand female offenders.[68]
After serving four years on the bench in Edmonton (see Figure 14), however,
Murphy published "A Straight Talk on Courts," which provided her
Maclean's readers with a less than sympathetic portrait of the female offender. Dividing the women she encountered in her court into two categories – those who were criminal by choice and those who were criminal
because they were mentally defective or feeble-minded – Murphy wrote
that she believed the former could be cured by enforced institutionaliza-
tion and the severance of all ties with their peers. The latter, in contrast,
needed to be segregated and isolated from society so that their traits could
not be passed on to future generations.[69]

    Murphy's understanding of the female offender drew upon eugen-
ics theory and Spencerian notions of racial hierarchy that postulated a

connection between feeble-mindedness, sexual promiscuity, and crime.[70] Between 1907 and 1918, Helen MacMurchy, a female physician and inspector of the feeble-minded in Ontario, had published a series of annual reports and a monograph titled *The Almosts: A Study of the Feeble-Minded* that advocated the segregation of mental defectives. If the courts allowed the feeble-minded to roam free, she argued, their inherent tendency to lead dissolute lives would result in more illegitimate births, the spread of venereal disease, and the mongrelization of the race. Legal officials and physicians once again envisaged the prostitute as a threat to the nation's moral and physical health: venereal disease caused feeble-mindedness, feeble-mindedness led to prostitution, and prostitutes spread venereal disease throughout society and to their offspring. MacMurchy cautioned: "It is impossible to calculate what even one feeble-minded woman may cost the public when her vast possibilities for evil as a producer of paupers and criminals are realized."[71]

MacMurchy supported her theories with questionable and vague statistics that suggested that 29 to 97 percent of prostitutes were mentally defective.[72] First-wave feminists such as Nellie McClung and Murphy similarly heightened fears about miscegenation and female delinquency when they produced narratives of narcoticism such as *The Black Candle* (1922) and *Painted Fires* (1925), which depicted young working-class and immigrant girls being drawn into lives of crime and promiscuity through the pernicious influence of dissolute flappers, Asian men, and cab drivers.[73] Because of these new pseudo-medical and psychiatric discourses, the distinctions between working-class and immigrant girls, occasional prostitutes, unwed mothers, and the feeble-minded collapsed in the interwar years.[74] This development would not only influence how judges and juries responded to complainants in sex crime trials and the female accused in infanticide and abortion cases (see Chapters 5 and 7); it also shaped prosecutorial patterns in police courts as magistrates and police officers, armed with new legislation, attempted to deal with prostitution in the 1920s and 1930s. During the Depression, reform groups did address the socioeconomic causes of prostitution, but the systemic causes of the sex trade were obscured by Christian ethics and larger societal fears that centred on the potential consequences of unregulated female sexuality. The WCTU, the Young Woman's Christian Association, and the National Council of Women, alongside socialists and trade union activists, once again predicted that low levels of relief and depressed wages would leave "normal" women with few options but to sin or starve.[75]

POLICING, PROSECUTION, AND RESISTANCE, 1886 TO 1940

How did the police respond to reform campaigns, and how did prostitutes respond to the regulatory practices to which those campaigns gave birth? With the exception of unique narratives such as *Madeleine: An Autobiography* and the testimony of individual prostitutes before the Robson Commission, the answer lies in rather oblique criminal registers and case files that recorded the day-to-day operation of the police and superior courts. Ironically, moral panics about white slavery and social evil occurred during decades when women made up a small (and possibly declining) percentage of offenders prosecuted in Canada.[76] Between 1886 and 1940, female offenders stood accused in less than 5 percent of indictable offences prosecuted in the supreme courts of the prairie judicial districts examined (see Table 1). As was the case with Aboriginal women, the majority of women's confrontations with the criminal justice system took place in local courts before JPs and magistrates. Even there, cases involving female

TABLE 1   Female offenders and the superior courts, 1886-1940

	Regina 1886-1931	Battleford 1908-38	Dauphin 1917-40	Macleod 1889-1940	Wetaskiwin 1914-38	Winnipeg 1886-1940
Total offenders	1,005	503	523	715	2,604	3,569
Female (N)	28	15	11	27	32	124
Female (%)	2.8	3	2.1	3.7	1.5	4.2

NOTES: These figures were tabulated using case files, docket books, and criminal registers of the respective courts. They include charges that ended in dismissal and cases that went to trial.
SOURCES: SCNWT (Western Assiniboia), SCS and SCKB (Regina), 1886-1932, R-1286 and R-1287, SAB; the judicial district of Battleford is included for comparative purposes only, Docket Books, SAB; Criminal Register, MCKB (Dauphin), 1917-1940 , GR 4576, L-4-15, PAM; SCNWT and SCA (Southern Alberta and Macleod), 1886-1940, Acc. 78.235, PAA; SCA (Wetaskiwin), 1914-1938, Acc. 81.198, PAA; Criminal Register, MCKB (Eastern Manitoba/Winnipeg), 1886-1940, GR 3636, M-1196, and GR 4576, L-4-15, PAM.

TABLE 2   Female offenders, superior and police courts, Edmonton, 1892-1939

	1892-1909	1910-19	1920-29	1930-39
Total offenders	3,455	3,193	7,052	3,602
Female (N)	135	456	526	179
Female (%)	4	14	7.5	4.6

SOURCES: SCNWT (Northern Alberta), 1886-1906, and SCA (Edmonton), 1907-1940, Acc. 83.1, PAA. This case file series includes records from the Edmonton Police Court.

TABLE 3   Female offenders, reported summary offences, Winnipeg Police Court

	1886	1894	1902	1910	1918*	1926*	1934*
Total offenders	1,450	1,240	2,149	9,434	3,517	7,452	9,235
Female (N)	267	109	146	504	258	416	665
Female (%)	18.4	8.7	6.8	5.3	7.3	5.5	7.2

* Because of the high volume of the court's business after the First World War, figures for 1918, 1926, and 1934 are based only on returns for six alternate months, beginning with January – numbers would have been approximately doubled.

SOURCES: City of Winnipeg Police Court, Record Books, 1886-1916, GR 651, M-1210-1220; and 1917-1954, GR 513, PAM.

defendants constituted only a small proportion of the courts' business. In the Edmonton superior and police courts, for instance, female offenders accounted for 4 percent of charged offenders between 1892 and 1914, 14 percent between 1910 and 1919, and 6 percent between 1920 and 1940 (see Table 2). The criminal registers for Winnipeg likewise reveal female offenders as a relative rarity in the city's police court. While the reported female crime rate achieved a high of 18.4 percent in the 1880s, it stabilized at roughly 6 percent of the total through the first four decades of the twentieth century (see Table 3).[77]

As these statistics suggest, prosecution patterns in prairie criminal courts reveal more about social concerns and changing patterns of enforcement than they do about female offenders, their lives, or their motivations. The relatively high percentage of women prosecuted in Winnipeg in the 1880s and in Edmonton during the First World War reflected the success of moral and social reform campaigns. When the treatment of female offenders by police and police courts is broken down into eight-year intervals and by category, the degree to which law enforcement was shaped by the social concerns of pressure groups is clear (see Table 4). Police and magistrates used the four largest prosecution categories – being an inmate of a bawdy house, keeping a bawdy house, being drunk and disorderly, and vagrancy – to regulate the behaviour and movement of prostitutes, particularly during periods of unofficial segregation, when the police prided themselves on dealing harshly with prostitutes who made a public nuisance of themselves. Female recidivists moved in and out of magistrates' court and prison on all four charges. By 1918, however, prostitution had ceased to be the primary concern of law enforcement agencies and was instead absorbed and dealt with within a larger system of socialized justice. Prostitution and prostitution-related offences, consequently, accounted for a decreasing

TABLE 4   Types of crimes as percentage of total female offences, Winnipeg
Police Court

Offence	1886	1894	1902	1910	1918*	1926*	1934*
Inmate of bawdy house	39	15	10	12	2	1	0.75
Drunk and disorderly	26	62	36	22	16.3	16	5
Keeper of bawdy house	18	2	9	9	3.9	0.7	5.7
Vagrancy	8	6.4	2.7	20.2	12	7	4
Theft	4	3	13	8.3	15.5	15	7
Liquor prohibitions	2.2	1	3.4	–	4.3	11	18
Insult/threat	1.8	0.9	2.7	3.4	3.4	1.2	–
Assault	1.4	7.3	8.2	6.5	10	5.2	–
Damage	0.3	3	1.3	1.3	–	0.5	–
Sunday non-observance	0.3	–	–	0.5	0.3	–	–
Bylaw infractions	0.3	–	3.4	6.7	19	2	–
Refuse wages	–	2.8	2.7	7.5	2	–	–
Traffic violation	–	–	–	–	5	37	51
Total number	267	109	146	504	258	416	665

* Percentages for 1918, 1926, and 1934 are based on returns from six alternate months
(see note with Table 3).
SOURCES: City of Winnipeg Police Court, Record Books, 1886-1916, GR 651, M-1210-1220;
and 1917-1940, GR 513, PAM.

majority of female crime between 1886 and 1914 – declining from 91 percent
of committals in 1886 to 34 percent of committals in 1918.[78]
    Patterns of arrest and conviction for prostitution-related offences in
Winnipeg and Edmonton between 1886 and 1940 followed the contours
of the debate between social purity advocates, feminists, and the police
as to the best and most efficient way to deal with prostitution. However,
regardless of whether the police were pursuing a pattern of tolerance or
suppression, the gender and class biases of the emerging settler society and
the attitudes of law enforcement officials remained the same: the common
prostitute, rather than the male client or female keeper, received the harshest penalties. The Winnipeg Police Court's record book for 1886 reveals
arrest and conviction strategies and patterns that would be repeated
through to the First World War. By 1886, Silcox's first morality crusade
against prostitution had wound down and the Thomas Street red-light
district – which housed approximately one hundred prostitutes, including
Madeleine, in six houses – had been in operation for three years. In the

TABLE 5   Ratio of female to male arrests for inmates and keepers of bawdy houses,
Winnipeg Police Court

Year	Inmates		Keepers	
	Female	Male	Female	Male
1886	103	60	50	6
1894	16	7	4	4
1902	15	7	18	0
1910	60	9	42	8
1918*	5	20	10	5
1926*	4	13	3	2
1934*	5	9	38	4

* Figures for 1918, 1926, and 1934 are based on returns from six alternate months (see note
with Table 3) – numbers would have been approximately doubled.
SOURCES: City of Winnipeg Police Court, Record Books, 1886-1916, GR 651, M-1210-1220;
and 1917-1940, GR 513, PAM.

four-year period between the founding of the district and the appointment
of John McRae as chief of police in 1887, the police subjected its keepers
and inmates to sporadic raids, which not only heightened the prostitute's
visibility as an anomalous figure in the city's public spaces but also enhanced
the stigma attached to the fallen woman.[79]

The police arrested fifty women and six men for keeping a common
bawdy house in 1886 (see Table 5). The magistrate subjected the vast majority to fines or release on bail. Only thirteen of the fifty female keepers
served prison sentences ranging from twenty-one days to three months.
By contrast, the magistrate committed 8 of the 60 men and 20 of the 103
women that the police had arrested as alleged inmates of a common bawdy
house. The magistrate reserved the harshest penalties for prostitutes charged
under the vagrancy or drunk and disorderly provisions of the Criminal
Code. Of the twenty-six women that the police arrested for vagrancy,
sixteen served sentences of two to three months, while two were asked to
leave town. Mary Trottier, a Metis woman who had been charged for
abortion in 1881 and worked as an occasional prostitute in the flats, was
convicted for being drunk and disorderly in January and August, for being
an inmate of a common bawdy house in March, and for keeping a common bawdy house and vagrancy in March and April. She served a total of
fifty-six days in jail and paid $4.50 in fines.[80] Arrest and conviction patterns
reinforced the hierarchical structure of the sex trade; for instance, indigenous and indigent men and women who could not afford to pay fines faced
the law's harshest penalties.

These prosecutorial and law enforcement trends became even more pronounced under Chief John McRae's tenure, when the social purity and moral reform campaigns against segregated prostitution gathered momentum. Between 1894 and 1910, arrests for prostitution-related offences dropped significantly. However, with the exception of the brief period between the Thomas Street raid in 1904 and the establishment of the Point Douglas district in 1909 (a period during which the police tried to contain the spread of prostitution throughout the city), the police pursued a two-tiered system of regulation influenced, on the one hand, by the sexual double standard and, on the other, by the brothel owners' wealth, status as property owners, and willingness to adhere to an unwritten system of regulation through taxation. In 1894, none of the Thomas Street brothel owners and only three of their inmates served prison sentences on conviction, and in 1902, the police arrested only three women for vagrancy. These prosecutorial trends suggest strongly that the police and magistrates used the Criminal Code's vagrancy provisions to regulate prostitutes who worked outside the boundaries of the segregated district. In 1910, when a red-light district had once again been established at Point Douglas, only three keepers and five inmates of bawdy houses served time in prison. The vast majority paid fines, received reprimands, or had their charges withdrawn.

Although Madeleine denied the allegations of graft that reform advocates laid against the police, brothel owners and working prostitutes who testified at the Robson Commission spoke openly of the taxation system that had evolved in Winnipeg. Minnie Woods, Winnipeg's most famous and likely wealthiest madam, for instance, disclosed that when Chief McRae suggested in 1909 that she help the police establish the Point Douglas area, she bought a house on Rachel Street for $6,000. When the commissioner asked Woods to respond to Reverend Shearer's allegations of graft, she disclosed that her lawyer had appeared in magistrates' court on three separate occasions since spring and had paid fines on her behalf to the amount of $1,088 for keeping a common bawdy house.[81] On each occasion, the police court register records that the magistrate also charged the brothel inmates but punished them with minimal fines of $20 upon conviction.[82]

Prior to the Robson Commission, the Edmonton Police Court adhered to a similar business model of unofficial taxation and regulation. Police and municipal officials generally tolerated prostitution, with fines, until social reform advocates, led by Mrs. E.E. Marshall, demanded that Chief A.C. Lancey enforce the law. Ethel Spencer, for example, appeared in court five times between 22 November and 9 December 1909 on charges of keeping a common bawdy house or selling liquor without a licence.

She pleaded guilty to all charges and paid fines between $25 and $50 for each offence. The dismantlement of the red-light district brought little change and even fewer punishments. Between August 1909 and March 1910, the Edmonton Police engaged in at least six raids on known brothels and arrested up to forty keepers and inmates during each raid. The majority of the women pleaded guilty and paid minimal fines and then reappeared before Magistrate G.S. Worsley in the months that followed.[83]

Although social purity and moral reform advocates such as Shearer, Du Val, and members of the WCTU drew the public's attention to the system of mutual toleration that had developed between the police and brothel owners, they failed to acknowledge how the subculture of prostitution, in its modern form, paralleled the hierarchical structure of society. Madeleine's contempt for the common prostitute or streetwalker, which she expressed in her memoir, was a central facet of her self-identity: "The social gulf between the first-class courtesan and those who have become the dregs of prostitution is as great as the gulf between the sheltered woman in her home and the streetwalker."[84] In Winnipeg, Chief McRae concurred and prided himself on the harsh treatment that his men and the magistrate meted out to women who tried to work outside the bounds of the Thomas Street segregated area.[85] Although the record books of the police courts reveal little about the realities of, and motivations for, these women's lives, their arrest records tell their own story. Sophie Howard appeared in the police court ten times in 1894 on charges of drunkenness, assault and battery, being an inmate of a bawdy house, vagrancy, and wilful damage to private property. In only one instance did she have enough money to pay the $6.50 fine; she spent a total of 273 days in jail that year.[86]

As historian Joan Sangster discovered when she researched female crime in Peterborough, Ontario, in the interwar years, the majority of female recidivists – women who may or may not have worked as occasional prostitutes – were poor, single, homeless alcoholics who needed shelter and a place to detoxify. Eliza Inkster, a thirty-year-old unmarried woman with no known occupation, was arrested seven times in 1886 on drunk and disorderly and vagrancy charges; in each case, the Winnipeg police magistrate sentenced her to a minimum of twenty-one days in jail with hard labour. On 3 May, when the police arrested Inkster for the theft of a watch, the magistrate sentenced her to three months in jail. As was the case with many female recidivists, Inkster appeared chronically in the courts, but she received increasingly lighter sentences. When the police arrested her three times in 1894 for public drunkenness, the magistrate either reprimanded her, demanded that she pay a fine, or asked her to leave town.[87] Charlotte Glover's circumstances were similarly tragic. Although my examination of the police court record books was confined to eight-year intervals, Glover first appeared in magistrates' court in May 1894 on charges of public drunkenness and vagrancy and continued to appear before the magistrate on a regular basis in 1902. Sadly, she disappeared from the record altogether in September 1910.[88] Police and magistrates exerted tremendous authority over the lives and experiences of women who had been rendered powerless by a blend of status and circumstance.

It was women such as Howard and Glover, rather than procurers or madams, who experienced the full force of the law in the wake of the white slavery moral panics. Contrary to reformers' expectations, the sexual double standard and the class biases that shaped policing and prosecution patterns became more pronounced following amendments to the Criminal Code in 1913 and 1915. In the superior courts of the five selected judicial districts, only seven men and women were charged under the new procuring provisions. Only two of the cases, *R. v. Herzer* (1913) and *R. v. Roberts* (1922), went to trial and resulted in conviction. In the first case, which involved a married couple who stood accused before the Supreme Court of Alberta in Edmonton, the husband was sentenced to serve one year in a federal penitentiary while his wife was released on a suspended sentence. The latter case, which was heard in the Saskatchewan Court of King's Bench in Regina, involved two men, one an itinerant labourer and the other a waiter. Based on the testimony of a "known prostitute" and one of her customers, the judge sentenced both defendants to serve one year in prison and receive six lashes in the last six months of the sentence.[89]

Prosecution patterns in the Winnipeg and Edmonton police courts paralleled those of the superior courts. Few of the men and women who were charged with keeping a common bawdy house, being found in a common bawdy house, or procuring or living off the avails of prostitution faced punishment following the war. In a six-month sample for 1918, the Winnipeg Police Court magistrate convicted and fined only one-fifth of the men who the police charged with being found in a bawdy house. The magistrate likewise dealt leniently with ten women charged with keeping a common bawdy house: he reprimanded eight, excused another who pleaded guilty, and made the final brothel owner pay a minimal fine of fifty-two dollars (see Table 5). The significant exception to this prosecutorial trend occurred during the Depression, when the police and the magistrates, perhaps in response to suggestions and warnings that depressed economic conditions would draw women into sexually exploitative situations, cracked down heavily on female keepers of bawdy houses. Of the thirty-eight women who the police arrested in the sample months for 1934, twenty-one were convicted and sentenced to six months in prison. An alternative explanation is that madams were increasingly unable to pay fines as economic conditions worsened. Similarly, the relative lack of vagrancy arrests in the 1930s might reflect the overburdened state of the city's jails, but it also suggests sympathy, on the part of legal officials, for the plight of working-class women.[90]

A number of divergent trends contributed to the uneven enforcement and prosecution of the prostitution provisions in the interwar years. On the one hand, declining arrest rates reflected the reconfiguration of prostitution as a medico-moral problem rather than a social evil, a return to selective tolerance and the sexual double standard, and the withdrawal of prostitution from public space, with the advent of the telephone and the automobile.[91] Prostitution also ceased to be of central importance as the demographic imbalance between men and women adjusted and the white settler society envisaged by policy and nation makers came to fruition. On the other hand, the active resistance of male and female brothel owners and male clients with money also played a role. The Robson Commission put an end to the system of cooperation between prostitutes and police that had flooded the courts with prostitution-related cases between 1883 and 1910. Ironically, Magistrate Daly and Chief McRae repeatedly warned and reminded social reformers and officials during the Robson Commission that prostitutes had rights too.[92] Daly argued that unless the accused pleaded guilty or a theft was involved, the evidentiary requirements in prostitution-related cases made it virtually impossible for prosecutors to convict. In the war years and interwar decades, sixteen men, mostly itinerant labourers, accused working-class women or prostitutes of luring them into rooming-houses and automobiles with the promise of sex – only to steal from them. These cases, some of which ended in physical harm or murder, became high-profile occasions for judges and juries in the superior courts to draw attention to the worst excesses of prostitution and unregulated male sexuality by imposing harsh punishments and penalties. In 1917, for example, Alfred Nye arrived in Winnipeg, cashed his cheque, and asked a taxi driver to take him to a woman. The driver took Nye to the Norwood Hotel, where he met Jenny Lebansky. After drinking with a number of men and women, Nye and Lebansky settled on a price for her sexual services and went for a drive to the outskirts of town, where Lebansky and a male companion assaulted Nye, stole $300, and left him lying in the ditch. Lebansky was convicted, received a two-year suspended sentence, and was released on her own recognizance for $2,000.[93]

Although cases such as Lebansky's typically ended in conviction, Daly maintained that it was more common, particularly during the brief period of non-tolerance between 1904 and 1909, for prostitutes to express their contempt for changing policy by refusing to plead guilty to charges of keeping or residing in a bawdy house. By doing so, they forced the police and prosecutors to produce direct evidence that an offence had been committed.[94] According to Daly, the evidentiary requirements of Canada's prostitution laws required police to provide sufficient evidence that the act of prostitution had occurred in a specific house before they could obtain a search warrant. In response, the Morality Division of the Winnipeg Police Force, which was created specifically to regulate vice in the Point Douglas segregated district, began to hire men to act as stool pigeons. It discovered, however, that these men proved to be unreliable witnesses because they could be charged with conspiracy to commit a crime. If the police did manage to obtain sufficient evidence, and a magistrate issued a warrant, the prosecution then had to prove that an overt or specific act of prostitution had taken place.[95] Daly backed up his assessment of the law by referring to *R. v. St. Clair* and *R. v. Osberg*, cases that followed the English case *Singleton v. Elliston*.[96] Without direct evidence of prostitution, Daly concluded, prosecutors had no recourse but to charge keepers, inmates, and habitual frequenters with vagrancy under section 238 of the Criminal Code.[97]

Prostitutes and brothel owners who could afford legal counsel defied, or outright manipulated, the law by either refusing to plead guilty or launching appeals of convictions. On 22 May 1912, for instance, Magistrate G.S. Worsley of the Edmonton Police Court dismissed charges against Mrs. Louis Moore of keeping and being an inmate of a common bawdy house on the grounds of insufficient evidence. Only one witness, Thomas George, appeared for the prosecution, and he testified that he had met Moore on the street, accompanied her home, and paid nine dollars for her sexual services. Although the court found Moore's husband and another man guilty of being inmates of a common bawdy house, there was no direct evidence that a commercial sexual exchange had taken place.[98] Amy Morris, a brothel owner who testified before the Robson Commission, told the court that she had appeared before a magistrate on many occasions but had refused to plead guilty. She preferred instead to appeal with *habeas corpus* and *certiorari* proceedings.[99] Daly disclosed that prostitutes commonly manipulated the system in this manner. Once the brothel owner or inmate provided two men as sureties, the magistrate freed her from jail on bail. As soon as the appeal court met to hear the case, however, the woman would fail to appear and the court would discover that the sureties had been straw men.[100]

Men who could afford legal counsel likewise evaded punishment by challenging police practices or appealing decisions. In Edmonton's police court, for instance, eight miners who were accused of frequenting or permitting their premises to be used as a disorderly house simply pleaded guilty and paid minimal fines. By contrast, Charles Langston, who had been charged with frequenting a bawdy house in Edmonton, told Magistrate Emily Murphy that his case had been brought illegally before the court. When Murphy ignored the plea, found the defendant guilty, and fined him seventy-five dollars and the costs of the court, Langston hired a lawyer to appeal the conviction on the grounds that the police had produced no evidence that the domicile was in fact a common bawdy house. Justice William Carlos Ives of the Supreme Court of Alberta in Edmonton heard the appeal and quashed the conviction.[101]

As had been the case prior to the Robson Commission and criminal law amendments, it was working-class women and, to a lesser degree, itinerant working-class men who lacked the social status or wealth to pay fines or hire defence counsel who experienced the increased regulatory force of the prostitution provisions and the turn toward socialized justice. Beginning in 1910, when the campaign against the Point Douglas segregated district was at its height, Daly, inspired by social reformers and new medico-moral theories of female criminality, began to sentence working-class women who had been arrested on prostitution-related charges, but who "demonstrated evidence of redeemability," to the Salvation Army's Industrial and Rescue Home for Women or to the Catholic Home of the Good Shepherd. Adjutant McElhany and his wife, who believed that prostitutes lacked discipline and self-control, ran the Salvation Army's home. They taught inmates industrial and domestic arts, encouraged their charges to renounce their associates, and attempted to instill in working prostitutes a respect for Christian moral values and the saving power of Jesus.[102]

A significant number of the women singled out for reformation by Daly and the Salvation Army actively resisted their reform efforts, forcing McElhany and his wife to quickly abandon all hope for rescue work. As part of their campaign to bring to light instances of white slavery in the heart of Winnipeg's red-light district, McElhany, his wife, and members of the League of Mercy entered the Point Douglas district to save a girl allegedly enslaved by debt and addiction to luxury and opium. Contrary to the reformers' expectations, the girl, much like Madeleine, refused assistance. The couple's attempt to persuade other red-light inmates to choose reformation over prostitution likewise met with failure.[103] More coercive measures were in order. On 26 August 1910, Daly sentenced Ruby Rowe to one year at the industrial home for vagrancy. Less than two months later, Rowe escaped; following her re-arrest, the magistrate released her on bail. Rowe then proceeded to get gloriously drunk and managed to attract a large crowd in front of the courthouse before the police carried her away by express wagon. The police again charged Rowe with vagrancy, and Magistrate Daly sentenced her to serve six months in the Eastern Judicial District jail with hard labour. When Rowe's escape case came up for trial at the Winnipeg Court of King's Bench on 7 March 1911, she demanded the court's lenience on the grounds that she was a hard-working woman. The judge ignored her plea and sentenced her to one month in prison. When Magistrate Daly testified before the Robson Commission, he lamented that Rowe was "again walking the streets."[104] The Winnipeg Police Court record books for 1910 list the names of ten other women who escaped from the home within weeks of their committal.[105]

Although prostitutes such as Rowe managed to resist police and magisterial efforts to regulate their behaviour, the records of the Edmonton Police Court, where Emily Murphy sat on the bench, suggest that resistance became more difficult in the interwar decades. In 1920, the Edmonton police arrested thirteen men for procuring or living off the avails of prostitution, and ten men for being found in a common bawdy house. Police similarly charged eight women with keeping a common bawdy house, and twenty-seven women for being an inmate of a bawdy house or a common prostitute under the vagrancy provisions. Although many of the men pleaded guilty and paid fines ranging from $10 to $100, depending upon the seriousness of the crime, the majority of the women were subjected to physical examinations under the Act for the Prevention of Venereal Disease, which had been passed by provincial legislators in 1918 on the urging of reformers and social hygienists. The act permitted the provincial medical officer of health to have any person committed to jail following a conviction to submit to an examination for venereal disease.[106] In the Edmonton Police Court, however, Murphy consistently had women (and a few men) who had been arrested for, but not convicted of, vagrancy or being found in a bawdy house remanded for examination. On 13 March 1919, a woman charged with being a common prostitute pleaded not guilty. Four days later, Murphy remanded her for examination. When the accused tested negative, Murphy withdrew the charge. By contrast, those women who tested positive or could not pay fines were subjected to prison sentences that ranged from three to six months. Ellen McKenzie, who tested positive for syphilis and gonorrhea and pleaded guilty to using a hotel room for the purposes of prostitution, was sentenced by Murphy to three months in the provincial jail and then bound over to keep the peace for $1,000.[107] By 1922, however, this strategy of identifying and punishing fallen women who were labelled carriers of contagion waned. As was the case in Winnipeg, the Edmonton Police Court did record a resurgence of arrests for keeping a common bawdy house between 1935 and the outbreak of the Second World War.

CONCLUSION

In late-nineteenth- and early-twentieth-century narratives of the prairie West, the pioneer woman struggles alongside her husband to raise a family and develop the homestead. Or, if she is a member of the urban middle class, she strives to reform and alleviate social and moral conditions in the city and women's unequal status before the law. The pioneer woman is rarely depicted as a woman who would engage in acts of prostitution, theft, and violence. Popular discourses, much like criminal trials, have the power to address perceived social disorders and disguise real social inequalities. Middle-class reformers objected to the publication of *Madeleine: An Autobiography* not only because they viewed the memoir as an outrage against public morality but also because its author had the audacity to represent herself as an individual whose life experiences and character did not conform to the virgin or whore archetypes then available to women. Madeleine was exceptional because she had the leisure, financial security, and wherewithal to write and publish an account of her experiences. Like the majority of prostitutes at the turn of the twentieth century, however, her increasingly visible presence in prairie towns, red-light districts, and public thoroughfares challenged the boundaries of the public-private divide that defined the liberal economic order.

As British criminologist Susan Edwards argues, turn-of-the-century theories of female prostitution placed a paradoxical image of female sexuality at the centre of Western culture.[108] Contradictory images of women as chaste yet unchaste, good yet bad, virgin yet whore played themselves out on the Prairies when the campaign to eradicate prostitution and venereal disease, initiated by physicians and sanitary engineers, gradually transformed into campaigns to either regulate deviant and disorderly women or save hapless women from the white slave trade's unscrupulous pimps and procurers. The belief that the moral and social foundations of empire and nation were in danger of dissolution fuelled this transformation, and, consequently, debates about prostitution reflected competing visions of the role of the state in public and private domains and the role of sexuality and the family in the nation. Members of the Winnipeg Ministerial Association and the Citizen's Committee for the Suppression of Vice, along with women's organization such as the WCTU and the National Council of Women of Canada, agreed that prostitution needed to be eradicated to contain sex within lawful marriages. They also agreed that the best way to achieve this was by expanding state authority to regulate the behaviour of women *and* men who engaged in private and commercial sexual exchanges that fell outside of lawful marriage and by addressing uneven enforcement practices that derived from the sexual double standard. Women's organizations and feminists in particular constructed the prostitute as the passive victim of corrupt politicians and policemen, of lust-filled and licentious immigrant and working-class men, and, following the First World War, of mental and genetic degeneracy. Hoping to shore up the family and create a stable settler society by confining sex to marriage and restraining the excesses of a rugged, frontier masculinity, social and moral reform advocates demanded increased state intervention for the protection of young girls and women. They sought to reinforce the family as an institution during a period when the tides of urban industrialization, secularization, the rise of the New Woman, and a new, more assertive masculine ideal were increasingly challenging their dominance and relevance. Their campaign to eradicate prostitution solidified and legitimized middle-class women and evangelical clergymen as the region's moral authorities but masked systemic inequalities that precluded many working-class and immigrant women from living up to their ideals.

Historians Joan Sangster and Carolyn Strange have used criminal case files to move beyond the prevailing rhetoric of protection to map how the confluence of reform campaigns and criminal law amendments resulted in the increased regulation of working-class women and prostitutes in early-twentieth-century Ontario. The same pattern emerged on the Prairies as law enforcement officials – who adhered to a vision of a rugged, frontier masculinity that was at odds with the ideals of Christian reform advocates and feminists – attempted to remove prostitution from the public sphere to preserve the spatial boundaries and social hierarchies of colonialism and nation building. The degree to which the agenda of law enforcement

agencies and lawmakers meshed with the imperatives of the liberal economic order was reflected in the criminal law amendments and arrest and
conviction patterns that followed the Robson Commission on Social Vice
(1910). Although it can be argued that it was the police and magistrates
alone who recognized that prostitutes had legal rights in the new carceral
regime, legislation and evidentiary requirements ensured that regular
prostitutes, rather than property-owning or affluent brothel owners or
male customers, would bear the full force of the law. Working-class women
and prostitutes in the interwar years increasingly found themselves caught
up in a new system of socialized justice that kept indigent and sexually
promiscuous women off the public streets by sweeping them into industrial
homes that inundated female offenders with the Christian and middle-class
values of self-discipline, piety, and women's place in the public sphere.
Although Christian and feminist reformers resisted application of the
sexual double standard and demanded that male pimps and customers be
subjected to the full force of the law, the enforcement of prostitution and
procuring laws paralleled the outcome of the "hired hand" cases that would
inundate the courts in the interwar years, with sexually promiscuous white
women being placed one rung above Aboriginal women, but one rung
below their working-class male counterparts.

Urban industrialization forced prostitution from the city's margins and
the fringes of rural communities to the heart of the public sphere, where
the prostitute became symptom and signifier of the worst excesses of
modernity and its perceived threat to the Christian family. The criminal
registers and case files, social surveys, and reform tracts that emerged from
myriad conflicts and negotiations between prostitutes, police, reform
agencies, and legal officials, however, tell a tale of working-class women,
like Madeleine, who actively coped with, responded to, and resisted the
regulatory impulse that accompanied the dislocations of urban industrialization. The meanings that were attached to these women's confrontations
by dominant groups and the media reinforced stereotypes of prostitutes
in particular, and women in general, as either vicious, unmanageable examples of their sex or as pitiable, passive creatures. Just as representations
of Aboriginal women as dangerous and dissolute threats to empire racialized the settlement process, the construction of prostitution as the social
evil of the era sexualized and feminized the process of urban industrialization on the Prairies (hired hand cases would do the same thing in the
countryside). These discursive practices drew attention away from the sex
trade's systemic causes and, to a lesser degree, the behaviour of men who

participated in it, enhancing the regulatory scope of the criminal law over women's behaviour and sexuality to preserve the public as a male space; however, campaigns to eradicate prostitution also helped middle-class women carve out a space for respectable femininity.

4

The Farmer, the Pioneer Woman, and the Hired Hand

Sexual Violence, Seduction, and the Boundaries of Class

In October 1907, an assize jury at Morden, Manitoba, condemned Lawrence Gowland, a British agricultural labourer, to death by hanging after a jury found the accused guilty of the rape and murder of Georgina Brown. At the trial, the victim's brother, John Brown, testified that he had left his Turtle Mountain homestead at noon on 22 May to buy supplies in town. When he departed, his twenty-year-old English farmhand sat smoking a cigarette on the front porch, while his sister, Georgina, was preparing to visit a neighbour. When the brother returned, he found a trail of blood that led from the kitchen upstairs to his bedroom, where he discovered Gowland bleeding on the bed. Brown rushed to find his sister, only to learn that she had never arrived at the neighbour's farm. It was not until he returned to the homestead that Brown found Georgina's nearly decapitated body in her bedroom. Further investigation by the coroner, police, and neighbours produced the murder weapon, a razor blade, and evidence that Georgina had been "criminally assaulted." After he recovered from his wound, Gowland confessed to the coroner and a constable that he had slit Brown's throat, raped the victim as she died, and then tried to kill himself.[1]

Gowland's contrition, youth, and race would have typically guaranteed him a fair trial or, if convicted, a reduced sentence. Unfortunately, his trial occurred at a time when the wide-open immigration policies of Frank Oliver, federal minister of the interior, had turned the attention of middle-class politicians and social reform advocates to the problem of working-class immigrants from Britain. Philanthropists, in concert with the British and

Canadian governments, responded to the crisis by creating numerous child rescue agencies, immigration schemes, and training programs to transform unskilled urban workers into farmers. The most famous of these organizations, the Barnardo's Homes, sought to turn "myriads of degraded lives into honourable and useful careers" by training children to work in rural Ontario and prairie Canada. Between 1870 and 1920, nearly seventy thousand destitute British children and youths entered the country under these agencies' auspices, and by 1914, 20 percent of all male immigrants to the Prairies were potential agricultural labourers.[2] Middle-class Canadians and prairie farmers responded to these schemes quickly and negatively. In early 1888, Dr. C. Ferguson told a House of Commons standing committee on agriculture and colonization that British orphans were "the offal of the most depraved characters in the cities of the old country." Two years later, Ontario's Royal Commission on the Prison and Reformatory System reported that "very many of them went wrong through hereditary traits," swelling the ranks of the criminal class by corrupting others through evil habits.[3] When the police arrested and charged a youth in Brandon, Manitoba, with the murder of his employer a few years later, journalists and politicians insisted that he hailed from the nearby Barnardo Industrial Farm. Although the accused was Canadian born and bred, the grand jury blamed English orphan children and youths for escalating crime rates in the Brandon area, and journalists in Ontario, who accepted inaccurate reports of the case, denounced the immigration of British labouring children and youths.[4] By 1907, when Lawrence Gowland stood trial for murder in Turtle Mountain's small farming community, the region's social reform advocates and commentators envisaged all working-class British immigrants as threats to prairie social development. In *Strangers within Our Gates: The Problem of the Immigrant* (1909), James Woodsworth agreed that English immigration was necessary to maintain British traditions in Canada, yet he lamented, "The trouble has been largely with the *class* of immigrants who have come ... we need farmers and labourers, they send us the failures of the cities." Backing up his argument with manipulated statistics from Winnipeg's Police Court, Woodsworth asserted that only saloons and criminal courts gained when Canada welcomed Britain's working class.[5]

For prairie dwellers, legal authorities, and servants of the court, the violent rape and murder of Georgina Brown on an isolated farmstead in rural Manitoba confirmed and compounded these suspicions. At the preliminary hearing, John Brown deposed that on the Sunday before the murder he had caught Gowland spying on his sister through a hole in her bedroom wall. The prosecution likewise produced physical evidence that the murder was more than a lover's quarrel gone wrong when the medical examiner disclosed that Brown had been a virgin. Gowland later confessed to a Manitoba Provincial Police officer that Brown had provoked his actions by calling him a "dirty English brat ... because I brought in dirt on my boots." Journalists played up the disparities between the accused and his victim by contrasting Gowland's youth, ethnicity, and lack of moral conscience with "Miss Brown's" social status and virtue.[6]

Although Gowland's guilt was beyond doubt, the court's treatment of him was less than just. In a decade when serious murder or rape cases lasted a minimum of two days, Gowland's trial lasted a mere forty-five minutes. When the accused made it known that he could not afford a defence attorney, the attorney general made it clear that the Manitoba government would not cover the cost. When Gowland disastrously pleaded guilty to the charge of murder, Justice Frank H. Phippen had to ask the accused to withdraw the plea, as was required by the Criminal Code. Although Justice Phippen later charged the jury to forget Gowland's original plea, the damage was done. During the trial, Gowland hurt his case further by failing to cross-examine witnesses or address the jury on his own behalf. Phippen later informed the secretary of state of the Department of Justice that he could not recall the last time an accused went undefended by counsel. Nevertheless, the judge did not believe that the government should extend the prerogative of mercy in the case, because the accused was "one of those unfortunates with little moral responsibility, whose passions and temper when roused are beyond their control, but who are nevertheless fully responsible for their acts."[7] Gowland's spiritual adviser, C.W. Finch, also wrote to the minister of justice and informed him that the accused had arrived in Canada from England in 1905 and worked as a "faithful farm servant." Gowland's behaviour, Finch believed, stemmed from his upbringing among London's working class and his lack of parental supervision in Canada. Following this lacklustre clemency campaign, Lawrence Gowland met his death on the scaffold on 13 December 1907.[8]

By the outbreak of the First World War, economic developments, an influx of immigrants from southern and eastern Europe, and cases such as *Gowland* ensured that all prairie agricultural labourers suffered poor reputations. Historian Cecilia Danysk has traced how bachelor homesteaders and farm labourers – once considered accepted and necessary figures on prairie farms – came to be known pejoratively as hired hands as pioneers transformed homesteads into family farms.[9] Organizations such as the Salvation Army represented hired men as moral and physical threats to farm women and children. Its mission to rural youth warned that hired men were "very likely to be men of low ideals and evil practices," and it advised parents to guard their sons from temptation into bestiality, which was urged by "the vile talk of farm hands."[10] By 1915, officials with the Saskatchewan Department of Agriculture felt compelled to publish "Practical Pointers for Farm Hands," which tried to construct physical boundaries between farm labourers and farm women. Rule 38 warned the potential labourer to be at all times decent in conduct, clean in appearance, and gentlemanly in demeanour. He was never to call elder daughters by their first names unless requested to drop such formalities. Rule 40 forbade him from calling the wife by her first name, "no matter how young and pretty she is nor how much she does to make you feel at home ... if she likes to have you call her by name, so much the more you should refrain, she's in need of a little training herself."[11]

Historians have revealed that the development of a capitalist market economy on settlement frontiers was often accompanied by heightened tensions and criminal conflicts between houseboys, farm labourers, and white women. The scarcity of free or cheap farm land by 1911 on the Canadian Prairies likewise heightened previously contained tensions between capital and labour.[12] This chapter traces how these tensions spilled over to influence the reporting and prosecution of sex crimes such as *Gowland* – cases of unlawful common knowledge, indecent assault, rape, or seduction – among farmers, their wives and daughters, and hired hands (see Table 6). How did judges and juries respond when men of poor general reputation entered the docket on charges of rape or seduction? What happened if their victim also failed to meet the ideals of the emerging patriarchal and capitalistic countryside? Historian Dirk Hoerder, who is concerned with how hierarchy was constructed and how attitudes toward the body changed within colonial and nation-building projects, has observed that women and working-class men came to be defined increasingly by parts of their bodies rather than as citizens in liberal economic frameworks: "The male work ethic and female chastity [a form of property in itself] defined men by muscles and women by reproductive organs."[13] Historians of masculinity have also argued that the determinants of honourable and dishonourable masculinity, much like those of honourable and dishonourable femininity, were highly class specific.[14] This chapter shows how sex crime prosecutions in rural communities at once reflected and reinforced these developments. It reveals how criminal courts, by helping to establish the norms of male and female heterosexuality and by

TABLE 6   Sex crimes as percentage of total charges, 1886-1940

District	Regina (1886-1940)	Battleford (1908-38)	Dauphin (1917-40)	Winnipeg (1889-1905)	Macleod (1886-1940)
Total charges	1,005	503	523	715	2,914
Sex crimes (N)	106	57	32	29	207
Sex crimes (%)	11	11.3	6.1	4.1	7.1

NOTES: Edmonton and Wetaskiwin districts are excluded because the records for these districts include summary offences. However, 101 cases of rape and indecent assault came before the courts in the period studied. Statistics for incest were also excluded.

SOURCES: SCNWT, SCS, SCKB (Western Assiniboia and Regina), R-1286 and R-1287, and SCS and SCKB (Battleford), Docket Books, SAB; Criminal Register, MCKB (Eastern Manitoba/Winnipeg), GR 3636, and Criminal Register, MCKB (Dauphin), GR 4576, L-4-15, PAM; SCNWT and SCA (Southern Alberta and Macleod), Acc. 78.235, PAA.

setting limits on who could marry a farmer's daughter, shored up both gender- and class-based inequalities in the rural countryside.

A MOST SERIOUS CHARGE:
POPULAR AND LEGAL UNDERSTANDINGS OF SEXUAL VIOLENCE

By the time Lawrence Gowland stood accused of rape and murder, prairie writers and propagandists were already representing prairie Canada as a rural, pastoral idyll. Proponents of the country-life ideology, which pervaded the rural press, claimed that country living produced only the "bravest men, the most valiant soldiers and a class of citizens least given of all to evil design."[15] The outcome of high-profile cases such as *Bourassa*, *Evanse*, and the Rosalie trials (see Chapters 1 and 2) also allowed legal authorities and officials to assert with confidence that the West was a haven for women. In 1895, a Crown prosecutor in Manitoba's Court of Queen's Bench assured the jury and public alike that settlers would have little to fear in terms of protecting their wives and daughters from physical harm and sexual violence. His declaration followed the 1895 trial of Joseph Henault, an unmarried fisherman who had been charged with having unlawful carnal knowledge of a girl under the age of fourteen. In his address to the jury, Crown counsel dwelled upon the gravity of the charge and the fortunate circumstance that cases of sexual violence appeared to be infrequent in Manitoba's courts. The alleged offence, he noted, had taken place in the rural municipality of St. Laurent, an area in which the

officers of the law were not numerous and "where people have to trust to
each other mutually for the protection of their persons and their property."[16]
After only fifteen minutes of deliberation, the jury found Henault guilty,
and the judge sentenced him to eight months in jail with hard labour.[17]

Although the editors of the *Free Press* chose to openly discuss the subject
of sexual violence in this instance, social and moral reform advocates,
first-wave feminists, and journalists rarely discussed or debated the issue.
In 1913, for instance, Mary E. Crawford, a physician and feminist from
Manitoba, published *The Legal Status of Women in Manitoba,* in which she
criticized the patriarchal assumptions of Canadian law by comparing the
maximum punishments in sex crime cases with those for property offences.
Crawford noted, for instance, that while a man convicted of abducting a
girl under the age of sixteen could serve a maximum of five years in prison,
a judge could sentence a man found guilty of stealing a cow to fourteen
years in prison.[18] Although feminists such as Crawford raised awareness
about the class and gender biases of Canadian criminal law and society, the
criminal law and the criminal courts remained areas of the public domain
deemed unsuitable for respectable women (with the exception of those
few women who were appointed to the bench of the juvenile and police
courts). The general public, therefore, remained largely ignorant of what
went on in criminal courts on a daily basis. After 1900, most sex crime
prosecutions took place in camera to protect the modesty of the victims.
Constrained by this limitation, reporters invariably noted that the accused
had been acquitted or convicted of "a most serious charge" but claimed
that the details of the case were unfit to print.

The *Regina Leader's* coverage of sex crime cases suggests that this trend
was more than a retreat to Victorian and Edwardian sensibilities. Although
judges and juries in the Regina superior courts heard 106 indictable sex
crime cases between 1887 and 1931, the editors chose to cover only 34 of
them. Whereas twenty-two articles described cases that ended in conviction, the remaining twelve items were newsworthy only because the accused
had been acquitted, even though he conformed to popular representations
of the criminal or rapist, particularly in the interwar years when the sexual
psychopath gripped the imaginations of the populace and the psychiatry
profession. While one headline read "Coloured Man Gets His Liberty,"
another announced "Charge against Greek Is Dismissed in Court."[19]

Newspaper coverage of sex crime prosecutions simultaneously reflected
and shaped popular understandings of sexual violence in prairie communities. Individual newspaper articles and trials – like that of George
Evanse – suggested that the law did not discriminate on the basis of race,

class, or ethnicity. The general tone and presentation of the coverage furthered the impression that sexual violence against western women was relatively rare and that, when it did occur, the courts responded swiftly and harshly to punish the typically foreign or working-class offender. In reality, the outcome of each case hinged upon the divergent, and often contradictory, understandings of sexual violence held by the parties involved: the victim, her family, the accused, the judge, the jury, and expert witnesses.[20]

At the highest level, magistrates and judges adhered to definitions of sexual violence that were entrenched in Canada's criminal law and the English common law tradition of judicial precedent.[21] The law of rape had evolved, at least theoretically, to protect women from sexual violence. The 1892 Criminal Code defined rape as "the act of a man having carnal knowledge of a woman who is not his wife without her consent or with consent which is extorted by threats or fear of bodily harm."[22] Rape was an indictable offence, and upon conviction the accused could suffer the penalty of death or life imprisonment. If the jury found him guilty of attempted rape, the accused was liable to serve a maximum sentence of seven years in prison.[23] In 1920 and 1921, influenced by new fears of sexual predators and the threat that urbanization and immigration posed to children and youths, legislators amended the Criminal Code to add whipping as a discretionary punishment in cases of rape and its attempt.[24]

By the late nineteenth century, the criminal law had developed substantively to protect women from sexual violence. In practice, the presumption of innocence of the accused placed the onus on the female complainant to disprove her consent. Typically, if the victim could not prove that she had resisted the assault – either by corroboration or direct physical evidence of a violent struggle – judges and juries assumed consent.[25] Over the course of the first two decades of the twentieth century, legislators extended the strict evidentiary requirements of rape law to cases of statutory rape – known then as unlawful carnal knowledge. As Justice Richardson advised in his charge to the jury during the 1892 Bourassa trial, because unlawful carnal knowledge cases involved girls under the age of consent (which was fourteen until 1920 and sixteen thereafter), the prosecution did not need to produce evidence of physical coercion. The 1920 amendments to the Criminal Code did stipulate, however, that girls between the ages of fourteen and sixteen should be of previously chaste character and that "no person ... shall be convicted upon the evidence of one witness, unless such witness is corroborated in some material particular by evidence implicating the accused."[26] Upon conviction, the accused was liable to serve a maximum life term in prison with a whipping.[27] If the jury found the accused guilty of attempted unlawful carnal knowledge, he could serve a maximum of two years in prison.

Complainants in seduction trials were likewise hampered in making their case by evidentiary constraints. Seduction became a criminal offence in Canada in 1886 on the urging of social reformers such as Liberal MP John Charlton and members of the Society for the Protection of Women and Children, who sought to eradicate prostitution and the sexual exploitation of single working-class and immigrant women.[28] By denying young, single women control over their sexuality, the legislation blurred the line between consensual sex and rape, and between the public and private spheres, allowing parents, family courts, and reform agencies to regulate girls' sexuality so as to restrict sexual relations and childbirth to marriage.[29] Unlike the legal definition of rape and unlawful carnal knowledge, the definition of the crime of seduction specifically required complainants of all ages to be of previously chaste character. In addition, if the complainant was over the age of sixteen, the prosecution had to prove that the seduction had taken place under promise of marriage. In all cases, Crown counsel was required to provide corroboratory evidence. If a conviction resulted, the accused was liable to serve a maximum penalty of two years in prison.[30]

The evidentiary requirements in sex crime cases encouraged the criminal courts to put the victim's character, rather than the deeds of the accused, on trial.[31] Magistrates' and judges' understandings of consent were historically determined and based on gendered understandings of human behaviour, character, and sexuality.[32] As Aboriginal complainants' confrontations with police, judges, and juries attest (see Chapter 2), one of the most pervasive criminal law assumptions was that women and girls, regardless of race, were inherently untruthful when they testified about sexual assault.[33] C.S. Greaves, a nineteenth-century Canadian authority on rape law, epitomized contemporary judicial attitudes when he commented: "A very long experience in criminal courts satisfies me that the majority of charges of rape are false, and that innocent persons are put in great peril by them; and for the most part no one except the man and woman are alleged to be present, and consequently it is open to the woman to fabricate any story she likes without fear of contradiction by anyone except the prisoner."[34]

The degree to which prejudicial attitudes toward sex crime complainants pervaded prairie society became apparent in 1894 when George Earle was tried for attempted rape in the Manitoba Court of Queen's Bench. Taking the stand in his own defence, Earle argued that he had been sexually intimate with the woman in question but that she had been a consenting party to the act. In his charge to the jury, the judge complimented the Crown and the defence on the masterly manner in which they had presented the details of the case, but he warned the jury that although the details of the sexual encounter were "heinously immoral," they were not that grave if the woman had consented. The judge asked the jury to address three issues when they deliberated on the issue of consent: Did the prosecutrix have any spite against the prisoner? Did she have anything to gain by bringing the case before the courts? Had defence counsel proven that the complainant was of previously unchaste character?[35]

The judiciary's willingness to use or question a woman's chastity as a test of her veracity led feminists in the 1970s to develop universalistic theories and explanations of sexual violence that linked it to the maintenance of patriarchal power. In her classic study *Against Our Will* (1975), Susan Brownmiller argued that low conviction rates in sex crime prosecutions increased women's vulnerability to rape: criminal trials enhanced cultural and legal perceptions of women's bodies as male property, thereby ensuring that all women remained subordinate.[36] Lorene Clark and Debra Lewis responded to, but departed from, Brownmiller's thesis by highlighting the class dimension of sexual violence and its prosecution. Rape laws, they argued, not only preserved women's bodies and sexuality for exclusive ownership by men, they also preserved them for those men who could afford to acquire and maintain them. Because working-class men lacked purchasing power, Clark and Lewis argued, they resorted to physical violence.[37] Although Clark and Lewis' analysis failed to account for, or explain, cases in which prominent upper- or middle-class men commit acts of sexual violence, they did cause scholars to question how political economy influenced sexual violence and its prosecution.

As the outcome of sex crime cases involving Aboriginal victims and accused attests, sexual violence, and the criminal courts' treatment of it, served complex functions in colonial contexts and developing societies. On the one hand, sexual violence was wrong in women's eyes not simply because it threatened their physical safety but also because it could bring shame upon them and destroy their moral standing in the community. In an age when middle-class and Anglo-Canadian judges and juries placed weight upon a woman's adherence to the ideal of female chastity outside of marriage, sexual shame determined whether a woman confronted her assailant – in person or in the court – or remained silent.[38] The female complainant's racial and economic status relative to the accused also determined whether she would seek recourse in the courts and how her complaint would be received. On the other hand, trial outcomes could also be shaped by middle-class ideals of masculinity that operated to define, or set limits upon, which men should, and could, have access to women's bodies. In her study of rape in York County, Ontario, between 1880 and 1930, for instance, historian Carolyn Strange turned the discussion of sexual violence on its head by asking the question, why were some men convicted? She discovered that the class, status, and ethnicity of the accused played a vital role in rape trials. Judges and juries were more likely to punish the accused if he represented a segment of the population deemed a threat to the moral, social, and political foundations of Ontario society. Strange argues that because rape trials are bound up in wider disputes over power and inequality, they expose broader social tensions that may appear to be unrelated to heterosexual conflict.[39] On the Prairies, sex crime prosecutions operated simultaneously to punish farm women whose sexual behaviour threatened the patriarchal foundations of the family farm and to set boundaries for single working-class men's sexual and social relationships with farm wives or their daughters. Both trends hastened the construction of normative masculinity and femininity as a bulwark against the challenges of modernity that were overtaking rural prairie communities.

A FARMER AND A FAMILY MAN:
PROSECUTORIAL TRENDS, CONVICTION PATTERNS, AND THEIR MEANINGS

Although prairie dwellers associated country living with moral purity and social regeneration, sexual violence and contraventions of sexual mores were a regular occurrence in rural settings. As was the case in northern and rural Ontario in the same decades, many acts of sexual violence and seduction took place not on the darkened streets of burgeoning cities but in the privacy of the patriarchal home and family farm.[40] Between 1886 and 1940, 473 women in the selected judicial districts accused men of either raping, indecently assaulting, or seducing them: 295 of these alleged offences involved farm women and girls as complainants. When compared to other regions and historical periods in Canada, where conviction rates ranged from a low of 2.3 percent in nineteenth-century Montreal to a high of 51 percent in Ontario between 1880 and 1929, western prosecutors and juries achieved convictions and brought in guilty verdicts at a higher than

TABLE 7   Conviction patterns, sex crime prosecutions: Agricultural labourers
vs. farmers

Outcome	Agricultural labourers	Farmers/farmers' sons
Convicted	53 (51%)	60 (39%)
Convicted of lesser offence	4 (4%)	–
Not guilty	25 (24%)	60 (39%)
No resolution	22 (21%)	33 (22%)
Total (out of 257)	104	153

SOURCES: SCNWT and SCA (Northern Alberta and Edmonton), 1886-1914, Acc. 83.1, PAA;
SCNWT and SCA (Southern Alberta and Macleod), 1886-1940, Acc. 78.235, PAA; SCA
(Wetaskiwin), 1914-1938, Acc. 81.198, PAA; Criminal Register, MCKB (Eastern Manitoba/
Winnipeg), 1886-1940, GR 3636, M-1196, PAM; Criminal Register, MCKB (Dauphin), 1917-
1940, GR 4576, L-4-15, PAM; SCNWT, SCS, SCKB (Western Assiniboia and Regina), 1886-
1932, R-1286 and R-1287, SAB.

average rate: convictions occurred in 46 percent of reported cases, and if
cases that did not proceed to trial are excluded, the conviction rate was 58
percent (see Table 7). In British Columbia, which was undergoing similar
demographic, economic, and cultural transformations, men were likewise
convicted in a slight majority of the 455 cases that went before a grand
jury or the Supreme Court between 1885 and 1940.[41]

High rates of conviction on the Prairies resulted almost entirely from
the overrepresentation and over-incarceration of agricultural labourers.
Although farm labourers made up no more than one-fifth of the rural
population at any given time, they stood as the accused in approximately
40 percent of the rape and indecent assault cases and 55 percent of seduction and abduction trials that occurred in rural areas. Conviction rates
and sentencing patterns suggest strongly that judges and rural juries –
which consisted predominantly of property-owning, Anglo-Canadian men
– were predisposed to believe farm women's stories of sexual violence if
the accused was a farm labourer. Not only were 55 percent of agricultural
labourers convicted (the conviction rate rises to 70 percent if cases that
did not proceed to trial are discounted), but the western judiciary also
proved more than willing to punish sex offenders harshly. Sentences in
these cases ranged from the six months with hard labour served by Ralph
Sheel, who was found guilty of attempting to have unlawful carnal knowledge of his employer's daughter near Milestone, Saskatchewan, to the ten
years and a whipping served by Archibald Daignault for rape in 1931.[42]

By contrast, farmers and farmers' sons fared much better. They were convicted in only 39 percent of the cases in which they faced a judge or jury at trial. When cases that did not proceed to trial are discounted, however, the conviction rate rises to 50 percent. In the vast majority of cases, farmers were either fined or served suspended sentences upon conviction for indecent assault or attempted rape. Even in those cases in which the prosecution established that a violent sexual assault had occurred and the jury brought in a guilty verdict, judges limited punishment to no more than a few months in jail. The few exceptions to this trend betray the role that judicial bias played in sentencing. In 1920, for example, a judge of the Winnipeg Court of King's Bench sentenced Arthur Daignault, a Metis farmer from St. Vital, Manitoba, to seven years' imprisonment on two counts of attempted rape.[43]

Criminal case files likewise reveal the role that class bias played in the prosecution of seduction on the Prairies. Statistics for Canada in general indicate that the conviction rate for seduction rose from 9 percent at the turn of the twentieth century to 34 percent by the end of the First World War.[44] In the prairie districts examined, agricultural labourers stood as the accused in twenty-one seduction and abduction trial: juries found three-quarters of them guilty, and judges typically sentenced them to three to six months in prison with hard labour. Although juries likewise found fifteen of the farmers or farmers' sons accused of seduction guilty, judges again failed to bring the full force of the law to bear in their cases: most received a suspended sentence or a minimal fine. Newspaper coverage of sex crime prosecutions in general suggests that the occasional conviction and imprisonment of a farmer or a married man for rape, seduction, or indecent assault was considered newsworthy because it happened so infrequently. In 1920, when a judge sentenced William Marcour, a farmer from Strasbourg, Saskatchewan, to fifteen months in prison for attempted rape, the headline read "Given 15 Months for Rape Attempt: Jury Convicts Wm. Marcour ... a Married Man with 7 Children."[45] Conviction and sentencing patterns reveal a serious reluctance on the part of all-male judges and juries to disrupt the operation of a family farm simply on the word of a woman, particularly if it meant that another man's family would be left unprotected and financially vulnerable.

Judges' and juries' differential treatment of agricultural labourers and farmers facing trial for acts of heterosexual violence reflected economic, demographic, and cultural changes that were creating new social tensions in rural communities by the time of the First World War. Paralleling prosecutorial trends across Canada, approximately two-thirds of the hired hand cases (and all of the seduction cases) came to the authorities' attention in the brief period between 1914 and 1930, when the social reform, labour, and first-wave feminist movements were at their height.[46] The economic and social dislocations that accompanied and gave birth to these movements worked in concert with criminal cases such as *Gowland* to exaggerate in the imaginations of westerners the threat that farm labourers posed to farm women, the family farm, and rural communities. Because the war revived the region's agricultural sector – wheat production doubled to exceed 360 million bushels, and the number of farms increased by more than 25 percent – prairie farmers' demands for more labour coincided with thousands of the region's young men leaving for the front.[47] Government officials and policy makers feared that only the most cowardly, unmanly, and degenerate men would remain behind. Furthermore, when soldiers returned from the front following the war, the region's sparsely settled and underdeveloped farm land had been transformed into mature agricultural and capitalistic communities.[48] The disappearance of free or cheap farm land enhanced the hired hand's declining status in rural communities. By the interwar decades, thousands of immigrants who had headed west as would-be farmers found themselves among the ranks of the wage-earning working class: they earned low wages, suffered high levels of job insecurity, and tended to be transient. In 1920, a Manitoba government publication characterized agricultural labourers as "men who had failed in pretty nearly every walk of life."[49]

Members of farm families likewise came to hold a dim view of hired hands by the 1920s. In 1922, the women's section of the *Grain Grower's Guide* ran a now famous contest in which farm women were asked, "Do you want your daughter to marry a farmer?"[50] The overwhelming majority of respondents answered the question in the affirmative – revealing a fundamental satisfaction with a rural lifestyle rooted in the intimate circle of the immediate family, extended family, and neighbours. The letters reflected the agrarian community's adherence to a country-life ideology that served as a defence mechanism against the perils and pleasures of the city and the threat that industry posed to agriculture in the 1920s. In this context, farmers began to perceive agricultural labourers – poor, itinerant, and often foreign – as, at best, poor country cousins or, at worst, outsiders to the community who posed a threat to succession patterns based on patriarchal models and the moral and sexual integrity of farm women.[51] By typecasting the itinerant labourer as an indiscriminate sexual predator, social reformers, government officials, and farmers also located the cause of sexual violence and heterosexual conflict outside the family and tight-knit farming communities. Government officials and social reformers, therefore, felt compelled to encourage farmers, their wives, and their daughters to maintain a strict social distance from hired men who, in the homestead period, often shared the family's living space. By the 1920s, most farmers thought little of housing their employees in barns, tool sheds, and bunkhouses.[52]

The vilification of agricultural labourers also reflected changes occurring in the industrial and agricultural sectors that appeared to pose serious threats to the financial and social independence of farmers. As was the case in other rural districts in colonial contexts, heightened fear of escalating crime rates, which focused on the detrimental presence of itinerant labourers in rural communities, reflected socio-economic developments that produced new tensions between capital and labour. In nineteenth-century rural Illinois, for instance, the denigration of the hired hand occurred as the Midwest was swiftly integrated into an industrial economy controlled by monopoly capitalism. For the farmer, who had relinquished his independence to corporate monopolies, the changes were disturbing and coalesced in populist and third-party movements. Farmers became increasingly reliant on debt to finance machinery and stock at the same time that birth control was limiting family size and their children's productive labour was being lost to compulsory education and rural out-migration. These developments increased farm families' reliance on agricultural labourers, who worked on a cash-for-work basis. Historian Susan Sessions Rugh, who has studied these developments, notes that as farmers increasingly turned to the formal legal system to resolve their disputes with labour, they unwittingly increased state authority over behaviour that had been regulated previously by the church, the family, or the community.[53]

On the early-twentieth-century Prairies, agrarian reform and protest movements centred on eastern political domination – symbolized by the National Policy – which, farmers argued, sheltered eastern manufacturers and the Canadian Pacific Railway and forced prairie farmers to sell their produce on an open market and pay high tariffs on manufactured imports. Agricultural expansion during the Great War also increased farm indebtedness and western discontent.[54] Exclusion from the decision-making process, combined with the exigencies of rural living and commercial farming, gave birth to class consciousness among farmers and the formation of a distinct agrarian prairie culture. In the 1910s and 1920s, this consciousness found expression in the country-life movement, in the Social Gospel, and in farmers' organizations and political parties such as the United Farmers of Alberta and Manitoba, the Saskatchewan Grain Growers, and the national Progressive Party.[55] Farm organizations and parties excluded agricultural labourers from their ranks but welcomed participation by women's organizations. Women, however, were to contain their involvement to activities deemed appropriate to their sex.[56]

The eruption of the agrarian revolt and reform on the Prairies in fact signalled the breakdown of the agrarian myth of the virtuous and independent yeoman farmer and symbolized a new spirit of cooperation among farmers that was inspired by the urban Social Gospel movement.[57] The hired hand cases that came before the criminal courts, consequently, signalled not only the emergence of new social tensions between capital and labour but also a new willingness on the part of farmers to allow the state to resolve disputes that emerged from these tensions. As farmers and their families turned increasingly to the criminal courts for restitution of perceived personal wrongs, judges and juries were placed in a unique position to hasten the transformation of class relations and relations between the sexes, as well as the construction of competing masculinities and femininities.

By the outbreak of the First World War, farm women and their families believed that there was less shame attached to (and perhaps felt justified in) laying a charge of sexual assault against men who possessed bad reputations in the community. The typical accused in hired hand cases contravened the ideals of normative masculinity that were being refashioned on the Prairies by popular authors, the judiciary, legislators, and patriarchal heads of households. He was between the ages of twenty-eight and thirty-two, had recently emigrated from an eastern European country, and typically adhered to the Catholic or Greek Orthodox faith. Agricultural labourers were as likely to be married as single, but their wives still resided in the Old World or lived in small North American towns or cities, where they engaged in waged labour. If the farmhand had been fortunate, he had some formal education at the elementary-school level; many, however, were illiterate.[58] As the proliferation of these men among the ranks of accused and convicted sexual offenders attests, certain men were as likely as women to fare poorly in the criminal courts, particularly when the complainant's social status and moral purity could be contrasted favourably to his failure to meet the ideals of prairie masculinity.

THE WOMAN'S WORD AGAINST THE MAN'S:
HARNESSING FEMALE SEXUALITY TO COMPETING MASCULINITIES

Given that agricultural labourers suffered overwhelming negative reputations in prairie communities by the First World War, when (and under what circumstances) were their explanations of sexual violence and heterosexual conflict believed? A number of agricultural labourers were able to successfully harness the country-life ideology and deep-seated notions of masculine and patriarchal prerogatives in their favour by casting doubt upon their victim's sexual integrity or social standing.[59] This strategy worked to great success if the complainant was a farm wife from a marginalized immigrant community rather than the underage daughter of an English Canadian farmer. In early August 1917, for instance, Annie Nagey, a Hungarian wife and mother who farmed in the Regina district, complained to the local justice of the peace that her family's former hired hand, Josef Kozma, had raped her on the grounds of the family farm. Kozma allegedly locked Nagey's children in the house before assaulting her, violently and sexually, in the barn. The trial took place before the Saskatchewan Court of King's Bench at Regina on 18 September 1917, and the jury acquitted the accused.[60] The *Morning Leader* described the case as follows: "It was the old story of the woman's word against the man's. The charge was brought by Mrs. Annie Nagey, of Quinton, wife of the accused's employer. An outraged husband with a gun and a murderous looking butcher knife in the hands of the accused figured in the story. All the parties to the case were Hungarians and the evidence had to be taken through an interpreter."[61]

The article's author implied that the jury acquitted Kozma of all charges despite his status as a hired hand. The reporter also managed to cast doubt on Annie Nagey's honesty and character without actually describing the particulars of the case. The victim's sex, marital status, and ethnicity alone sufficed to explain the jury's verdict. Annie Nagey was a Hungarian immigrant whose lack of familiarity with the language and laws of the court must have been a liability in wartime Canada. Her ethnicity, combined with evidence of violent conflict between her husband and the hired man, did not work in her favour. In addition, the complainant lived on a farm where, aside from her children, social interaction was restricted to her husband, the hired hand, and the occasional visit from a neighbour. At the preliminary hearing held at Punnichy, Saskatchewan, Nagey deposed before the justice of the peace, H. Butcher, that she had struggled with Joe Kozma and screamed for help, but the accused had locked her children in the house. Nagey then tried to enhance her credibility by deposing that, because of illness, she had been unable to fight off her attacker. Nagey unwittingly undermined her testimony further by admitting that she had not been wearing underpants at the time of the assault. Ripped, torn, and semen-stained drawers were commonly entered as evidence in the early nineteenth century, and the prosecution's ability to produce them often made or broke a case. Defence counsel, consequently, manipulated this failure to meet the unwritten evidentiary requirements of the case with the absence of the victim's husband to suggest that Nagey had been sexually available to the accused.[62]

In his own defence, Josef Kozma claimed that he had conducted an illicit affair with Nagey whenever her husband travelled away from the farm on business. Defence counsel also introduced evidence that Nagey had failed to report the rape until one month after the alleged incident occurred, suggesting that the complainant, or her husband, laid the charge out of spite or discovery.[63] Kozma's defence played upon deep-seated fears that farm labourers constituted a threat to the sanctity of the family farm. During the preliminary hearing, it became apparent to the court that Kozma habitually slept and ate in the farmhouse and that the farmer frequently left his wife alone with his employee. Because Nagey was a married woman and mother, the onus fell upon her to uphold standards of sexual morality in her husband's absence. The relatively lengthy coverage that the case received in the press, combined with the jury's verdict of not guilty, transformed the court proceedings into a classroom through which Anglo-Canadian judges and juries could impose, or teach, their own vision of sexual morality, femininity, and appropriate class relations on marginalized immigrant communities.

The degree to which the criminal courts could serve as classrooms for the imposition of normative femininity and sexual morality had likewise been apparent six years earlier when the police charged an immigrant hired hand with having unlawful carnal knowledge of an underage girl. Unlike the Bourassa case of 1892, in which Justice Richardson advised the jury that the Aboriginal girl's consent was not at issue, the justices of the peace in the Sachatski case allowed the defence to cast doubt upon the complainant's virtue. On 25 October 1911, police charged Fedor Sachatski, a hired hand, with having unlawful carnal knowledge of eight-year-old Marie Schmigorski near Wostok, Alberta. Tina Gonko, age nine, corroborated Schmigorski's testimony but also disclosed that the complainant's mother had encouraged her daughter to sleep with the accused: "Mrs. Schmigorski told her daughter Marie to go to bed with uncle and he would give her some money and she cried and would not go and her mother whipped

her and she went to bed with him and through the night I heard her crying."[64] Although the complainant, with corroboration, produced enough
evidence to proceed to trial, the attorney general withdrew the charge,
signalling to the community that unchaste immigrant girls, no matter
their age or the circumstances of the sexual relationship, were unworthy
of the courts' protection.

Following the war, defence counsel for German farm labourer Edward
Gebhardt, perhaps having learned the lessons of the Kozma and Sachatski
cases, used a similar strategy to earn a not-guilty verdict for his client, who
was charged with raping four girls under the age of fourteen. The complainants, two sets of sisters, provided independent and corroborative
evidence that Gebhardt had habitually assaulted them between 1918 and
1922, when their parents went to town.[65] As in *Sachatski,* the JP, prior to
the hearing, determined whether the underage children understood the
importance of telling the truth and the religious nature of an oath. In
most cases, children's depositions were received but not sworn, and the
justice demanded corroboration by some other material evidence.[66] During
this hearing, however, lengthy cross-examinations by defence counsel J.E.
Doer ended when one of the complainants disclosed that her eighteen-
year-old brother had participated in some of the assaults. Although the
admission corroborated the girls' accusations, the defence manipulated
the information to imply that the complainants and their families completely lacked moral rectitude. Defence counsel also manipulated the
lengthy period of time that had elapsed between the first assault and the
complaint to imply that the girls had engaged in consensual sexual relations with the accused.[67]

Sachatski and *Gebhardt* highlight how certain agricultural labourers and
their defence attorneys could construct the accused as victims of immoral,
promiscuous women to overcome the hired hand's generally poor reputation in prairie communities. But this strategy was successful only if the
complainant belonged to a culturally or economically marginalized sector
of the population. Although the outcomes and defence strategies of
Sachatski and *Gebhardt* conformed to the prosecution patterns and performative scripts of rape cases in Western, patriarchal societies in these
decades, the majority of hired hands learned that the courtroom could
just as easily become a forum where prosecutors, judges, and juries could
test, and find wanting, the accused's masculinity and morality. In January
and February 1911, four farmhands were charged with having unlawful
carnal knowledge of Matilda Susan, Maggie Elvina, and Nellie May

Mangelman – three girls under the age of consent.[68] Three of the accusations resulted in not-guilty verdicts or dismissals because the prosecution
lacked sufficient evidence or, more typically, because the defence portrayed
the complainants as sexually deviant.[69] In one telling case, however, a jury
decided to convict Carl Paul, even though the complainant and her family
failed to measure up to the ideals of the patriarchal family farm and the
morally upright prairie woman.

In the first case, thirteen-year-old Matilda Susan Mangelman, a domestic
servant, alleged that Phillip Connelly, an agricultural labourer, had unlawful carnal knowledge of her in the summer of 1910, when her employer
went for hay. The substance of Mangelman's deposition transgressed the
prevailing ideal of female chastity and virtue. Contrary to the court's expectations, Mangelman did not deny knowledge of what had physically
occurred during the assault. She instead explained to the court, candidly
and graphically, the mechanics of the sexual encounter. She also admitted
that Connelly had given her five dollars following the incident, which she
turned over to her mother without complaint. Connelly's and Mangelman's
employer, farmer J.A. Fleming, damaged the complainant's case further
by deposing on the accused's behalf that the "girl has a poor reputation
for telling the truth."[70] During the prosecution's cross-examination,
Mangelman again failed to gain the JP's sympathy when she admitted that
she had also had sexual intercourse with Carl Paul, William Wysk, and
John Kowalika while they were employed as threshers on her mother's
farm. Just as young Tina Gonko had done during the hearing of the
Schmigorski case, Mangelman ended her deposition by claiming that her
mother had been fully aware of her behaviour and may have encouraged
it: "I did not think that this was very serious ... I give all my money to my
mother."[71] The jury acquitted Connelly of all charges. The Supreme Court
of Alberta, however, later tried Wysk and Kowalika for the rape of Matilda's
younger sister, Maggie Elvina. In Kowalika's case, the jury found the accused not guilty when the defence established that the victim was sexually
promiscuous and suffered from the effects of venereal disease.[72]

Although the Mangelman family's sexual morality appeared to run
against the grain of turn-of-the-century Victorian and Edwardian sensibilities, the Supreme Court of Alberta did finally decide in its favour
when, in a complete reversal of the Connelly verdict, it convicted Carl Paul
for the rape of Matilda Susan Mangelman.[73] Mangelman deposed at the
hearing that the accused had sexually assaulted her in the summer of 1909,
when the couple was alone butchering meat. When her sister, Nellie May,

tried to help her, Matilda claimed that Paul had also raped her brutally. The jury convicted Paul on the strength of the sister's corroborative testimony. On 18 May 1911, however, Paul successfully appealed the conviction (and his twelve-year sentence) on the grounds that Justice William Charles Simmons had allowed the prosecution to unlawfully elicit, from Nellie May, evidence of similar and subsequent acts. The Supreme Court of Alberta retried the case on 26 May 1913, but the jury again brought in a guilty verdict. The judge increased the sentence to fifteen years in a penitentiary.[74]

Carl Paul's sentence was one of the harshest meted out to a sexual offender on the Prairies prior to the Second World War.[75] Paul's status as an agricultural labourer with a poor reputation in Bruce, Alberta, outweighed Matilda Susan Mangelman's failure to conform to middle-class ideals of morality. At the time of Paul's conviction, he was serving a two-year prison term for cattle theft.[76] Upon sentencing in the Mangelman case, the *Edmonton Journal* reported sensationally that Paul had been found guilty under the most "revolting circumstances" and that the accused – who had a "very black record" – had also been arrested several years earlier as a suspect in the murder of the Mangelman girls' father. Upon the accused's release, the reporter continued, Paul had continued to live with Mrs. Mangelman until she committed suicide just prior to her daughters' involvement in the rape trials.[77] Paul's trial (and the tragic events that led up to it) sensationally embodied everything that the press, public, and policy makers had come to expect of agricultural labourers and non-British immigrant families by the second decade of the twentieth century.

Agricultural labourers could, however, find themselves convicted and sentenced even when the prosecution and complainants met few of the evidentiary requirements of rape law. In 1915, Hafia Ukryniuk accused a twenty-five-year-old Austrian farm labourer, Steve Hryciuk, of raping her while her husband was away from their Manitoba homestead. Like Hungarian farm wife Annie Nagey, whose case would occur only two years later, Ukryniuk testified that the accused had forced her to consent to sexual relations by pointing a revolver at her and threatening to kill her. Although Ukryniuk reported the incident to her husband immediately upon his return home, the prosecution could produce no physical evidence of the assault, and the victim's testimony remained uncorroborated by an eyewitness. In his own defence, Hryciuk testified that Ukryniuk herself had initiated the sexual episode: "She was lying on the bed and pulled up her dress and said come on – after, she said 'let's have a little more.'"[78] The jury – perhaps doubting the truth of the accused's claims – convicted, and the judge sentenced him to five years in prison.

As the outcome of *Hryciuk* attests, the prairie judiciary and juries were less likely to accept the "she asked for it" argument when the accused failed to measure up to the prevailing masculine ideal. As was the case throughout North America in the early twentieth century, middle-class, property-owning men viewed their ability to rein in strong masculine passions – through character and force of will – as a mark of character that differentiated them from their working-class or immigrant counterparts. Historians Angus McLaren and Gail Bederman have noted, furthermore, that middle-class men legitimized their strength and authority over subordinate masculinities – and women – through institutions such as the criminal courts and legal processes like the criminal trial.[79] On the Prairies, the judiciary's and ordinary jurymen's willingness to turn to the criminal courts to assert their vision of reconstituted imperial masculinity became apparent in 1923, when a fifteen-year-old domestic servant from Saskatchewan successfully proved a charge of rape against agricultural labourer Patrick George Coghlan. At the preliminary hearing, held at the Saskatchewan Provincial Police Court in July, Rosie Lanz deposed that the accused had come to the Riggat farm, where she worked near Kronau, on the pretence that he needed a glass of water. When the accused's behaviour caused Lanz to become suspicious, the complainant ran outside, but Coghlan dragged her back into the house, where the sexual assault took place. Although the prosecution produced no eyewitnesses to the assault, Lanz complained immediately to the accused's foreman and produced ripped and stained clothing at the preliminary hearing.

In response to the complainant's deposition, the defence tried to establish that the half hour that had elapsed between the alleged rape and the complaint constituted enough time for Lanz to make up a story. Given the gendered biases of evidentiary law in rape proceedings, Coghlan might have swayed the jury to his side; however, in his statement to the police, the accused contended that he had been suffering the effects of alcohol when Lanz lured him into the farmhouse, allegedly to listen to music. Coghlan also argued that Lanz had lied about her age and, by her actions, suggested she was amenable to sex.[80] Coghlan's use of off-colour language in the courtroom – in addition to his unabashed use of alcohol in a period of prohibition – contrasted unfavourably with expert medical testimony, which proved that the complainant remained a virgin.[81] Although prairie juries tended to find even the most violent proven sexual offenders guilty of a lesser charge, in this instance the Saskatchewan Court of King's Bench jury convicted Coghlan of rape and sentenced him to ten years in Prince Albert Penitentiary with hard labour.[82]

Five years earlier, the degree to which the courts could become a playground for competing masculinities had become more than apparent when John Bowie, an agricultural labourer who worked in Alberta's Wetaskiwin Judicial District, likewise offended the sensibilities of the male officers and jury of the court. After filing a complaint of unlawful carnal knowledge against Bowie, complainant Mary Moran, who was between the ages of fourteen and sixteen, deposed that she had permitted the accused to take her out on a date; however, when it came time for Bowie to drive her home, the accused instead drove into the country, pushed her into the back seat of the car, and sexually assaulted her. As Coghlan would attempt five years later, Bowie tried to sway the all-male jury to his side by arguing that Moran had asked for it. But, he informed the court, given that the complainant had been a virgin, he would be willing to marry her. Depositions by witnesses for the prosecution, however, revealed at the hearing and trial that Bowie had reported the details of his conquest to at least three men whose testimony revealed the accused as a braggart and coward. While one witness deposed that Bowie had disclosed that he was "going to have a lot of screwing before he went overseas," another revealed that the accused had admitted he would rather go to jail than to war. The complainant's family, the judge, and the court ignored Bowie's willingness to marry Moran. The jury found the accused guilty of unlawful carnal knowledge. Justice William Carlos Ives granted Bowie his wish and sentenced the twenty-one-year-old from Hardisty, Alberta, to a maximum sentence of two years in prison.[83]

Court(ing) Conflicts: Seduction and Abduction on Trial

An agricultural labourer's failure to measure up to prevailing ideals of normative masculinity likewise shaped prosecution and conviction patterns in seduction and abduction cases. Laying a charge of seduction or abduction proved to be, for many farm families, a cheap and effective way to impede an interloping hired hand's ability to advance economically and socially by marrying their daughter. Seduction and abduction prosecutions, consequently, served as a means for land-holding immigrants who lived in marginalized ethnic communities to solidify their position in the emerging socio-economic hierarchy of the countryside. Trials of seduction and abduction open a window not only on gender and class divisions and tensions in prairie social development but also on generational conflicts between immigrant parents and their daughters. The romantic involvements that quite naturally evolved between hired hands and farm girls also served as platforms for farm families to regulate young women's sexuality to maintain patriarchal privileges and prerogatives. Once these cases entered a court of law, they transformed into duels between competing masculinities that emerged out of much larger contests over land and labour in a region that had once been envisaged as a landscape that would free women and labour from the chains that had bound them in the Old World. The frequency with which seduction and abduction cases appeared before the courts suggests that the contest between farmers and hired hands over access to women's bodies was part of the larger working-class men's movement that sought to resist emerging class divisions on the Prairies.

The complex interplay of these diverse, but interrelated, contests for power became apparent in 1927, when Andrew Daradics, a Ukrainian farmer from Arbury, Saskatchewan, accused his hired hand, Louis Fabian, of seducing his seventeen-year-old daughter. Daradics testified that his daughter had engaged in sexual relations with the family's hired hand from the spring of 1926 through to March 1927, when the couple ran away together. At the preliminary hearing, however, Annie Daradics challenged her father's authority by informing the court that her father had promised her in marriage to a friend and neighbour if she proved to be a breeder. She also disclosed that her father's failure to pay Fabian his wages had compelled the labourer to quit his job and take his employer's daughter, who was carrying his child, away with him. Because she reviled her father's choice of husband, Annie admitted that she was more than willing to leave with the accused. Although her consent was irrelevant to the case, Annie's admission that she "came to court to compel Louis to pay something for the child" forced the prosecution to withdraw the charge on 5 April 1927.[84]

Although the Fabian case never went to trial, it shared much in common with more successful seduction and abduction prosecutions. In all but the rarest cases, the involved parties had emigrated from an eastern European country, from Ukraine in particular.[85] Deep-seated biases held by dominant groups, judges, and juries only partially explain Ukrainian farm labourers' overrepresentation in these cases: gender, generational, and class divisions within the immigrant community also influenced the outcome.[86] Historian Frances Swyripa, who has studied historical sexual assault and seduction cases that occurred in the Vegreville bloc settlement east of Edmonton, for instance, discovered that Ukrainian girls did not simply acquiesce in their families' and community's expectations for them – they developed strategies to negotiate their own destinies. Some girls turned to the criminal courts to force their sexual attacker, fiancé, or lover to marry them or pay child support, while others refused to marry their seducers. Although the Criminal Code defined seduction as a criminal offence to be prosecuted by the Crown, Ukrainian immigrants treated it privately, as a civil offence, with restitution made directly to the victim.[87] Canadian judges and juries, however, tended to view their efforts, and any exchange of money that might have resulted, as attempts to evade punishment or state regulation.[88]

Seduction and abduction cases also involved land-holding Ukrainian farmers who had moved to Canada to improve their own and their children's lives; consequently, economic considerations and the desire for increased social standing fuelled their complaints. As Andrew Daradics' treatment of his daughter and recourse to the courts illustrates, many Ukrainian parents did not want their daughters to become involved with or marry the hired man – even when he was part of their own immigrant community. Although Canadian judges and juries proved more than willing to convict and punish eastern Europeans accused of violent crimes, in abduction and seduction cases they supported parents' initiatives, even when the daughter's sexual behaviour placed her outside the norms of ideal femininity. Agricultural labourer George Lorreg learned this lesson in 1916, when his employer of nearly six months, Ukrainian farmer Martin Hoffman, accused him of abducting his underage daughter from the family farm near Regina.

Adhering to the evidentiary requirements of the law of abduction meant that the prosecution in *Lorreg* had to establish that the accused had taken Ludwiga Hoffman "out of the possession and against the will" of her parents. Ludwiga's consent was immaterial to the case – as was the accused's knowledge of her age. If convicted, Lorreg potentially faced five years in prison.[89] At the preliminary hearing, Ludwiga's mother, Carrie Hoffman, deposed that she had caught the accused in her daughter's bed on three separate occasions before the abduction occurred on 17 July. Hoffman also informed the court that her daughter had consented to a sexual relationship with another agricultural labourer three years previously. On the urging of defence counsel, Hoffman disclosed that her husband had physically punished Ludwiga for her indiscretions and written her out of the family Bible because she was a "hoor." Although she admitted that it was true that her husband owed George Lorreg $148, Hoffman ended her deposition by contending that the hired hand had done irredeemable damage to her family's fortunes: "She [Ludwiga] could have taken any good farmer's son, and he made shame for all the family."[90] Ludwiga Hoffman did not deny her mother's accusations, but she did put forward a promise of marriage from Lorreg as justification for her behaviour. She also defended the accused's behaviour by admitting that he had agreed to run off with her only when she threatened to commit suicide. Police testimony corroborated Ludwiga's narrative of events: the couple was arrested in Southey, Saskatchewan, when they tried to obtain a marriage licence. Given this damaging testimony, which placed Ludwiga Hoffman outside the bounds of chaste womanhood demanded by the law of abduction, the officers of the court and the jury supported the parents' demands for restitution by convicting Lorreg of unlawful carnal knowledge and sentencing him to three months in prison with hard labour.[91]

Ludwiga Hoffman's conflicted testimony and behaviour reveal the degree to which contests over property and power could shape farm girls' intimate experiences and overshadow their personal interests in a court of law. Three years after the Lorreg trial, a farm daughter's transgressions took second place to her parents' conflict with their hired hand. In 1919 Haski Pulaski, a farmer from the rural municipality of Rosser, Manitoba, learned of his daughter's relations with the hired hand only when she became pregnant. After Pulaski laid an information against Mike Rudnicki, and the police arrested the labourer for seduction, Rudnicki justified his behaviour by claiming, "The girl was after me all the time and I could not help it. I wanted to get married but the old man would not let me ... I had connection with her twice and the old man refused to allow me to marry her because of that."[92] Defence counsel at the hearing established that the father had withheld his daughter's hand in marriage in a bid to force Rudnicki to enter a period of indentured servitude for two years. Pulaski justified his actions by arguing that the accused would have brought no property to the marriage but hoped to gain some in return. Defence counsel responded by attacking Pulaski's character and credibility, suggesting that the farmer had threatened to press charges unless the accused paid him $100. When counsel concluded the cross-examination by asking Pulaski why, despite everything that had occurred, he was now willing to let his daughter marry the accused, the father responded that it was the only way for his family to save face in the community. Although defence counsel made a strong argument that monetary motivations and external factors had compelled Pulaski to lay an information against his employee, the farmer's situation appeared to resonate with a Winnipeg jury and judge: the jury convicted and the judge sentenced Rudnicki to serve four months with hard labour.[93] Whether the couple later married is unknown.

CONCLUSION

Acts of sexual violence, seduction, and abduction in prairie Canada, as elsewhere, typically occurred in private. As one journalist pointed out so succinctly, in all but the most exceptional cases it was "the woman's word against the man's." Just as North West Mounted Police personnel, Indian agents, and JPs tended to view complainants in sex crime prosecutions through a lens darkened by colonial discourses on a dangerous, dissolute Aboriginal womanhood, all-male judges and juries allowed turn-of-the-century ideals about middle-class femininity and legal discourses on rape to colour their response to those farm women and girls who sought recourse in the courts for rape, indecent assault, seduction, or abduction. Yet higher-than-average conviction rates, and the overrepresentation of agricultural labourers among the ranks of the convicted following the First World War, illustrate the powerful, determining role that political economy, class tensions, and contests over power between men could play in sex crime prosecutions. Although a woman's or girl's proven morality and social status could influence the judge's and jury's belief in her credibility, a man's failure to conform to the ideal of muscular, hard-working, and morally upright masculinity could sway the judge's and jury's sympathies in the complainant's or, in the case of abduction and seduction, her parents' favour. In either case, these hired hand cases belie popular representations of the region that use the image of the prairie farmhouse – nestled in the woods or seemingly floating on the plains – to mark the passing of an era when people's lives were simple, innocent, and based on solid family values. Criminal case files open a window on stories, narratives, and acts of sexual violence and seduction that occurred not in the darkened alleyways of prairie cities but in farmyards and farmhouses. These cases stand as a testament to the fact that many farm women and girls risked considerable social censure to seek retribution in the courts for sexual violence committed against them by men in their employ. Although the truth behind their allegations will never be known, we do know that the judiciary and all-male juries often transformed their complaints of sexual violence into an opportunity to punish women who did not – by virtue of their ethnicity, social standing, or sexual morality – conform to the sexually pure, morally upright feminine ideal. Similarly, in their ability to chasten, punish, and discipline agricultural labourers who had aspirations beyond their stations, seduction and abduction cases were but one part of a complex process by which immigrant farmers turned to the criminal courts and the state to negotiate a position for themselves in prairie society.[94] Sexual violence and the intimate, consequently, played an integral role in the construction of Canada's prairie settler society.

Although policy makers such as Nicholas Flood Davin had advertised the region as a paradise in which immigrants could be delivered from Old World barriers to social and economic success, in reality they sought a society built upon the foundations of Anglo-Saxon and Protestant values and the small-scale family farm. To them, the hard-working and self-sacrificing pioneer woman – usually depicted at work in her garden or alone on the desolate prairie, often with a child at her side – was an integral component for the future success of that society. By contrast, the bachelor homesteader and agricultural labourer (often of recent immigrant status) had become, by the First World War, superfluous to utopian visions of the West. The stories of conflict that emerge from the hired hand cases reveal a society in the process of developing new masculine and feminine ideals grounded in the social, economic, and political foundations of a patriarchal, capitalistic countryside. Consequently, during a period when juries only occasionally punished sexual violence against women, the hired hand was more likely to be convicted than acquitted for sexual transgressions. He escaped punishment only when his female victim had herself turned her back on the values of a region that first-wave feminist and judge Emily Murphy had once described as "a paradise of blossoms – a very garden of the Lord."[95] Although the complex process by which women's and girls' sexuality was regulated by the day-to-prosecution of sex crime offences was often overshadowed by larger contests for power between farmers and labourers, it was more overt in burgeoning urban centres, where struggles for power between police, social reformers, feminists, and politicians over prostitution carried over to influence the prosecution of drug offences, abortion, and sex crimes in the interwar years.

5

For Family, Nation, and Empire

Policing Drugs, Abortion, and Heterosexuality in the Interwar City

N
arratives about the dangerous and dissolute itinerant labourer, and the campaign to eradicate prostitution and the white slavery panics to which he helped give birth, drew public and official attention to the potential problem of single, working-class women and girls in the city. Lectures, sermons, police raids, and public inquiries on sin and iniquity in the city also contradicted pre-war booster literature that lauded the economic growth and material success of prairie towns and cities but ignored the social and economic dislocations that accompanied a 700 percent growth rate from the turn of the century. J.S. Woodsworth's social survey *Strangers within Our Gates,* the Thomas Street raid, the Robson Commission on Social Vice, and the *Grain Growers' Guide*'s contest "Do You Want Your Daughter to Marry a Farmer?" helped to construct the city as counterculture. They depicted the city not only as the point of origin for basic social problems – such as prostitution and immigrant slums – but also as one of the most menacing threats to the region's progress. After the war, economic and social developments and the new carceral regime that followed the moral panic over white slavery caused social observers, feminists, and law officials to envisage the city as the site of new sexual threats and moral dangers that threatened the stability of households, the sanctity of the family, and the sexual and psychological well-being of impressionable youths. The pre-war and wartime campaign to eradicate prostitution, however, had also sexualized the city and problematized the role of women in its social spaces. Prostitutes and suffragists used a combination of resistance, negotiation, and accommodation to

carve a place for themselves in the public sphere, but within the new carceral regime that emerged from this struggle, single young girls and women in the city – more so than their white, male counterparts – were envisaged as threats to region, nation, and empire.[1]

In 1925, Nellie McClung – a prominent novelist, politician, and suffragist – gave popular expression to these fears when she published *Painted Fires,* a novel that relates the trials and tribulations of Helmi Milander, a young, single, Finnish girl who immigrated to North America in search of a better life. "For years I had wanted to write an immigration story in the form of a novel," McClung wrote in her autobiography. "I wanted to portray the struggles of a young girl who found herself in Canada dependent upon her own resources with everything to learn, including the language."[2] McClung wanted to persuade her fellow feminists, influential members of women's organizations, and concerned citizens that nothing bad would happen if Canada's immigration laws were expanded to allow non-British, single women into the country to fill domestic service jobs. Although assisted emigration for British girls had been the norm from 1896 to 1925, under the Railway Agreement Act of 1925 the women's section of the Department of Immigration was encouraged to place and recruit domestics from non-preferred countries. The Canadian government expected potential immigrants under the agreement to pay their own way with future earnings. Whereas 60 percent of immigrant domestics to the West had been British in 1921, 58 percent were eastern European by 1931.[3]

McClung wrote *Painted Fires* while she was a member of Alberta's Legislative Assembly, and the novel was an outlet for her social and political activism. The book expressed both her hopes for and disillusionment with social conditions, social reform, and feminism following the war, and it revealed her uneasy reception of the new working girl, the Jazz Age, and flapper culture, which were becoming more visible in prairie cities.[4] Just as pre-war and wartime representations of the prostitute vacillated between the two dichotomous images of the whore of Babylon and the lost lamb of the flock, McClung depicted Helmi as a sexually precocious adolescent whose respectability was threatened by unscrupulous, rapacious immigrant men. McClung also shared her feminist colleagues' disdain for the patriarchal underpinnings of the law. In incident after incident throughout *Painted Fires,* McClung's heroine is victimized by an unsympathetic criminal justice system controlled by conservative, autocratic, and ethnocentric judges concerned only with preserving the sexual double standard and the middle-class, Anglo-Canadian status quo. McClung's novel, however, introduced a new discursive element: Helmi falls under the pernicious influence of a middle-class, childless housewife and heroin addict who tries to control her own body and sexuality through illegal abortion.

McClung's portrait of Helmi was considered so authentic that the novel was translated into Finnish, published in Helsinki, and remained in print until 1945.[5] McClung based the novel on research she completed in Alberta's Provincial Library, where she drew upon popular, academic, and judicial discourses on the criminal courts, the immigrant experience, adolescence, and the drug trade. Although McClung hoped to draw attention to the plight of young, working-class girls and immigrants, the novel also reflected popular fears about Canada's declining birth rate and potential for race suicide; the moral and degenerative effects of drug abuse, miscegenation, and the spread of venereal disease; and the potentially harmful impact of urbanization and mechanization on Canadian households. In response to these perceived problems, middle-class Anglo-Canadians, social commentators, and public policy officials increasingly idealized marriage and family, and they advocated increased state regulation of premarital sexuality, adolescence, and family matters. These preoccupations shaped how law enforcement officials, judges, and juries responded when they were called upon to investigate or pass judgment on alleged violations of drug and abortion laws or on sex crime cases in the interwar decades.

FLAMING YOUTH AND NARRATIVES OF NARCOTICISM

In *Painted Fires,* when Helmi Milander arrives in the United States, the Promised Land, she discovers her aunt (and role model) living in St. Paul, Minnesota, subject to an abusive husband and wasted by infection caused by a botched abortion. To protect her niece from the clutches of dangerous and dissolute men, Helmi's aunt arranges for her to take a job as a waitress in a Winnipeg hotel. Upon her arrival in the city, Helmi meets Anna Milander, another Finnish immigrant, two years in Canada, who belongs to a working-class brotherhood, spouts communist propaganda, and unabashedly embraces the materialistic pop culture of the 1920s: "Anna dreamed pleasantly of the golden age ... when there would be leisure and luxuries for the workers and confusion for the capitalists, when railways and streetcars and theatres and all the sources of pleasure would be free as air."[6] Anna's fate, however, served as a cautionary tale to the young Helmi: following a labour demonstration, Anna was charged, convicted, and jailed for having maliciously and with intent to harm hurled a stone at a policeman.

Four months later, Helmi, who spends her free Sundays walking in the countryside and absorbing its regenerative effects, is miraculously saved from a fate worse than death when Abigail J. Moore – on her way home from the Girls' Friendly Home for delinquent girls, where she volunteers – disrupts two ill-kempt and poorly dressed strangers who try to take sexual advantage of Helmi's isolation. Moore, a New Woman, is a member of the Presbyterian Church and the Ladies' Aid Society. She takes Helmi under her wing and plans, eventually, to adopt the young girl. Moore hopes to provide her charge with a wholesome, Christian home environment, and she enrolls Helmi in the girls' auxiliary of the Methodist Church and the Canadian Girls in Training, which, like the British Girl Guide movement upon which it was modelled, was conceived as an antidote to the girl problem in Canadian cities.[7] Moore arranges for the wife of her neighbour, Dr. St. John, a man she had known in England, to teach Helmi English. Eva St. John, a middle-aged housewife, proves to be a dangerous influence on the impressionable youth. St. John lives in the lap of luxury, embraces the flapper lifestyle, and spends her days in an opium-induced haze. Each week, St. John takes Helmi to picture shows, where the young girl sees "ladies in trailing beaded dresses and shining jewels, leaving their elegant homes to go with their lovers, and smart young stenographers ... who married the old man's wayward son ... Then and there Helmi determined she would be a stenographer."[8]

The impressionable youth faces complete social and moral ruin when Eva St. John, suffering illness following an abortion, asks Helmi to get her "medicine" from a Chinese physician who lives above a laundry in Winnipeg's North End. After receiving the drugs from Dr. Sam, Helmi stops in to eat at the Shanghai Chop Suey House, which is raided by police who arrest Helmi for drug possession under the Opium and Drug Act. Neither St. John nor her neighbours come to Helmi's defence, and they justify their neglect on the grounds that they expected no better from a foreigner. The Reverend Edward Terry of the Young Methodist Church, a minister with the physique of a "light-weight boxing champion," believes in Helmi's innocence, however, and he speaks on her behalf before the Winnipeg Police Court. Magistrate Windsor, a "gray-haired, florid-faced old man," is not disposed to listen to Helmi or Rev. Terry, who, the magistrate feels, looks too young to be a minister. Upon hearing that Helmi had resisted arrest, Windsor exclaims, "Well, Sir, she will have to learn to respect an officer of the law. These foreigners have no respect for the King's uniform, and I take it as my duty to teach them."[9] When Rev. Terry accuses the magistrate of prejudice, Windsor replies, "Finns are all naturally red,

and I don't trust them ... Being a preacher doesn't give you much chance
to know your fellow man. I see them here in the raw; the veneer is all off
when they come here. I know them, and in every case the women are the
worst."[10] During the trial, when a member of a women's organization to
which Helmi belongs testifies to her good character, Windsor presents the
court with a tirade on women's status and women's clubs, which he believes
are responsible for the moral decline of young women:

> They don't work anymore – they just gad around to picture shows and get
> into trouble, and the women's organizations encourage them instead of
> trying to restrain them. The old-fashioned girl stayed at home and worked
> with her mother. But now the mothers are out reforming the world, and
> the girls are on the street or in their clubs. I blame the club women of this
> city for the devilment that goes on among the young people, for the home
> is gone. I tell you, there's no religion in the homes any more, no respect for
> law – nothing but birth control clubs, political clubs, bridge clubs, while
> the young girls and boys steal cars, joy ride and snuff dope.[11]

Windsor convicts Helmi and sentences her to three months in Stony
Mountain Penitentiary. She serves her time, however, at the Girls' Friendly
Home.

Although McClung tried to foster sympathy for the plight of immigrant
domestic servants and to undermine conservative attempts to link social
problems to the feminist movement, the plot and narrative structure of
Painted Fires played upon prevalent discourses on the crisis of the family,
which tended to centre on the problem of urban youths. In the 1920s,
moral and sexual mores appeared to be relaxing as divorce rates rose and
as parents lost control of their children to public education, new employment opportunities in the city, and the emergence of an adolescent culture
that revolved around American leisure activities: dance halls, picture shows,
and consumerism.[12] Although the fate of the Empire no longer consumed
reform advocates (as it did during the early campaigns to eradicate prostitution), when first-wave feminists (such as McClung), psychologists, social
workers, law officials, and policy makers linked popular amusement to
rising rates of sexual and moral delinquency among youths, they gave birth
to a "multifarious critique that intertwined these 'problems' with the larger
issues of citizenship, national welfare, and the nature of modernity."[13]

Michel Foucault and Philippe Ariès have argued that the association
of normative adolescence with sexual innocence delineated a key stage in

the historical formation of a distinct concept of childhood.[14] The cultural construction of adolescence as a social problem in the interwar years owed much to G. Stanley Hall's pioneering work on youth culture in America, *Adolescence: Its Psychology and Its Relation to Physiology, Anthropology, Sociology, Sex, Crime, Religion, and Education.* Published in 1904, the work spurred the emergence of the child study movement prior to the war, and it focused attention, for the first time, on the psychological dimension of child development. Like turn-of-the-century discourses on Aboriginal, working-class, and middle-class masculinities, Hall relied on recapitulation theory – the notion that a child's development echoed the Darwinian evolutionary pattern from the primitive to the civilized – to construct a vision of adolescence as a distinct phase in individual development. Hall believed that puberty initiated adolescence, which he defined as a rapid spurt of growth in mind, body, and feeling that broke the child's stable personality. Heterosexuality emerged during this stage, but the child did not understand it. Without the stabilizing influence of a normal home life and regulated leisure activities, the adolescents would, Hall argued, descend into a state of psychosis characterized by physical and mental anarchy.[15]

In Canada, the perceived problem of flaming youth was constructed in such a way as to target immigrant and working-class children in the city. Reform advocates, social workers, and psychologists believed that first-generation immigrants adhered to rural and communal traditions that would, inevitably, clash with their children's wish to participate in the new urban youth culture. They predicted an intergenerational clash of wills that would contribute to broken homes and rising rates of juvenile delinquency.[16] These nascent fears were expressed through the child rescue movement in the late nineteenth century, and they became part of public policy when parliamentarians passed the Juvenile Delinquent's Act in 1908. Legislators sought to check delinquent tendencies through the creation of a system of justice, centred on juvenile and family courts, that would re-socialize immigrant and working-class children in conflict with the law.[17] In February 1922, Ethel MacLachlan, juvenile court judge in Regina, enhanced the perception that juvenile delinquency was on the rise when she reported that 1,045 boys and girls had come through her jurisdiction the previous year: children, she argued, were now committing "all the offences that adults are usually guilty of."[18]

Early child psychology found a receptive audience among middle-class parents and social reformers who latched on to it as an explanation for the public displays of sexuality that they witnessed among adolescent girls and young, unmarried women in the city. In prairie Canada, as elsewhere, psychological explanations of girls' behaviour took on new meaning in the interwar decades because feminists and social reformers could no longer employ the white slave trade as an explanatory model. By the First World War, the psychological immaturity of adolescent girls – and their perceived lack of responsibility for sexual behaviour – was a part of reformers' and legislators' rationale for increasing the age of consent for girls from fourteen to sixteen, and from sixteen to eighteen in cases of seduction without promise of marriage, which became law in 1920.[19] As the spotlight shifted from prostitution to sexual deviance among adolescents and the unmarried, the regulatory scope of institutions and the law over working-class and immigrant youths widened. While educators designed sexual education courses to foster inner discipline among boys and girls, police departments appointed female officers and matrons to monitor girls' and young women's behaviour in dance halls, ice-cream parlours, and after-school activities. Numerous institutions, programs, and organizations, premised on the assumption that adolescents needed to be taught middle-class and Christian civic and moral values, emerged in the interwar decades, including movie censorship boards, public-schooling regulations that raised the school-leaving age, domestic science and industrial training, Girl Guides and Boy Scouts, the YWCA and YMCA, the Canadian Girls in Training, and the Canadian Council of Child Welfare.[20]

Popular perceptions of the moral and sexual dangers posed by the city also reflected changes occurring in the region's economy. As farmers became increasingly reliant on agricultural labour, mechanization, and credit financing, farm women and girls' productive labour became less necessary to the maintenance of the family farm. Although social reformers and magistrates across Canada remarked upon the problem of youth in the city and linked it to immigration, statistics suggest that it was rural, Canadian-born female youths who contributed to the region's burgeoning urban populations in the interwar years. In 1921, for instance, adolescents made up 8 percent of the male and 26 percent of the female labour forces in Edmonton. Over the next decade, youths between the ages of ten and nineteen increased from 17 to 20 percent of the city's population. Although males outnumbered females in prairie cities until the First World War, the gender balance shifted in favour of females in the interwar years. In 1926, the male-to-female ratio was 967 to 1,000 in Winnipeg and 978 to 1,000 in Regina. This gender imbalance reflected the realities of the region's postwar political economy: while girls and young women tended to find work in the service, clerical, and manufacturing sectors, boys were more likely to find employment in the agricultural sector as labourers. Because this youthful influx had a decidedly feminine cast, social observers tended to perceive it as a potential social problem.[21]

Contrary to psychological depictions of modern adolescence as a time of leisure, 42 percent of Edmonton's youths engaged in waged labour in 1921; ten years later, 57 percent did so. Publicly expressed anxieties that associated city living and urban employment with female sexual immorality increased as cyclical downturns plagued the economy and limited women's employment opportunities in the 1920s. In 1921, 93 percent of Edmonton's female labour force worked in manufacturing, trades, service, and clerical occupations. Ten years later, the majority worked as domestic servants, waiters, salespersons, and typists – jobs that were low waged and, in the case of domestic and food service, outside the bounds of protective labour legislation.[22] Many feared that these economic trends were creating an economic and social climate that would once again drive women to prostitution. Although the three prairie provinces passed minimum-wage legislation for women between 1917 and 1919, the legislation offered single women only a living wage. Girls under the age of eighteen received significantly less, since legislators assumed that they would live at home. The notion of a social minimum that underlay this legislation presumed a transitory single woman worker whose ultimate destiny was marriage and motherhood.[23]

McClung's novel drew attention to the plight of young immigrant women in prairie cities, yet *Painted Fires* was also one of the most complex and nuanced examples of the narratives of narcoticism that dominated popular discourses on female sexuality, race, and nation building in the 1920s. The novel's depiction of the drug trade and its effects drew heavily upon Emily Murphy's exposé, *The Black Candle,* which was based on the magistrate's experience in Edmonton's police court and her forays into British Columbia's Chinatowns. The book was published as a serial in *Maclean's* before it was released as a full-length monograph in 1922.[24] Murphy's narrative and McClung's depiction of Dr. Sam and the Shanghai Chop Suey House drew on and enhanced popular perceptions of Asian Canadian men as deceitful, dangerous opium addicts and traffickers who posed a sexual threat to white women. These stereotypes were harnessed by reform advocates, women's organizations, and labour groups to lend weight to their demands for anti-Asian immigration policies and labour legislation, anti-drug legislation, white women's labour laws, and the regulation of Chinatowns.[25] Yet narratives of narcoticism were more than a simple attempt to enhance racial boundaries. Although white, middle-class social commentators and reformers linked substance abuse and the drug traffic to Chinese immigrants, they also feared that opium use was on the rise among middle-class urban dwellers who eschewed alcohol as a working-class and immigrant vice. Their fears were echoed by physicians, who pushed for anti-drug legislation in their campaign to assert their role as protectors of the nation's health and moral values.[26]

DRUG LAW ENFORCEMENT:
REGULATING CHINESE MASCULINITY AND CROSS-RACIAL SEXUAL
RELATIONSHIPS

In 1911, the Canadian government responded to pressure and passed the Opium and Drug Act, which made it a criminal offence to smoke or possess opium for non-medicinal purposes. Following the achievement of women's suffrage and prohibition during the war, anti-drug advocates such as McClung and Murphy demanded further regulation on the grounds that women would turn to drugs to reduce the stress of modern life and urban living. They also feared that state-regulated prohibition of alcohol consumption would cause opium use to filter down from middle-class to working-class immigrants. They predicted the downfall of women, the decline of the family, and the moral and physical degeneration of society as the female addict, driven by desperation, turned to prostitution and sexual relationships with Asian Canadian and African American men to support her habit. Their arguments prompted amendments to the Opium and Drug Act in 1920 and police crackdowns and press crusades against the drug trade for the remainder of the decade.[27]

Enforcement of the Opium and Drug Act, in turn, reinforced stereotypes: in the year ending 30 September 1921, Chinese Canadians stood accused in 1,211 of the 1,864 cases that resulted in conviction.[28] By no means did conviction rates paint an accurate portrait of drug usage on the Prairies; rather, they reflected the prejudices and fears of municipal law enforcement agencies. Although anti-drug advocates suspected that narcotics use was on the rise among immigrant and working-class females, police charged few women under the Opium and Drug Act. The Edmonton Police Court, for instance, convicted only eight women in the 1910s, nine in the 1920s, and three in the 1930s.[29] In Winnipeg, only seven women – six Canadian

Protestants and one Polish Catholic – stood accused in the district's Court of King's Bench on drug-related charges between 1924 and 1937. Their case files and case histories belie the accuracy of narratives of narcoticism and reveal that such representations of dissolute Asian Canadian men and opium-addicted women were built upon intrusive police tactics and uneven law enforcement. The case files paint an alternative portrait, one in which law enforcement officials were more preoccupied with regulating and policing immigrant men and cross-racial sexual relationships than they were with enforcing the Drug and Opium Act.

In 1924, the Winnipeg police caught Valerie Sherwood, in the company of a man, breaking and entering into the Louis K. Liggett Company. The couple was in the process of stealing a shelf of narcotics that included heroin, tincture of opium, and Novocain. Sherwood, a housewife originally from Alabama, declared her occupation as drug addict. The Winnipeg Court of King's Bench found her guilty only of shop breaking and sentenced her to six months in jail.[30] Five years later, the Morality Department charged Dolly and William Lazaruk with drug possession. The Lazaruks operated a restaurant together, and when the police raided the Polish couple's living quarters above the restaurant, they found drugs hidden on the outer edge of a windowsill. Although Dolly convinced the jury that she knew nothing about the drugs in question, the jury found William guilty, and the judge sentenced him to serve two years in Manitoba Penitentiary with a $500 fine.[31]

Judges and juries reserved the harshest penalties for alleged addicts whose sexual relationships transgressed racial boundaries. In 1929, a jury convicted three single women – known to the police under aliases and presumably prostitutes – of drug possession, and the judge sentenced them each to between two and three years in Manitoba Penitentiary. The Morality Department had raided their place of residence and found the women, in the company of Lim Tung, in possession of heroin. At the preliminary hearing, held before Sir Hugh J. Macdonald of the Winnipeg Police Court, the police emphasized that they had caught Lim Tung "pulling up his pants" in a room separate from the women. The women had been apprehended wearing only nightclothes. Morality Department officers also admitted that they had lied about their identity to gain admittance to the house, and although they found syringes, spoons, and droppers in one of the women's rooms, the heroin itself was found outside a window. When the women's defence attorney established that the "china boy" had been closest to the window where the drugs were disposed, the appeal court quashed the convictions of two of the women.[32]

Two years later, the Morality Department's mishandling of a case that involved a white woman and three Asian men resulted in the attorney general withdrawing the charge. On 11 June 1931, William Robson and two other officers with the Morality Department went to Capital Laundry to execute a search warrant for drugs. At the preliminary hearing before magistrate R.B. Graham, Robson deposed that one of the accused, Gin Get, was downstairs when the warrant was read. In cross-examination, the defence asked if the accused, a "china boy," had been able to understand the warrant, which the officer had read to him in English. Robson then presented evidence that he had discovered another Asian man, "Wesley Jim," in an upstairs bedroom with Irene Ross, a white woman. Robson's fellow officers then called him downstairs, where he discovered three packages of heroin in the ironing room and four packages in a laundry parcel. In cross-examination, Robson admitted that the laundry's proprietor and the other accused, "Jim Chong," had remained in the summer kitchen throughout the investigation and were nowhere near the laundry. Irene Ross, Robson admitted further, had only been at the laundry for thirty minutes before she left to go buy beer. When Officer Cragg made his deposition, he stated that he had found Ross in bed with "Wesley Lee." At this point in the hearing, Magistrate Graham interrupted the proceedings and castigated the Morality Department: the officers had failed to refer to the accused by their names, which appeared on the docket as Jim Sam, Jim Shung, and Jim Gim Goon. The charges against Ross, Shung, and Gim Goon were dropped, and a jury found Jim Sam not guilty.[33]

"Is It Such a Bad Crime As That?"
Regulating Reproduction and Popular Resistance to the Criminalization of Abortion

In late August 1914, Samuel Bates, a Winnipeg ironworker, was given the court's protection to make a deposition against Russell and Maud Dumas, abortionists charged with the murder of Maria Kissock. At the preliminary hearing, which was held before Sir Hugh J. Macdonald in Winnipeg's Police Court between 23 August and 3 September, Bates informed the court that he was responsible for the victim's pregnancy and had tried to protect her by arranging an abortion at Dr. Dumas' office in early August. Like many women who underwent illegal abortions, Kissock developed septic peritonitis that went untreated and resulted in her death. When the prosecuting attorney asked Bates if he understood that abortion was a crime, he replied,

A: I didn't think it was as bad a crime as that.
Q: You didn't think it was a crime?
A: How should I know, I am not a doctor.
Q: Have you any conscience?
A: I had enough to know how the girl was feeling.[34]

Despite Bates's testimony, the prosecution failed to establish that Dr. Dumas and his wife possessed the instruments that caused Kissock's abortion. Crown counsel and the Winnipeg City Police also failed to produce a dying declaration by the victim. The jury acquitted the couple of all charges on 17 November 1914. Less than a year later, however, the police and the prosecution put together enough evidence to convict the couple of manslaughter and attempted abortion on the person of Annie Zawiderski. The judge sentenced them to five years each in prison.[35]

Legislators did not decriminalize the use of contraceptives and certain medically approved abortions until the late 1960s. Prior to that decade, Canada had a law code that has been described as "less liberal than that of Great Britain and close in spirit to the notorious Comstock laws of the United States."[36] Under the 1892 Criminal Code, persons convicted of attempting to procure a miscarriage on a woman were liable to life imprisonment, while the pregnant woman faced a maximum sentence of seven years in prison.[37] The legislation also prescribed two years in prison for those who sold or disseminated abortifacients or provided instruments to procure abortion on women, regardless of whether the woman was pregnant.[38]

Canada's criminal law provisions against birth control and abortion were enacted in response to pressure from social reform advocates, physicians, and politicians who became increasingly aware that Canadians had been limiting reproduction since the mid-nineteenth century. Canada's birth rate declined approximately 30 percent between 1851 and 1891. Although this downward trend was offset by the turn-of-the-century immigration wave to the Prairies, it resumed following the war. The nation's declining birth rate enhanced fears of race suicide and moral and social degeneracy because social observers linked birth control (as both cause and effect) to the trials of modernity associated with urbanization, rural depopulation, immigration, and feminism.[39] Emily Murphy considered birth control the height of degeneracy, and other social commentators tended to contrast urban middle-class housewives' willingness to limit their family size unfavourably with the fecundity of working-class and immigrant girls and women.[40] Nineteenth-century physicians in central and eastern Canada had, in fact, lobbied for the criminalization of abortion to offset the declining birth rate of the respectable classes.[41] Statistics for the prairie region supported these fears. In Regina, British-born citizens, who comprised three-quarters of the city's population in 1921, made up only two-thirds of the population in 1931. British dominance likewise declined in Winnipeg, but not as severely as it had in the decade preceding the war.[42] While some conservative critics laid the blame for declining birth rates on the doorstep of the modern woman, feminists in Canada hesitated to publicly support women's reproductive rights because they feared that the issue's controversial nature would hamper their quest for political equality. In 1929, for instance, Georgina Sackville of Innisfail, Alberta, published two tracts in defence of the rhythm method of birth control. Sackville condoned birth control as a personal option in marriage, but birth control advocacy remained ideologically at odds with maternal feminism, which accepted – if not embraced – women's reproductive role and maternal function.[43]

As Samuel Bates's resistance to the idea that he had committed a crime when he helped Maria Kissock terminate an unwanted pregnancy suggests, the criminal courts became sites for the further performance of hegemony and resistance when judges and juries dealt with individuals such as Bates, Kissock, and Zawiderski – youths and young adults who risked permanent damage to their bodies, health, and reputation (not to mention life imprisonment) to avoid the shame and stigma of bearing a child outside the sanctity of marriage. Between 1886 and 1940, forty-four cases of abortion came before the superior courts in the selected judicial districts. As was the case in other North American cities, 86 percent of these cases were prosecuted in the 1920s and 1930s, when urbanization, the expansion of municipal police forces, the proliferation of social hygiene discourse in medical and legal circles, and state intervention in medical practice – which required physicians to report suspected abortion cases to the police – brought them to the attention of legal authorities.[44] Whereas only 36 percent of the forty-four abortion charges laid by the North West Mounted Police between 1874 and 1916 resulted in conviction, judges and juries in the five districts convicted and punished 61 percent of offenders in the interwar years.[45] The police and Crown counsels tended to follow pre-war precedent by prosecuting the abortionist rather than the woman upon whom the abortion was performed. Aggressive postwar crackdowns and elaborate police investigations, however, drew a wider array of individuals into the purview of the criminal court.[46] In 1921, for instance, juries in the Saskatchewan Court of King's Bench found two women upon whom abortions had been performed guilty of attempted abortion. Mary Hay's and Mary Beauman's cases were part of an elaborate five-trial series of actions that centred on the activities of Jeanette Swift, a married woman, nurse, and suspected abortionist, and William H. Bundy, an advertising manager who allegedly procured Swift's clients. Throughout the trials, the accused made voluntary statements to the police, pleaded guilty to the charges, and testified against one another to receive reduced sentences. The cases drew the public's and the state's attention to the prevalence of abortion in prairie cities and highlighted the disparate meanings that were attached to its occurrence by prosecutors, the judiciary, and ordinary citizens.

On 1 December 1920, the police arrested Mary Hay at Jeanette Swift's house on Angus Street in Regina. During Hay's preliminary hearing, which was held three weeks later before Magistrate J.H. Heffernan, Swift deposed that William Bundy had called from his office three times to arrange an appointment with Hay. Swift met Hay, whom she described as a married woman and milliner from a rural municipality, at Bundy's office, and the two women arranged to meet again at Swift's house. Swift admitted that she repeatedly, over a two-week period, used a catheter on Hay to induce a miscarriage. The procedure, according to Swift, never worked, but Swift charged Hay sixty dollars for her efforts.

Following her arrest, Hay provided the police with a voluntary written statement. Hay had arrived in Regina on 25 November 1920 and met Bundy at a physician's office. Hay admitted that she paid Swift for her services, but she claimed that Bundy received no payment for his aid. In her own defence, Hay explained her circumstances to the court: "My husband knew I was coming to have this abortion procured, he said if I wanted to have it done I could suit myself. My reason for wanting this abortion procured is I am in the milinery [sic] business, and my husband has only one foot and is crippled so I thought three of a family is enough."[47] At the trial, which was held on 15 January 1921, no one appeared for the accused, Hay pleaded guilty, and she received a twelve-month suspended sentence upon entering into a recognizance for $500.

Mary Hay also served as a key witness for the prosecution when William Bundy was charged with attempting to procure an abortion on Hay and another woman, Margaret Fowler. Fowler was extended the benefit of the

Canadian Evidence Act to testify at Bundy's preliminary hearing, where
she disclosed the series of incidents and meetings that brought her into
Bundy's sphere. Unlike Hay, Fowler was a widow with children who ran
a boarding house in Regina. In June 1920, she thought she had "got into
trouble" and asked John Hughes, her boarder and likely father of the child,
to get medicine from a physician. Hughes procured tablets from Dr.
McCutheon. When the pills failed to induce miscarriage, Fowler received
a phone call from Bundy and arranged an appointment with Jeanette
Swift. Fowler proceeded immediately to Swift's house "for the sake of my
children."[48] On two separate occasions, Swift used a long instrument on
Fowler until a miscarriage occurred on 1 July. Fowler admitted that she
paid Swift ten dollars after the first procedure. John Hughes corroborated
Hay's deposition when he testified that he had met Bundy at Dr.
McCutheon's office and arranged for him to contact Fowler. Prior to that
meeting, Hughes had met with three different physicians who refused to
help him and advised him to let the pregnancy progress. When Fowler
told Hughes about Jeanette Swift, the boarder arranged to meet Bundy at
Swift's home, where he paid the man twenty dollars for his services.

    Officer Hayes deposed that he had proceeded to Bundy's office on 13
December 1920, where he read Swift's statement to the accused, received
a voluntary statement in return, and proceeded to make an arrest.
According to Bundy, Hughes had asked him to arrange an abortion for
Mrs. Fowler; in return, Bundy had received thirty dollars, half of which
he turned over to Jeanette Swift. Swift, who was given the benefit of the
Canadian Evidence Act, refused to disclose the identity of the first woman
she treated, but she claimed that Sadie Carroll was the first woman sent
to her by Bundy. Carroll stayed at Swift's home for six weeks, and the
woman's boyfriend paid the nurse twenty-five dollars after the abortion
occurred. Given the damaging effect of Fowler's, Swift's, and Hayes's sworn
statements and depositions, Bundy pleaded guilty to all charges, and Justice
MacKay sentenced him to serve eight months in the provincial jail with
hard labour. John Hughes, who was arraigned on the same day, also pleaded
guilty to attempting to procure an abortion on Margaret Fowler. Hughes
was an assistant car foreman with the Canadian National Railway and a
married man. He was sentenced to four months in the provincial jail and
fined $100.[49]

    In a statement made to the police on 13 December 1920, Jeanette Swift
catalogued the many clients that had been sent to her by Bundy and another man, William Flood. Most were married women from rural areas,
but a few, such as Sadie Carroll and Mary Beauman, were young, single

women who worked either in the clerical sector or as domestic servants. Carroll had herself tried to induce an abortion; when her efforts met with no success, she turned to Swift as a last resort. By contrast, Beauman was introduced to Swift by William Flood, who learned of the nurse's business through word of mouth. Swift pleaded guilty to an attempt to procure abortions on Margaret Fowler and Mary Hay, and she was sentenced to six months in Prince Albert Penitentiary on each charge. Beauman, like Hay, received a twelve-month suspended sentence and was released on her own recognizance for $500.[50]

The Jeanette Swift abortion trials represent the realities of abortion and its legal enforcement in prairie Canada during the interwar years. Although abortion was typically represented as a female crime, criminal case files reveal husbands, boyfriends, and fathers procuring the means to induce illegal miscarriages. Most husbands claimed that they only wanted to protect their wives from the physical and financial problems associated with frequent childbirth and too many children, while other men, married and single, argued that they wanted to hide the shame of having a child born out of wedlock. In extreme cases, men acted, either personally or with the aid of an abortionist, to hide evidence of incest and rape. In 1939, for instance, Anthony Lycka was sentenced in the Supreme Court of Alberta in the Macleod Judicial District to serve three years in Prince Albert Penitentiary for attempting to procure a miscarriage on his daughter, Helen Lycka. It was proven at trial that Lycka was the father of his daughter's child.[51]

With the exception of men such as Lycka, prosecutors, judges, and juries tended to treat male accomplices to abortion with remarkable leniency: in the majority of cases, no charges were laid, and when they were, the accused was subjected to minimal punishment. Prosecutors and judges recognized and accepted that boyfriends and husbands were often the only witnesses to abortion transactions and procedures. In return for these men's testimony against physicians and abortionists, public prosecutors were willing to give male accomplices the court's protection. As was the case in prostitution-related cases, the sexual double standard and a certain un-willingness to interfere in the most intimate aspects of the patriarchal family also shaped trial outcomes, particularly in cases where a conviction or lengthy sentence would disrupt a male breadwinner's wage-earning potential. These extra-legal considerations became apparent in 1932, when Winnipegger Charles Miller, a Scottish machinist and married man, was charged with two counts of having used an instrument or other means to procure abortion on Margaret Dinney. Dinney's sexual morality played a determining role in the outcome of the trial. At the preliminary hearing, which was held before magistrate R.B. Graham in the Winnipeg Police Court, Dinney, age fourteen, deposed that she had visited the machinist frequently at his shop. Dinney claimed that Miller propositioned her for sex in early April. When she refused on the grounds that he was a married man, Miller raped her and threatened her with bodily harm if she told anyone. Dinney admitted in cross-examination, however, that she later returned to Miller's shop on two separate occasions. When Dinney told Miller that she was pregnant, he procured slippery elm bark from a local pharmacy, sharpened it to a point, and proceeded to perform an abortion. Dinney's aunt corroborated her testimony, and two of Miller's friends deposed that the accused had admitted to performing the abortion and asked them to lie if they were asked about his relationship with Dinney. A jury in the Manitoba Court of King's Bench convicted Miller, but the judge sentenced him only to six months with hard labour in provincial jail.[52]

Because the majority of women involved in aiding or abetting abortions were married with children, judges, juries, and law enforcement agencies likewise proved reluctant to bring the full force of the law against them. In 1922, two married women, Ethel Walton and Alice Holden of Winnipeg, were charged with conspiracy to commit, and using means to procure, an abortion on Lillian Caswell, an English elevator operator and widow who died from advanced septicemia while in Walton's and Holden's care.[53] As was the case during the Swift trials, Walton and Holden served as key witnesses in the Crown's case against Dr. Robert B.W. Canning, who was accused of being responsible for Caswell's death. Walton was given the protection of the court, and she testified that a Mrs. Daley had brought Caswell to her home in mid-December 1920. Walton, who had the previous year allowed Canning to perform an abortion on her, took Caswell to see the doctor. Canning, who represented himself as a mechanotherapist and an expert in electrotherapeutics, subjected Caswell to electric-shock therapies that caused internal burns and wounds that later developed infection. Walton took Caswell to Alice Holden's home, where she helped the other woman care for Caswell until she died one day after Christmas. Both women testified that Caswell had aborted the child and that they had flushed the evidence down the toilet. When their cases came to trial on 16 June 1922, Holden and Walton pleaded guilty to the second charge, and each woman received a suspended one-year sentence. By contrast, a judge and jury in the Manitoba Court of King's Bench found Canning guilty of manslaughter and sentenced him to serve five years in Manitoba Penitentiary.[54]

Canada's draconian criminal legislation against abortion emerged as a result of Anglo-Canadian and middle-class fears about race and class suicide and perceived fears about the plight of the single girl in the city. Conviction rates and sentencing patterns in abortion cases on the Prairies suggest, at best, a desultory response to legal infractions on the part of judges and juries because, with the exception of male abortionists such as Canning, the individuals who came before them as accused or witnesses rarely conformed to prevailing myth and discourse. When revealed in a court of law, the desperate actions of ordinary citizens attested to the remarkable success of legal prohibitions against abortion and the success of attempts to limit sex and reproduction within lawful marriage. Individuals such as Samuel Bates, Mary Hay, Mary Beauman, and John Hughes actively resisted the idea that an unplanned pregnancy should lead to an unwanted marriage or child. Yet their subsequent involvement in public and humiliating abortion trials must have served as a cautionary tale to future generations.[55]

Judges and juries could afford to extend mercy to the few husbands, boyfriends, and women who stood accused in the criminal courts because, in a significant number of cases, their actions, either directly or indirectly, resulted in the death of a woman. The Jeanette Swift trials were unusual in that they came to the attention of police authorities via word of mouth. Given the underground nature of abortion-related offences, abortionists' activities became public knowledge only when a physician, hospital, or the woman herself reported that an illegal abortion had resulted in medical complications or death.[56] In fourteen of the forty-four cases, the accused was charged with manslaughter in addition to abortion-related offences. The harshest sentences fell on those middle-class men and women, such as Swift and Canning, who used their superior education to subvert state and medical control over reproduction and women's bodies and, consequently, the reproduction of their own class.

DANCING, DRINKING, AND DRIVING WITH THE DEFENDANT

Although popular anxieties about the sexual emancipation of women and girls in the city had an uneven impact on abortion prosecutions, they profoundly influenced judges' and juries' responses to rape, unlawful carnal knowledge, and seduction cases in the city in the 1920s and 1930s. Sex crime prosecutions in prairie cities paralleled developments in other Canadian regions. Whereas xenophobia and classism rendered foreign-born men and agricultural labourers vulnerable to conviction in both Ontario and the Prairies in the 1910s, juries and judges in both regions found cases that exemplified the dangers of big city life troubling in the interwar decades.[57] Unlike men prosecuted for sex crimes in Ontario, however, men in prairie cities were less likely to face conviction in the 1920s and 1930s, when professional discourses on female sexual delinquency filtered down to all levels of society. Although juvenile and family courts emerged in the period – ostensibly to dispense a more compassionate or socialized form of justice shaped by the psychiatric and social work professions – the circulation of professional discourses resulted in more probationary surveillance and the preventative incarceration of working-class girls.[58] Magistrate Daly's willingness to send young women convicted of vagrancy and prostitution-related offences to the Salvation Army's Industrial and Rescue Home for Women or the Catholic Home of the Good Shepherd in the war years signalled the beginnings of this trend (see Chapter 3).

In *Painted Fires*, Nellie McClung unveiled discrepancies between the rhetoric of protection and the realities of punishment through her depiction of the Girls' Friendly Home, where Helmi was incarcerated. The home had been run originally by a progressive female matron who instituted a merit system, dispensed with uniforms, and took girls to movies or for drives in the countryside. The matron was soon dismissed by an all-male board composed of Protestant ministers: "She gave the Board members positive chills by the things she said about the double standard of morals which was made by men to shield men, and went on to tell them that many of her girls were innocent young things from the country who had come to work in the city to help the family at home, and had fallen victim to men's lust and hypocrisy: The very men who had led them astray, fathers of families some of them, and regarded as respectable men in society, no doubt now spoke of these girls as 'fallen women.'"[59] The board decided that a man should run the school with the aid of a female assistant, and it instituted a new disciplinary regime to break girls of their pride and transform them into respectable women.[60]

McClung's novel offered a Christian, feminist critique of the new carceral regime for women that emerged after the war. By choosing a Finnish heroine and depicting her trials and tribulations with empathy and accuracy, McClung also wanted to defuse middle-class anxieties about Finnish immigrant women – who demonstrated a marked preference for urban life, financial independence, common law marriage, birth control, and socialism – as a potential threat to Canadian society.[61] Yet the novel perpetuated stereotypes of working-class and immigrant girls – and the nature of sexual assault in the city – that governed women's reception in criminal courts when they stood as complainants in sex crime cases. Although McClung criticized the sexual double standard that left women vulnerable to rape and seduction in their own homes and communities, Helmi was almost raped by two strangers while walking alone in the countryside. Throughout the novel, Helmi runs a gauntlet of potential perils and pleasures, from automobiles and picture shows to narcotics, flapper culture, and the new pink-collar professions. In prairie communities – as in other emerging settler societies in which the land, patriarchy, and country-life ideology exerted a powerful influence over regional identity and culture – popular representations of the city as a site for the potential moral ruin of young women and the family enhanced the ability of defence attorneys to demolish the character and credibility of complainants in sex crime prosecutions.[62]

The prosecution of sexual assault in prairie cities, as indicated in Table 8, was characterized by low conviction rates, lengthy and intrusive cross-examinations, the so-called expert testimony of urban physicians, and moral posturing on the part of male, middle-class, conservative judges. Between 1886 and 1940, women or girls reported 178 cases of rape, indecent assault, unlawful carnal knowledge, and seduction in the selected districts. The majority of these urban cases occurred during the First World War and the interwar decades, and they reflected the dislocations and upheavals that accompanied unprecedented urban expansion in the region. Just as the criminal law of sexual assault served the interests of the patriarchal family farm by setting boundaries on working-class men's ability to engage in intimate relationships with farm women and girls, so it also operated to protect patriarchy and family in urban centres by regulating

TABLE 8   Sex crime prosecutions, urban centres, 1886-1940

	N	%
Convicted	80	45
Not guilty	76	42
No resolution	19	11
Unknown	3	2
Total number of cases	178	100

SOURCES: SCNWT (Western Assiniboia), SCS and SCKB (Regina), 1886-1932, R-1286 and R-1287, SAB; Criminal Register, MCKB (Dauphin), 1917-1940 , GR 4576, L-4-15, PAM; Criminal Register, MCKB (Eastern Manitoba/Winnipeg), 1886-1940, GR 3636, M-1196, and GR 4576, L-4-15, PAM; SCNWT and SCA (Southern Alberta and Macleod), 1886-1940, Acc. 78.235, PAA; SCA (Wetaskiwin), 1914-1938, Acc. 81.198, PAA.

the sexuality of immigrant and working-class girls and women. The prairie judiciary, however, also tried to enforce conformity to middle-class ideas of masculinity as the standard of civilized behaviour during an era when the labour and feminist movements actively challenged its dominance.

Juries and judges reserved convictions and harsh sentences for cases that involved accused who fit the stereotype of the rapist as stranger or sexual predator and, consequently, meshed with narratives of the dangerous city. The criminal courts thus served as sites where the image "of the pleasure-seeking working girl competed with that of the dangerous stranger."[63] In 1919, for instance, a jury in the Manitoba Court of King's Bench, Winnipeg, found Marvin Suggitt, a twenty-nine-year-old married man, guilty after accusations of rape were laid by Florence Lillian Stewart. Justice T. Gill sentenced Suggitt to serve fifteen years in Manitoba Penitentiary.[64] At the preliminary hearing, which was held before Magistrate Noble of Winnipeg's Police Court in early February, Stewart deposed that on the evening of 27 January 1919, she had worked at Government Telephones until 11:00 p.m., when she took the train car home. Stewart testified that when she got off the train, a man appeared from nowhere and chased her into Logan Park, where he threw her over a wire fence, hit her in the face, and twisted a dirty handkerchief into her mouth to suppress her screams. Following the rape, Stewart ran home, screaming for her father. When Stewart's father saw the bruises on her body, he reported the case to the police and provided them with his daughter's ripped and torn clothing.

Two physicians corroborated Stewart's deposition when they presented evidence that Stewart suffered from a torn hymen and bruises and that the accused had abrasions and scratches on his hands. Another witness, Annie Corderley, deposed that she had heard rumours about the case and could testify that she had seen Suggitt follow Stewart off the streetcar. The police investigation centred on Suggitt's eyeglasses. Investigators found a lens at the scene of the crime, and they later established that Suggitt had recently taken his eyewear for repair to a local jeweller and optician. The provincial bacteriologist confirmed that Stewart's skirt and the accused's underwear contained traces of blood and semen, and the prosecution provided evidence that Suggitt had been in the possession of pornographic postcards when the rape was committed.[65]

Suggitt's defence attorney tried to discredit Stewart's testimony by questioning why she had chosen to work and travel alone in the city at night. Stewart replied that she was sixteen years old but had left school in Grade 6 because her father, who was a sheet-metal worker, required her labour at home. She had, however, been working split shifts as a telephone operator for six months to augment the family income. Stewart disclosed that she had, indeed, been hesitant to travel home alone on the night in question because the Winnipeg General Strike was in progress. Stewart understood that the situation was volatile and asked her brother, a soldier, to meet her where she got off the streetcar. Unfortunately, her brother did not arrive in time. Defence counsel then tried to discredit the prosecution's medical evidence by suggesting that the complainant could have torn her hymen by engaging in vigorous athletics.[66] If Marvin Suggitt was the perfect rapist, however, Florence Lillian Stewart was the perfect rape victim. In addition to corroborative testimony, the prosecution was able to adduce evidence of physical struggle and an immediate complaint. Stewart refused to be cowed by the defence, and she established herself as a hard-working, virtuous, working-class girl.

Working-class girls who appeared to flirt with the perils and pleasures of the city did not fare as well. In 1926, the Saskatchewan Court of King's Bench tried two men for unlawful carnal knowledge of and sexual assault on young, immigrant, and working-class women. On 4 and 5 February 1926, Tom Manos was tried and found not guilty of having unlawful carnal knowledge of Tessie Benko, a fifteen-year-old girl. Although legislators had increased the age of consent for girls to sixteen in 1920, the complainant had to be of previously chaste character and provide corroborative testimony.[67] After 1925, further amendments to the Criminal Code stipulated that "no person could be convicted upon the evidence of one witness, unless such witness is corroborated in some material particular by evidence implicating the accused."[68] At the preliminary hearing of the Manos case, which was held in the Regina Police Court on 19 October 1925, Tessie Benko deposed that she worked in Regina as a domestic servant and waitress. On the afternoon of 12 October, Benko, along with her friend Lillian Forbes, attended Bible class and then proceeded to the popular downtown street mall on Scarth Street, where two men, Ray Fraser and Jack McIntyre, introduced themselves. The girls arranged to meet the men after dinner. Benko deposed that McIntyre met them at the arranged time and place and convinced the girls to follow him to a suite at a local hotel, where Fraser was supposedly staying with his mother. When they arrived at the room, however, they discovered Fraser alone with a woman named Florence Harding. Tom Manos arrived soon thereafter. The three couples danced, drank alcohol, and went for a late dinner at the Parkview Café, which was owned by Manos. When they returned to the hotel, Benko claimed that Manos asked her to have sex with him. She refused because she was too sick from drinking. The next day, the two girls breakfasted with McIntyre and Manos, went for a drive with the two men, and returned to the hotel suite to listen to the gramophone. It was that evening, Benko explained, that she had "sexual connections" with the accused.[69]

Witnesses for the prosecution included Dr. M.R. Bow, who testified that Benko suffered from a ruptured hymen and had behaved with modesty during the physical examination. Amelia Benko, the victim's mother, established that her daughter was fifteen. In cross-examination, however, Manos' attorney, M. Anderson, coaxed Amelia Benko to admit that her daughter was often disobedient and refused to go to high school. During the cross-examination of the complainant, Anderson cast doubt on Tessie Benko's moral character and chastity and insinuated that she was a common prostitute. Anderson asked Benko if she or Manos had paid for the meals they shared and if she had accepted money from the accused. Anderson also adduced evidence that the two girls used aliases when out with boys and had gone to picture shows and concerts with RCMP recruits on at least two separate occasions.

Jack McIntyre, who was a married man with a child, deposed that he and Fraser had met the two girls not on Scarth Street but at the Palace of Sweets in the Palace Café. When the girls asked him and his companion to join them at their booth, McIntyre disclosed that they did so willingly because they did not consider Benko or her friend decent women. McIntyre admitted that he had sexual intercourse with Forbes, who was fourteen, while Manos had sexual connections with Benko.[70] When the jury brought a not-guilty verdict, Chief Justice Maclean chastised the accused for his behaviour and warned Manos to refrain from entertaining young flappers in his rooms in the future.[71]

Three days after Manos' trial, a jury found John A. MacDonald of Moose Jaw not guilty of the rape of Annie Darvo, a twenty-two-year-old Austro-French woman. Darvo, who was an employee at Tom Manos' Parkview Café, deposed at the preliminary hearing, which was held before Magistrate Heffernan in the Regina Police Court in mid-September, that she had arrived in Canada eight months previous and had since held three jobs working as a waitress and domestic servant. On the evening of 14 September, Darvo's friend Margaret Maher picked her up from Mrs. McGillvray's boarding house, where she was staying, and invited her to a party at a local hotel. When Darvo got into the car, she met the accused and another man who accompanied them to the hotel. Darvo told the court that she had been uneasy about the situation, but she accepted two drinks, which made her ill, after the party arrived at the hotel room. Darvo asked MacDonald to drive her home, but the accused told her that he was in no condition to do so. Maher and the other man, James McBennett, then got undressed and took one of the room's two beds, and they asked Darvo to join MacDonald in the other. Darvo argued that the alcohol had made her insensible; when she came to her senses, she discovered MacDonald having sexual connections with her. Both men later took her home. The following day she reported the incident to the police and visited a physician.[72]

At the preliminary hearing, Dr. D.S. Johnson provided evidence that Darvo had recently suffered a ruptured hymen, and the hotel's night clerk deposed that the accused and McBennett had paid for the room in advance and registered under aliases. Although James McBennett and Margaret Maher appeared as witnesses for the defence, their depositions corroborated Darvo's testimony. McBennett, who was a lumberman from Moose Jaw, told the court that he and MacDonald had phoned Maher, who also worked at the Parkview Café, to inform her that they would be coming to town and that MacDonald would need a girl. On the evening in question, however, MacDonald told McBennett that he did not think that Darvo had been "on parties" before. During cross-examination by Crown Prosecutor Herbert E. Sampson, McBennett admitted that he had shared a long sexual relationship with Maher, that MacDonald had given Darvo not two but three drinks, that MacDonald had exclaimed that there was "something wrong with the girl," and that Maher had repeatedly encouraged Darvo to be a mixer and have sex with MacDonald. In her deposition, Maher agreed that Darvo had been scared when they arrived at the hotel and had acted like a baby.[73]

MacDonald's attorney, W.E. Knowles, employed the same strategies during the cross-examination of the prosecution's witnesses that Anderson had used to great effect during the Manos trial. Knowles asked Dr. Johnson if it was possible that Darvo's hymen had been ruptured by a metal instrument or by a man's fingers if he was intoxicated. Knowles asked Darvo if it had, in fact, not been Maher who raped her. When Darvo said no, Knowles asked her if she had not been in the habit of walking the streets with Maher. When Darvo again replied in the negative, Knowles suggested that she had been frightened at the hotel only because she knew that if a police officer saw her, he would think she was a prostitute. Knowles completed his examination by suggesting that Darvo was truly ignorant if she did not know that when a girl went to a boy's room it was for sex: "Will you agree with this, you got just what you expected?"[74]

When a judge and jury heard the case in the Saskatchewan Court of King's Bench, the trial revolved around the issue of Darvo's consent. Both MacDonald and McBennett testified that Darvo had been intoxicated but not to the point where she was incapacitated. Defence counsel then addressed the jury and told the men that it was not the moral aspects of the case that were in question but whether Darvo had willingly had sexual relations with the accused. In Knowles's opinion, "A woman who would go to such a place, and allow herself to get into such a compromising situation without even calling for help – was not taking reasonable precautions to protect that precious thing, the loss of which she has so bewailed in court."[75] Given the nature of popular middle-class anxieties in the 1920s, the Crown prosecutor's rebuttal was weak. Sampson told the court that consent was an act of will and he expressed the opinion that alcohol could rob a person of all willpower. Sampson also asked jury members to take the complainant's foreign origins and weak intelligence into consideration when they deliberated on the issue of consent. In his charge to the jury, Justice J.F.L. Embury asked the jury to bear in mind that the "mere articulation of the word 'no' did not mean non-consent if, by actions, a person gave willing submission." One would assume, he continued, that an ordinary woman in similar circumstances would scream for help or physically fight off her assailant.[76] The jury acquitted MacDonald of rape but asked Justice Embury to censure the accused for his unmanly conduct: "You know what the jury means. Your conscience should tell you. If it doesn't, no words of mine will be of any avail. Your conduct in this matter is the most disgusting that I have ever come across in a court room. If you ever come before me again and are found guilty, I'll not forget about this, either."[77]

Throughout the 1920s, and into the 1930s, a woman's willingness to attend picture shows, eat in public cafés, walk the streets, take rides in automobiles with men, and consume alcohol was represented by defence attorneys as reasonable grounds to argue that she had consented to rape or, in cases of unlawful carnal knowledge or seduction, that she had not been of previously chaste character. Unlike sex crime prosecutions in rural communities (see Chapter 4), seduction cases in the city rarely made it to the trial stage, and when they did they rarely resulted in conviction. At a preliminary hearing held in the Regina Police Court in 1923, for instance, Hazel King complained that Weldon Mulligan, who was engaged to be married, had seduced and impregnated her. King, who was between the ages of sixteen and eighteen and worked as a domestic servant for Mrs.

Crocket, deposed that she had met Mulligan at a skating rink at the beginning of June. The accused took her to his home, and the couple had sexual
intercourse, which caused her to bleed and vomit. On the second occasion,
which occurred in late June, the complainant attended a dance and then
met Mulligan on Scarth Street. The couple then proceeded to Mulligan's
rooms near the Chicago Postal Studio, where he worked.[78]

Mulligan's attorney cast doubt on King's assertion that she had been
of previously chaste character. When Ada King, the complainant's mother,
testified that the accused had accepted responsibility for the pregnancy
and offered to arrange for an abortion or adoption, defence counsel asked
her if Hazel had been in the habit of going to picture shows with other
girls. King admitted that her daughter had once gone to a show with a
boy named Dick Hannah. In his cross-examination of Hazel King,
Mulligan's attorney asked King if she had ever discussed venereal disease
with his client. When King replied in the affirmative, he asked, "Weren't
some of the conversations – not nice? ... You talked to a stranger about
sex, venereal disease, and pregnancy? ... Did you tell him about a guy in
Moose Jaw who was 'jazzing' you but went away?"[79] Unlike farm families,
who successfully used the Criminal Code's seduction provisions to impede
a hired hand's ability to marry their daughters, Hazel King, a domestic
servant and the daughter of a working-class widow with six children, appeared to be a sexually deviant girl who was manipulating the justice system
to force a respectable and engaged man to marry her. On 15 February 1924,
Justice C.J. Brown withdrew the charge from the jury.[80]

In 1938, a particularly violent gang rape case in Winnipeg likewise revolved around the issue of whether the complainant's willingness to get
into an automobile and drink alcohol with strange men constituted consent. In late February, the police arrested six men for the rape of Jessie
Kulik. The accused men were between the ages of eighteen and twenty-five,
and they held diverse jobs – some hired themselves out as occasional farm
labourers and carpenters; others worked as bookkeepers and deliverymen.
A jury in Manitoba's Court of King's Bench found all six men guilty of
rape, and Justice A.K. Dysart sentenced each to serve between five and
seven years in Manitoba Penitentiary with a whipping. Four of the men,
however, successfully appealed the decision.[81]

Jessie Kulik deposed at the preliminary hearing, which was heard over
two days in early December by Magistrate R.B. Graham of the Winnipeg
Police Court, that she had attended a wedding with her sister on the evening of 7 November. The girls stayed until 2 a.m. and accepted a ride home

from William Sawka and his friends because the streetcars were no longer running. Kulik told the court that she had asked the driver to drop them at a specific location. Sawka, however, ignored the instructions, threw her sister out of the car, and drove in the opposite direction. When the car stopped, the men pulled Kulik from the vehicle, hit her, and called her obscene names. Kulik told the court that she could not cry out for help because Sawka had tied her mouth shut with a hanky. Kulik believed that a number of the men raped her, but she had trouble identifying specific individuals because she had passed out at one point. At the end of the incident, the men drove Kulik back to the city and dropped her off at Jubilee Avenue. She proceeded to a nearby house, where a woman helped her clean up and wash her clothes.[82]

In cross-examination, Kulik agreed that she had arrived at the wedding at 7:30 p.m., drank some beer, and danced once with Sawka. Stanley Dyck, who appeared as a witness for the defence and was tried separately from the other men, offered a counternarrative to Kulik's story. Dyck told the court that he and his friends had left the wedding at 9 p.m. but returned at 3:30 a.m, at which time they offered the two girls a ride home. According to Dyck, Jessie agreed to go for a drive, and they dropped the younger sister off at home. The party then left the city and drove out into the bush, where they had to stop the car because Kulik was "feeling a little good." When Dyck got out of the vehicle to urinate, he witnessed Kulik having sexual relations with Sawka. The complainant never hollered for help: "In fact, what I saw was that she gave it to him and she was kissing him in the car and everything."[83] Dyck testified that the older Lakoski brother wanted to go next, but he came back to the car to get a condom when Kulik refused to have sex with him otherwise. Joe Dworanoski then had his turn. According to Dyck, Pete Lakoski and John Fright remained in the car for the entire incident.[84] Given the nature of Dyck's testimony, Kulik was recalled and asked whether she had willingly engaged in sex with the men in question. When Kulik said no, she was again asked to explain how much alcohol she had consumed. Kulik admitted that she had consumed six glasses of beer.

Kulik saw a physician, Athol Gordon, on 10 November. The physician deposed that Kulik still suffered from severe bruising on her arms, thighs, and face three days after the alleged rapes. An internal examination revealed evidence of internal bleeding from recent lacerations. Mabel Kulik, who appeared for the Crown, corroborated her sister's testimony when she stated that the six men had coaxed them to enter the car with assurances that a ride from them would be safer than taking a taxi. Walter Wozony, who lived at the Northern Hotel, also stated that the two girls had asked him if he knew of anyone who could drive them home. A Winnipeg police detective made a deposition to the effect that the girls had asked him how to get home; after he told them that he could not help them, the officer saw a number of men in a 1934 Ford pull up and offer them a ride.[85]

Four of the six accused later had their convictions overturned on appeal. Jessie's inability, because of her impaired state, to identify the accused shaped the outcome, as did the complainant's lack of credibility in the eyes of the judge and jury. At the conclusion of the first trials, Justice Dysart did, however, take the opportunity to castigate the men for their behaviour: "This crime is the worst that has ever come to my attention. It is very hard to understand that in this day civilized people could do such a thing. Not one of you had the manhood to stand up for the girl or to intercede. Her arms were twisted to compel her silence, she was thrown around and not one of you protested. You will find out that neither the public opinion nor the law of this country will stand for such a thing."[86]

Only eight months after Dysart's pronouncement, the police charged six men for the rape of Jennie Pearl. Only two of the cases resulted in convictions, and they too were dismissed on appeal. With the exception of Peter Kissick, who had dated Pearl, the accused were strangers to the complainant. It took the police, prosecution, and Pearl months to track down and identify the men in police lineups; however, it was never certain if they had truly been the assailants.[87]

Only one complainant in the urban cases examined resisted the trend toward intrusive and demeaning cross-examinations. In 1928, Dorothy Thompson, a twenty-two-year-old graduate nurse from Regina, charged Frank O'Reilly, a twenty-one-year-old printer, with rape. At the preliminary hearing, which was held in the RCMP Police Court on 26 July 1928 before Stewart Gibson, JP, Thompson deposed that on the evening of 22 July she had accepted a ride home to Moose Jaw from the accused. Thompson had met the accused a year earlier during a dinner date with his brother at the O'Reilly family home. On the night in question, a mile outside of the city limits, the accused pulled off the road and proceeded to rape Thompson. Following the assault, Thompson ran to the safety of a nearby farmhouse. During the cross-examination, Thompson actively resisted the defence attorney's attempt to cast doubt on her moral character and the truth of her claims:

Q: Did you ever have sex with the accused previous to Sunday? No.
Q: You have been to drinking parties with him? No.

Q: You and the accused drank before you went out in the car? No.
Q: As a matter of fact you are 100 per cent pure? Yes.
Q: Did you ever have sex with anyone prior to that night? No.
Q: Why were you downtown at night? I went to have lunch at the Cameo Café.
Q: And his male organ entered your female organ against your will? Yes.
Q: You are a graduate nurse and you want us to believe that? Why, of course.
Q: As a matter of fact you have been a girl that has been drinking considerably in the last six months? I have not.
Q: Where you room, you can go in and out unchaperoned? Yes.
Q: Have you had VD? No.
Q: Did you consent? No.[88]

Thompson's superior education, medical knowledge, and maturity gave her the confidence to counter medical and social discourses on female sexuality in the 1920s and 1930s. In her estimation, accepting a ride home from a young man known to her was not an invitation to rape; rather, she simply stated that O'Reilly turned out to be not "such a friend" after all. Thompson also rejected the idea, prevalent among physicians and the judiciary, that rape was a physical impossibility if the woman truly resisted.

During the preliminary hearing, O'Reilly's attorney tried to harness in his client's favour medical discourses on rape that had influenced the outcome of rape proceedings in eastern Canada and the United States since the mid-nineteenth century but had little influence in prairie legal and medical circles until the 1920s. In 1835, American physician Theodric Romeyn Beck published *Elements of Medical Jurisprudence* to universal acclaim. Physicians and attorneys throughout the Western industrializing world welcomed the text because Beck weighed in on whether rape was a medical and physical possibility:

> I have intimated that doubts exist whether rape can be consummated on a grown female in good health and strength. It has been anxiously inquired whether this violence, if properly resisted ... can be compelled? ... I am strongly inclined to doubt its probability. The opinion of medical jurists generally is very decisive against it. An attempt ... may be possible, but the *consummation* of a rape ... seems impossible, unless some very extraordinary circumstances occur. For a woman always possesses sufficient power, by drawing back her limbs, and by the force of her hands, to prevent the insertion of the penis, whilst she can keep her resolution entire.[89]

Thompson, a graduate nurse, maintained few doubts that medical jurisprudence was incorrect. The jury, by contrast, accepted dominant medical
opinion: it found Frank O'Reilly guilty only of attempted rape, and the
judge sentenced him to serve five months in prison with hard labour.[90]

CONCLUSION

In the interwar decades, physicians, legal officials, and legislators held
young women and girls to increasingly rigid standards of sexual behaviour.
Nellie McClung suggested in her autobiography *The Stream Runs Fast* and
her novel *Painted Fires* that these diverse pressure groups believed that the
passage of the Opium Drug Act, the criminalization of abortion, and more
expansive age-of-consent laws would better protect women and girls from
the perils and pleasures of modernity. In practice, medico-moral and legal
discourses and legislation that singled out female sexuality for special
attention and linked it to larger concerns for family, region, or nation
blurred the line between leisure activities and occasional prostitution. Girls
and young women who embraced aspects of the new youth culture became,
in the eyes of officials, women who demonstrated little concern for their
moral or social reputations.[91] Complainants in sex crime trials discovered
that the social, economic, and intellectual developments that had given
birth to their newly won independence – a widening job market, financial
independence, leisure, and feminism – were condemned by judges and
juries as responsible for their moral and sexual ruin. Girls and women who
exhibited even a glimmer of sexual desire ceased to be victims and became,
instead, deviant women in need of regulation, punishment, or public
shaming. Only those women who could be represented as passive and
chaste victims of the rapacious assaults of strange men, women such as
Florence Lillian Stewart, were deemed suitable recipients of the criminal
courts' protection.

The rhetoric of protection masked not only, as some historians argue,
the extent that drug, abortion, and rape provisions in Canadian criminal
law enhanced the regulatory scope of the law over female sexuality, reproduction, and behaviour in the new carceral regime that followed the moral
panics over white slavery and prostitution; it also cloaked the degree to
which the criminal courts became sites for competing conceptions of the
state and the performance of hegemonic masculinity, familialism, and
resistance in the interwar decades.[92] Police forces on the Prairies used the
Opium and Drug Act to regulate and punish Asian men who transgressed

societal and legal prohibitions against cross-cultural social and sexual relationships. Although police officials accepted the sexual double standard
and resisted the idea that the state should play a role in the bedrooms of
the nation during the prostitution debates, they embraced the idea that
state authority should extend to the intimate lives of Asian Canadian
bachelor men. Similarly, the criminalization of birth control and abortion
operated not only to regulate women's bodies and sexuality but also to
protect the political and social order – symbolized by the nuclear family
– by ensuring that young men and women would limit sex to marriage
and, when that failed and pregnancy resulted, by forcing men to accept
their responsibilities.[93]

By their very nature, criminal case files contain countless narratives of
resistance to law enforcement practices and criminal sanctions against
birth control and extra-marital sex, which suggests that cultural attitudes
and sexual identities were being actively negotiated. While Asian Canadian
men such as Jim Sam, Jim Shung, and Jim Gim Goon asserted their rights
to a fair trial and criminal investigation under the Opium Act, married
men and women such as Mary Hay and her husband asserted their right
to set limits on the number of children they would and could bear and
maintain. Unmarried men and women such as Samuel Bates and Maria
Kissock likewise defended their right to enjoy a sexual or social relationship without the benefit of marriage, as did those girls who felt no shame
when they laid charges of rape and seduction against men with whom they
had initially agreed to date, dance, drink, or drive. Although instances of
it were rare, women such as Jeanette Swift and Dorothy Thompson also
actively challenged the idea that physicians were the sole experts and exclusive controllers of women's bodies and female reproduction.

The judicial lectures on morality and masculinity that tended to follow
the completion of sex crime trials also suggest that the birth of adolescent
popular culture in the interwar decades forced legal officials and average
men and women to, if not accept, at least address new attitudes toward
female sexual and social behaviour. Although historians such as Angus
McLaren and Gail Bederman have argued that middle-class discourses on
masculinity tended to serve hegemonic functions, the western Canadian
judiciary appeared to deem acceptable some sexual and social freedom on
the part of adolescent girls by castigating men and boys who took advantage
of them.[94] As American historian Stephen Robertson has argued in his
work on sex crimes in New York at the turn of the twentieth century,
campaigns to increase the age of consent were not simply attempts to
regulate female sexuality – they were also unsuccessful attempts, made

by social reformers and legislators, to extend the concept of childhood, and the protection it afforded, to female adolescents. The outcomes of statutory rape cases, however, demonstrate that judges and juries often had trouble fitting the new activities of adolescent girls into their older rural ideas about childhood.[95] By constructing the city as the counter-culture, as a site of moral and sexual danger for girls and women, country-life ideologists and prairie social commentators and reform advocates often overlooked the real challenges, dangers, and tribulations that ordinary men and women faced in a period of intense economic, social, and intel-lectual dislocation. Representations of the sinful, seductive city likewise drew attention away from the hardships, conflicts, and dangers that farm women experienced within the most private, sacrosanct sphere of the emerging liberal economic order – the family.

6

The Might of a Good Strong Hand

Domestic Violence, Wife Murder, and Incest

On the evening of 1 September 1923, medical staff at a local hospital in the mining community of Coleman, Alberta, treated Tammy Oswald for a broken arm and multiple wounds to the head and torso. Upon investigation, Alberta Provincial Police investigators stationed at nearby Blairmore learned that Oswald's neighbours had witnessed the attack and that the assailant, the victim's husband, had fled to the United States to avoid prosecution. Upon recovery, Tammy Oswald deposed at a preliminary hearing that she, along with her friend Mrs. Garveaux, had arranged to leave her husband. Unfortunately, Oswald's husband intercepted the two women. When he learned of his wife's decision to leave him, the husband stabbed her with a knife and beat her with a brick. Oswald admitted during cross-examination that she had suffered a poor marriage from the time she was forced to marry, twenty-one years earlier in Hungary. Oswald's children testified that they had tried to stop their father from beating their mother, but he overpowered them and hit them with household furniture. Oswald's neighbours – Thomas Flyer, Arthur Kay, and Thomas Johnson – likewise came to the woman's assistance, but the three men admitted that they initially ignored the conflict because they had "heard it all before."[1] The *Lethbridge Herald,* which reported the incident, focused on the community's response. The reporter described the events leading up to the conflict and the ensuing struggle: "They wrestled with one another, all the while, the husband made slashes in her body. The neighbours were not attracted until someone cried with a loud voice 'murder.'"[2] The article concluded that "the incident has disturbed the community frightfully as Mr. L. Oswald was a man of quiet disposition to all who met him and Mrs. Oswald was respected by all who knew her."[3] Although the prosecution presented evidence that Lewis Oswald repeatedly beat his wife, the accused (who returned from the United States for the hearing and the trial) was sentenced by Justice Thomas Mitchell Tweedie to serve thirty days in jail, rather than a maximum penalty of three years in prison.[4]

Judges and juries in the selected judicial districts heard twenty-two cases of wife murder and seventy-seven cases of incest (most were sexual abuse cases) in the settlement period and interwar years, and magistrates and the police dealt with instances of domestic discord or abuse daily. High-profile cases of domestic and intimate violence, such as Oswald, contradicted the myth of companionate marriage and a pioneering partnership between men and women by exposing the patriarchal underpinnings of prairie society and the dark side of utopian visions of the West as the site for a reinvigorated masculinity. Accusations of domestic and intimate violence in this era also disrupted the assumption that crime was primarily a public-sphere activity, and the subsequent enactment of extensive criminal legislation directed at policing domestic and intimate sexual relations signalled a reformulation of the public-private divide and of patriarchy in emerging welfare states. As social reformers and feminists challenged the laissez-faire state's patriarchal-authoritarian model of the family, a liberal welfare model of the family emerged that was based on the assumption that the state needed to intervene if the patriarch abused his power.[5]

Did judges and juries simply reinforce the assumptions upon which prairie society was built, or did these cases become the occasion for more complex acts of resistance, acquiescence, and negotiation that paralleled wider developments? Historians of domestic and intimate violence in central and eastern Canada and other Western societies have traced how men charged with domestic violence or the sexual abuse of their children could expect lenient treatment because magistrates, judges, and jurors took the male breadwinner's right to earn a family wage into consideration when they judged a case. As in rape and sexual assault cases, the victim's sexual morality and adherence to middle-class domestic ideologies also came under scrutiny and influenced which women were deserving of legal protection. The late nineteenth and early twentieth centuries, however, were also characterized by a growing intolerance of violence in everyday life.[6] While some historians have argued that this critique of violence did not extend to the domestic sphere,[7] others have shown how the behaviour of working-class or immigrant men did come increasingly under the scrutiny of middle-class feminist reformers and their male counterparts as they renegotiated "the public."[8]

Magistrates in Winnipeg's police court in the selected years (see Table 9) heard 338 domestic violence cases. Few resulted in conviction or a prison sentence. Judges and juries in prairie Canada, however, were more willing than their eastern counterparts to convict and punish men accused of incest or of murdering their wives. Unlike accused wife murderers in Ontario, who were typically Anglo-Canadian and middle-class professionals, defendants on the Prairies were more likely to be rural farm labourers or farmers from eastern Europe.[9] In addition, given the strength of the country-life ideology and utopian visions of rural life, incest and wife murder cases did not result, as they often did in Ontario, in public discourses on rural backwardness.[10] Instead, these cases, like cases of sexual violence that involved agricultural labourers or Aboriginal men (see Chapters 2 and 4), became occasions for judges, jurors, and members of the local community to comment on and contest immigrant and working-class masculinity, femininity, and domestic arrangements. They also reveal how larger contests over power and property – between feminists, farmers, policy makers, and ordinary men and women – played out in daily life and, under certain circumstances, created conditions in which sexual and physical violence was an accepted, if not condoned, feature of family life and life in prairie communities.

POPULAR, LEGAL, AND JUDICIAL ATTITUDES TOWARD WIFE BEATING AND INCEST

In 1894 and 1895, Richard Burton Deane, a North West Mounted Police superintendent stationed at Lethbridge, made frequent reports to his superiors on the criminal courts' treatment of Thomas Elliot, a man widely known throughout the area as a liquor trader and wife beater. On the first occasion, Elliot attacked his wife with a pitchfork and wounded her so severely that she was bedridden for weeks. After pleading guilty to unlawfully wounding his wife and dropping a "penitential tear or two," Elliot received a sentence of three months in prison with hard labour. Upon his release, his wife again accused him of threatening to kill her and nearly choking her to death. Although Mrs. Elliot planned to obtain sureties of the peace, she lost courage at the last moment and asked Deane to let the incident pass. Deane reported that Elliot had been committed for trial, but he believed that the man would likely kill his wife one day because the judge had no power to order a judicial separation. When the case came before Justice Charles B. Rouleau, Elliot was acquitted. Rouleau defended his decision on the grounds that he looked upon the matter as a family quarrel and believed that Elliot had already been punished – he had spent six weeks in the guardroom.[11]

Justice Rouleau's decision reflected popular, legal, and judicial attitudes toward domestic violence in the late nineteenth and early twentieth centuries. Until the mid-nineteenth century, Canadian law reflected the English common law assumption that wives did not require the courts' protection because they were under the guardianship of their husbands. As a *feme covert*, the married woman (and her children) were defined legally as the property of the husband – as were the means of production, land, and wealth in the family economy. Wife abuse was one of the harshest "manifestations of a husband's real or perceived proprietary rights."[12] Battered wives and women whose husbands "wilfully and without lawful excuse" refused to support them, however, could seek redress in the civil courts and claim alimony for their maintenance during marital separation. Perhaps in recognition that the expense of civil actions precluded poor and working-class women from receiving protection, Canadian legislators modified criminal legislation. After 1869, a husband who wilfully and without lawful excuse caused bodily harm or life endangerment by refusing to provide his wife and children with necessities – food, clothing, and shelter – could be charged with a criminal offence that carried a maximum penalty of three years' imprisonment.[13]

The Manitoba legislature likewise tried to alleviate some of the limitations of Canadian law when it passed the Married Women's Protection Act in 1902. The same social concerns that drove the anti-prostitution campaigns shaped the legislation. An increased awareness that Canada's divorce rate was on the rise combined with the growing number of children admitted to the care of Children's Aid Societies to convince reformers and legislators that the state should be employed to coerce husbands to stay at home and accept their responsibilities as breadwinners.[14] Under the provisions of the Manitoba legislation, a deserted wife could have her husband summoned to magistrates' court for a weekly support order, but she had to prove that her husband had wilfully refused or neglected to maintain her. The Manitoba legislation was liberal for its time because the wife could assert desertion even if she herself had separated from her husband. The wife had to prove, however, that her desertion had been provoked by abuse, habitual drunkenness, or non-support. The court could grant custody of the children to the wife, but she would lose both financial support and custody if her husband proved that she had committed one act of adultery, before or after the magistrate issued the court order.[15] Saskatchewan passed similar legislation in 1910.

By the eve of the First World War, prairie women who sought support or protection from abusive or negligent husbands or partners had a few more options. The Criminal Code was amended in 1913 because of lobbying efforts by the Associated Charities of Toronto, which was supported by the National Council of Women, the Brandon Charity Association, the Associated Charities of Winnipeg, and the Moral and Social Reform Council of Canada. Legislators extended the definition of non-support by omitting references to death, danger, or injury, and cohabitation became *prima facie* evidence that the man was married. Similarly, any recognition of children on the part of the father became *prima facie* evidence that the children were legitimate.[16]

Although magistrates and the police were reluctant to intervene in marital relations or cases of domestic discord, they did provide women and children who suffered excessive cruelty with some legal protection. The majority of women in Canada sought redress in the criminal courts for offences that ranged from threats and intimidation to various degrees of assault.[17] Wife battery fell under section 262 of the 1892 Criminal Code, "Assaults Occasioning Actual Bodily Harm," which became section 295 in 1906. Upon conviction, the accused would be liable to a maximum penalty of three years in prison. In 1909, amendments to section 292, "Indecent Assault on Female," made it an indictable offence for a man to "assault and beat his wife or any other female and thereby occasion her actual bodily harm." The judge could add a whipping to the punishment at his own discretion.[18]

Young girls who were abused sexually by their fathers, stepfathers, or godfathers could always charge them with rape, indecent assault, or unlawful carnal knowledge. The 1892 Criminal Code also made available the newly created crime of incest. First introduced in 1890, the law on incest made sexual intercourse or cohabitation between grandparents or parents and children, or between brothers and sisters, a criminal offence if the parties were aware of their consanguinity. If sexual relations occurred under restraint, fear, or duress, however, the courts could not charge or punish the female party to the crime. The legislation made convicted offenders liable to fourteen years in prison and a whipping.[19] In Canada and Great Britain, sexual abuse of children increasingly fell under the rubric of incest at the turn of the century because lawmakers, influenced by social hygiene rhetoric, were primarily concerned with the dangerous effects that in-breeding could have on the moral and physical health of citizens of the nation. A small number of legislators did warn, however, that the legislation, in practice, could unjustly punish and criminalize the victim and asked that young females not be liable for punishment. But familial sexual abuse, as broadly defined, simply was not part of social or legal thinking at the time.[20]

Many of the amendments to Canada's criminal legislation came as a direct result of social reform, temperance, and first-wave feminist critiques of social conditions in Canada. Although second-wave feminists commonly claimed that family violence was not "discovered" until the 1970s, it had been constructed as a social problem by the middle class in most Western nations by the 1870s.[21] In Canada, as in the United States and Britain, popular discussions of wife abuse emerged out of the movement to prevent cruelty to animals, which occurred simultaneously with the temperance, social reform, and feminist movements. In eastern and central Canada, nineteenth-century temperance advocates linked wife battering to alcohol abuse in a causal chain that led directly from urbanization and industrialization to the behaviour of working-class men and working-class leisure. Influenced by the middle-class ideals of separate spheres for men and women, temperance advocates did not explore the individual, social, or psychological causes of alcoholism, nor did they perceive the problem of wife abuse as stemming from anything but alcohol abuse and female victimization.[22] The plight of abused women did enter public discourses in Canada in a more general way, however, when Adelaide Hunter Hoodless founded the Women's Institutes in 1897. The institutes were among the first organizations to acknowledge and attempt to alleviate the poverty, isolation, and loneliness suffered by rural women. In combination with farm women's organizations, the institutes publicly recognized pioneer women's hardships during an era when they went unacknowledged in utopian literature and were overshadowed by the more vocal social reform movement that focused public attention on the dangerous, dissolute city. Margaret Graham, a settler from Ontario, established the first Women's Institute in western Canada in 1909.[23]

Recognition of wife abuse as a social problem in prairie Canada was particularly intense, largely because it was linked in the popular imagination with the region's immigrant problem, which fuelled temperance and feminist arguments for social reform and women's suffrage prior to the First World War. Just as government pamphlets and popular authors such as James S. Woodsworth and Ralph Connor represented unmarried immigrant agricultural labourers as a threat to the sexual morality of farm families, so too did they represent their married counterparts as particularly prone to alcoholism and family violence. In Woodsworth's and Connor's estimation, the immigrant's proclivities made him a frequent visitor to the police courts on charges of wife battery, desertion, and neglect. First-wave feminists and prohibitionists such as Nellie McClung were even more outspoken in their denunciation of this male, working-class, and immigrant vice. In *The Stream Runs Fast,* McClung reflected upon the Woman's Christian Temperance Union's and suffragists' tendency to equate social ills with alcohol abuse: "No one could deny that women and children were the sufferers from the liquor traffic; any fun that came from drinking belonged to men exclusively."[24] McClung argued that she and her companions had honestly believed that women, because they appeared to have more inner strength and positive outlets for their energies than men, would never become drinkers. She admitted that the sight of women lined up before liquor stores came as a blow to the assumptions that underlay her understandings of masculinity and femininity.[25]

First-wave feminists drew attention to the plight of female victims of male, alcohol-induced aggression to enhance their demands for prohibition and female suffrage. By the First World War, however, it was the ethnocentric bias of their arguments that resonated with Anglo-Canadian and Protestant politicians and voters who were now willing, during wartime, to enlist the state to enforce reform measures. Prohibitionists and feminists not only argued that drunken men made poor soldiers, they also asked the question, why should immigrant and foreign men, who tended toward alcohol abuse and wife battery, be eligible to vote when women were not?[26] Prohibitionists identified the liquor traffic with the kaiser, and they depicted him as waging war on married women and children.[27]

With the achievement of prohibition and suffrage legislation during the First World War, discussions of domestic violence receded from public debates in Canada and did not return until the second-wave feminist movement once again broke the silence in the 1970s. Discussions of family violence occasionally surfaced in social welfare circles and in campaigns for the creation of family courts, but the interwar period witnessed a return to forms of masculine humour that reflected misogynist views of women and marriage.[28] However, a number of sensational husband murder trials that took place in prairie Canada during the 1920s resulted in heated public debates about domestic violence and gender inequality in patriarchal societies and the status of farm women (see Chapter 7). The use of criminal records to shed light on domestic violence against women is limiting to the degree that it reveals only the experiences of families who, because of their poverty, could not conceal the realities of domestic violence in their homes. Yet criminal records also provide evidence that working-class, rural, and immigrant women, in their daily lives and actions, used the criminal courts to continue the critique of patriarchal norms well after their plight had ceased to be of public interest.

MAGISTERIAL AND JUDICIAL RESPONSES TO WIFE BATTERING

In 1903, the police charged Theresa Singer of the Red Deer district in Alberta with shooting with the intent to harm Gabriel Saloge, a man who had accompanied her husband when he came to retrieve her following her desertion.[29] Singer's extreme response to her husband's strategy of intimidation reflected rural women's vulnerability to domestic violence, but it was not typical of prairie women's responses in general. Superior court judges occasionally heard cases of domestic violence in their courts, but the details of these cases suggest that many women simply suffered in silence until a family member or neighbour intervened and drew the police and the criminal courts into the dispute-resolution process. In other cases, wives such as Mrs. Elliot would have their husbands summoned to magistrates' court on a regular basis. Criminal records contain many references to recidivists whose predilection for violence eventually resulted in murder or manslaughter convictions. The majority of these cases occurred on isolated farms in rural communities. Although battered women fared poorly in Winnipeg's magistrates' court, the frequency with which urban working-class and immigrant women laid complaints suggests that the police court's geographic accessibility to urban housewives might have caused some men to think twice about using physical coercion to temper wifely insubordination.[30]

The prosecution and treatment of domestic violence and cases of non-maintenance in Winnipeg's Police Court were driven by contradictory impulses: on the one hand, social reform and feminist critiques of working-class culture opened the door to state intervention in the private sphere; on the other, some police and magistrates favoured the preservation of patriarchal households as the building blocks of the liberal economic order. Police court record books for selected years suggest that few women reported cases of domestic violence – or, alternatively, that their complaints did not reach a receptive audience – until the social reform and feminist

TABLE 9   Domestic abuse and neglect cases, Winnipeg Police Court

	1886	1894	1902	1910	1918*	1926*	1934*
Wife battering	5	–	1	37	15	28	48
Assault of female	1	1	–	55	3	6	17
Non-support	1	–	–	3	17	40	60
Total (338)	7	1	1	95	35	74	125

* Figures for 1918, 1926, and 1934 include only the returns from alternate months – numbers would have been at least doubled for all categories in these years.
SOURCES: City of Winnipeg Police Court, Record Books, 1886-1916, GR 651, M-1210-20; and 1917-1940, GR 513, PAM.

movements gathered steam in the immediate pre-war period (see Table 9). Winnipeg's burgeoning population, and the emergence of the city's North End as an immigrant and working-class enclave, also led to a dramatic increase in the number of complaints made by poor and working-class women in the eight-year interval between 1902 and 1910. Between 1909 and 1910, the Winnipeg Police Force increased in number from approximately one hundred to three hundred officers. More officers on the ground enhanced the force's ability to regulate labour unrest, ethnic tensions, and prostitution- and alcohol-related offences, but it also made individual police officers and the magistrates' court more accessible to women. In 1908, for instance, the city constructed a new police station on the corner of Magnus Avenue and Charles Street, which was in the heart of the North End.[31]

Record books also show that magistrates took women's complaints less seriously over time (see Table 10). Although magistrates convicted a significant majority of the men accused of neglect or assault on a woman or wife in 1910, by 1934 they committed and sentenced only a small minority: the majority of complaints ended in withdrawn charges or dismissals.[32] Although women increasingly took advantage (particularly during the Depression) of the Manitoba Women's Protection Act and amendments to the Criminal Code as strategies to evade abusive husbands and support their children, fewer than ten were awarded maintenance payments by the court. Although legislators had amended the criminal law to protect working-class women from domestic violence, women who charged their husbands with assault or non-support – regardless of whether their cases were successful – learned that criminal prosecutions came with their own hidden costs and punishments. In cases that resulted in withdrawn or dismissed charges, for instance, the magistrate often required the husband

TABLE 10   Prosecution and sentencing patterns, domestic violence, Winnipeg
Police Court

	1886	1894	1902	1910	1918[1]	1926[1]	1934[1]
DS/NCP/WD[2]	2	–	–	29	17	45	92
Acquitted	–	–	–	1	–	–	–
Convicted	5	1	1	65	18	29	33
Fine/support	3	–	–	24	9	8	13
BKP[3]	1	–	–	19	7	8	16
Jailed	1	1	–	14	2	6	1
Suspended	–	–	1	3	–	3	1
Reprimand	–	–	–	5	–	4	2
Total (338)	7	1	1	95	35	74	125

1 Figures for 1918, 1926, and 1934 include only the returns from alternate months – numbers
  would have been at least doubled for all categories in these years.
2 Dismissed, no charge preferred, or charge withdrawn.
3 Bound over to keep the peace.
SOURCES: City of Winnipeg Police Court, Record Books, 1886-1916, GR 651, M-1210-20; and
1917-1940, GR 513, PAM.

to pay for the costs of the court. And in the majority of cases in which
husbands either pleaded or were found guilty, the magistrate made the
accused pay minimal fines or released him on peace bonds. The latter
practice required the husband to put up collateral and sign a bond agreeing
that in future he would report to the police, support his wife and children,
and practise temperance. In both cases, the working-class woman, often
dependent on her husband's wages, lost valuable household income and
achieved little beyond aggravating her husband.

   Cases that appeared in the superior courts reveal that husbands who
chronically beat their wives also had little to fear from juries or judges. In
1915, for instance, a concerned neighbour reported a case of wife beating
in Winnipeg's North End. The arresting officer deposed at the preliminary
hearing that the accused, S. Goddelin, had responded to the charge with
the comment: "That is nothing, she has had me arrested about ten times
now, she comes the next day and takes me out, I don't care." A jury in the
Court of King's Bench found Goddelin guilty, but the judge served him
only with a suspended sentence and a $100 fine.[33]

   As was the case in Ontario in the same period, judges and magistrates
in the interwar decades preferred, if not prided themselves on, preserving

the privacy and the economic stability of the family by promoting informal dispute resolution that would preserve the breadwinner's earning potential.[34] But magistrates also accepted the patriarch's prerogative to physically discipline his wife. In the Winnipeg Police Court, the majority of men who served prison sentences between 1886 and 1934 for crimes committed against a female were not convicted on charges of wife beating or non-support; rather, they served time for assaulting women who were not members of their families. In 1910, for example, the magistrate convicted and jailed fourteen men for assaulting women. The ten men who assaulted women who were not their wives were convicted and sentenced to serve six months in the Eastern Judicial District Gaol. By contrast, magistrates tended to jail only those husbands who appeared frequently in their court. Fred Stone, for instance, appeared in the Winnipeg Police Court three times in 1910, pleaded guilty to all charges, and paid $22.25 in fines in the first instance, paid $5.00 and provided sureties to keep the peace in the second, and served a sentence of two months in prison with hard labour in the third.[35]

"If I Ever Touched Her Again She Would Not Tell of It": Wife Murder

Winnipeg Police Court records reveal little about the domestic conflicts or circumstances that led women and their husbands to the criminal courts. The depositions from victims of, and witnesses to, the forty-one cases of wife battery and twenty-two cases of wife murder that came before the superior courts in the selected districts include telling moments and utterances that show how precipitating incidents that resulted in violence often had deep roots in larger contestations for power between husbands and wives and between duelling forms of masculinity. In 1888, for instance, William Webb, an English immigrant and laundry owner who lived in Brandon, Manitoba, confessed to shooting and killing his wife, Mary Jane, under circumstances of extreme provocation: his wife, he declared, had been a scold and a nag. Nearly five years earlier, the police had arrested Webb for assaulting his wife. Webb spent one night in jail and claimed that he thereafter suffered his wife's taunts about the incident on a regular basis. In what was to become a self-fulfilling prophecy, Webb admitted to the police that he had once told his wife that "if I ever touched her again she would not tell of it." Webb was hanged for murder on 28 December 1888.[36]

Webb's case file, like those from all murder cases that resulted in conviction, was sent to Ottawa, where the governor general in council decided whether to extend or withhold the prerogative of mercy. Although routine legal documents rarely give a voice to battered women or the men who abused them, the legal process in capital cases afforded the husband the opportunity – often with the assistance of expert witnesses, such as psychiatrists – to tell his side of the story, which circulated throughout communities during clemency campaigns and in newspapers. Women's experiences and responses to abuse, by contrast, can be known only to the extent that their children, friends, family, and neighbours revealed them in depositions and trial testimonies. Although the legal record is biased in this respect, capital case files and superior court records reveal both the causes of and communal attitudes toward domestic violence that suggest the outer limits to which families, communities, and the judiciary would go to preserve the privacy of the patriarchal family. When juries and the public deliberated on or debated cases of spousal murder, they often confused the social category of character with the legal category of provocation.[37] Their response to individual cases, therefore, can be read as an indirect answer to a question that, if asked directly, most prairie dwellers would have likely answered with the response "never." When, and under what circumstances, was battery or murder justifiable?

Spousal murder trials contain countless hidden transcripts of women's resistance to abusive husbands and to laws and practices that protected their husband's interests. Ironically, juries' and the public's sympathy for the plight of these women often depended on whether their behaviour and appearance conformed to hegemonic notions of femininity. However, although a wife's failure to fulfil her domestic or sexual responsibilities could render her culpable in her own murder, a husband's failure to measure up to the masculine ideal influenced his ability to garner the sympathy of judges and juries, which, in turn, influenced whether the prerogative of mercy would be extended in his case. Capital case files reveal judges, juries, and prairie communities actively enforcing, contesting, or negotiating gender roles and domestic relations in a moral and political atmosphere that protected the privacy of the family but increasingly frowned upon public manifestations of violence in everyday life.[38]

Perhaps reflecting the isolation of rural life on the Prairies, and the limitations of law enforcement in agricultural communities, the majority of cases in which domestic violence resulted in murder occurred on isolated homesteads and farms. Of the twenty-two husbands who were convicted of murder during the period, only five lived and worked in urban centres. The remainder either rented or owned farmland.[39] In a number of these cases, contested property rights and the hardships associated with home-steading and farming fuelled disputes that escalated into murder. Spousal murder trials, as historian Martin Wiener has observed, can be approached as the working-class, or plebeian, counterpart to the better-known political contest over women's rights and feminism.[40] In 1909, for instance, a jury convicted, and the government hanged, Herycko Zbyhley, a Ukrainian farmer from Mundare, Alberta, for murder. Zbyhley pleaded guilty to the charge after disclosing to the police that he had chopped his wife to pieces with an axe. During the trial, which was held on 19 and 20 October 1909 before Justice Arthur L. Sifton and a six-man jury, it became clear that Zbyhley's animus toward his wife had been fuelled by her demand for half of the proceeds from the sale of the family homestead. The jury learned that Zbyhley's wife had deserted him in September. When she arrived at her son's farm, she had only a trunk and $300 in her possession. Zbyhley quickly tracked down his wife and accused her of theft. Anna Zbyhley – the papers described her as larger and stronger than her husband, who was "a little, bent old man of sixty-one years" – calmly told her husband to sue her in court for the money.[41]

Five years later, disputes over labour, land, and sexual power likewise contributed to conflicts that resulted in John Ireland's being convicted and hanged for murder in Noseby, Saskatchewan. Ireland, a forty-year-old American farmer who journalists described as a partial invalid, had threatened to kill his wife, Jesse, when he grew suspicious of her relation-ship with the family's hired hand. During the trial, which was held on 21 October 1914 in the Supreme Court of Saskatchewan before Justice Lamont, Margaret Clay, the victim's sister, testified that she had witnessed a number of disputes and beatings while she stayed with the couple in April and May of 1914. On one occasion, Clay's son ran and told her that Ireland had beaten his wife. When Clay arrived at the scene, she found Jesse crying and hiding from her husband in the tool shed. After Ireland accused his wife of having inappropriate sexual relations with Willie Smith, the hired hand, he tried to evict her from his property. Jesse, however, refused to leave on the grounds that her money and labour had contributed to both the house and the farm. Ireland pulled his wife's hair and tried to choke her. According to Ireland, Clay's willingness to meddle in his marriage and other troubles reached a point where he overheard his wife exclaim, "It is easier to be a sport[ing woman] than to be on the prairie." When Clay tried to help Jesse leave her husband, Ireland tried to evict Clay from his property. On the evening of 24 May, after writing a letter to Clay's husband in which he declared that his sister-in-law's influence over his wife had driven him to extreme measures, Ireland shot his wife in the back of the head while she was doing the dishes.[42] John Ireland, an American who was likely familiar with his country's unwritten law regarding adultery and justifiable violence (see Chapter 7), clearly believed that the behaviour of his wife and sister-in-law was justifiable grounds for murder.

Other convicted wife murderers excused their actions and petitioned for clemency on the grounds that their domestic problems had emerged out of the hardships and frustrations they experienced farming in the Canadian West. During the Depression, legal and political authorities were particularly predisposed to sympathize with these arguments. In 1934, for instance, Harvey Clare, a government-appointed alienist (a psychiatrist who specialized in legal aspects of mental illness), recommended that the government extend the prerogative of mercy in the case of Arthur Karl Poets, a Belgian immigrant who had locked his wife, her in-laws, and his children in their Saskatchewan farmhouse before he set it on fire. When his wife and family managed to escape, Poets axed his wife to death while she held their child in her arms. The couple, Clare argued, had a history of domestic violence because they lived in the driest part of southern Saskatchewan, had had two babies in swift succession, and had crops that had failed completely for four or five years in a row. Poets, too proud to apply for relief, had supported his family by trade and barter, which often took him away from the homestead for significant stretches of time. During one absence, Poets' mother-in-law and brothers-in-law convinced his wife to come live with them at their farm. Clare concluded that economic hardship, combined with Florence's interfering relatives, had caused Poets to doubt his wife's fidelity. Echoing Clare's assessment of the case, the entire population of the Manor District, including women, petitioned the governor general on Poets' behalf. On 1 March 1935, the governor general, by Order-in-Council, commuted Poets' sentence to life imprisonment.[43]

Although many convicted murderers attempted to justify their actions as the result of economic hardship and their wife's dissatisfaction with the unequal distribution of power in their marriage, defendants in at least six murder and three wife battery cases also put forward, much as Poets did, their wife's alleged unfaithfulness as a motivating factor in the commission of their crime.[44] In 1915, for instance, Marius Paulsen, a Norwegian car-penter and soldier who lived in Eunice, Alberta, shot his wife, Wilhelmina, because he believed she had given birth to another man's child. A headline in the *Edmonton Journal* declared, "Jealousy, that green-eyed monster ...

is again the cause of another domestic tragedy."[45] When the Supreme Court of Alberta tried the case on 21 and 22 January 1916, Justice Horace Harvey warned the jury that a woman's adultery was no excuse for murder. Although the jury convicted the accused, the clemency campaign on Paulsen's behalf met with success: Paulsen served only nine years of his life sentence. The willingness of government officials, legal authorities, and prairie communities to take wifely infidelity into account when they considered the issue of provocation in wife murder cases reflected the degree to which notions of female sexuality as a commodity that belonged to the husband permeated society. When played out in the media and during clemency campaigns, the drama of a husband's jealous rage brought on by his wife's alleged unfaithfulness tended also to obscure the systemic causes of domestic violence.

In many cases, domestic violence escalated to murder when husbands became angry after their wives stepped out of their prescribed role as submissive and dependent helpmates. On the evening of 23 February 1902, for instance, Usup Saloman, a Ukrainian farmer from Stuartburn, Manitoba, beat his wife to death with a trawl during a domestic disagreement. The Manitoba Court of King's Bench tried the case, and the jury convicted the accused, but the government reduced the death sentence to life imprisonment following a successful clemency campaign mounted by farmers and farm labourers within the Ukrainian community. In a plea for remission dated 15 January 1915, Saloman – much like Aboriginal defendants – tried to harness the cultural defence in his favour by arguing that in Ukraine it had been a husband's right to beat his wife when she was disobedient: "When we came to Canada we lived happily for a long time all our neighbours were Austrians, a white woman came who spoke our language she told my wife about freedom of women in Canada and got her to rebel against me, my wife began to leave home and stay away nights; then she began to stay away for a week or more at a time. I punished her for this badness." Saloman then described the night of the murder: "I went to bed my wife began quarrelling. She said, 'If a wore [sic] came in the room you would not be too tired ... You brought your niece and her husband out here so you could use her as a wore.' I got out of bed and beat her, I was so angry I beat her too hard and killed her ... Had I known the law of the country as I now know it I would have taken her to magistrate or divorced her."[46]

Saloman's defence attorney, Ross Sutherland, informed the secretary of state that Frances Saloman had been a woman of "vile temper and bad tongue." Even worse, he continued, she was lazy, indolent, and showed little interest in her home or children: her husband was required to do the "washing, baking, general house work and caring for the children."[47] In other words, the woman had stripped her husband of his masculinity. Saloman's frequent pleas for remission on the grounds that Frances Saloman had been a poor wife and mother, the motherless state of his children who were in a Winnipeg orphanage, and the fact that Saloman had already spent thirteen years in penitentiary contributed to his release on probation in 1915. He was granted a ticket-of-leave three years later.

Usup Saloman's pleas for sympathy and mercy manipulated representations of first-generation Ukrainian women as primitive barriers to the advancement of the nation-building project. The early years of settlement were particularly hard for these women, who suffered from isolation, limited access to services, and the language barrier. Pioneer conditions not only preserved but also enhanced women's traditional role within the socio-economic unit of the Ukrainian family, forcing them to perform heavier work and spend more time in the fields than they had in Ukraine. The Church Women's Missionary Society of the Methodist Church drew attention to the plight of Ukrainian women when it opened its first mission in the bloc settlements of eastern Alberta in 1904. Religious, ethnic, and gender biases, however, underscored its mission to Christianize and civilize the Ukrainian population by converting women and girls – segments of the population it deemed particularly "irreligious, corrupted, corruptible, intemperate, and unhygienic."[48]

Frances Saloman's refusal to fulfil her domestic duties as wife and mother resulted in domestic conflict, frequent beatings, and, ultimately, her death. Her circumstances bore similarities to eight other murder and five other wife battery cases in which women resisted abuse and defied societal expectations by leaving their husbands on an informal basis or through the more formal means of judicial separation. In 1935, for instance, the Supreme Court tried, convicted, and hanged William Hawryliuk, a Ukrainian farmer of Youngstown, Alberta, for wife murder. Hawryliuk had beaten his wife to death with hoof trimmers and tried to set her on fire with gasoline. During the trial and clemency campaign, the defence and Hawryliuk's supporters argued that the accused had suffered undue provocation because his wife had left him repeatedly, sometimes taking the children with her, for up to four months at a time. During the trial, however, the prosecution produced evidence showing that Hawryliuk had, since 1929, been convicted in magistrates' court five times for wife battering, neglect, and theft.[49]

Other women resisted domestic and sexual violence by verbally defying their husband's authority and, in extreme situations, turning to the courts for help. In 1929, Mary Bodz, a farm wife from Pine River, Manitoba, laid charges of incest against her husband and disclosed that he had fathered her daughter's child. Although Bodz pleaded guilty to the incest charge, he argued before the Manitoba Court of King's Bench in Dauphin that his wife had laid the complaint as retribution for the fact that she had not wanted to emigrate from Ukraine. He believed that she planned to sell the farm and return to her homeland.[50] Although Justice Bonnycastle sentenced Bodz to serve five years in prison, remissions officers released him on a ticket-of-leave in June 1931. When Bodz returned to the family farm, his wife told him to go to hell and locked him out of the house. Bodz slept in the barn for the duration of his wife's life. On the evening of the murder, 26 July 1931, Bodz asked his wife where she had been during the day and why she had not cooked supper. She replied by lifting her skirts and telling him to "kiss her ass." Bodz told the police that he beat his wife to death for her defiance.[51]

Bodz was tried and convicted before Justice J.E. Adamson and a jury in the Manitoba Court of King's Bench. The clemency campaign on behalf of the accused was almost non-existent, and Bodz met his death on the scaffold on 3 February 1932. Justice Adamson's charge to the jury, along with his trial summary to the secretary of state, played a determining role in the decision. In his charge, Adamson concluded, "It would be too thin a thing indeed when a man does his wife to death, to step into a box and say, she made me angry." In the trial summary, Adamson expressed the opinion that Bodz had committed murder in revenge against his wife for her role in the incest prosecution. He likewise discounted Bodz's plea of drunkenness as "simply grasping at a straw."[52] Adamson's understanding of the case, however, diverged from that of local law enforcement officials. Sergeant G.A. Renton of the Manitoba Provincial Police believed that Bodz's actions could be justified because the man's wife had failed to "do as much as she could have to enable her husband to make good." She had, he continued, withheld her domestic and sexual services from her husband: "Had [she] been just a little forbearing, he would not be in the present dilemma."[53]

Evidence of a wife's refusal to submit to her husband clearly served as a matter for grave consideration when individuals deliberated on the issue of motivation in cases of wife battery and murder, and the victim's character played a significant role in determining whether her husband's death sentence would be commuted. The governor general in council chose to commute the death sentence to life imprisonment in seven of the twenty-two wife murder cases. The wife's character, when measured against hegemonic notions of prairie femininity, played a role, but so too did the husband's standing in the community. Saloman's defence attorney informed the minister of justice that "the general consensus among the best citizens is in favour of the sentence of death being commuted ... as they feel that the poor unfortunate wretch was goaded on until human nature could stand it no longer and the belief is that in punishing his wife he had no intention of inflicting such serious blows."[54] With the exception of Bodz, men who beat their wives to death were granted the prerogative of mercy by the Canadian government. While there was a strictly legal justification for these decisions – namely, that the Crown had difficulty establishing premeditation because the murder was committed in the heat of the moment – the commutations also reflected the legal authorities' acceptance of wife battering, particularly if the victim failed to conform to middle-class conceptions of proper womanhood. The executive chose to hang William Hawryliuk for murder even though Justice Thomas Mitchell Tweedie advised them that Hawryliuk was a "highly provoked man" because his wife had left him on numerous occasions. Tweedie chose to overlook the fact that Hawryliuk had repeatedly answered to charges of wife battering, theft, and verbal abuse in magistrates' court.[55]

The preponderance of men who beat their wives to death among those granted clemency reveals that the defendant's choice of weapon could and did influence his treatment and reception in the courtroom and the wider court of public opinion. This was particularly true in cases in which the details of the murder proved to be an affront to the judge's notions of masculinity. In 1917, for instance, a farmer from Schuler, Alberta, named Adam Neigel was charged with murder. Neigel had fallen in love with his neighbour's wife and then proceeded to poison his own. His trial proved to be one of the lengthier and more sensational cases of wife murder in the settlement period. In both his charge to the jury and during sentencing, Justice James Duncan Hyndman commented that murder by poisoning was "one of the most fiendish and devilish" ways to take another's life because "it differs from murder by outward violence when the murdered person has a chance to defend himself."[56] Poisoning by murder also differed from more outward forms of violence because contemporaries viewed it as the female crime par excellence.[57] It appears that Hyndman not only overlooked the victim's sex but also suggested that murder was more acceptable if undertaken with gentlemanly dispatch. Neigel was hanged on 22 March 1918.

An accused's failure to meet middle-class standards of masculinity could influence the judge and jury in a number of subtle ways. In nine of the cases in which the death penalty took effect, the judge and public alike questioned the accused's ability to control his wife and fulfil his obligations as husband. Judges took a dim view of men who engaged in adultery. In Neigel's case, Justice Hyndman reminded the jury of the sacredness of the marital bond, and he advised the men to consider the accused's adultery as direct evidence of his guilt.[58] In other cases, Crown counsels would make a point of portraying the accused as weak-willed, henpecked men who could control their wives only by killing them. In *Zbyhley*, a neighbour testified for the defence that the accused had sliced off his penis and one testicle with a razor after axing his wife to death. Although the defence introduced Zbyhley's self-inflicted violence as *prima facie* evidence of the accused's insanity, Justice Arthur L. Sifton informed the minister of justice in a memorandum that the incident was more likely the result of "a deep despondency."[59] Sifton's interpretation of Zbyhley's behaviour meshed well with media characterizations of the accused as a pathetic little man.

The defendant's racial or ethnic background also influenced his reception in Canadian courts. Immigrants from eastern Europe, particularly Ukraine, accounted for 50 percent of the wife murder cases studied. Even though immigrants of Ukrainian origin made up an increasing percentage of the western Canadian population – by the First World War they had moved from eighth to fourth place among ethnic-origin categories – they were still highly overrepresented in wife murder and other cases.[60] Alternatively, Anglo-Canadian men were under-represented, standing as the accused in only three of the cases studied. Evidence suggests that juries tended to find Anglo-Canadian men, such as Phillip Hart – a rancher from Burmis, Alberta, who shot his wife in 1915 – guilty of manslaughter. Hart had a number of witnesses who testified that he was a fine, upstanding citizen "except when he was mad at his wife." He was sentenced to three years in the Alberta Penitentiary.[61]

By contrast, neither Anglo-Canadian judges nor juries were predisposed to treat eastern European defendants with any degree of sympathy. Only two of the twelve eastern European defendants had their sentences commuted to life imprisonment: ethnic stereotypes often served in place of real character evidence or considerations of motivation in many of the cases. In Zbyhley's case, newspaper accounts of the trial and the testimony of expert witnesses emphasized his Ukrainian heritage as evidence of his low moral character.[62] In Neigel's case, which took place at the height of mented

the First World War near Schuler, Alberta, Justice Hyndman asked the jury to consider what he felt was the low state of morality in the German-Russian community. In his petition to the minister of justice on Neigel's behalf, the Reverend P.F. Beaton tried to engage the sympathy of government officials by noting that the German-Russians at Schuler had moved to Canada four or five years earlier after failing to prove up in the American West. He added that "they had now passed through the pioneer hardship and poverty period of the prairie homesteader twice."[63] Beaton also advised the minister of justice that ethnocentrism had prejudiced the presentation of the accused's case before the jury. Beaton had been bothered in particular by Justice Hyndman's charge: "The fact of his [Neigel's] being a German was enough to prejudice, at least to a degree, the general run of British Alberta juries at this time of Anti-German feeling."[64]

A CRIME WITHOUT A NAME:
"INCEST" – THE SEXUAL ABUSE OF FEMALE CHILDREN

The perceived low state of morality in eastern European farming communities was a central consideration in the incest cases that came to the attention of legal authorities and the courts. Although the sexual abuse of children fell outside of popular and legal understandings of family violence in the late nineteenth and early twentieth centuries, criminal courts dealt with instances of it on a regular basis under the rubric of incest. The treatment of these cases in prairie communities may have been unique in this respect. Between 1890 and 1929, for instance, prosecutors deemed only twenty-five incest charges as serious or contentious enough to come before the criminal assize of Peterborough County, Ontario: a mere five resulted in convictions.[65] In roughly the same period, eight men in York County, Ontario, were indicted for incestuous rape: six were convicted.[66] And in British Columbia, the assize courts dealt with thirty-two incest cases between 1885 and 1940.[67] By contrast, in the five selected prairie districts, the superior or district or county courts heard seventy-one incest cases. Forty-two of them resulted in guilty verdicts, with the accused serving from a minimum of one to a maximum of ten years in prison with hard labour and a whipping.[68] The diversity and rural nature of the prairie population may explain the courts' response. Conviction rates, for instance, tended to be higher in Ontario's rural communities. On the one hand, the prosecution in Ontario could successfully exploit stereotypes of rural depravity and backwardness in the complainant's favour; on the other, magistrates and JPs in rural areas were more likely to know the accused and the complainant and their general reputations in the community. In contrast (and not surprisingly, given the nature of British Columbia's economy and demographic realities), two-thirds of the cases that came before the courts in British Columbia involved complainants and victims who lived in urban areas. The outcome of the cases, however, reflected the entrenched belief that incest was the monopoly of the poor and minorities.[69] Given the strength of the country-life ideology in prairie communities, incest was not associated with rural depravity and backwardness per se but rather with the low state of morality in rural immigrant and working-class families.

Yet evidentiary requirements and the sexual double standard largely determined whether the justice of the peace would take the female complainant's accusations seriously. As was the case in the prosecution of wife murder and beating, the same biases that operated in sex crime trials influenced the courts' treatment of girls who laid charges of incest against their fathers. In the minority of cases that resulted in dismissals or not-guilty verdicts, the daughter's unchaste state, reputation for lying, and age were adduced as evidence of consent, as was the family's – particularly the mother's – unwillingness to corroborate her daughter's story.[70] If the complainant was over the age of sixteen, the defence also tended to malign her sexual reputation. In 1903, for instance, Thomas Breen's wife accused him of impregnating their eighteen-year-old daughter and then causing her to miscarry by working her too hard on the farm. Although a younger sister corroborated the complainant's accusation of sexual abuse, a neighbour deposed that the daughter's reputation for chastity was good but that her reputation for telling the truth was bad. A physician testified that sexual intercourse had occurred but that it had been consensual.[71]

Medical testimony as to the daughter's chaste state could, conversely, be used by the defence as evidence that incest had not occurred. In these cases, which resulted in dismissal, it became apparent that the incest provisions in criminal legislation did little to protect girls who suffered sexual abuse that did not extend to penetration. In 1905, a jury in the Manitoba Court of King's Bench acquitted Cornelius Hebert of Winnipeg on the grounds that his wife had denied her stepdaughter's accusations and that the prosecution had provided no direct evidence that sexual intercourse had occurred. Medical testimony had in fact revealed that the daughter remained a virgin. The complainant, however, had simply told her employer that her father often touched her improperly.[72] The emphasis that members

of the jury and judges placed on the mother's testimony can also be interpreted as an unwillingness to take into consideration women's and children's
economic dependence. In 1910, for instance, Mary Barret withdrew charges
against her husband because, she claimed, she had been jealous of the
attention her husband paid her daughter and had mistakenly laid an information against him. Carl Hanson, a neighbour who reported the case,
deposed that Mrs. Barret had told him that she would not lay an information because she feared the punishment and its consequences for her family
would far outweigh the severity of the crime.[73]

   In contrast to cases that resulted in dismissals, acquittals, or withdrawn
charges, cases that resulted in conviction often involved daughters who
could be represented either as the passive victims of their parents' domestic
conflicts or as the victims of their bachelor father's uncontrollable lust.
Unexplained pregnancies, community disapproval, and family testimony
held the most weight with judges and juries, as did the defendant's social
and economic status.[74] In 1918, for instance, Justice Newlands of the
Saskatchewan Court of King's Bench sentenced William Smith, an American farmer from Dilke, to three years in Prince Albert Penitentiary. At
the trial, his daughter, age twelve, testified that her mother had died,
leaving the children alone with their father in a three-bedroom house. As
was the case with many of the sexual abuse victims who were believed by
the courts, the daughter gained the sympathy of the court when she hesitated to tell specifically what had happened to her.[75]

   In certain cases, the victim's refusal to be interrogated could be extreme,
and this resistance to court proceedings stands as testimony to the degree
to which women's identities were bound to prescriptions of female chastity,
not to mention the moral force that public shame could hold over their
lives. Complainants' resistance to legal intrusions in their lives also illustrates the intimate connections that existed between the privacy and
presumed moral sanctity of the family and its capacity for sexual abuse:
female children had to reconcile the demands of being chaste with the
imperative to obey one's father.[76] In 1916, for instance, Annie Spence refused
to testify or take an oath at her father's preliminary hearing in Winnipeg's
Police Court. The magistrate committed her to a detention centre until
she cooperated. Spence, however, refused to testify until the magistrate
agreed to clear the court of spectators.

   Spence's case had come to the authorities' attention via a complaint
made by Agnes Johnson, the accused's former sister-in-law. Johnson deposed that Spence, along with Annie, his daughter by his first marriage,

had come to stay with her while his wife was in hospital. She thought it odd that Spence refused to sleep without his daughter and, upon investigation, learned that the girl was pregnant. In cross-examination, Annie told the court that, had Johnson not coerced her, she would never have accused her father of wrongdoing. On further prompting, Annie admitted that she still cared for her father because he gave her everything she wanted.[77] Spence pleaded guilty to the charge, and the judge sentenced him to five years in a federal penitentiary with twenty lashes.

In other cases, one daughter's courage to make a formal complaint against her father would be backed by the mother and corroborating testimony from her sisters. In 1913, for instance, a jury in the Supreme Court of Alberta found Stewart Spencer, an American farmer from Kitscobey, guilty of incest, and the judge sentenced him to two years in prison. The daughter initiated the case when she walked to town from the family farm and made a formal complaint to a friend of the family. The daughter deposed that the sexual abuse had gone on for years, despite the fact that her mother did her best to protect her. The abuse escalated, however, when her mother went to live with her sister during the latter's confinement. At the trial, both the mother and an older sister, also the victim of sexual abuse, testified on the complainant's behalf.[78] In a 1928 case against Henry Holtz, which occurred in New Sarepta, Alberta, the mother herself made the initial complaint. Married for seventeen years and the mother of nine children, Holtz deposed at the preliminary hearing that she had often left her daughter alone with her husband following arguments that resulted in her husband beating her. She claimed that she would have made a complaint sooner, but her husband's physical abuse kept her and the children in a constant state of fear. Holtz added that she only made it to town once a year. A jury at the Supreme Court convicted Henry Holtz of both indecent assault and incest. The judge sentenced him to one year in prison on both counts.[79]

Although many women and children defied expectation and laid complaints of incest against husbands or fathers, their experiences never resulted in a public debate on incest or the sexual abuse of children in prairie Canada. Neither Holtz's nor any of the cases studied received media attention because parties to the cases, officers of the court, and journalists accepted the prevailing liberal notion that the family was private and knowledge of incest should be confined to that sphere.[80] One exception, however, reveals the extreme measures that some families were willing to take to disguise sexual abuse in the home. The case also highlights the class- and race-based stereotypes that governed popular perceptions of the crime. In March 1922, police charged William Frederick Grover, an English farmer, of murdering his daughter's child (allegedly Grover's) in Brandon, Manitoba. A jury in the Manitoba Court of King's Bench found Grover guilty of murder, and the judge sentenced him to hang. During the trial, the prosecution produced evidence that the child was Grover's and that, to hide evidence of his daughter's sexual abuse, Grover and his wife had arranged to have the pregnancy aborted. When a physician refused to perform the procedure, however, Grover had his daughter, Ada, placed in the Brandon Maternity Home. Ada testified that her parents had arranged to give the child to a family in Neepawa. The Grovers picked up the child from the maternity home on 4 January 1922, and the body of the child, which had been suffocated to death, was found the next day beneath boxes and crates at the CPR railway station.[81]

The clemency campaign on Grover's behalf unveiled communal fears and anxieties that shaped the treatment of other incest cases that came before the courts. Many petitioners asked the minister of justice to exercise the prerogative of mercy on account of Grover's age and status as a father: he was a sixty-eight-year-old man with twelve children. By contrast, Grover's defence attorney echoed the legal authorities' attitudes toward the 1907 *Gowland* case when he argued that his client's sentence should be commuted because he was mentally and morally defective. The only evidence that the attorney had for this claim was that Grover had arrived in Canada as a Barnardo boy. Of the eight Grover children that were still living, he continued, three of them, including Ada, were "morons": "While the accused is responsible in a criminal sense, yet the real responsibility is I believe to be traced back to unjust social conditions producing the slums of London, England, where Grover was born and passed his early life."[82] M.F. Gallagher, writing on behalf of the deputy minister of justice, agreed, but he felt that "it would be unusual to hang a man of his age, unless the circumstances of the case were exceptionally revolting." Gallagher believed that Grover's motive was not sordid; he had "acted to save his family from dishonour."[83] The governor general reduced Grover's sentence to life imprisonment at Stony Mountain Penitentiary.

As was the case in other Canadian regions and settler societies, legal and political authorities adhered to a narrow definition of incest that limited it to cases of sexual violence that threatened to produce children of blood relations. The legal establishment's and the public's perception of incest cases perpetrated by men such as Grover was coloured by contemporary eugenics theory and postwar jitters about race suicide.[84] These fears help to explain why a daughter's pregnancy often carried more evidentiary weight than her testimony in incest cases, even when it was impossible to determine the identity of the child's father. Sensational trials, such as Grover's, also obscured the realities of sexual abuse in prairie communities by enhancing popular stereotypes that associated sexual deviancy with the urban and immigrant working class. The criminal record shows that sexual abuse of female children remained a common, if unacknowledged, problem in urban and rural, working-class and middle-class, eastern European and Anglo-Canadian households. Justices of the peace, judges, and juries took girls' complaints of sexual abuse by their fathers seriously, but for the wrong reasons.

Conclusion

On 13 June 1929, Constable Willmott Maddison of the Alberta Provincial Police was called to investigate an attempted suicide on the Russell farm near Blairmore. Rose Russell, the accused, had tried to kill herself by swallowing Lysol. Russell told Maddison that she had left her husband on three different occasions because he had beaten her. The next time it happened, she promised, she would "do him up and not myself." Maddison's report acknowledged that the Russells had been in the APP office on previous occasions, but that little could be done since Russell refused to lay charges against her husband. In this instance, the husband had beaten his wife because she had beaten their daughters. Rose Russell wanted to know if "there be such a thing as getting a separation from my husband, keeping the children, and having him support them." Rose told the police that she had married her husband at sixteen and had had four children by the time she was twenty-three. Her husband, who made $5.50 a day, gave her no allowance for herself or her children. Justice William Carlos Ives, upon hearing Russell's testimony, discharged the accused.[85]

Acts of sexual and physical violence such as Russell's and Grover's show that, for many women and girls, the prairie West was not a land of freedom or opportunity. The contests for power and property between husbands and wives that were recorded in depositions and trial testimonies reveal the dark side of a settlement process framed by the desire to create a new society based on the liberal economic order and a reinvigorated masculinity. The temperance and prohibition movements raised some public awareness of wife beating as an unacceptable practice and a social ill. Yet these movements did very little to alleviate the condition of beaten or battered wives in rural areas, women whose suffering was increased by isolation, ignorance of the law, fear, and their economic dependence on their husbands. Combinations of these circumstances made farm women and their daughters hesitant to seek out the protection of the police or the courts. Although contemporary socialist feminists commonly argue that the emergence of the urban-industrial household increased women's economic dependence on – and vulnerability to abuse by – men, the criminal records from four levels of criminal courts on the Prairies do not support this supposition.[86] Instances of wife beating in rural areas were severe and chronic, and they could result in the death of the wife or, at the other extreme, in the wife's attempted suicide. Moreover, this evidence of rural domestic violence is likely no more than the tip of the iceberg.[87]

By contrast, the records of the Winnipeg Police Court suggest that even though magistrates tended to condone wife beating and acted in what they felt was the best interest of the family, the accessibility of police courts, combined with criminal law amendments, gave urban working-class women recourse to the criminal courts, which they frequently and increasingly used. Contrary to middle-class discourses on alcoholism and domestic violence, women and girls who suffered physical and sexual abuse at the hands of their husbands and fathers in urban and rural areas were much more than passive victims. Criminal records contain evidence of women's everyday resistance to and defiance of a legal system that failed to acknowledge their contributions to farm life by providing them with equal access to and ownership of homestead property. Wife murder cases provide glimpses of women who resisted their husband's abuse – and dominant ideologies of female domesticity – by refusing to perform their household tasks, by fighting back physically and verbally, and by simply leaving their husbands on a permanent or temporary basis. Daughters and mothers also used the incest provisions of the Criminal Code to stop instances of sexual abuse in their own homes. By doing so, they actively resisted entrenched notions that violent crime was a public sphere activity and that the family, as the heart of the private domain, was sacrosanct. Yet the "reformation of the private" that resulted was an uneven process, one that was shaped more by concerns for the preservation of the Anglo-Saxon race, the patriarchal family, and hegemonic masculinity than the protection of women and children. The contradictions that existed in the criminal prosecution of domestic violence cases between 1886 and 1940 reflect a society, and a justice system, struggling to come to terms with feminist critiques of a patriarchal legal structure and culture. It is revealing that few cases of child beating came before the courts in this period. Canadians had only begun to deconstruct the foundations of patriarchy

by acknowledging the rights of women; it had not yet completely acknowledged the rights of children.

In the domestic violence, murder, and sexual abuse cases that did come
to light in courts of law, two impulses merged to produce uneven prosecutorial trends. On the one hand, magistrates, judges, and juries tended
to take most seriously the complaints of women and girls who fit the
mould of hegemonic femininity. Bad wives and unchaste daughters, in
contrast, were represented – in cross-examination, clemency campaigns,
and newspaper articles – as being culpable in their own death or abuse at
the hands of fathers or husbands.[88] On the other hand, law and government officials were more than willing to undermine the patriarchal-
authoritarian family model if the husband or father failed to live up to
the standards of reinstituted masculinity envisaged by the region's promoters. Membership in a marginalized ethnic or working-class community,
or evidence of sexual impropriety, meant that male judges, juries, and
officials were less likely to consider the accused worthy of protection from
prosecution and punishment. As the overrepresentation of eastern European men, Ukrainians in particular, among the ranks of convicted and
hanged wife murderers attests, proceedings in the courtroom and the
meanings that observers attached to them in clemency campaigns and
journalistic treatments transformed the most private acts into cautionary
tales and lessons on the dangers of nonconformity. When the person who
entered the docket was a woman facing charges of husband or child murder,
however, the proceedings caused ordinary prairie dwellers, officials, and
policy makers to seriously consider the nature of the family, the role of
the state, the status of women and children, and discriminatory practices
in the criminal justice system.

7

She Is to Be Pitied, Not Punished

The Murderess, the Woman Question, and the Capital Punishment Debate

On the evening of 14 November 1915, the Reverend C.F. Potter, a Unitarian minister of Edmonton, graced his congregation with a rousing sermon titled "Mrs. Hawkes and Capital Punishment." One month earlier, on 7 October, a Wetaskiwin jury had convicted and a judge had sentenced Jenny Hawkes to hang for the murder of Rosella Stoley, her husband's mistress. Many members of the public were outraged by the decision. Potter, however, cautioned his audience to assign blame where it was due: "The trouble is not with judge or jury, but with ourselves. We are questioning whether or not capital punishment is always justifiable when murder is committed; and even whether or not it is ever justifiable."[1] Potter advised his congregation that, contrary to some arguments, he believed considerations of sex played a fundamental role each and every time an accused's culpability was debated by judges, members of a criminal trial jury, or officials or politicians attached to the Department of Justice: "I venture to disagree with my friends and to assert that the question of sex does enter into this particular case, and every case where women are tried under our present system. Who wronged Mrs. Hawkes in the first instance? A man. Who arrested her? A man. Who judged her? A man. Who were on the jury? Men only. Who made the laws which judge and jury had to obey? Men. Who will the chaplain be to attend her to the scaffold? A man. Who will spring the trap that will kill her? A man." Potter concluded his sermon by exclaiming, "Is this justice?"[2]

Traditional narratives of capital punishment frequently identify the emergence of the Canadian abolitionist movement with W. Ross Thatcher's

introduction of Bill No. 2 in the House of Commons in 1950.[3] The minister of justice, governor general, members of the federal cabinet, and the
public, however, debated the morality and utility of the death penalty –
and usually found it wanting – each time a jury found a woman guilty of
murder and a judge sentenced her to hang. Modern historians are interested
in how nation-states founded on the notion of the rule of law justified
executive modifications of punishment in the past. Ordinary citizens on
the Prairies grappled with this issue when they engaged in discussion and
followed the trials of women accused of murder or infanticide or when
they participated in the clemency campaigns for the ten prairie women
who were condemned to death prior to 1940. Nine of the cases occurred
either at the height of the campaigns for women's suffrage and the homestead dower or soon after women achieved the vote, years when the very
foundations of prairie society were being questioned. As the Reverend
Potter's sermon suggests, judges responded to first-wave feminists' demands
for legal and political equality by advising juries to set aside their notions
of chivalry and ignore the issue of the accused's sex when they considered
the issue of murder.

Prairie dwellers in general found it difficult, if not impossible, to discount
the gendered dimensions of murder trials that involved female offenders
because the narratives of sex and violence that emerged from the courtroom
either contravened entrenched ideas about gender, crime, and violence or
cast the accused in the role of victim to abusive, rapacious, or adulterous
men. In prairie Canada, as in all Western nations and regions, women who
killed their husbands or children came to symbolize a world turned upside
down, a world in which women violated the male prerogative of violence,
challenged the idea of crime as a public activity perpetrated largely by
members of ethnic minorities or the working class, and generally ignored
the scripts written for a docile, passive womanhood. As was the case in
wife murder cases, the details of domestic discord, sexual impropriety, and
violence also belied utopian visions of the Prairies as a region of triumphant democracy and a reinstituted masculinity. Murder trials and clemency
campaigns, consequently, became a stage on which larger societal fears
and anxieties played.[4] What did it mean for society in general when women,
believed to be inherently maternal and nurturing, killed their husbands,
lovers, or infants?[5] Conversely, what did it mean when the state condemned
individuals who were thought to be the weaker sex to death?

By the First World War, first-wave feminists, religious leaders, and social
reform advocates argued that the murderess was both sign and symbol of

an unjust and patriarchal legal system that rendered married women economically and physically dependent on their husbands' good will.[6] While murderess cases provided first-wave feminists with fuel for their argument that the achievement of women's political equality and suffrage would ensure social justice and a fair deal for all, conservatives and anti-feminists manipulated murderess trials to forecast the breakdown of marriage and the family – the dissolution of the ties that held together the liberal economic order. After prairie women won the vote in early 1916, a number of conservative critics began to argue that women such as Hawkes should be prepared to accept the pains as well as the pleasures of citizen-ship, and they pointed to instances of men dying on the scaffold as ex-amples of gender discrimination. Did these debates and developments affect the reception and treatment of violent female offenders and their victims in the courtroom and the wider court of public opinion? Did chivalry win the day, or did female offenders and their defence counsels learn that the strategies that women had long employed to evade punish-ment could no longer be used to great effect, that women could now expect the same treatment that was meted out to wife murderers?

GETTING AWAY WITH MURDER?
MURDERED MEN, CHILD MURDER, AND CHIVALRIC JUSTICE

Feminist historians and sociologists have long argued that the criminal courts' tendency to apply gendered or chivalric systems of justice was little more than paternalism in disguise.[7] Female accused, much like Aboriginal men accused of murder or infanticide (see Chapter 2), could manipulate patriarchal legal systems and evade punishment by portraying themselves as wounded individuals: as mentally or morally weak, passive, or abused wives and abandoned mothers. Male judges, jurors, and politicians, imbued with white, middle-class notions of chivalry, typically chose to pity rather than punish the accused. Murderess cases, when played out in the media, tended to reinforce rather than challenge entrenched notions of hegemonic femininity. F. Murray Greenwood and Beverley Boissery, who have used capital case files to explore the historical treatment of convicted murderesses in Canada, argue that judges, juries, and the government tended to treat husband murderers more harshly than wife murderers; however, they con-tend that a system of sham chivalry was applied to protect individual women, at the expense of stereotyping them as weak-minded and passive.[8]

To a certain degree, the answer to the question, did chivalry truly prevail in murderess trials in prairie Canada? depends on which cases and files are assessed. Capital cases such as *R. v. Hawkes* resulted in conviction and sparked debate because the offender either refused to play the victim or, for a variety of reasons, failed to harness stereotypes about women in her favour. Although capital case files provide the richest textual source for exploring defence strategies and attitudes toward violent female offenders in the Prairies, the majority of murder and infanticide cases that involved female offenders never resulted in murder convictions. Between 1889 and 1940, eighteen women in the selected judicial districts were either acquitted of charges of murder or shooting with intent to kill or they were found guilty only of manslaughter.[9] In addition, none of the twenty-four women who stood accused of committing infanticide received a murder conviction. By contrast, William Grover was convicted and had his death sentence commuted to life in prison (see Chapter 6). A few of the cases that involved women were clear cases of accidental or unintentional death; in others, a combination of chivalric justice, the social and economic status of the accused, and the character and status of the victim shaped the outcome. In the Regina judicial district in the twenty-year period ending in 1932, for instance, six women were accused, and found not guilty, of shooting with intent to kill, conspiracy to murder, and murder.[10] With the exception of Jenny Solomon, all of the perpetrators were Anglo-Canadian farm wives whose profile and crimes were often at variance with images of the violent criminal as masculine, immigrant, or working-class.

Jenny Solomon, a thirty-two-year-old Romanian housewife, was tried on 11 and 12 September 1928 on charges of shooting with the intent to kill and the unlawful wounding of her husband. On the evening of 1 May 1928, Solomon shot her husband in the back of the head with a revolver. At the time of the shooting, her husband had been eating pastries at the kitchen table of their Regina home. Although the case was clearly not one of self-defence, Solomon's attorney did portray his client as the victim of a controlling and abusive husband. During the preliminary hearing, held before Magistrate J.H. Heffernan in the Regina Police Court, defence counsel demolished Fred Solomon's credibility by producing evidence that he was a known drinker and woman beater: the police court had convicted Solomon previously for assaulting his mother-in-law. The *Morning Leader* provided full-length coverage of the trial, focusing in particular on Solomon's lengthy recital of the physical abuse she suffered at the hands of her husband: "Mrs. Solomon was conducted by counsel through a harrowing recital of her domestic troubles in laying a foundation for defence to the two charges and her evidence was punctuated at times with sobs and hesitancy in relating some of the more intimate details. At one time, while Mrs. Solomon's mother was giving evidence, both women broke down for a few seconds."[11] The jury brought in a guilty verdict on the lesser charge. Jury members stated that the defence's presentation of the case had convinced them that Solomon had intended only to scare her husband, not kill him, and they accepted the accused's testimony that she did not recall if she had drawn the hammer on the gun. Under the revised statutes of the Criminal Code, Solomon would have been liable to spend three years in prison, but Justice J.F.L. Embury suspended her sentence on the grounds that there had been no evidence of intent.[12]

One of the most sensational and gripping trials to come before the Regina courts played upon the notions of wounded womanhood and chivalry to spectacular effect. On 4 February 1913, a jury found twenty-two-year-old Amy Christine Warwick, an English farm wife, not guilty of a conspiracy to murder her aged husband.[13] As reported by the *Morning Leader*, Ralph Warwick's death and his wife's trial had all the elements of a ghastly romance: "Somewhat over a year ago a girl called Lizzie Swain came to live in the district of Invermay, a few miles north and west of the town of Pense. Amy Christine Johnson was the girl's name but she was not so known then ... She met a man whose name was Stanley Price, and after some few months went to live with him ... There was another man. His name was Ralph Warwick ... Last September she married Warwick ... Today, Warwick's body, a mangled caricature of the human frame, rests in the Stoney Beach Cemetery; Price has sought a suicide's grave."[14] Herbert E. Sampson, agent for the attorney general, argued that Amy Warwick (alias Lizzie Swain) had met Stanley Price, a young man of twenty-four, while working for W.J. Newman near Belle Plaine, Saskatchewan. The two lovers hatched a sinister plot whereby Swain would marry Ralph Warwick, Stanley would murder him, and the couple would then establish themselves in the Peace River district with Warwick's money. At trial, Mrs. Trodden, a friend of the accused, testified that when Stanley Price's suicide became common knowledge, Warwick confessed to her that Price had killed her husband with a two-by-four and then dragged the body into the stable so it would look like the horses had trampled him to death. Another Crown witness, Mrs. Howd of Dilke, testified that on the same day that Warwick was murdered, 8 November 1912, Amy Warwick had entered her shop, told her that her husband habitually beat his horses, and declared, "I would not be surprised if one day he was found dead under their hooves."[15]

FIGURE 15   This courtroom drawing of Amy Warwick, who
was acquitted of murder in 1913, accompanied coverage of her
murder trial in the *Regina Morning Leader.*

Despite the evidence of premeditation that Sampson compiled against
Warwick, Warwick's defence attorney, J.F. Bryant, managed to turn the
case in his client's favour. During the coroner's inquest into Stanley Price's
suicide, Warwick had admitted that she and Price had planned to kill her
husband: "The bargain struck me as cold blooded, still I carried it through."[16]
At her trial for murder, however, Chief Justice Frederick William Haultain
declared the statement inadmissible after Bryant argued that Warwick had
made the admission while under arrest. In addition, Bryant argued that
the Royal North West Mounted Police had arrested Warwick without a
warrant. Despite this setback, Sampson managed to introduce a letter
written by the accused to Price's cousin that clearly implicated Warwick
in a conspiracy to murder her husband.

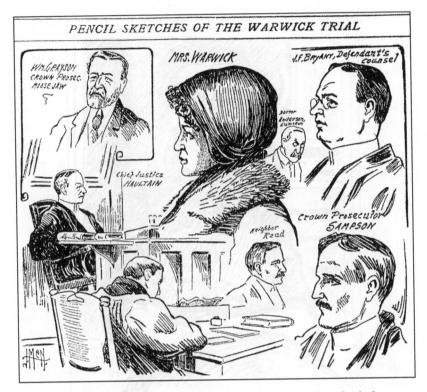

FIGURE 16   An artist's sketches of the main players in the Warwick trial, which appeared in the *Regina Morning Leader* in 1913.

Through the careful cross-examination of witnesses for the prosecution, and during Warwick's testimony on her own behalf, Bryant represented Warwick as a passive victim to Price's machinations. Newspapers followed suit and coloured their accounts of the trial with illustrations of a defenceless, pitiable Warwick (see Figures 15 and 16). When cross-examined, Mrs. Trodden testified that Price had had such a hold over Warwick's "girl wife" that she was afraid to disobey him. Trodden claimed that Price carried a gun and was such a "strong thinking man" that he appeared to have hypnotized the accused. Dr. Shaw, a witness for the defence, testified that the accused was "of a mentality easily influenced by another person."[17] When the jury acquitted the accused after two hours' deliberation, Chief Justice Haultain chastised Warwick and expressed the hope "that the experience had been a sufficient warning to her to shun even the appearance of wrong doing."[18]

By donning the mantle of wounded womanhood, Solomon and Warwick swayed the opinion of judges, journalists, and juries to attain acquittals. Mrs. Dean Davis, a working-class woman whom a jury in the Supreme Court of Alberta found guilty of manslaughter, was not so fortunate. Davis was tried on 27 October 1913 in Edmonton for the murder of Sydney Pallant, her lover. Davis admitted unabashedly that she had shot Pallant. Her attorney, Harry Robertson, however, argued that Davis was the "victim of the machinations of both her husband and the dead man ... she should be pitied rather than blamed."[19] Defence counsel in this case might have gone too far in his attempts to play upon the sympathies and prejudices of the jury. Two witnesses for the defence testified that Mrs. Davis had lived with both her husband and Pallant. Pallant, they argued, made his living as a pimp, drawing women such as Davis into prostitution through alcohol and drug addiction. The jury took only twenty minutes to come to a decision of manslaughter. Unlike Justice Embury in *Solomon*, Justice William Simmons sentenced Davis to twelve years' imprisonment.[20] Although the defence had tried to employ narratives of the white slave trade and narcoticism to good effect, Davis – as a married, working-class woman with no children – was not deemed worthy of the full application of chivalric justice.

By contrast, even though their behaviour contravened the ideals of normative femininity, only the most exceptional and monstrous of women would have failed to garner the judge's or jury's sympathy upon being charged with infanticide. Under the provisions of the Canadian Criminal Code, women suspected of committing infanticide could be charged with murder, the concealment of birth, or neglect. Proving the former, however, was difficult because the prosecution had to establish that the infant had existed separately from its mother after its birth.[21] As a corrective to the strict evidentiary requirements for murder, the police and the attorney general could also charge women with concealment of birth, which involved disposing "of the dead body of any child in any manner with intent to conceal the fact that its mother was delivered of it, whether the child died before, or during, or after birth." Unlike murder, which was a capital offence, concealment was an indictable offence, and women convicted of concealment were liable to a maximum of two years in prison.[22] Also in contrast to the murder provisions of the Criminal Code, which were theoretically gender blind, the concealment provisions, medical jurisprudence, and evidentiary requirements created an extra layer of institutional practices that promoted the differential treatment of women who murdered children.[23]

TABLE 11   Outcome of child murder or concealment of birth cases, female
offenders, 1896-1940

	Murder/concealment	Concealment
Convicted	–	6
Acquitted	5	2
Dismissed	–	3
Guilty of manslaughter	1	–
Guilty of concealment	6	–
Total (23)	12	11

SOURCES: SCNWT (Western Assiniboia), SCS and SCKB (Regina), 1886-1932, R-1286 and
R-1287, SAB; Criminal Register, MCKB (Dauphin), 1917-1940 , GR 4576, L-4-15, PAM;
Criminal Register, MCKB (Eastern Manitoba/Winnipeg), 1886-1940, GR 3636, M-1196, and
GR 4576, L-4-15, PAM; SCNWT and SCA (Southern Alberta and Macleod), 1886-1940,
Acc. 78.235, PAA; SCA (Wetaskiwin), 1914-1938, Acc. 81.198, PAA.

Prosecutors charged twenty-three women in the selected districts with
infanticide-related crimes between 1896 and 1940: only half of them stood
trial for murder, and juries either acquitted the accused or found her
guilty of the lesser charges of manslaughter or concealment (see Table 11).
The two individuals who were convicted for child murder were not female
offenders but married farmers: William Grover (see Chapter 6) and Jesse
Hammond. Jesse Hammond was found guilty of murdering his newborn
child on his farm in Wynard, Saskatchewan. His sister-in-law, who lived
with the Hammonds, was the mother. As was the case with Grover,
Hammond was depicted as a degenerate of the lowest order.[24] By contrast,
the majority of women charged with infanticide or concealment were
single, unmarried girls under the age of twenty who had recently arrived
in Canada from eastern Europe. As domestic servants or farm labourers,
the women would have lacked the money, education, and network of
friends and contacts needed to procure an abortion. Their unmarried
state might also have increased their chances of detection since married
women rarely needed to conceal a pregnancy. A married woman could
also claim, without much fear of discovery, that her child had died of
natural causes.[25]

Criminal trial juries convicted on reduced charges in at least half of the
cases that came before them, and female child murderers rarely suffered
harsh penalties. In a number of cases, the accused pleaded guilty to concealment and received a suspended sentence. In December 1932, for instance, Anna Duryba of Broadview, Saskatchewan, pleaded guilty to

concealment. In her statement to the police, made in November, she stated that she had arrived in Quebec from Poland in 1928. She decided to emigrate because her father had died, and she hoped to take advantage of opportunities in the New World. (She had no idea where, or if, her mother was living.) After settling in with her aunt and uncle on their farm near Broadview, Duryba worked as a farm labourer on a neighbour's farm. It was during this time that she had sex with three unnamed men. Duryba admitted that she gave birth to a child in the barn on 30 October 1932, placed it in a suitcase, hid the suitcase in the granary, and burned the afterbirth. When her aunt and uncle later asked her what she had done with the child, she told them, and they reported the death to the police. Judge Hannon of the District Court of Regina gave her a six-month suspended sentence.[26]

Prosecutors often had to content themselves with reduced charges and lenient sentences because trial juries, and sometimes judges, were unwilling to sentence women to death, particularly in cases that involved fathers who failed to meet their socially prescribed obligations.[27] In August 1905, for instance, Tina Arischuk of Winnipeg was charged with murder after her infant's body was found in the Red River. The police found three witnesses who had seen Arischuk wandering near the river, and Jacob Seel of the Winnipeg Police later found the accused lying on the riverbank with blood on her skirts. Bloody footprints led from an outdoor privy on Manitoba Avenue to the river, and the coroner reported that the child had died of suffocation from drowning.[28] During the trial, held before Justice Perdue and a jury in the Winnipeg Court of King's Bench on 1 November 1905, there was no defence for the accused, and Justice Perdue acted on her behalf. Although Arischuk had admitted her guilt to Seel, Perdue declared the accused's statement inadmissible. The jury found Arischuk guilty of manslaughter, with a strong recommendation for mercy. Perdue sentenced her to three years in prison. It was the harshest penalty meted out to a woman charged with an infanticide-related case prior to 1940.[29]

In 1940, however, one prairie woman's conviction for child murder brought to light the difficulties that prosecutors faced in obtaining convictions in child murder cases that involved female offenders. The case also resulted in a clemency campaign and retrial that gained the attention of the nation and helped convince legislators to amend the Criminal Code in 1948 to make infanticide a special category of murder. On 24 and 25 September 1940, a jury in Yorkton, Saskatchewan, found Annie Rubletz guilty of killing her child on her brother-in-law's farm near Hyas, Saskatchewan. The RCMP became aware of the case when they received an anonymous letter at their Sturgis headquarters on 5 August. Upon investigation they learned that Norma Tetlock – the daughter of Leslie Tetlock, who was the child's father and Rubletz's brother-in-law – had sent the letter. At the time of the birth, Leslie Tetlock had been in jail, but when he returned to his farm, his wife and Rubletz showed him where they had buried the child. Although the police charged Rubletz originally with concealment, they later received, on 27 August, a voluntary sworn statement from Rubletz in which she admitted that her child had been alive at birth and that she had smothered it to death. The police then charged the accused with murder. Justice Hector Macdonald, who presided over the first trial, later advised the secretary of state that the jury had been completely resistant to convicting Rubletz of murder. After ten minutes of deliberation, he recounted, the jury withdrew and asked him if Rubletz had been given counsel prior to making her voluntary statement. The men returned again to ask him if they had to accept the statement as voluntary. In a final attempt to avoid a murder conviction, the jury asked Macdonald if they could reduce the charge to concealment. Only after Macdonald replied that they could not did the jury find the accused guilty of murder. Macdonald concluded his assessment of the case by recommending clemency on account of the accused's youthfulness and "the sordid circumstances surrounding her life and the unmoral atmosphere in which she was evidently brought up."[30] He rationalized his handling of the case by arguing that he had feared jury nullification.[31]

The clemency campaign on Rubletz's behalf gave public expression to popular attitudes about the crime of child murder, and it exposed the race, class, and gender biases that continued to permeate prairie society.[32] Cecil G. Schmidt, barrister and clerk of the Westminster Church in Saskatoon, argued that Rubletz was a girl of low mentality, born of deplorable home conditions, whose hanging would have a lamentable effect on public consciousness.[33] Percy Farebroker of Kamsack likewise advised the government that Rubletz was "somewhat low in mentality" and of "weak character." During the trial, for instance, Rubletz had admitted that she had previously given birth to her brother's child and that her older sister had had a child at age fourteen. Rubletz's parents, Farebroker claimed, were Ukrainians of low moral and mental intelligence who could not afford to clothe their children or send them to school. The father spent most winters in jail for bootlegging.[34]

The Cara Amica Club, a young businesswomen's association, urged the minister of justice to extend clemency in Rubletz's case on account of her sex and her youth. Reflecting new attitudes toward adolescence and childhood, they also counselled him that capital punishment should be abolished for all individuals under the age of twenty-one. Petitioners who put forward Rubletz's sex as an argument in her favour contended that a single girl in Rubletz's condition was rarely responsible for her actions: her desperation negated criminal intent. The majority of petitions, however, asked for clemency on the grounds that the punishment was too harsh, and they derided the gendered biases of a criminal justice system that punished the victim and not the real villain, her seducer. Miss Anna C. Murray of the Woman's Christian Temperance Union (WCTU) advised the minister of justice that a harsh punishment would not deter future acts – it would only lead to more secrecy.[35]

A few petitioners argued, conversely, that the law should take its course. A woman who identified herself as "another mother" advised the government to ignore the "sob sister stuff": "There is something very brutal in a girl's nature who will deliberately murder her own baby ... Why throw so much blame on the men when so many girls are willing to sink to the lowest ebbs? Women should be the moral uplifters of the human race while men are the breadwinners."[36] Mrs. E. Eaton of Regina depicted Rubletz as a common prostitute and advocated sterilization as the only solution. Stanley H. Morrison asked, "Doesn't the girl need a psychiatrist and guidance rather than death?"[37]

Despite these arguments, Rubletz appealed her conviction on the grounds that her statement had not been voluntary, that the death of her child might have been accidental, and that the judge had erred when he told the jury they could not reduce the charge. When the appeal court quashed her conviction on 22 November 1942, Rubletz pleaded guilty to concealment and served one year in Battleford Prison. The attorney general of Saskatchewan sent a recommendation to Ottawa, forwarded with thousands of petitions, that Canada amend its Criminal Code to provide for a special case of infanticide, as in England.[38] The federal government enacted this legislation in 1948. Forty years later, however, the Law Reform Commission of Canada and the Butler Committee recommended that the legislation be abolished on the grounds that it was discriminatory. As Judith Osborne argues in her study of contemporary debates on the infanticide provision, with the passing of infanticide legislation, it became ingrained in law that women were not to be accorded full responsibility for their actions.[39] Legislators in 1948 sought to overcome jurors' unwillingness to convict women for murder; they did so by giving legal expression to theories of female criminality that rooted it in women's physiology. By doing so, they made it easier for juries and the public to overlook or

disregard the social, economic, and cultural motivations that drove women
to commit infanticide or murder in the first place.

EQUAL RIGHTS AND THE UNWRITTEN LAW:
HUSBAND MURDERERS AND THEIR CLEMENCY CAMPAIGNS

Chivalric justice applied in the majority of murder cases that involved
female offenders between 1912 and 1942, but ten prairie women committed
violent murders that appeared – at least to a jury of their male peers – to
have no justification. The public, however, did not agree. When Jenny
Hawkes was convicted and sentenced to hang for the murder of Rosella
Stoley in 1915, an anonymous man inquired in the pages of the *Calgary
Herald:* "Where is chivalry? Have all the men of the country gone to the
front, that we who remain sit idly by and approve of such a sentence?"[40]
In the end, chivalry of a sort prevailed. In response to clemency campaigns
mounted by the public, journalists, and pressure groups, the executive
decided that the law should run its course in only two of the ten cases:
Hilda Blake and Florence Lassandro died on the scaffold in 1899 and 1922,
respectively.[41] By contrast, during the same period, twenty-two of the
thirty-eight men (58 percent) who were found guilty by juries of murdering
prairie women suffered the death penalty. Nationally, men were twenty-
five times more likely to face conviction for murder than women, and
the proportion of executions to life sentences for men hovered at around
50 percent.[42] Despite the realities of a criminal justice system in which the
prerogative of mercy was extended to convicted murderers on a regular
basis, the majority of Canadians continued to support capital punishment
as a deterrent to crime – and as an integral aspect of the English common
law tradition – until the mid-1950s.[43] Many Canadians, in fact, prided
themselves on the severity of their penal code when compared to that of
other nations.[44] Most agreed, however, that Canada, as a "civilized nation,"
should not subject the weaker sex to the death penalty.

   With the exception of the trials for murder of Hilda Blake and Florence
Lassandro, murderess cases led to acrimonious public debates about the
application of capital punishment to women and to retrials or remissions
of sentences. An accused found guilty of manslaughter could end up serving more jail time than a woman who had been convicted for murder (see
Table 12). In 1923, for instance, Irene May Christensen faced a retrial for
the murder of her husband. The second jury found her guilty of manslaughter, and the judge sentenced her to fifteen years in prison.[45] By

TABLE 12   Outcome of murder trials involving female offenders that resulted in conviction, prairie Canada, 1886-1940

Case	Location	Ethnicity	Victim	Sentence	Motive
Christensen (1923)	Dapp, AB	American	Husband	Retrial, manslaughter, 15 years	Abuse
Smith (1935)	Duck Lake, SK	Metis	Husband	Retrial, unfit to stand trial	Quarrel
Hawkes (1915)	Camrose, AB	American	Rosella Stoley	10 years	Jealousy
Maloney (1916)	Hamiota, MB	Ukrainian	Mary Ann Hamilton	15 years	Monetary
Shulman (1919)	Calder, SK	Ukrainian	Husband	12 years	Jealousy/ abuse
Jackson (1920)	Swan River, AB	English Canadian	Husband	Life	Another man
Tratch (1924)	Fish Creek, SK	Ukrainian	Husband	Life	Another man
Dranchuk (1934)	Flat Lake, AB	Polish	Husband	Life	Quarrel
Blake (1899)	Brandon, MB	British	Mary Lane	Death	Jealousy
Lassandro (1922)	Coleman, AB	Italian	Stephen Lawson	Death	Retribution

SOURCE: Department of Justice, Capital Case Files, RG 13, Library and Archives Canada.

contrast, juries convicted both Hawkes (1915) and Grapena Shulman (1919) for murder, but the governor general in council commuted their sentences to ten and twelve years, respectively.[46] In the case of three other convicted murderesses – Sarah Jane (Sadie) Jackson (discussed in Chapter 2), Catherine Tratch, and Dina Dranchuk – the death penalty was commuted to a life sentence.[47] A number of factors – including the political climate at the time of the trial, the defence strategy, and the character and status of the accused and her relationship with the victim – had an impact on the strength of the clemency campaigns and the outcome of the case.

Arguments in favour of commutation in the Hawkes and Shulman cases resonated with legal authorities and government officials. The cases occurred at the height of the social reform movement. Women's organizations were at their most powerful and, under the leadership of Emily Murphy and the United Farm Women of Alberta, the campaign for women's homestead dower had gained the attention of Alberta's legislators.[48] First-wave feminists such as Nellie McClung and Murphy spoke eloquently on Hawkes's and Shulman's behalf in the hopes that their arguments would also sway public opinion in favour of legislation that would guarantee married women property rights. Some contemporary feminist historians have characterized maternal feminists as conservative, middle-class, white women who championed reform and female suffrage to maintain the status quo. Maternal feminist rhetoric, they argue, also tended to reaffirm women's subordinate status in society because it did not question that women's primary role was in the private sphere.[49] Yet suffrage and social reform activists also used equal rights rhetoric to secure their goals, and by claiming rights beyond the domestic sphere, they challenged male authority in the public sphere and in the home.[50] Although both types of arguments were brought to bear on the Hawkes and Shulman cases, equal rights rhetoric prevailed.

On 13 March 1915, Jenny Hawkes, an American farm wife, armed herself with a revolver, entered her Lewisville homestead near Camrose, Alberta, and fired six shots into her husband's mistress, Rosella Stoley. The defence introduced the bulk of evidence at her trial, which took place before Justice William Carlos Ives and a jury of American immigrant farmers in early October. Various witnesses described in detail the physical and emotional abuse that Hawkes had suffered during her marriage. When Hawkes testified on her own behalf, she explained that her husband had invited Rosella Stoley for a visit at Christmas. During that visit, she overheard her husband tell Stoley that he hoped he never got as tired of her as he had of his wife. Not long after, the entire Stoley family – including Rosella's husband, William, and the children – moved into the Hawkes homestead. Hawkes collected his personal belongings and a stove and moved to the Stoley side of the partition. Jenny Hawkes testified that she had repeatedly witnessed her husband having sexual intercourse with Mrs. Stoley through a hole in the partition wall. On one occasion she overheard the couple planning to have her committed to an insane asylum. When Hawkes confronted her husband, he threatened to shoot her if she did not let him sleep with his mistress. He also told her that he could beat her – or do anything he wanted to her – and the law would be on his side. On 2 March, Hawkes's husband evicted her from the family homestead, forcing her to live with her son-in-law, David Rosser. Hawkes claimed that on the day of the murder she had returned to the homestead to gather some personal items. She could not, however, remember any of the events that occurred after Rosella Stoley told her she was unwelcome.[51]

In contrast to most prairie men and women who stood trial for murder in these decades, Hawkes was represented by two high-profile lawyers, W. J. Loggie and R. W. Manley, who were hired by her daughter. Defence counsel argued that Hawkes had suffered from a fit of temporary insanity brought on by her husband's treatment of her. The strategy was not entirely successful, however, because the accused had not killed her husband but, rather, his mistress. The jury deliberated for an hour and a half and returned a verdict of guilty, with a strong recommendation for mercy on the grounds that (1) the victim had been sleeping with the accused's husband, and (2) her husband's infidelity had caused Hawkes to enter into a state of mental incapacity.[52] Hawkes appealed the conviction on the grounds that Justice Ives had unfairly refused to admit evidence of her husband's immorality as evidence of her state of mind. The appeal was unsuccessful. Justice Beck, who dissented, stated that he truly believed that Hawkes could not re-member committing the crime because medical experts had adduced evidence that she had suffered from hysterical or epileptic amnesia. Women, he believed, were more apt to develop the condition since they were less rational than men.[53]

When the papers announced on 8 November 1915 that Hawkes's convic-tion would not be overturned on appeal, the public's reaction was swift and negative. That same evening, the executive of the Local Council of Women in Edmonton met in the Hudson's Bay Company Palm Room to discuss the case. Members resolved that Jenny Hawkes should be pitied, not punished; her husband, Rosella Stoley, and the Canadian legal system were to blame for the tragedy. The council decided to petition the Do-minion Council of Women to lobby the federal government to enact a law that would punish any husband who brought another woman into the family home for immoral purposes.[54] Four days later, the Reverend Potter argued in his sermon that the Canadian justice system did not protect women's interests but discriminated against them at every level. Potter's sermon was intended as a rebuttal of Emily Murphy's arguments, which she had presented at a meeting held on Hawkes's behalf on the evening of 12 November. During that meeting, Murphy argued that the accused's sex should not be brought into play during the clemency cam-paign on Hawkes's behalf: "We do not ask this mercy on any sex plea; we realize that there is no sex in sin and there is no sex in soul. What is black for a man, must not be shaded into grey for a woman."[55] Murphy argued that Hawkes, "an old, work-withered woman," had suffered great provoca-tion at the hands of a degenerate husband and a woman who was a pitiless usurper. Murphy, who would remain at the forefront of the campaign to better women's legal position, argued that the Alberta Married Women's Relief Act of 1910, which she had been instrumental in having passed, had not gone far enough to protect women's legal rights in marriage. The legislation granted a married woman the right to apply to the courts for relief if, by the terms of her husband's will, she received less of his estate than she would have if he died intestate. Provincial law provided that where a man died without a will, and where there were no children, his widow received his entire estate.[56]

The day after Murphy's appeal, E.J. Keerley expressed similar sentiments in a letter to the governor general. Keerley believed that Hawkes, having no law to protect her, had no choice but to take the law into her own hands. Keerley, like many petitioners to the Department of Justice, noted that if Hawkes had been a man, her actions would have been excused by the unwritten law. In late October 1915, for instance, a man in Nelson, British Columbia, had been unconditionally released after killing his wife's lover. Keerley included in his petition a newspaper clipping titled "Case of Mrs. Hawkes and the Law for Women in Alberta," which he felt expressed public opinion in the Province of Alberta. The article quoted the Anglican bishop of Calgary's sermon on the Hawkes case, which had been given on the evening of 12 November: "In the whole history of British justice, no male murderer ever invoked the unwritten law of civilization with the peculiar force and tragic helplessness of Mrs. Hawkes. No man was ever placed in such a position – under Alberta law no man could be in such a position unless he were feeble-minded or an infant."[57] The article detailed Jenny Hawkes's legal and economic dependence upon her husband: Hawkes could not prevent her husband from selling the homestead without her permission; the separation and alimony process was "tedious, precarious, and expensive"; and the Married Women's Home Protection Act of 1915 did not give a married woman the right to control the home property or say who could live on it. Hawkes, the author argued, had simply reversed the application of the unwritten law. He concluded, "It is time women shouldered arms for home defence from other menaces than the Germans."[58]

Petitioners also appealed to unwritten law in Grapena Shulman's case following her conviction for murder on 17 January 1919. Appeals to unwritten law referred to the practice of allowing a husband the right to kill his wife's lover if he acted immediately upon catching the man in a compromising position with his wife. A number of cases in California in the 1880s and 1890s had made it apparent that some settler societies also supported what they felt was a woman's natural right to defend her personal honour against men who violated the sanctity of the family.[59] In a sense, murder trials such as *Hawkes* and *Shulman* can be approached as the flip side, or female version, of the hired hand cases that flooded the courts in the same period. Shulman's defence was constructed to highlight women's unequal status in Canadian marriage law and the extent to which inadequate laws rendered women vulnerable to abuse. Shulman confessed that on 28 September 1918 she had shot her husband in the head while he lay sleeping. "My husband beat me for the last time the same week he died," she said. Shulman, a Ukrainian mother of five who farmed near Calder, Saskatchewan, testified that her husband beat her regularly, that she had left him frequently over a seven-year period, and that he had habitually committed adultery during their marriage. In 1913 and 1914, she disclosed, her husband had gone so far as to welcome his mistress into their home. Two days before the murder, John Shulman kicked his pregnant wife in the stomach so hard that she suffered a miscarriage.[60]

In letters to the editor and petitions to the Department of Justice, many Albertans, prompted by the guilty verdicts in the Hawkes and Shulman cases, commented on the uneven application of the unwritten law in Canada. The article in the *Calgary Herald* referred to by Keerley, which drew parallels between the Hawkes case and the one in British Columbia, stated: "A jury acquitted a man who killed another man who had been visiting his wife in his absence at work. And the judge in commenting on the verdict trusted that the case would be a warning to any other man who might set out to destroy another man's home."[61] The author noted that although acquittals of this kind failed to promote confidence in the jury system, a commutation of Hawkes's sentence could restore faith in Canadian criminal justice, while at the same time avoiding the application of an American convention.

Premier Arthur Lewis Sifton, a former lawyer and chief justice of Alberta, followed the clemency campaign on Hawkes's behalf closely and objected strenuously to the tone of the campaign and the direction of arguments that appealed to unwritten law. In a letter published in the *Edmonton Bulletin,* Sifton advised the public that it should not blame Justice Ives and the jury in Jenny Hawkes's case. He reminded readers that Hawkes had murdered a woman in front of witnesses, violently and deliberately. In his estimation, the jury had no choice but to bring forward a guilty verdict. Sifton's reaction to the case can be interpreted either as an argument for gender equality or as a condemnation of women who challenged the male monopoly on violence. Political considerations also shaped Sifton's response. In his memorandum to the minister of justice, Justice

William Carlos Ives echoed Sifton's fears when he highly recommended mercy in Hawkes's case because the accused's home town, Lewisville, Alberta, was populated predominantly by Americans who were apt, he argued, to be influenced by their own laws. Ives argued that justice tempered by mercy would ensure impartiality in future trials and maintain faith in British Canadian law.[62]

Jenny Hawkes, who was from Ohio, disagreed. When a journalist informed Hawkes that her sentence had been commuted to ten years in prison, she replied: "This is a queer country on women isn't it? I mean that the laws are queer, when a husband can bring another woman into his home and not be punished. Take this one message from me to your Canadian women: Ask them to work hard for laws that will make it a serious crime for a husband to bring a strange woman into his home and force his wife to live with her, or else to become a homeless, unprovided for wanderer on the face of the earth."[63] Neither Hawkes nor Shulman conformed to the classic stereotype of the wounded woman. Although both women suffered at the hands of abusive and unfaithful husbands, they did not represent themselves as fragile or passive victims. Their convictions and death sentences, consequently, gave birth to clemency campaigns that moved beyond simple demands for the application of chivalric justice to demands in which the underlying framework of the liberal economic order and the male monopoly on property and violence were questioned.

FIRST-WAVE FEMINISM ON TRIAL: THE INTERWAR YEARS

Following the achievement of women's suffrage in the prairie provinces in early 1916, and throughout the interwar period, new voices emerged in debates about violence and capital punishment in prairie communities and Canadian society. In September 1934, for instance, an Edmonton jury found Dina Dranchuk, a Polish mother of two, guilty of beating her husband to death with an axe. Despite the violent nature of the crime, the jury tempered its verdict with a strong recommendation for mercy. A variety of Depression-related labour and social welfare organizations – including the Women's Auxiliary to the Unemployed Married Men's Association, the Calgary Labour Party, and the Calgary Council of Child and Family Welfare – then petitioned the federal government on the accused's behalf. As in the Hawkes and Shulman cases, women's organizations such as the WCTU and the United Farm Women of Alberta also made appeals on her behalf. Many believed that the Depression, which placed women in a position of virtual "insanity from looking down empty flour barrels," caused Dranchuk to quarrel with her husband over money and health care. Others emphasized the location of the Dranchuk homestead, in the northern wilderness between Athabasca Landing and St. Paul, and represented Dranchuk as a particularly ignorant foreign woman.[64]

On 25 October 1934, however, a correspondent to the *Calgary Albertan*, who identified himself as "A Mere Man," opposed the clemency campaign on Dranchuk's behalf. The author argued that the Calgary Local Council of Women's recommendation for a commutation of the death penalty was based solely on the accused's uncorroborated allegations of brutality by the victim. In the letter writer's reading of the case, the accused had not claimed that her husband committed adultery; she had simply testified that he had refused to let her sell two pigs so that she could buy medicine for an "imaginary" illness. Overlooking the larger contest for property rights that precipitated the outbreak of violence in the case, the author pointed to the execution of male accused as evidence of gender discrimination, and he claimed that the criminal justice system in Canada operated on the assumption that a woman, and especially a wife and a mother, could do no wrong: "If a man murders his wife or is even suspected of murdering her ... he is a brute and must be hanged, but if she murders him, no matter how atrociously, oh, well, he is a brute anyway and brought it all on himself, while she is a downtrodden sort and must be let off."[65] Another letter to the editor of the *Albertan* weighed in on the treatment of violent female offenders: "It is not really hard to explain. The fact is that women, though they have secured equal rights with men, are still a little unwilling to assume equal obligations."[66] This writer concluded: "If the law is to be asked to consider the proposition that death is too extreme a penalty for a woman it must also be asked to consider whether anyone should be required to pay it."[67]

The opinions expressed in the *Calgary Albertan* were more than a simple lament, on behalf of white, middle-class men, for a bygone age. The controversy that surrounded murderess trials in the interwar period reflected the ambiguities, contradictions, and uncertainties of women's status in the 1920s and 1930s. Although members of the social reform and suffrage movements had predicted that a new day of reform and social advancement for women would follow female enfranchisement, the postwar era witnessed new assertions that the place of women was still in the home. Organizations such as the Girl Guides, the Girls and Boys Clubs of Canada, and the Canadian Girls in Training emerged during the Roaring Twenties to instil independence in young women. Yet they simultaneously emphasized the girls' future roles as wives and mothers.[68] During the Depression, plummeting wages, deteriorating working conditions, and declining union membership challenged women's right to engage in waged labour. As the crisis grew and the national unemployment rate blossomed, the deep-seated prejudice against married women working intensified.[69]

In this context, petitions to the minister of justice once again emphasized that capital punishment should not be applied to women – particularly if the accused was a wife and mother. In Sarah Jackson's case (which took place on the fringes of civilization; see Chapter 2), for instance, judicial attitudes opposed to the application of gendered justice competed with popular reassertions that the courts and the government should apply chivalric justice to all cases that involved violent female offenders. In his charge to the jury, Justice William Walsh described Jackson's crime as "gruesome beyond description" and advised members of the jury to ignore their "innate chivalry" and guard their hearts against a "feeling of sentiment or a mistaken feeling of pity."[70] Despite Walsh's warnings, the jury convicted Jackson but strongly recommended mercy. Nellie McClung supported the petition circulated by the Salvation Army on Jackson's behalf because she felt that capital punishment in general, and the hanging of women in particular, caused communal wounds that would not heal quickly. In Jackson's case, McClung believed that the exercise of executive clemency would prove to be of most benefit to the accused's seven children. Jackson, she argued, was a woman of a low grade of intelligence and underdeveloped mentality: Christian influence and proper discipline would cause her to repent her evil deed and become a model citizen.[71] Louise C. McKinney, member of the Legislative Assembly of Alberta, successfully argued that although there was no doubt in her mind (given Jackson's sexual relationship with an Aboriginal man) that the accused was a confirmed prostitute, the interests of the children would best be served by a life term in prison.[72]

In extreme instances, such as the case of Catherine Tratch, a Ukrainian mother of eight who was found guilty of poisoning her husband to death on 6 February 1924, petitioners did – as "A Mere Man" claimed – argue that motherhood could expiate all sins. Tratch admitted to feeding her husband strychnine in the kitchen of their homestead near Fish Creek, Saskatchewan, but she claimed that she had acted on the urging of a neighbour, Theodore Oleskiw. When Tratch stood trial in the Saskatchewan

Court of King's Bench in Prince Albert, before Justice J.F.L. Embury, defence counsel called no witnesses but instead made a passionate plea on behalf of a wife and mother. Justice Embury advised the minister of justice that public opinion supported the accused, but he warned that "such an opinion is based upon ignorance." Embury explained that the crime was one of the most "damnable perpetrated in this western country" and described Tratch's actions as deliberate, cowardly, and unjustifiable. He did concede, however, that two facts stood in the accused's favour: she was a woman, and she was a Ukrainian whose "environment has created in her, as among many belonging to her race, an indifference to the value of human life."[73]

During the trial and clemency campaign, counsel for the defence, J. Harvey Hearn, argued that Tratch had fallen victim to the machinations of Oleskiw, whose property ran adjacent to the Tratch homestead. Tratch, he claimed, had been susceptible to Oleskiw's wiles because her parents had forced her, at the age of fourteen, to marry a man twenty years her senior whom she disliked intensely. Nevertheless, Tratch had unfailingly performed her duties as wife and mother, producing eight children by the time she was thirty-eight. Hearn concluded that even though the accused was now a mature woman, her race, early marriage, and lack of education rendered her incapable of acting on her own initiative.[74] Despite Justice Embury's advice, Tratch's sentence was commuted to life imprisonment on 18 May 1924.

Three days before the governor general in council made its decision in the Tratch case, John Kidman of the Canadian Prisoners' Welfare Association asked the minister of justice to consider the following: "One point some of us had desired to emphasize was that there is something repulsive in hanging a woman when she has contributed to the welfare of the community by bringing eight children into the world ... Both the Roman Catholic Church and the Church of England have in their rubrics services which acknowledge that a woman's life is imperilled and divinely preserved every time that she passes through the maternal experience."[75] Tratch employed a similar argument in her own defence when she made her first petition for parole to the minister of justice in March 1929. Expressing great sorrow for her crime, Tratch argued that she was a mother of eight whose sons needed her to keep house for them. She also reminded the government that her children owned eleven thousand acres between them and that she herself was a significant taxpayer.[76] Tratch was released from prison by a ticket-of-leave on 2 June 1938.

A DEGRADING AND REVOLTING SPECTACLE: FEMALE HANGINGS –
THE LIMITS OF CHIVALRY AND FIRST-WAVE FEMINISM

Although it appeared that prairie women could, quite literally, get away with murder, a spirit of female solidarity and male chivalry did not blanket every woman convicted of that crime. On 30 April 1923, the Canadian Prisoners' Welfare Association, which was opposed to capital punishment in all cases, entered a final appeal to Prime Minister William Lyon Mackenzie King on behalf of Florence Lassandro, who had been sentenced to hang: "We desire to enter a final appeal that the degrading and revolting spectacle of hanging a woman in the twentieth century should not be permitted under your regime. It is now twenty-four years since any occurrence in Canada. A similar event in England recently caused widespread sorrow. We are aware that local sentiment, especially on the part of women, is for hanging, but suggest that the spirit of revenge should be checked rather than encouraged by a Christian state."[77] The association tried to influence the federal government to extend its prerogative of mercy in Lassandro's case by reminding its members that Canada had not hanged a woman since it entered the age of modernity. Hilda Blake – who was hanged at Brandon, Manitoba, in 1899 for the murder of her mistress, Mary Lane – was an exception to the rule.

Although they are not representative, Blake's and Lassandro's cases are significant because their outcome reflected the limits of chivalry and patriarchy in prairie society and legal culture, not to mention the ethnic and class biases that underscored the attitudes of some first-wave feminists. On 7 February 1923, Mrs. Dorothy A. Anderson of Calgary wrote to the minister of justice on Lassandro's behalf. She noted that the usual petitions and pleas that circulated on behalf of female murderers had not followed Lassandro's conviction. Anderson expressed no doubt that Lassandro was a criminal, but she opposed the death penalty as anathema to a Christian society.[78] Unlike the majority of women convicted of murder prior to the Second World War, neither Florence Lassandro nor Hilda Blake, who were both childless, could claim motherhood or wounded womanhood as a defence for their crimes. More significantly, both women were associated with minority groups that were considered the most undesirable in Canadian society.

Hilda Blake came to Canada as one of the growing number of destitute British orphans sent to the country in the late nineteenth century. Throughout the 1890s, Blake worked as a domestic servant in a variety of homes in Brandon and western Manitoba, until she was hired by Robert Lane, a socially prominent member of Brandon society, on 15 July 1898. One year later, on 5 July, Blake confessed to shooting Lane's wife – a thirty-two-year-old mother of four children who was expecting a fifth – because she was jealous of the relationship that the woman shared with her husband. Two weeks before her execution, which was scheduled to take place in late December, Blake claimed that she had murdered Mary Lane with the expectation that Robert Lane would make her his wife.[79]

During Blake's trial, which took place on 15 November 1899 before Justice Killam, and the subsequent clemency campaign, her ethnicity and working-class background shaped public and judicial evaluations of her character. Although the WCTU of Brandon circulated a petition requesting that the death sentence be commuted to life imprisonment, a number of women rose and left the meeting when the petition was proposed. In Winnipeg, Dr. Amelia Yeomans – who was one of the first licensed female physicians in Canada, a dedicated proponent of social purity, a member of the WCTU, and one of the leading maternal feminists of her generation – became the leading protagonist in Blake's case. Her arguments on Blake's behalf, however, were anything but complimentary. After spending an hour with the accused on 25 November 1899, Yeomans concluded that Blake was a moral lunatic or degenerate whose sentence should be commuted because she bore no moral responsibility for her action and because the interests of society would be better served if Blake was studied scientifically. Yet Yeomans also argued that it was both unfair and immoral to hang women because they did not enjoy the right to formulate the laws to which they were subject.[80] Despite these arguments in her favour, Blake was executed on 27 December 1899.[81]

Although her case occurred twenty-two years later, Florence Lassandro shared much in common with Hilda Blake. At the time of her trial, Lassandro remained childless, she remained accused of murdering a prominent individual, and she belonged to an ethnic community that was believed to be actively involved in corrupting the morals of prairie society. In late November and early December 1922, the Supreme Court of Alberta, Calgary, tried Lassandro alongside Emilio Picariello, "the biggest bootlegger of the Crow's Nest Pass," for the murder of Stephen Lawson, a war veteran and Alberta Provincial Police constable. Born Philomena Costanzo in Consenza, southern Italy, Lassandro and her family had immigrated to the Crow's Nest Pass region in 1911. Her father worked initially on the railway, but he later settled at Fernie, where he became a coal miner. In 1915, Costanzo's parents arranged for their fourteen-year-old daughter to marry an Italian immigrant ten years her senior. The couple moved to Philadelphia, where the husband became involved in Mafia-related crimes. Philomena fled to the Crow's Nest Pass region two years later and assumed the name Florence Lassandro.[82]

Lassandro worked as a waitress at Emilio Picariello's hotel and as a nursemaid to his children. She became involved in Picariello's liquor-smuggling operation, which boomed during the prohibition era. Lassandro, along with Picariello's son Stephen, served as police decoys by pretending to be lovers while liquor exchanges were being made. Picariello believed that the Alberta Provincial Police (APP) would be less likely to fire upon his men if a woman was present. On the evening of 21 September 1922, however, Stephen Picariello was wounded during a high-speed chase with the APP. The police later arrested Lassandro and Emilio Picariello for the retribution-style murder of Lawson. The trial was transferred to Calgary because public sentiment in the Crow's Nest Pass was strongly against the accused. Because neither accused presented evidence on his or her own behalf, it never became clear who killed Lawson. According to Lassandro's original statement to the police, she herself had asked to accompany Picariello to Coleman and was responsible for bringing along the .38 that killed the victim. Just hours prior to her hanging, however, Lassandro confessed to her mother that Picariello had fired all of the shots. Picariello had advised her to take the blame because "women don't hang in Canada."[83]

Lassandro's Italian heritage and association with liquor interests placed her solidly within the enemy camp of most social reform activists. In 1909, James S. Woodsworth had warned Canadians of the pernicious influence of Italians in *Strangers within Our Gates*: "AN ITALIAN! The figure that flashed before the mind's eye is probably that of an organ-grinder with his monkey. That was the impression we first received, and it is difficult to substitute another. Italian immigrants! The figure of the organ man fades away, and we see dark, uncertain figures, and someone whispers, 'The Mafia – the Black Hand.'"[84] The Canadian Prisoners' Welfare Association (CPWA) went so far as to argue that Lassandro's ethnicity constituted grounds for forgiveness: she came from a race of people whose ignorance precluded them from understanding proscriptions against liquor.[85]

Dr. Moore, a petitioner from Cross Creek, New Brunswick, and members of the Calgary Labour Congress echoed the CPWA's sentiments when they pressured the minister of justice to either pardon Lassandro or admit that the age of chivalry had truly died. Moore made a reference to the recent execution of Edith Cavell, a British nurse who had been stationed at the Red Cross hospital in Brussels during the First World War. On

5 August 1915, during the German occupation of Brussels, Cavell was arrested for having sheltered two hundred British, French, and Belgian soldiers in her home. Although American and Spanish authorities tried to postpone her execution, she was shot by a firing squad on 12 October 1915. Cavell's execution aroused widespread indignation, and Moore counselled the minister of justice to avoid a similar occurrence in Canada.[86]

The public reaction to Lassandro's sentence indicates that if chivalry had not yet died, it did not apply to women such as Lassandro. In a lengthy and argumentative letter to Minister of Justice Lomer Gouin, dated 12 December 1922, J.W.D. Turner, a lawyer with the Alberta provincial government, argued that although the idea of carrying out the death sentence seemed worse if the convicted murderer was a woman, given the context of the time, attitudes were in need of adjustment: "Women [in the past] were on the whole, content to be engaged domestically ... Theirs was the retiring but inestimably valuable lot of the German 'Hausfrau' ... If therefore women will [now] occupy themselves with all those things (law, Bench, franchise, etc.), taking the places side by side with men as their equal in all things, including even part in the framing and administration of our own laws, surely women should be equally subject to those laws in the event of their offending against them."[87] Emily Murphy concurred. In a letter to Prime Minister King, Murphy argued that although she was opposed to capital punishment in general, Florence Lassandro had killed a police official and should, therefore, experience the full measure of the law. In contrast to her qualified championing of Jenny Hawkes, Murphy protested the executive's application of a gendered system of justice in capital cases involving women: "I also desire to protest against the pernicious doctrine that because a person who commits a murder is a woman that person should escape from capital punishment. As women we claim the privileges of citizenship for our sex, and we accordingly are prepared to take upon ourselves the weight of the penalties as well."[88]

Picariello and Lassandro appealed their conviction before the Supreme Court of Canada, which unanimously dismissed the appeal on 11 April 1923. The governor general did not commute Lassandro's sentence, and Lassandro was hanged on 2 May 1923. Federal legal authorities had responded to the jury's and judicial and public opinion. In his report to the secretary of state, Justice Walsh stated that he did not recommend commutation "for the man in any case ... The only thing that can be said for Lassandro is that she is a woman."[89] Lassandro's case file included clippings that suggested North America was suffering the effects of a crime wave. The *Montreal Gazette* reported on 1 May 1922 that a recent wave of urban crime had resulted in a number of police murders. It also disclosed that the newspapers of larger American cities daily chronicled incidents in which men were killed by bandits or members of gangs.[90]

The Italian community believed unquestioningly that Picariello and Lassandro were hanged to serve as an example to liquor interests. One Italian journalist noted that English-language newspapers liked to point out that it had been twenty-four years since a woman was hanged in Canada. He contended that clemency had been granted to these women because they were English. Lassandro, by contrast, was an Italian bootlegger: "The sacred Churches and Protestant organisations, influential in other cases did not intercede ... To be contaminated by bootlegging ... no pity was to be shown."[91]

CONCLUSION

In the war years and interwar decades, chivalry won the day in the treatment of violent offenders in prairie courts and communities. As in other settler societies and Canadian regions, the majority of women who entered the docket following accusations of murder or child murder donned the mantle of wounded womanhood to evade punishment. Like male Aboriginal defendants who stood accused of similar charges and used the cultural defence to great effect, this defence strategy reaffirmed hegemonic notions of femininity, saving a few individuals at the expense of many. The interwar period closed with a reaffirmation of late-nineteenth-century theories of female criminality that were premised on assumptions of women's inherent mental and physiological inferiority. Yet the trials of women such as Jenny Hawkes, Grapena Shulman, Hilda Blake, and Florence Lassandro, women who refused to play the victim at a moment when the movement for women's suffrage and the homestead dower were at their height, became occasions for feminists, legal officials, politicians, and members of the public to either resist or embrace inequalities in prairie society and law that the trials and the individual experiences of these women exposed. As historian Martin J. Wiener has argued, domestic disputes and conflicts that resulted in spousal murder, murder, or infanticide often paralleled more public struggles between feminists and the legal and political establishments.[92] The cases also caused ordinary citizens, lawmakers, and officials to grapple with the issue of when, or if, violence – whether committed by an individual or the state (in the form of capital punishment) – was justifiable. As the uneven treatment of accused female offenders shows, these questions were mediated by prejudicial explanations of crime and a concern for the preservation of the liberal economic order.

In those cases where the offender was neither a wife nor a mother, or where her victims were of a higher social or economic status, feminists and officials rarely interceded on the accused's behalf. Hilda Blake and Florence Lassandro were hanged because they were working-class, immigrant women who killed members of the middle-class, Anglo-Canadian, social and legal establishment: a female employer and a police officer. By contrast, convicted murderesses such as Hawkes and Shulman, whose clemency campaigns ended in commutations of death sentences and shorter prison terms, owed their treatment to their privileged status as wives and mothers and to the fact that it could be argued they had resorted to violence for the best of motives: to preserve the family farm from harm from interloping, promiscuous women and from negligent husbands who had abdicated their rights and duties as rural patriarchs. Finally, unmarried, immigrant, and working-class women who killed their babies or concealed the births to avoid unwanted motherhood were accorded the most lenient treatment because their actions constituted no real threat to the social order. Since the courts had yet to establish the rights of infants and the unborn, society deemed these women's desperate actions to be in the best interests of the family and the nation. As was the case in the parallel campaign to eradicate prostitution as a social ill in prairie cities, social commentators and community members often represented the female child murderer as the hapless, passive victim of an aggressive or negligent male seducer. Although Lassandro's and Blake's class, ethnicity, and unmarried status placed them outside the realm of respectable womanhood, the actions of female child murderers were viewed as pitiable strategies to avoid the public shame attached to unwed motherhood. As historian Marilyn Francis has argued in her study of child murder in England, the choice of infanticide or murder "confirmed the power that the social order had over these women's lives."[93]

Conclusion

The Canadian Prairies are defined by space: wide-open skies and limitless horizons. In 1891, Nicholas Flood Davin – a Conservative MP, newsman, and Canadian expansionist – enhanced this image when he, along with other regional promoters, promised potential immigrants fruitful land, happy homes, and freedom from Old World constraints. Within three decades, over 1.5 million European, American, and Canadian immigrants answered the call. Some of them undoubtedly found what they sought; others did not, and in this book I have explored the experiences of those less fortunate. Criminal case files in key contact zones expose the dark side of the settlement process, which has been obscured by older conceptions of Canadian history and the sensational story of the mythic Mountie and the mild West he allegedly produced. As historian Steven Maynard, in his discussion of sexuality and violence in Canadian history, reminds us, what we, as a nation, choose to forget is as important as what we choose to remember and memorialize.[1] Hundreds of criminal cases and trials that involved women as victims or perpetrators provide an entry into the intimate world of the farmer, the pioneer woman, and the hired hand; of sexual and domestic violence in Aboriginal and non-Aboriginal populations; of prostitutes and reformers, of "sin" and seduction; of working-class and immigrant masculinities; and of sensational murders that gained local and national attention. Prosecution patterns, trial outcomes, and the narratives that emerged from the courtroom or in the media provide clues to unlock how sexuality, violence, and the law shaped colonialism and nation building in Canada.

At the turn of the twentieth century, the North American Prairies were viewed by economists, policy makers, and financiers as the basis of the modern world. The American and Canadian Wests formed part of a web of frontier neo-Europes that stretched to South Africa, New Zealand, Australia, Russia, and Argentina. These frontiers were drawn into imperial projects by a specific view of land: land could be grasped from indigenous peoples if newcomers promised to add value to it and make it bear fruit, and if a legal framework was put in place to ensure that men – individuals of modest means – could acquire property.[2] Dreams of imperial expansion came to reside on settlement frontiers, but so too did dreams of nation. The incorporation of the West in Canada and the United States was a deliberate exercise in nation building, and the monogamous, patriarchal family was viewed as a building block of the nation that was as important as the transnational railway, the national policy, and the arrival of the North West Mounted Police. But, as a number of historians have pointed out, the project of liberal rule – defined by Ian McKay as the implantation of a specific economic-political logic of liberalism – and the transformation of the prairie West into a white, manly space was not a natural process. Nor did it go uncontested.[3] First-wave feminists campaigned for the vote and access to land on the same basis as men, and some First Nations and immigrant groups adhered to alternative views of marriage, divorce, and sexuality.[4]

The criminal justice system in prairie Canada served as a clearing house in which dominant ideas about the individual, the family, and society came up against countervailing notions and produced "common sense" understandings of land, family, gender, sexuality, race, class, and settler society. While the international boundary line and the arrival of the North West Mounted Police (NWMP) carved out geographic spaces that distinguished the Canadian and American nations, "other lines, distinguishing 'Indians' from 'whites,' Indian land from white land, femininity from masculinity, [and property owners from labourers] were equally necessary ... because both nations depended upon assumptions about race, space, and gender to make all of their demarcations meaningful."[5] Yet, whereas westerners in the United States turned their backs on historical ties with Europe, newcomer elites north of the forty-ninth parallel embraced the relationship and culture they shared with Britain. The creation of judicial districts and the erection of courthouses translated into a new mental universe populated by officials who appeared to possess a socially ordained right to rule.[6] The rhetoric that accompanied the arrival of the NWMP and early criminal trials that involved women helped the Canadian state project an image of a protective, peaceable kingdom, even as it condoned violence and sexual impropriety under certain circumstances and erected hierarchies of difference and social barriers in the emerging settler society.

British Canadian trial judges used sensational trials to signal to Aboriginal peoples and settlers alike that violence and the vigilante-style justice of the American West would not be countenanced in prairie Canada and that the rule of law would be applied universally, irrespective of race, social class, or gender. When a trial jury in Calgary, which harboured a large American immigrant population, appeared to condone the murder of an Aboriginal woman in 1889, Justice Charles Rouleau cast himself as a defender of Aboriginal womanhood, overturned the decision, and cautioned Calgarians to overlook the victim's race when they deliberated on the issue of murder. In 1890, Chief Justice Hugh Richardson of the Supreme Court of the North-West Territories likewise charged jury members to overlook Harriet Thorne's status as an Aboriginal woman when they assessed her accusations of rape against a white settler, George Evanse, and to afford the victim as much consideration as if she were "the highest lady in the land."[7] Two decades later, when the campaign for women's suffrage and homestead dower was at its height and some prairie dwellers were wont to draw upon American notions of the unwritten law to justify murders committed by two abused farm wives who had taken the law into their own hands to preserve the sanctity of their marriages, judges and politicians similarly interceded in the cases to ensure that prairie dwellers maintained faith in the superiority of British Canadian justice over its American counterpart.

These relatively rare yet high-profile trials helped to consolidate the prairie West's place as a peaceable kingdom in imperial and nation-building schemes. They also drew attention away from less sensational, more routine, policing practices, legal strategies, and prosecutorial patterns that reinforced boundaries and divisions between Native and newcomer, capital and labour, and the private and public spheres. Judicial claims to impartiality were belied by the haste with which criminal cases were dispatched in magistrates' and trial courts. Trials and jury deliberations seldom took more than a few hours, charges to the jury and jury decisions rarely centred on intricate considerations of substantive law and evidence, and only in the most extreme situations – such as cases of husband murder or the rape of Harriet Thorne, a "respectable" Aboriginal woman – did they generate debates about law and the systemic inequalities that were the foundations of the liberal economic order and the white, manly, settler society envisaged by the region's promoters and policy makers. The ranks of charged or convicted offenders were filled with indigent and Aboriginal women, agricultural labourers, and immigrant men – individuals who either failed to heed the lines of demarcation that were deemed essential to nation and empire or failed to meet new standards of middle-class femininity and masculinity that were embodied by judges, jury members, and social and moral reformers. By virtue of law or their alleged behaviour, these individuals were deemed unworthy of the unwritten rights of citizenship that accrued to property-owning individuals, particularly protection from prosecution in a criminal court and state intervention should they become the victims of violence.

Police, Indian agents, and JPs used the status provisions of the Indian Act, along with liquor and trespassing laws, to pursue and punish Aboriginal and mixed-blood women, such as Sarah and Bertha Thomas, who resisted the notion that newly constructed racial categories and reserve boundaries should preclude them from engaging in behaviour – consuming alcohol, visiting relatives, or entering into cross-racial sexual relationships – routinely carried out by white settlers without fear of punishment. Policing practices and criminal law provisions that criminalized the colonized helped to construct the Aboriginal woman as dangerous and dissolute; they also guaranteed that magistrates, judges, and juries would not, contrary to Justice Richardson's claims, take individual Aboriginal women's accusations of sexual or physical violence suffered at the hands of Aboriginal men seriously. Murder, rape, and incest trials that involved Aboriginal victims and accused contributed to the process by which depictions of Aboriginal men as sexual predators who posed a threat to white womanhood were replaced with new, non-threatening images of Aboriginal masculinity. Aboriginal men who were drawn into an alien justice system with foreign methods of dispute resolution often put forward (on the advice of their defence counsels) ignorance of the law, drunkenness, or culture as mitigating circumstances in the commission of their crimes. The strategy was successful. But it cast Aboriginal defendants as ignorant, infantile stock characters and white judges and jury members as wise, learned father figures. The treatment of Aboriginal defendants served as a powerful lesson to Native and newcomer alike – that discretion, as an aspect of a criminal justice system founded on the British principles of majesty and terror tempered by mercy, had taken root in the countryside.[8] It would play an important role in the construction of racial categories and class divisions, and it would police the boundaries between the private and public spheres. The depictions of Aboriginal masculinity that emerged from the courtroom for consumption by the larger settler society helped to justify official policies that imposed the patriarchal, monogamous family model in reserve communities.

A desire to secure the patriarchal foundation of the emerging capitalistic countryside and the protection of property (and its owners) trumped other considerations when police, judges, and juries dealt with cases of domestic or sexual violence. In Aboriginal communities, the Indian Act and unofficial policies of the Department of Indian Affairs (DIA) encouraged Indian agents to police, punish, or discourage behaviour that fell outside of monogamy and lifelong union. Many of the cases of wife beating, non-support, and desertion that came to the attention of law and government officials attached to the Kainai Reserve in southern Alberta reflected Aboriginal peoples' resistance to these policies or their unintended consequences. Members of the NWMP, Aboriginal scouts, and DIA officials increasingly interceded on Aboriginal men's behalf to resolve disputes that would have ended in sanctioned divorce, separation, or reconciliation under Aboriginal law.

By contrast, in white settler communities, where the delimitation of land and power to individual men preceded settlement, magistrates and judges were reluctant to convict in sexual and domestic violence cases if the accused proved himself to be an upstanding farmer or a family man. Criminal records are filled with evidence of domestic disputes that emerged from women's active resistance to and defiance of a legal system that treated them as little more than their husband's or father's property and failed to acknowledge their contributions to farm life by providing them with equal access to and ownership of homestead property. But prosecution patterns in magistrates' and trial courts show that men who beat another man's wife or daughter were more likely to receive convictions and harsh penalties than men who beat their own. An unwillingness to disrupt the sanctity of the private, patriarchal family or undermine masculine privilege meant that many acts of violence perpetrated on girls and women would go unpunished – within limits.

Trials for sexual or domestic violence that resulted in conviction and lengthy prison terms or the death penalty were trials of masculinity that darkened the lines between capital and labour and between Anglo-Canadians and others. Although the region's promoters and politicians had originally envisaged a settlement frontier dotted at regular intervals by stalwart British, Canadian, or western European farmers and their families, demands for labour and increasingly expansive immigration policies tipped the balance in favour of unmarried, itinerant men who moved in and out of the region's burgeoning cities, and eastern Europeans who took up homesteads in bloc settlements. Beginning in the 1880s, the NWMP, city councils, and some magistrates made allowances for the demographic imbalance by adopting a pragmatic approach to prostitution. They viewed an unofficial system of regulation as the most efficient way to meet the needs of rugged, frontier masculinity and to protect virtuous women and the public sphere from its excesses. By the First World War, however, the campaign to eradicate prostitution and the consolidation of the countryside were accompanied by new, middle-class notions of masculinity and marriage and less fluid class distinctions. Farm wives or their daughters who accused immigrant agricultural labourers of rape, sexual assault, or seduction were taken seriously, and their cases often ended with some of the harshest sentences meted out to sexual offenders prior to the Second World War. Similarly, parents who employed the seduction provisions of the Criminal Code to prevent an interloping hired hand from marrying their daughter often received the full sympathy of police, judges, juries, and JPs. Legal and government officials were also less likely to apply discretionary justice or extend the prerogative of mercy to immigrant farmers, such as Herycko Zbyhley, who were accused of wife beating, murder, or incest.

In the absence of incontrovertible physical evidence, prosecuting attorneys introduced, to good effect, character evidence that placed the accused outside the protective bounds of proper, middle-class masculinity in sexual and domestic violence cases. Sometimes, such as in Lawrence Gowland's trial for rape and murder, the defendant's association with the English working-class or assisted immigration schemes for orphans was enough to ensure that he would not receive a fair trial. In other cases, judges and juries took a dim view of accused who engaged in sexual activity outside of marriage, used off-colour language, indulged in drink, or engaged in behaviour that could be construed as a cowardly avoidance of civic or familial responsibility. Even the choice of weapon in cases of wife murder could influence the accused's reception in a court of law: poisoning one's wife was deemed one of the most pernicious crimes known to man, whereas beating her, or shooting her, could be justified under some circumstances. In the courtroom and the larger court of public opinion, trials of masculinity extended to husband murder cases in which certain victims (particularly those whom defence counsels could portray as unfit for the rights and privileges of family and citizenship by virtue of their status as members of marginalized immigrant groups or because of their "brutish" or "weak-willed" behaviour) were deemed culpable in their own murders, with the result that the murderess received a lenient sentence or commutation of a death sentence.

Masculinity was on trial but, as feminist historians of criminal justice systems have argued and shown over the last four decades, so too was femininity. As Jennifer Henderson argues in her exploration of settler feminism and race making in Canada, the pioneer woman did not reside outside of culture and the machinations of power in the emerging liberal economic order: she "occupied the site of the *norm.*"[9] Although first-wave feminists and male social and moral reform advocates mounted a concerted campaign to abolish the sexual double standard, to hold men to the same moral and sexual standards as women, and to eradicate social problems such as prostitution that the double standard encouraged, the farther away a female complainant or offender was from the hegemonic ideal of the hard-working and subservient pioneer wife and mother, a figure that embodied the white life for two, the less likely she was to receive the court's protection or evade punishment for her indiscretions or violent acts. Reformers in Winnipeg caused red-light districts to be shut down and prompted the passage of new criminal law provisions to encourage the punishment of procurers, madams, and male inmates of bawdy houses. Prosecutorial patterns in the interwar decades, however, suggest that law enforcement officials and police continued to adhere to older notions of property, frontier masculinity, and the sexual double standard that encouraged the arrest and incarceration of common prostitutes rather than their male clients or property-owning madams. The white-slave scares and anti-prostitution campaigns, perhaps inadvertently, encouraged this trend: they helped to establish settler feminists as moral icons and to carve out a place in the public sphere for respectable women, yet they did so by representing the city as counterculture, drawing attention to and problematizing the sexuality of unmarried women and female youths who increasingly lived, worked, and played in its confines.

Because of the diversity of and disparities among various groups in prairie communities, judges and juries were predisposed to take women's accusations of sexual and physical abuse seriously. Yet even men who suffered poor reputations – Aboriginal men, eastern European farmers, and agricultural labourers – could harness the sexual double standard and hegemonic femininity to evade punishment on charges of rape, wife beating, or murder. Defence counsels and accused who introduced evidence that the victim had engaged in sex outside the constraints of marriage or was a poor wife and mother could gain the sympathy of the judge, jury, or public. This strategy became more effective over time as ordinary citizens digested the lessons of trials past and (as a comparison of prosecution patterns and trial outcomes in rural and urban areas suggests) as proponents of the country-life ideology contrasted life in the city with life in the countryside and found it wanting. Complainants in rape, indecent assault, or seduction cases who were unmarried working girls, or women shown to enjoy picture shows, dances, driving, or drinking with men, found it difficult to counter negative readings of their leisure activities that interpreted them as immoral acts that threatened the very foundations of family and nation. As a result, they found it difficult to convince judges and juries of the truth of their claims of rape, indecent assault, or seduction. These trials offered middle-class judges opportunities to solidify their position as moral authorities; they strengthened the lines between middle- and working-class femininities, which in the Prairies were tied intimately to ethnicity and race; they served as cautionary tales for women who failed to toe the line; and they belied Jessie Saxby's promise that the region's manly titans would "treat ... women with a chivalry and tenderness which cannot fail to bind the feebler sex in willing chains."

As in other Western industrializing nations and regions, chivalry, or paternalism in disguise, did inform the treatment of female offenders. Just as male Aboriginal accused could harness the cultural defence in their favour, so too could prairie women don the mantle of wounded womanhood to evade punishment. Defence counsels and women who stood trial for abortion, infanticide, or husband murder frequently manipulated the ideology's underlying assumptions of an active and assertive masculinity and a passive and submissive femininity in their favour. While Anglo-Canadian and American farm wives, such as Amy Warwick, evoked pity and sympathy from all-male trial juries and the public by arguing that they had been driven to murder by the machinations and abuse of men, married women and single girls such as Mary Hay and Annie Rubletz escaped the maximum punishment for abortion and infanticide by claiming that their acts had been carried out in the best interests of preserving the institution of marriage and the nation or were the result of temporary insanity brought on by childbirth. Although their experiences of courtship, marriage, work, and family often departed from the middle-class ideal of separate spheres for men and women and companionate marriage, these women's trials enhanced notions of women as submissive, irrational, infantile, and irresponsible. As historian Jill Newton Ainsley observes in her study of insanity acquittals in nineteenth-century England, "What kind of mysterious agency was this?"[10]

Conclusion

237

But the application of chivalric justice was modified or undercut by the race, class, and ethnic tensions that underlay the making of the modern order. Prosecution patterns and trial outcomes show that in prairie Canada, more so than in more established regions, judges, juries, and magistrates took the female offender's marital status, race, age, and ethnicity into account when they deliberated on issues of motivation and intent. Aboriginal women and indigent women moved in and out of prison on various charges, and immigrant, working-class women such as Hilda Blake, Florence Lassandro, and Catherine Tratch were either hanged for murder or served life sentences.

As the differential treatment of complainants or accused in cases that involved women shows, the criminal justice system helped to regulate sex and violence outside of marriage and reproduce forms of inequality and Spencerian notions of crime that were necessary to colonialism and nation building in prairie Canada. The conception of the male, property-owning individual and the patriarchal, monogamous family model that accompanied the creation of a liberal economic order in the region conferred on a small minority of men and women protection from punishment, freedom from state intervention in their private lives, and the ability to demand justice from the state if they suffered sexual or physical violence at the hands of another. The myth of the mild West, and the peaceable kingdom it helped produce, emerged from a particular understanding of crime and violence: one that limited it to behaviour in the public sphere or behaviour that threatened private property. The sanctity of the private sphere *was* breached – in reserve communities and cases of incest in immigrant families, for instance – not to protect women or children from harm but to maintain the nation. However, the settlement of prairie Canada occurred during a period when colonial unrest, the rise of feminism, and the labour movement challenged the unequal foundations upon which the region was built, and these tensions spilled over to influence conflicts between Aboriginal people and settlers, labour and capital, husbands and wives, parents and children, and men and women and their interactions in the classroom of the courtroom.

Although systemic inequalities would not be addressed for decades – the Province of Alberta did not recognize women's right to an equal share in family property until 1979, and the consequences of Canada's Indian Act and policy remain with us – criminal cases and trials prior to the Second World War sparked observations, discussions, debates, and new understandings of sexuality, family, violence, personhood, and human rights. A few lawyers spoke out against abuses of justice committed by Indian agents and police in Aboriginal communities. First-wave feminists drew attention to the sexual double standard and its effect on women, and some judges and juries took their criticism into account when they considered cases of sexual violence, infanticide, or abortion and did not, out of hand, blame the female party. Women and girls defended their right to be protected from sexual and physical violence or negligence at the hands of strange men, fathers, or husbands, and some of their cases caused members of the public to ask questions. Should women now suffer the pains as well as the pleasures of citizenship? Is violence, regardless of whether it is committed by a woman or the state in the form of capital punishment, ever justifiable? Contemporary criminal trials and incidents, such as the Pamela George case (discussed in the Introduction), have raised similar allegations, debates, and concerns in contemporary prairie Canada. In 2000, Manitoba's First Nations demanded a study of racism in Winnipeg's police force following the deaths of two Metis women. They argued that the deaths could have been averted had police not ignored the women's repeated requests, made to 911, to intervene in a domestic dispute. That same year, two officers in Saskatoon, Saskatchewan, faced trial for assault and unlawful confinement after abandoning three Aboriginal men on the outskirts of the city in the dead of winter. One of the cases of abandonment occurred in 1990, but it was not until two more men were found frozen to death a decade later that the first victim's mother, an Aboriginal woman whose sons had been in trouble with the law, convinced legal authorities to listen to her concerns and launch a full investigation. These cases, much like criminal case files and trials from the distant past, serve as important reminders that the experiences of those forgotten, ignored, or marginalized can tell us as much about nation and community as those things we choose to praise and remember.

Notes

INTRODUCTION

1 "Natives Scorn Killers' Sentences," *Globe and Mail*, 31 January 1997.
2 "Pair Guilty in Slaying of Regina Prostitute," *Globe and Mail*, 21 December 1996; "Judge Accused of Bias," *Star Phoenix*, 21 February 1997. Defence counsel Aaron Fox noted that the issue of sexual assault and forcible confinement arose only in the context of whether the crime was first- or second-degree murder. Fox contended that Malone correctly directed the jury to consider the issue of consent only if it rejected a verdict of manslaughter: "Editorial Wrong, Lawyer Wants to Set Record Straight," *Leader Post*, 11 February 1997.
3 For full accounts of the murder and trial, see Sherene Razack, "Gendered Racial Violence and Spatialized Justice: The Murder of Pamela George," in *Race, Space, and the Law: Unmapping a White Settler Society*, ed. Sherene Razack (Toronto: Between the Lines, 2002), 121-56; "Pair Guilty in Slaying of Regina Prostitute," *Globe and Mail*, 21 December 1996; Albert Angus, "Saskatchewan Justice on Trial: The Pamela George Case," *Saskatchewan Indian* 27 (April 1997): 5, 23; Ron Bourgeault, "Pamela George: A Victim of History and Economic Racism," *Canadian Dimension* 31 (May-June 1997): 41-43; "Murder Victim's Family Angry," *Vancouver Sun*, 31 January 1997.
4 See Peggy Pascoe, "Western Women at the Cultural Crossroads," in *Trails: Towards a New Western History*, ed. Patricia Nelson Limerick, Clyde A. Milner II, and Charles E. Rankin (Lawrence: University of Kansas Press, 1991), 40-58. Pascoe recommended placing women of colour at the centre of historical investigation.
5 See Natalie Zemon Davis, "The Shapes of Social History," *Storia della storiografia* 17 (1990): 28-34.
6 For Canadian examples of these two approaches that I found particularly inspirational, see Karen Dubinsky and Franca Iacovetta, "Murder, Womanly Virtue, and Motherhood: The Case of Angelina Napolitano, 1911-1922," *Canadian Historical Review* 72 (December 1991): 505-31; Constance Backhouse, "Desperate Women and Compassionate Courts:

Infanticide in Nineteenth-Century Canada," *University of Toronto Law Journal* 34 (1984): 447-78; Joan Sangster, "'Pardon Tales' from Magistrate's Courts: Women, Crime, and the Court in Peterborough County, 1920-50," *Canadian Historical Review* 74 (June 1993): 505-31; Karen Dubinsky, *Improper Advances: Rape and Heterosexual Conflict in Ontario, 1880-1929* (Chicago: University of Chicago Press, 1993); Annalee Gölz, "'If a Man's Wife Does Not Obey Him, What Can He Do?' Marital Breakdown and Wife Abuse in Late Nineteenth-Century and Early Twentieth-Century Ontario," in *Law, Society, and the State: Essays in Modern Legal History,* ed. Louis A. Knafla and Susan W.S. Binnie (Toronto: University of Toronto Press, 1995), 323-50. Constance Backhouse's *Petticoats and Prejudice: Women and Law in Nineteenth-Century Canada* (Toronto: Women's Press, 1991), which was one of the few studies that considered women as both victims and offenders, was, and continues to be, an inspiration.

7   See Chapman's "'Til Death Do Us Part': Wife Beating in Alberta, 1905-1920," *Alberta History* 36 (Autumn 1988): 13-22; "Sex Crimes in the West, 1890-1920," *Alberta History* 35 (Autumn 1987): 6-21; and "Sex Crimes in Western Canada, 1890-1920" (PhD diss., University of Alberta, 1984). For studies that support what historian Kathryn McPherson calls the frontier-equality thesis, see Catherine Cleverdon, *The Woman Suffrage Movement in Canada* (1950; repr., Toronto: University of Toronto Press, 1974); Susan Jackel, ed., *A Flannel Shirt and Liberty: British Emigrant Gentlewomen in the Canadian West, 1880-1914* (Vancouver: UBC Press, 1982); James H. Gray, *Red Lights on the Prairies: The Bonanza Years When the Wide-Open Frontier Was a Hooker's Happy Hunting Ground* (1971; repr., Scarborough, ON: New American Library, 1973); and Carol Lee Bacchi, "Divided Allegiances: The Response of Farm and Labour Women to Suffrage," in *A Not Unreasonable Claim: Women and Reform in Canada, 1880-1920s,* ed. Linda Kealey (Toronto: Women's Press, 1979), 89-107. Finally, see Kathryn McPherson, "Was the 'Frontier' Good for Women? Historical Approaches to Women and Agricultural Settlement in the Prairie West, 1870-1925," *Atlantis* 25, 1 (2000): 75-86.

8   Douglas Owram, "*On the Case: Explorations in Social History:* A Roundtable Discussion," *Canadian Historical Review* 81 (June 2000): 275-76.

9   See Lorraine Gadoury and Antonio Lechasseur, "Persons Sentenced to Death in Canada, 1867-1976: An Inventory of Case Files in the Fonds of the Department of Justice (RG 13)" (Ottawa: National Archives of Canada, 1994).

10   The Provincial Archives of Manitoba has the most complete and inventoried collection of records. See Michele Fitzgerald, *A Research Guide to Court Records in the Provincial Archives of Manitoba* (Winnipeg: Legal Research Institute, 1994). The Alberta collection is equally extensive, yet the archives (with the exception of the Edmonton Judicial District) lack detailed finding aids. For an overview of the records, see Alberta Legal History Project, *Specimen File Selections and Analysis with Index* (Calgary: Alberta Law Foundation, 1984).

11   Bryan D. Palmer, "Foucault and the Historians: The Case of *On the Case,*" *Literary Review of Canada* (Summer 1999): 11-17.

12   Franca Iacovetta and Wendy Mitchinson, "Social History and Case File Research," in Iacovetta and Mitchinson, *On the Case,* 3.

13   Mariana Valverde's contribution to Owram, "*On the Case: Explorations in Social History:* A Roundtable Discussion," 268-69.

14   Ibid., 269.

15   Ibid.

16 Annalee E. Lepp, "Dis/membering the Family: Marital Breakdown, Domestic Conflict, and Family Violence in Ontario, 1830-1920" (PhD diss., Queen's University, 2001), 7-9.

17 *British North American Act,* 1867, s. 92(14). The pioneering work on the use of these records is Natalie Zemon Davis' *Fiction in the Archives: Pardon Tales and Their Tellers in Sixteenth-Century France* (Stanford: Stanford University Press, 1987). The prerogative of mercy and the nature of capital case files in Canada are discussed by Carolyn Strange in "Stories of Their Lives: The Historian and the Capital Case File," in Iacovetta and Mitchinson, *On the Case,* 25-48, and in "Discretionary Justice: Political Culture and the Death Penalty in New South Wales and Ontario, 1890-1920," in *Qualities of Mercy: Justice, Punishment, and Discretion,* ed. Carolyn Strange (Vancouver: UBC Press, 1996), 140-42; and by Kimberley White in *Negotiating Responsibility: Law, Murder, and States of Mind* (Vancouver: UBC Press, 2008), 17-27. See also Jonathan Swainger, "A Distant Edge of Authority: Capital Punishment and the Prerogative of Mercy in British Columbia, 1872-1880," in *Essays in the History of Canadian Law,* vol. 6, *British Columbia and the Yukon,* ed. Hamar Foster and John McLaren (Toronto: University of Toronto Press for the Osgoode Society for Canadian Legal History, 1995), 204-41; and Swainger's "Advisors to the Crown and the Prerogative of Mercy," in *The Canadian Department of Justice and the Completion of Confederation, 1867-78* (Vancouver: UBC Press, 2000), 56-78.

18 Strange, "Stories of Their Lives," 27; Palmer, "Foucault and the Historians," 13.

19 Karen Dubinsky, "Telling Stories about Dead People," in Iacovetta and Mitchinson, *On the Case,* 361.

20 Iacovetta and Mitchinson, "Social History and Case File Research," 8.

21 For examples of Canadian historians who have used a case study or microhistorical approach to examine these issues, see James W. St. G. Walker, "The Case for Morality: The Quong Wing Files," in Iacovetta and Mitchinson, *On the Case,* 217; Dubinsky and Iacovetta, "Murder, Womanly Virtue, and Motherhood," 505-31; Reinhold Kramer and Tom Mitchell, *Walk Towards the Gallows: The Tragedy of Hilda Blake, Hanged 1899* (Don Mills, ON: Oxford University Press, 2002); Constance Backhouse, *Colour-Coded: A Legal History of Racism in Canada, 1900-1950* (Toronto: University of Toronto Press for the Osgoode Society for Canadian Legal History, 1999); Kenneth Coates and William R. Morrison, *Strange Things Done: Murder in Yukon Territory* (Montreal and Kingston: McGill-Queen's University Press, 2004).

22 Sander Gilman, *Difference and Pathology: Stereotypes of Sexuality, Race, and Madness* (Ithaca, NY: Cornell University Press, 1995).

23 See, for instance, the articles in Edward Muir and Guido Ruggiero, eds., *Microhistory and the Lost Peoples of Europe,* trans. Eren Branch (Baltimore: Johns Hopkins University Press, 1991).

24 Garthine Walker, *Crime, Gender, and Social Order in Early Modern England* (Cambridge: Cambridge University Press, 2003), 4. For an exception to this observation, see Angus McLaren, *Trials of Masculinity: Policing Sexual Boundaries, 1870-1930* (Chicago: University of Chicago Press, 1997); and Martin J. Wiener has since published *Men of Blood: Violence, Manliness, and Criminal Justice in Victorian England* (New York: Cambridge University Press, 2004). Historical scholarship on women, gender, and crime is extensive and ever expanding. Margaret L. Arnot and Cornelie Usborne provide an excellent overview in "Why Gender and Crime? Aspects of an International Debate," in *Gender and Crime in Modern Europe,* ed. Margaret L. Arnot and Cornelie Usborne (London: University College London Press, 1999), 1-29.

25 Daiva Stasiulis and Nira Yuval-Davis, "Introduction: Beyond Dichotomies – Gender, Race, Ethnicity, and Class in Settler Societies," in *Unsettling Settler Societies: Articulations of Gender, Race, Ethnicity, and Class*, ed. Daiva Stasiulis and Nira Yuval-Davis (London: Sage Publications, 1995), 2; Anne McClintock, *Imperial Leather: Race, Gender, and Sexuality in the Colonial Contest* (New York: Routledge, 1995), 5; Diane Kirkby, ed., *Sex, Power, and Justice: Historical Perspectives on Law in Australia* (Melbourne: Oxford University Press, 1995), xvii.

26 Pascoe, "Western Women at the Cultural Crossroads," 46.

27 *Stanford Encyclopedia of Philosophy*, s.v., "Colonialism," http://plato.stanford.edu/entries/colonialism/. I distinguish between colonialism and imperialism. The term *imperialism* "draws attention to the way that one country exercises power over another, whether through settlement, sovereignty, or indirect mechanisms of control." Many scholars apply the term *internal colonialism* to white settler societies such as Canada. The term describes the network of legal, political, and economic constraints that were imposed on racialized others and ethnic minorities within the borders of nations that had founding myths and liberal democratic states that emphasized freedom and equality. See Stasiulis and Yuval-Davis, "Introduction: Beyond Dichotomies," 12.

28 Stuart Hall, *The Multicultural Question* (Milton Keynes, UK: Pavis Centre for Social and Cultural Research, 2001), 231.

29 Brad Asher, *Beyond the Reservation: Indians, Settlers, and the Law in Washington Territory, 1853-1889* (Norman: University of Oklahoma Press, 1999), 13.

30 George Robb and Nancy Erber, eds., *Disorder in the Court: Trials and Sexual Conflict at the Turn of the Century* (New York: New York University Press, 1999), 1-11.

CHAPTER 1: FRUITFUL LAND, HAPPY HOMES, MANLY TITANS

1 Quoted in Donald Smith, "Bloody Murder Almost Became Miscarriage of Justice," *Calgary Herald Sunday Magazine*, 23 July 1989, 15. The case has also been examined by Sarah Carter in "Categories and Terrains of Exclusion: Constructing the 'Indian Woman' in the Early Settlement Era in Western Canada," *Great Plains Quarterly* 13 (Summer 1993): 156-57; and by novelist Katherine Govier in *Between Men* (Markham, ON: Penguin Books Canada, 1987). For an in-depth discussion, see Lesley Erickson, "Murdered Women and Mythic Villains: The Criminal Case and the Imaginary Criminal in the Canadian West, 1886-1930," in *People and Place: Historical Influences on Legal Culture*, ed. Jonathan Swainger and Constance Backhouse (Vancouver: UBC Press, 2003), 95-119.

2 Quoted in Carter, "Categories and Terrains," 157.

3 As many historians acknowledge, the term *prairie West* is a misnomer, since it applies only to that small southern portion of the prairie provinces that lies at the tip of the northern Great Plains. Yet the term is useful for distinguishing the region from the colonies and province of British Columbia and for highlighting the region's unique economic and historical development: Gerald Friesen, *The Canadian Prairies: A History* (Toronto: University of Toronto Press, 1984), 3. For recent discussions about the place of the Prairies in Canada, and the region's status as an imagined community, see the Introduction and contributions to R. Douglas Francis and Chris Kitzan, eds., *The Prairie West as Promised Land* (Calgary: University of Calgary Press, 2007); Bill Waiser, "Introduction: Place, Process,

and the New Prairie Realities," *Canadian Historical Review* 84 (December 2003): 509-17; Gerald Friesen, "Defining the Prairies: Or, Why the Prairies Don't Exist," in *Toward Defining the Prairies: Region, Culture, and History,* ed. Robert Wardhaugh (Winnipeg: University of Manitoba Press, 2001), 19, 21-22; and John Herd Thompson, *Forging the Prairie West: The Illustrated History of Canada* (Toronto: Oxford University Press, 1998), ix-xii.

4 See Douglas M. Peers, "Is Humpty Dumpty Back Together Again? The Revival of Imperial History and the *Oxford History of the British Empire," Journal of World History* 13 (Fall 2002): 457-58; Daiva Stasiulis and Nira Yuval-Davis, "Introduction: Beyond Dichotomies – Gender, Race, Ethnicity, and Class in Settler Societies," in *Unsettling Settler Societies: Articulations of Gender, Race, Ethnicity, and Class,* ed. Daiva Stasiulis and Nira Yuval-Davis (London: Sage Publications, 1995), 1-2; Catherine Hall, "Introduction: Thinking the Postcolonial, Thinking the Empire," in *Cultures of Empire: A Reader; Colonizers in Britain and the Empire in the Nineteenth and Twentieth Centuries,* ed. Catherine Hall (New York: Routledge, 2000), 3; Phillip A. Buckner and R. Douglas Francis, eds., Introduction to *Rediscovering the British World* (Calgary: University of Calgary Press, 2005), 9-12. For a recent discussion of this trend in the writing of western Canadian or Prairie regional history, see Gerald Friesen, "Critical History in Western Canada, 1900–2000," in *The West and Beyond: New Perspectives on an Imagined Region,* ed. Alvin Finkel, Sarah Carter, and Peter Fontina (Edmonton: Athabasca University Press, 2010), 7-8.

5 Daiva Stasiulis and Radha Jhappan, "The Fractious Politics of a Settler Society: Canada," in Stasiulis and Yuval-Davis, *Unsettling Settler Societies,* 97.

6 Phillip A. Buckner, ed., Introduction to *Canada and the British Empire* (Oxford: Oxford University Press, 2008), 5-6; Phillip A. Buckner and R. Douglas Francis, eds., Introduction to *Canada and the British World* (Vancouver: UBC Press, 2006), 1-7.

7 In *Colonialism's Culture: Anthropology, Travel, and Government* (Princeton, NJ: Princeton University Press, 1994), Nicholas Thomas defines *colonial project* as "a socially transforma- tive endeavour that is localized, politicized, and partial, yet also engendered by larger historical developments and ways of narrating them" (104). Nation building involves imagining a national past and present, inventing traditions, and symbolically constructing community: see Benedict Anderson, *Imagined Communities: Reflections on the Origin and Spread of Nationalism* (London: Verso, 1991); and Anthony Cohen, *The Symbolic Con- struction of Community* (New York: Tavistock, 1985).

8 The following edited volumes provide good introductions to these literatures: Diane Kirkby and Catherine Coleborne, eds., *Law, History, Colonialism: The Reach of Empire* (Manchester, UK: Manchester University Press, 2001); Peter Fitzpatrick and Eve Darian-Smith, eds., *Laws of the Postcolonial* (Ann Arbor: University of Michigan Press, 1999); Mindie Lazarus- Black and Susan F. Hirsch, eds., *Contested States: Law, Hegemony and Resistance* (New York: Routledge, 1994); Ruth Roach Pierson and Nupur Chaudhuri, eds., *Nation, Empire, Colony: Historicizing Gender and Race* (Bloomington: Indiana University Press, 1998). In contrast to a purely cultural understanding of gender, this study adopts Gail Bederman's definition of gender as "a historical, ideological process through which individuals are positioned or position themselves as men or as women": *Manliness and Civilization: A Cultural History of Gender and Race in the United States, 1880-1917* (London: University of Chicago Press, 1995), 5-6, 13.

9 Sean Gouglas and John C. Weaver, "A Postcolonial Understanding of Law and Society: Exploring Criminal Trials in Colonial Queensland," *Australian Journal of Legal History*

7 (2003): 232; Douglas Hay, "Property, Authority, and the Criminal Law," in *Albion's Fatal Tree: Crime and Society in Eighteenth-Century England,* ed. Douglas Hay, Peter Linbaugh, John G. Rule, and E.P. Thompson (New York: Pantheon, 1975), 17; Simon Gikandi, *Maps of Englishness: Writing Identity in the Culture of Colonialism* (New York: Columbia University Press, 1996), 1-83. Jean and John L. Comaroff argue that colonial and nation-building projects rested on civilizing the primitive and the pauper: *Ethnography and the Historical Imagination* (Boulder, CO: Westview Press, 1992), 289.

10 Martin Chanock, *Law, Custom, and Social Order: The Colonial Experience in Malawi and Zambia* (Cambridge: Cambridge University Press, 1985), 4; Louis A. Knafla and Susan W.S. Binnie, "Beyond the State: Law and Legal Pluralism in the Making of Modern Societies," in *Law, Society, and the State: Essays in Modern Legal History,* ed. Louis A. Knafla and Susan W.S. Binnie (Toronto: University of Toronto Press, 1995), 5-7; Sally Merry Engle, *Colonizing Hawai'i: The Cultural Power of Law* (Princeton, NJ: Princeton University Press, 2000), 206, 264; Radhika Singha, *A Despotism of Law: Crime and Justice in Early Colonial India* (Oxford: Oxford University Press, 1998).

11 John L. Comaroff, "Colonialism, Culture, and the Law: A Foreword," *Law and Social Inquiry* 26 (Spring 2001): 307; Gouglas and Weaver, "A Postcolonial Understanding," 232-33.

12 David Spurr, *The Rhetoric of Empire: Colonial Discourse in Journalism, Travel Writing, and Imperial Administration* (Durham, NC: Duke University Press, 1993), 32.

13 Carolyn Strange and Tina Loo, *Making Good: Law and Moral Regulation in Canada, 1867-1939* (Toronto: University of Toronto Press, 1997), 4. A number of fine historiographical articles explore historians' move away from simplistic, top-down models of law in colonial contexts: Comaroff, "Colonialism, Culture, and the Law," 305-14; Sally Merry Engle, "From Law and Colonialism to Law and Globalization," *Law and Social Inquiry* 28 (Spring 2003): 569-90; Jeffrey R. Dudas, "Law and the American Frontier," *Law and Social Inquiry* 29 (Fall 2004): 860-61. Martin Chanock's own research has followed this trajectory; see *The Making of South African Legal Culture, 1902-1936: Fear, Favour, and Prejudice* (Cambridge: Cambridge University Press, 2001). Douglas Harris argues that the insights and theoretical perspectives of postcolonial history can be applied to situations of internal colonialism in North America: *Fish, Law, and Colonialism: The Legal Capture of Salmon in British Columbia* (Toronto: University of Toronto Press, 2001).

14 Comaroff and Comaroff, *Ethnography and the Historical Imagination,* 265. For an excellent overview of the burgeoning international literature on how intimate domains made the racial categories necessary for imperial rule, and how these insights are applicable to North American contexts, see Ann Laura Stoler's review essay, "Tense and Tender Ties: The Politics of Comparison in North American History and (Post) Colonial Studies," *Journal of American History* 88 (December 2001): 829-65. For a small sampling of this literature, see Anne McClintock, *Imperial Leather: Race, Gender, and Sexuality in the Colonial Contest* (New York: Routledge, 1995); Julie Ann Clancy-Smith and Frances Gouda, eds., *Domesticating the Empire: Race, Gender, and Family in French and Dutch Colonialism* (Charlottesville: University of Virginia Press, 1998); Kathleen Brown, *Good Wives, Nasty Wenches, and Anxious Patriarchs: Gender, Race, and Power in Colonial Virginia* (Chapel Hill: University of North Carolina Press, 1996); Albert Hurtado, *Intimate Frontiers: Sex, Gender, and Culture in Old California* (Albuquerque: University of New Mexico Press, 1999); Mark M. Carroll, *Homesteads Ungovernable: Families, Sex, Race, and the Law in Frontier Texas, 1823-1860* (Austin: University of Texas Press, 2001). Studies that examine efforts to manage sexual and domestic

relationships in the colonial and early settlement periods of the Canadian West include contributions to Katie Pickles and Myra Rutherdale, eds., *Contact Zones: Aboriginal and Settler Women in Canada's Colonial Past* (Vancouver: UBC Press, 2005); Adele Perry, *On the Edge of Empire: Gender, Race, and the Making of British Columbia, 1849-1871* (Toronto: University of Toronto Press, 2001); Myra Rutherdale, *Women and the White Man's God: Gender and Race in the Canadian Mission Field* (Vancouver: UBC Press, 2002); Sarah Carter, *The Importance of Being Monogamous: Marriage and Nation Building in Western Canada to 1915* (Edmonton: University of Alberta Press/Athabasca University Press, 2008), and *Capturing Women: The Manipulation of Cultural Imagery in Canada's Prairie West* (Montreal and Kingston: McGill-Queen's University Press, 1997); Sylvia Van Kirk, *"Many Tender Ties": Women in Fur-Trade Society, 1670-1870* (1980; repr., Winnipeg: Watson and Dwyer, 1991).

15 Martin Wagner, *A Sociology of Modernity: Liberty and Discipline* (London: Routledge, 1994), 55-69; Martin Daunton and Bernhard Rieger, *Meanings of Modernity: Britain and the Late-Victorian Era to World War II* (Oxford: Oxford University Press, 2001).

16 Hall, "Introduction," 5-9; Robert Dixon, *Writing the Colonial Adventure: Race, Gender, and Nation in Anglo-Australian Popular Fiction, 1875-1914* (Cambridge: Cambridge University Press, 1995), 2-5.

17 The responsibility for Indian affairs rested with various government departments between 1873 and 1966. The Department of Indian Affairs was established in 1880, and it fell under the direction of the Department of the Interior. The minister of the interior was also the superintendent-general of Indian affairs. See Sarah Carter, *Lost Harvests: Prairie Indian Reserve Farmers and Government Policy* (Montreal and Kingston: McGill-Queen's University Press, 1990), particularly Chapter 4, "Assault upon the 'Tribal' System: Government Policy after 1885."

18 Sidney L. Harring, *White Man's Law: Native People in Nineteenth-Century Canadian Jurisprudence* (Toronto: University of Toronto Press for the Osgoode Society for Canadian Legal History, 1998), 247; Sandra Estlin Bingaman, "The Trials of Poundmaker and Big Bear, 1885," *Saskatchewan History* 28, 3 (1975): 81-102.

19 Sarah Carter, *Aboriginal People and Colonizers of Western Canada to 1900* (Toronto: University of Toronto Press, 1999), 150. See Bill Waiser and Blair Stonechild, *Loyal Till Death: Indians and the North-West Rebellion* (Calgary: Fifth House, 1997), 192-237.

20 Macdonald to Edgar Dewdney, 20 November 1885, quoted in Waiser and Stonechild, *Loyal Till Death*, 221.

21 Jessie M.E. Saxby, "North-West for Girls," *Regina Leader*, 31 July 1888.

22 Nicholas Flood Davin, ed., *Homes for Millions: The Great Canadian North-West; Its Resources Fully Described* (Ottawa: n.p., 1891), 3.

23 John McLaren, A.R. Buck, and Nancy E. Wright, eds., *Despotic Dominion: Property Rights in British Settler Societies* (Vancouver: UBC Press, 2004); John C. Weaver, *The Great Land Rush and the Making of the Modern World, 1650-1900* (Montreal and Kingston: McGill-Queen's University Press, 2003), 5; William H. Katerberg, "A Northern Vision: Frontiers and the West in the Canadian and American Imagination," *American Review of Canadian Studies* 33 (Winter 2003): 546; Douglas Owram, *Promise of Eden: The Canadian Expansionist Movement and the Idea of the West, 1856-1900* (Toronto: University of Toronto Press, 1992), 149-67; R. Douglas Francis, *Images of the West: Changing Perceptions of the Prairies, 1690-1960* (Saskatoon: Western Producer Prairie Books, 1989), 90-95; and Francis and Kitzan, eds., *Prairie West as Promised Land*, ix-xxiv.

24 Ian McKay, "The Liberal Order Framework: A Prospectus for a Reconnaissance of Canadian History," *Canadian Historical Review* 81 (December 2000): 618-19, 621-22, 624-26. For extensive debate on the liberal order framework in Canadian history, see Jean-François Constant and Michele Ducharme, eds., *Liberalism and Hegemony: Debating the Canadian Liberal Revolution* (Toronto: University of Toronto Press, 2009).For examples of studies that explore the Canadian West within a liberal order framework, see Tina Loo, *Making Law, Order, and Authority in British Columbia, 1821-1871* (Toronto: University of Toronto Press, 1994); and Carter, *Lost Harvests.*

25 Ann Leger-Anderson, "Canadian Prairie Women's History: An Uncertain Enterprise," *Journal of the West* 37 (January 1998): 55. See also Nancy F. Cott, *Public Vows: A History of Marriage and the Nation* (Cambridge, MA: Harvard University Press, 2000), 2, 174, 226.

26 Anna Davin, "Imperialism and Motherhood," *History Workshop Journal* 5 (Spring 1978): 9-65; Vron Ware, *Beyond the Pale: White Women, Racism, and History* (London: Verso, 1992); Howard I. Kushner, "The Persistence of the Frontier Thesis: Gender, Myth, and Self-Destruction," in "Reinterpreting the American Experience: Women, Gender, and American Studies," special issue, Part 1, *Canadian Review of American Studies* 23 (1992): 53.

27 Lori Chambers, *Married Women and Property Law in Victorian Ontario* (Toronto: University of Toronto Press for the Osgoode Society for Canadian Legal History, 1997), 24; Christina Simmons, *Making Marriage Modern: Women's Sexuality from the Progressive Era to World War II* (Oxford: Oxford University Press, 2009).

28 Catherine Cavanaugh, "The Limitations of the Pioneering Partnership: The Alberta Campaign for Homestead Dower, 1909-1925," in *Making Western Canada: Essays on European Colonization and Settlement,* ed. Catherine Cavanaugh and Jeremy Mouat (Toronto: Garamond Press, 1996), 190-91; Margaret E. McCallum, "Prairie Women and the Struggle for a Dower Law, 1905-1920," in *Historical Perspectives on Law and Society in Canada,* ed. Tina Loo and Lorna R. McLean, 306-20 (Toronto: Copp Clark Longman, 1994), 306-8; Sandra Rollings-Magnusson, "Hidden Homesteaders: Women, the State, and Patriarchy in the Saskatchewan Wheat Economy, 1870-1930," *Prairie Forum* 24, 2 (1999): 171-83. Hilary Golder and Diane Kirkby discuss married women's property law in Commonwealth countries in "Mrs. Mayne and Her Boxing Kangaroo: A Married Woman Tests Her Property Rights in Colonial New South Wales," *Law and History Review* 21, 3 (2003): 585-604; and Chris Clarkson's *Domestic Reforms: Political Visions and Family Regulation in British Columbia* (Vancouver: UBC Press, 2008) discusses legislators' willingness to grant married women and children new rights in British Columbia. The colonial reconstruction of legal patriarchy in South Asia is traced, for example, in Erin P. Moore, *Gender, Law, and Resistance in India* (Tucson: University of Arizona Press, 1998).

29 Comaroff and Comaroff, *Ethnography and the Historical Imagination,* 266; Leonore Davidoff and Catherine Hall, *Family Fortunes: Men and Women of the English Middle Class, 1780-1850* (New York: Random House, 1987); Ruth W. Sandwell, "The Limits of Liberalism: The Liberal Reconnaissance and the History of the Family in Canada," *Canadian Historical Review* 84 (September 2003): 430-33.

30 Bettina Bradbury, "Colonial Comparisons: Rethinking Marriage, Civilization, and Nation in Nineteenth-Century White Settler Societies," in Buckner and Francis, *Rediscovering the British World,* 135.

31 Sandwell, "The Limits of Liberalism," 426 [quote]; Cott, *Public Vows,* 1.

32 C.A. Dawson and Eva R. Younge, *Pioneering in the Prairie Provinces: The Social Side of the Settlement Process* (Toronto: Macmillan, 1940), 310; Christopher A. Clarkson, "Property Law and Family Regulation in Pacific British North America, 1862-1873," *Histoire sociale/*

Social History 30 (November 1997): 387-89; Sarah Carter, Capturing Women: The Manipulation of Cultural Imagery in Canada's Prairie West (Montreal and Kingston: McGill-Queen's University Press), 1997, 4-10; Perry, On the Edge of Empire, 140-66.

33 Leonore Davidoff, "Gender and the 'Great Divide': Public and Private in British Gender History," Journal of Women's History 15 (Spring 2003): 11; Pierson and Chaudhuri, "Introduction," Nation, Empire, Colony, 4.

34 Stasiulis and Jhappan, "The Fractious Politics of a Settler Society," 97.

35 Anne M. Windholz, "An Emigrant and a Gentleman: Imperial Masculinity, British Magazines, and the Colony That Got Away," Victorian Studies 42 (Summer 1999/2000): 631-32; Dixon, Writing the Colonial Adventure, 2-5; Carter F. Hanson, "'Working in the West': The Canadian Prairie as Playground in Late-Victorian Literature," American Review of Canadian Studies 31 (Winter 2001): 658; Tina Loo, "Of Moose and Men: Hunting for Masculinities in British Columbia, 1880-1939," Western Historical Quarterly 32, 3 (2001): 296-319; Robert H. MacDonald, Sons of the Empire: The Frontier and the Boy Scout Movement, 1890-1918 (Toronto: University of Toronto Press, 1993).

36 Joane Nagel, "Masculinity and Nationalism: Gender and Sexuality in the Making of Nations," Ethnic and Racial Studies 21 (March 1998): 244-45. Although historians and theorists such as Anthony Rotundo, George L. Mosse, and Robert Connell disagree on how to approach men's history, they all agree that, at any given time, in any given place, there is a hegemonic masculinity that is more than an ideal; it is assumptive and natural: Anthony Rotundo, American Manhood: Transformations in Masculinity from the Revolution to the Modern Era (New York: Basic Books, 1993); George L. Mosse, The Image of Man: The Creation of Modern Masculinity (New York: Oxford University Press, 1996); Robert W. Connell, Masculinities (Berkeley: University of California Press, 1995).

37 Robert W. Connell, "Masculinities, Change, and Conflict in Global Society: Thinking about the Future of Men's Studies," Journal of Men's Studies 11 (2003): 249-66; Gail Bederman, Manliness and Civilization: A Cultural History of Gender and Race in the United States, 1880-1917 (Chicago: University of Chicago Press, 1996), 5-6, 13; Toby L. Ditz, "The New Men's History and the Peculiar Absence of Gendered Power: Some Remedies from Early American Gender History," Gender and History 16 (April 2004): 6; Mrinalini Sinha, Colonial Masculinity: The "Manly Englishman" and the "Effeminate Bengali" in the Late Nineteenth Century (Manchester, UK: Manchester University Press, 1995).

38 Ditz, "The New Men's History," 3-4. Elizabeth Vibert and Adele Perry explore the construction of masculinities in British Columbia in Vibert, Traders' Tales: Narratives of Cultural Encounters in the Columbia Plateau, 1807-1846 (Norman: University of Oklahoma Press, 1997), 245-73; and Perry, On the Edge of Empire, 20-21.

39 Nagel, "Masculinity and Nationalism," 247.

40 Hanson, "'Working in the West,'" 659.

41 Steve Hewitt, "The Masculine Mountie: The Royal Canadian Mounted Police as a Male Institution, 1914-1939," Journal of the Canadian Historical Association 7 (1996): 154-70; Michael Dawson, "'That Nice Red Coat Goes to My Head Like Champagne': Gender, Antimodernism, and the Mountie Image, 1880-1960," Journal of Canadian Studies 32 (1997): 119-39; Erickson, "Murdered Women and Mythic Villains," 95-119.

42 Martin J. Wiener, Reconstructing the Criminal: Culture, Law, and Policy in England, 1830-1914 (Cambridge: Cambridge University Press, 1990), Chapter 7, "The De-Moralizing of Criminality." Although Wiener argues that Britain's medico-psychiatric establishment was hostile to Lombroso's criminal anthropology, Neil Davie contends that their conception of the habitual criminal or recidivist rested upon the same assumptions as criminal

anthropology: "Criminal Man Revisited? Continuity and Change in British Criminology, c. 1865-1918," *Journal of Victorian Culture* 8 (Spring 2003): 1-32.

43   Ditz, "The New Men's History," 6-7.

44   The literature on the (North West) Royal Canadian Mounted Police is extensive. Proponents of the mild West include Wilbur F. Bowker, *A Consolidation of Fifty Years of Legal Writings, 1938-1988*, ed. Marjorie Bowker (Edmonton: University of Alberta Press, 1989), 448-59, 691-734; and, more judiciously, R.C. Macleod, *The North-West Mounted Police and Law Enforcement, 1873-1905* (Toronto: University of Toronto Press, 1976). For a historiographical overview, see Louis A. Knafla, "Introduction: Laws and Societies in the Anglo-Canadian North-West Frontier and Prairie Provinces, 1670-1940," in *Laws and Societies in the Canadian Prairie West, 1670-1940*, ed. Louis A. Knafla (Vancouver: UBC Press, 2005), 23-29; Jim Phillips, "The History of Canadian Criminal Justice, 1750-1920," in *Criminology: A Reader's Guide*, ed. Jane Gladstone, Richard Ericson, and Clifford Shearing (Toronto: Centre of Criminology, University of Toronto, 1991), 81-89; and Phillips' "Crime and Punishment in the Dominion of the North: Canada from New France to the Present," in *Crime History and Histories of Crime*, ed. Clive Emsley and Louis A. Knafla (Westport, CT: Greenwood Press, 1996), 163-99. Andrew R. Graybill has compared the NWMP's treatment of Plains Indians with that of the Texas Rangers and concluded that both constabularies pursued policies of coercion in the 1870s and 1880s: "Rangers, Mounties, and the Subjugation of Indigenous Peoples, 1870-1885," *Great Plains Quarterly* 24 (Spring 2004): 83-100. See also Graybill, *Policing the Great Plains: Rangers, Mounties, and the North American Frontier, 1875-1920* (Lincoln: University of Nebraska Press, 2007).

45   Terry L. Chapman, "Sex Crimes in Western Canada, 1890-1920" (PhD diss., University of Alberta, 1984); "Sex Crimes in the West, 1890-1920," *Alberta History* 35 (Autumn 1987): 6-21; "'Til Death Do Us Part': Wife Beating in Alberta, 1905-1920," *Alberta History* 36 (Autumn 1988): 13-22. A few historians have also explored single trials or written articles that examine how criminal cases involving women or the courts' treatment of women enhanced race, class, or gender divisions in prairie Canada: see Reinhold Kramer and Tom Mitchell, *Walk Towards the Gallows: The Tragedy of Hilda Blake, Hanged 1899* (Don Mills, ON: Oxford University Press, 2002); Frances Swyripa, "Negotiating Sex and Gender in the Ukrainian Bloc Settlement," *Prairie Forum* 20 (Fall 1995): 149-74; Erica Smith, "'Gentlemen, This Is No Ordinary Trial': Sexual Narratives in the Trial of the Reverend Corbett, Red River, 1863," in *Reading beyond Words: Contexts for Native History*, ed. Jennifer S.H. Brown and Elizabeth Vibert (Peterborough, ON: Broadview Press, 1996), 364-80; David Bright, "'Go Home. Straighten Up. Live Decent Lives': Female Vagrancy and Social Respectability in Alberta," *Prairie Forum* 28 (Fall 2003): 161-72; and David Bright, "Sexual Assaults in Calgary, Alberta, between the Wars," in *Criminal Justice History*, vol. 19, *Violent Crime in North America*, ed. Louis A. Knafla (Westport, CT: Greenwood Press, 2003), 105-30.

46   For a general discussion of the North American Wests and the myths on which they were built, see Carol L. Higham and Bob Thacker, eds., *One West, Two Myths: A Comparative Reader* (Calgary: University of Calgary Press, 2004). For discussions of violence on the American side of the border, see John Phillip Reid, *Policing the Elephant: Crime, Punishment, and Social Behaviour on the Overland Trail* (San Marino, CA: Huntington Library, 1997), and *Patterns of Vengeance: Crosscultural Homicide in the North American Fur Trade* (Pasadena, CA: North Judicial Circuit Historical Society, 1999); Robert Waite, "Violent Crime on the Western Frontier: The Experience of the Idaho Territory, 1863-1890," in *Violent Crime*

in North America, 53-74. On violence in the Canadian West, see contributions to John McLaren, Hamar Foster, and Chet Orloff, eds., *Law for the Elephant, Law for the Beaver: Essays in the Legal History of the North American West* (Regina: Canadian Plains Research Center, 1992); J.W. McClung, *Law West of the Bay* (Calgary: Legal Archives Society of Alberta, 1998), 90-95; Louis A. Knafla, "Violence on the Western Canadian Frontier: A Historical Perspective," in *Violence in Canada: Sociopolitical Perspectives*, ed. Jeffrey Ian Ross, 2nd ed. (Somerset, NJ: Transaction Publishers, 2004), 10-39; Warren B. Elofson "Law and Disorder on the Ranching Frontiers of Montana and Alberta/Assiniboia, 1870-1914," *Journal of the West* 42, 1 (2003): 40-51; Jonathan Swainger, "Creating the Peace: Crimes and Community Identity in Northeastern British Columbia, 1930-1950," in *Violent Crime in North America*, 131-54. David Peterson del Mar's *Beaten Down: A History of Interpersonal Violence in the West* (Seattle: University of Washington Press, 2002) does, however, signal a shift in focus by examining domestic violence in the Pacific Northwest within a cross-border framework.

47 For studies that focus on the transplantation of English law and the jurisdiction of Canadian courts on the Prairies (Rupert's Land) through to 1859, see Louis A. Knafla, "From Oral to Written Memory: The Common Law Tradition in Western Canada," in *Law and Justice in a New Land: Essays in Western Canadian Legal History*, ed. Louis A. Knafla (Toronto: Carswell, 1986), 31-77; Hamar Foster, "Long-Distance Justice: The Criminal Jurisdiction of Canadian Courts West of the Canadas, 1763-1859," *American Journal of Legal History* 34 (1990): 1-48; H. Robert Baker, "Creating Order in the Wilderness: Transplanting the English Law to Rupert's Land, 1835-51," *Law and History Review* 17 (Summer 1999): 209-46.

48 Myron C. Noonkester, "The Third British Empire: Transplanting the English Shire to Wales, Scotland, Ireland, and America," *Journal of British Studies* 36, 3 (1997): 257.

49 Frederick Read, "Early History of the Manitoba Courts," *Manitoba Bar News* 10 (October 1987): 471, 482-84; Knafla, "From Oral to Written Memory," 51-53; see also Jonathan Swainger, ed., *Alberta Supreme Court at 100: History and Authority* (Edmonton: University of Alberta Press for the Osgoode Society for Canadian Legal History, 2007).

50 Canadian Criminal Code, 1892 (CCC), 55 & 56 Vict., c. 29, ss. 539, 764, and 783; Peter H. Russell, *The Judiciary in Canada: The Third Branch of Government* (Toronto: McGraw-Hill Ryerson, 1987), 260-61, 266.

51 For a full explication of the duties undertaken and procedures followed by JPs, see David Carey, ed., *Carey's Manitoba Reports* (Calgary: Carswell, 1918), i-ix; and T. Mayne Daly, *Canadian Criminal Procedure as the Same Relates to Preliminary Hearings, Summary Convictions and Summary Trials*, 2nd ed., rev. George Patterson (Toronto: Carswell, 1915).

52 Linda Silver Dranoff, *Women in Canadian Life: Law* (Toronto: Fitzhenry and Whiteside, 1977), 95.

53 Richard A. Willie, *"These Legal Gentlemen": Lawyers in Manitoba: 1839-1900* (Winnipeg: Legal Research Institute, 1994), 284-87; Louis A. Knafla and Richard Klumpenhouwer, *Lords of the Western Bench: A Biographical History of the Supreme and District Courts of Alberta, 1876-1990* (Calgary: Legal Archives Society of Alberta, 1997); Jonathan Swainger, "Ideology, Social Capital, and Entrepreneurship," in *Beyond the Law: Lawyers and Business in Canada, 1830-1930*, ed. Carol Wilton (Toronto: Butterworths Canada for the Osgoode Society for Canadian Legal History, 1990), 377-402; Henry C. Klassen, "Lawyers, Finance, and Economic Development in Southwestern Alberta, 1884 to 1920," in *Beyond the Law*, 298-319; W. Wesley Pue, "Planting Legal Culture in Colonial Soil: Legal Professionalism in the Lands of the Beaver and Kangaroo," in *Shaping Nations: Constitutionalism and Society*

in Australia and Canada, ed. Linda Cardinal and David Headon (Ottawa: University of Ottawa Press, 2002), 91-115.

54 For good introductions to Indian policy in prairie Canada and the gradual shift in Canadian policy from cooperation to coercion, see J.R. Miller, *Skyscrapers Hide the Heavens: A History of Indian-White Relations in Canada,* 3rd ed. (Toronto: University of Toronto Press, 2000), Chapter 11, "The Policy of the Bible and the Plough"; and Carter, *Aboriginal People and Colonizers,* Chapter 8, "Turning Point: 1885 and After." For a discussion of policy in the late nineteenth century that emphasizes Aboriginal peoples' agency, see J.R. Miller, "Owen Glendower, Hotspur, and Canadian Indian Policy," in *Sweet Promises: A Reader on Indian-White Relations in Canada,* ed. J.R. Miller (Toronto: University of Toronto Press, 1991), 323-52. See also Robin Brownlie and Mary-Ellen Kelm's discussion of historians' emphasis on agency in "Desperately Seeking Absolution: Native Agency as Colonialist Alibi," *Canadian Historical Review* 75 (December 1994): 543-57; and Douglas Cole and J.R. Miller's response, "Desperately Seeking Absolution: Responses and a Reply," *Canadian Historical Review* 76 (December 1995): 628-43.

55 Harring, *White Man's Law,* 262.

56 Ibid., 263-64; John Lutz, "Relating to the Country: The Lekwammen and the Extension of European Settlement," in *Beyond the City Limits: Rural History in British Columbia,* ed. Ruth Sandwell (Vancouver: UBC Press, 1999), 23; Miller, *Skyscrapers Hide the Heavens,* 192-93; Katherine Pettipas, *Severing the Ties that Bind: Government Repression of Indigenous Religious Ceremonies on the Prairies* (Winnipeg: University of Manitoba Press, 1994), 238; J. Rick Ponting and Roger Gibbins, *Out of Irrelevance: A Socio-Political Introduction to Indian Affairs in Canada* (Toronto: Butterworths, 1980); B. Hogeveen, "An Intrusive and Corrective Government: Political Rationalities and the Governance of Plains Aboriginals, 1870-1890," in *Governable Places: Readings on Governmentality and Crime Control,* ed. Russell Smandych (Aldershot, UK: Dartmouth Publishing, 1999), 287-312. The 1894 amendments to the Indian Act reasserted earlier provisions by empowering Indian agents to be *ex officio* JPs for Indian Act offences and certain sections of the 1892 Criminal Code.

57 Carter, *Lost Harvests,* 144-47; Pettipas, *Severing the Ties that Bind,* 85-105; Miller, *Skyscrapers Hide the Heavens,* Chapter 11; Walter Hildebrandt, *Views from Fort Battleford: Constructed Visions of an Anglo-Canadian West* (Regina: Canadian Plains Research Center, 1994), 89-93.

58 Keith D. Smith, *Liberalism, Surveillance, and Resistance: Indigenous Communities in Western Canada, 1877-1927* (Edmonton: AU Press, 2009), Chapter 3, "'A Splendid Spirit of Cooperation': Churches, Police Forces, and the Department of Indian Affairs."

59 *Constitution Act, 1867* (U.K.), 30 & 31 Vict., c. 3, s. 91(24); Stasiulis and Jhappan, "The Fractious Politics," 98, 114; Ann McGrath and Winona Stevenson, "Gender, Race, and Policy: Aboriginal Women and the State in Canada and Australia," *Labour/Le Travail* 38 (Fall 1996): 37-53; Julia Emberley, "The Bourgeois Family, Aboriginal Women, and Colonial Governance in Canada: A Study in Feminist Historical and Cultural Materialism," *Signs* 27, 1 (2001): 59-85; Pamela White, "Restructuring the Domestic Sphere: Prairie Indian Women on Reserves – Image, Ideology, and State Policy, 1880-1930" (PhD diss., McGill University, 1987); McClintock, *Imperial Leather,* 36; Carter, *The Importance of Being Monogamous,* passim.

60 Quoted in Valerie Knowles, *Strangers at Our Gates: Canadian Immigration and Immigration Policy, 1540-1997,* rev. ed. (Toronto: Dundurn Press, 1997), 77.

61 Friesen, *The Canadian Prairies*, 242, 244, 246-47; Thompson, *Forging the Prairie West*, 71; Howard Palmer, "Reluctant Hosts: Anglo-Canadian Views of Multi-Culturalism in the Twentieth Century," in *Immigration in Canada: Historical Perspectives*, ed. Gerald Tulchinsky (Toronto: Copp Clark Longman, 1994), 301.

62 W.J.C. Cherwinski, "Wooden Horses and Rubber Cows: Training British Agricultural Labour for the Canadian Prairies, 1890-1930," *Historical Papers* 15, 1 (1980): 139; and Cherwinski, "In Search of Jake Trumper: The Farm Hand and the Prairie Farm Family," in *Building beyond the Homestead: Rural History on the Prairies*, ed. David C. Jones and Ian MacPherson (Calgary: University of Calgary Press, 1985), 114, 120-24; Cecilia Danysk, *Hired Hands: Labour and the Development of Prairie Agriculture, 1880-1930* (Toronto: McClelland and Stewart, 1994), 59, 162; Alan Artibise, *Winnipeg: An Illustrated History* (Toronto: James Lorimer, 1977), 68.

63 James S. Woodsworth, *Strangers within Our Gates: The Problem of the Immigrant* (1909; repr., Toronto: University of Toronto Press, 1972), and *My Neighbour: Urban Ills and Urban Reform, 1911* (Toronto: University of Toronto Press, 1972).

64 Dorothy Chunn, "Sex and Citizenship: (Hetero)Sexual Offences, Law, and 'White' Settler Society in British Columbia, 1885-1940," in *Contesting Canadian Citizenship: Historical Readings*, ed. Robert Adamoski, Dorothy Chunn, and Robert Menzies (Peterborough, ON: Broadview Press, 2002), 359. For a sample of the vast literature on these movements and the construction of the social, see Bruce Curtis, "Surveying the Social: Techniques, Practices, Power," *Histoire sociale/Social History* 35, 69 (May 2002): 83-108; Michel Foucault, *The History of Sexuality*, vol. 1 (New York: Random House, 1978); Alan Hunt, *Governing Morals: A Social History of Moral Regulation* (Cambridge: Cambridge University Press, 1999); Philippa Levine, *Prostitution, Race, and Politics: Policing Venereal Disease in the British Empire* (New York: Routledge, 2003); Judith Walkowitz, *Prostitution and Victorian Society: Women, Class, and the State* (Cambridge: Cambridge University Press, 1980).

65 Mariana Valverde, *The Age of Light, Soap, and Water: Moral Reform in English Canada, 1885-1925* (Toronto: McClelland and Stewart, 1991), 107-8. See Howard Palmer's *Patterns of Prejudice: A History of Nativism in Alberta* (Toronto: McClelland and Stewart, 1982), in which he champions the term's application to prairie Canada.

66 James G. Snell, "'The White Life for Two': The Defence of Marriage and Sexual Morality in Canada, 1890-1914," in *Canadian Family History: Selected Readings*, ed. Bettina Bradbury (Toronto: Copp Clark Pitman, 1992), 381-96; Angus McLaren, *Our Own Master Race: Eugenics in Canada, 1885-1945* (Toronto: McClelland and Stewart, 1990), 46-67; Dorothy Chunn, "Secrets and Lies: The Criminalization of Incest and the (Re)Formation of the 'Private' in British Columbia, 1890-1940," in *Regulating Lives: Historical Essays on the State, Society, the Individual, and the Law*, ed. John McLaren, Robert Menzies, and Dorothy Chunn (Vancouver: UBC Press, 2002), 120-22; Catherine MacKinnon, "Feminism, Marxism, Method, and the State: Toward a Feminist Jurisprudence," *Signs* 8, 4 (1983): 635-58; Joan Sangster, *Regulating Girls and Women: Sexuality, Family, and the Law in Ontario, 1920-1960* (Don Mills, ON: Oxford University Press, 2001); Carter, *The Importance of Being Monogamous*, 3-4.

67 In *Imperial Eyes: Travel Writing and Transculturation* (New York: Routledge, 1992), Mary Louise Pratt defines contact zones as "social spaces where disparate cultures meet, clash, and grapple with each other, often in highly asymmetrical relations of domination and subordination" (4). In *Colonial Proximities: Crossracial Encounters and Juridical Truths in*

British Columbia, 1871-1921 (Vancouver: UBC Press, 2009), Renisa Mawani adopts a broader understanding of the contact zone as a variegated site that reflected and produced multiple identities.

68 Clifford Geertz, *Local Knowledge: Further Essays in Interpretive Anthropology* (New York: Basic Books, 2000), 218-19, 232.

69 John L. Comaroff, "Foreword," in Lazarus-Black and Hirsch, *Contested States*, x.

70 As defined by Antonio Gramsci, the term *hegemony* refers to power that maintains structures of domination but is invisible: it is "power that naturalizes a social order, institution, or even an everyday practice so that 'how things are' seems inevitable and not the consequence of particular historical actors, classes, or events": Susan F. Hirsch and Mindie Lazarus-Black, "Performance and Paradox: Exploring Law's Role in Hegemony and Resistance," in Lazarus-Black and Hirsch, *Contested States*, 7.

71 Sally Merry Engle, "Courts as Performances: Domestic Violence Hearings in a Hawai'i Family Court," in Lazarus-Black and Hirsch, *Contested States*, 35-58; John L. Comaroff and Jean Comaroff, *Of Revelation and Revolution: Christianity, Colonialism, and Consciousness in South Africa*, vol. 1 (Chicago: University of Chicago Press, 1991), 23, 24-28; Sally Merry Engle, "Hegemony and Culture in Historical Anthropology: A Review Essay on Jean and John L. Comaroff's *Of Revelation and Revolution*," *American Historical Review* 108 (April 2003): 460-70; Jeffrey R. Dudas, "Law and the American Frontier," *Law and Social Inquiry* 29 (Fall 2004): 865. For excellent discussions of the cultural turn and its impact on the writing of legal history, see James W. St. G. Walker, *"Race," Rights and the Law in the Supreme Court of Canada* (Waterloo, ON: Wilfrid Laurier University Press for the Osgoode Society for Canadian Legal History, 1997), 38-45; and Sangster, *Regulating Girls and Women*, 1-16.

72 Timothy J. Gilfoyle provides an in-depth overview of historical approaches to prostitution in "Prostitutes in History: From Parables of Pornography to Metaphors of Modernity," *American Historical Review* 104 (February 1999): 117-41.

73 Ditz, "The New Men's History," 11-13; Konstantin Dierks, "Men's History, Gender History, or Cultural History?" *Gender and History* 14 (April 2002): 149-50; Mark E. Kann, *The Republic of Men: The American Founders, Gendered Language, and Patriarchal Politics* (New York: New York University Press, 1998), 28.

74 For a sampling of the extensive literature on these issues, see Carolyn J. Dean, *The Frail Social Body: Pornography, Homosexuality, and Other Fantasies in Interwar France* (Berkeley: University of California Press, 2000); Leonore Davidoff, "Regarding Some 'Old' Husbands' Tales: Public and Private in Feminist History," in *Feminism, the Public and the Private*, ed. Joan B. Landes (Oxford: Oxford University Press, 1998), 164-94; Cornelie Usborne, *The Politics of the Body in Weimar Germany: Women's Reproductive Rights and Duties* (Ann Arbor: University of Michigan Press, 1992); Marie-Louise Roberts, *Civilization without Sexes: Reconstructing Gender in Postwar France, 1917-1927* (Chicago: University of Chicago Press, 1994); Carolyn Strange, *Toronto's Girl Problem: The Perils and Pleasures of the City, 1880-1920* (Toronto: University of Toronto Press, 1995); Joan Sangster, *Regulating Girls and Women*, and *Girl Trouble: Female Delinquency in English Canada* (Toronto: Between the Lines, 2002).

75 Leslie J. Reagan, *When Abortion Was a Crime: Women, Medicine, and the Law in the United States, 1867-1973* (Berkeley: University of California Press, 1997), 3-4; Lorna McLean, "'Deserving' Wives and 'Drunken' Husbands: Wife Beating, Marital Conduct, and the Law in Ontario, 1850-1910," *Histoire sociale/Social History* 35, 69 (2002): 59-81; Jeffrey S. Adler, "'We've Got a Right to Fight, We're Married': Domestic Homicide in Chicago,

1875-1920," *Journal of Interdisciplinary History* 34 (Summer 2003): 28; Nancy Christie, *Engendering the State: Family, Work, and Welfare in Canada* (Toronto: University of Toronto Press, 2000); Carroll, *Homesteads Ungovernable*, xii; Jessie Ramey, "The Bloody Blonde and the Marble Woman: Gender and Power in the Case of Ruth Snyder," *Journal of Social History* 37, 3 (2004): 625-40.

<h2 style="text-align:center">Chapter 2: They Know No Better</h2>

1   "Criminal Court – Rape – Exemplary Punishment" and "A Revolting Crime," *Regina Leader*, 21 October 1890; *R. v. Evanse* (1890), Supreme Court of the North-West Territories (SCNWT), Western Assiniboia, R-1286, Saskatchewan Archives Board (SAB).
2   Nancy L. Paxton, *Writing under the Raj: Gender, Race, and Rape in the British Colonial Imagination, 1830-1947* (New Brunswick, NJ: Rutgers University Press, 1999), 344. See also Jock McCulloch, *Black Peril, White Virtue: Sexual Crime in Southern Rhodesia, 1902-1935* (Bloomington: Indiana University Press, 2000); Richard C. Trexler, *Sex and Conquest: Gendered Violence, Political Order and the European Conquest of the Americas* (Ithaca, NY: Cornell University Press, 1995).
3   Adele Perry, "The Autocracy of Love and the Legitimacy of Empire: Intimacy, Power, and Scandal in Nineteenth-Century Metlakahtlah," *Gender and History* 16, 2 (2004): 261-62. In the early 1960s, Frantz Fanon exposed rape as a master trope of colonial discourse and as a sign of colonizers' bad faith: *Wretched of the Earth*, trans. Constance Farrington (New York: Grove Weidenfeld, 1963), 254-58.
4   Anne McClintock, *Imperial Leather: Race, Gender, and Sexuality in the Colonial Contest* (New York: Routledge, 1995), 30.
5   For examples of these mid-nineteenth-century cases, see Adele Perry, *On the Edge of Empire: Gender, Race, and the Making of British Columbia, 1849-1871* (Toronto: University of Toronto Press, 2001), 65; Jean Barman, "Taming Aboriginal Sexuality: Gender, Power, and Race in British Columbia, 1850-1900," *BC Studies* 115/116 (Autumn/Winter 1997/1998): 237-66; Erica Smith, "'Gentlemen, This Is No Ordinary Trial': Sexual Narratives in the Trial of the Reverend Corbett, Red River, 1863," in *Reading beyond Words: Contexts for Native History*, ed. Jennifer S.H. Brown and Elizabeth Vibert (Peterborough, ON: Broadview Press, 1996), 364-80.
6   Sarah Carter, *Capturing Women: The Manipulation of Cultural Imagery in Canada's Prairie West* (Montreal and Kingston: McGill-Queen's University Press, 1997), 15-18; Jeremy C. Martens, "Settler Homes, Manhood and 'Houseboys': An Analysis of Natal's Rape Scare of 1886," *Journal of South African Studies* 28, 2 (2002): 379-400; Norman Etherington, "Natal's Black Rape Scare of the 1870s," *Journal of South African Studies* 15, 1 (1988): 36-53; Amirah Inglis, *"Not a White Woman Safe": Sexual Anxiety and Politics in Port Moresby, 1920-1934* (Canberra: Australian National University Press, 1974); Gail Bederman, *Manliness and Civilization: A Cultural History of Gender and Race in the United States, 1880-1917* (Chicago: University of Chicago Press, 1996), 46-47; Jenny Sharpe, "The Unspeakable Limits of Rape: Colonial Violence and Counter-Insurgency," *Genders* 10 (Spring 1991): 25-46.
7   Nathalie Kermoal, "Les rôles et les souffrances des femmes métisses lors de la Résistance de 1870 et de la Rébellion de 1885," *Prairie Forum* 19 (Fall 1994): 153-68; Carter, *Capturing Women*, 70-71.

8 Canadian Council on Social Development, "Social Challenges: The Well-Being of Aboriginal People," Crime Prevention through Social Development, http://www.ccsd.ca/cpsd/ccsd/c_ab.htm.

9 R.C. Macleod and Heather Rollason, "'Restrain the Lawless Savages': Native Defendants in the Criminal Courts of the North-West Territories, 1878-1885," *Journal of Historical Sociology* 10 (June 1997): 157-83; Sidney L. Harring, *White Man's Law: Native People in Nineteenth-Century Canadian Jurisprudence* (Toronto: University of Toronto Press for the Osgoode Society for Canadian Legal History, 1998), 243-45; A.C. Hamilton, C.M. Sinclair, and Gerald Friesen, "'Justice Systems' and Manitoba's Aboriginal People: An Historical Survey," in *River Road: Essays in Manitoba and Prairie History,* by Gerald Friesen (Winnipeg: University of Manitoba Press, 1996), 57; John N. Jennings, "The Northwest Mounted Police and Indian Policy, 1874-1896" (PhD diss., University of Toronto, 1979).

10 Elizabeth Furniss, *The Burden of History: Colonialism and Frontier Myth in a Rural Canadian Community* (Vancouver: UBC Press, 2000), 187; Arthur J. Ray, Jim Miller, and Frank Tough, *Bounty and Benevolence: A History of Saskatchewan Treaties* (Montreal and Kingston: McGill-Queen's University Press, 2000), 204-7.

11 James H. Gray, *Red Lights on the Prairie: The Bonanza Years When the Wide-Open Frontier Was a Hooker's Happy Hunting Ground* (1971, repr., Scarborough, ON: New American Library, 1973), 225-26; Carter, *Capturing Women,* 166-85.

12 For discussions of the importance of alcohol consumption to evolutionary anthropology, see Bonnie Duran, "Indigenous versus Colonial Discourse: Alcohol and American Indian Identity," in *Dressing in Feathers: The Construction of the Indian in American Popular Culture,* ed. S. Elizabeth Bird (Boulder, CO: Westview Press, 1996), 111-28; and Gilbert Quintero, "Making the Indian: Colonial Knowledge, Alcohol, and Native Americans," *American Indian Culture and Research Journal* 25, 4 (2001): 57-71.

13 Sarah Carter, *Lost Harvests: Prairie Indian Reserve Farmers and Government Policy* (Montreal and Kingston: McGill-Queen's University Press, 1990), 130-37; Paige Raibmon, "Theatres of Contact: The Kwakwaka'wakw Meet Colonialism in British Columbia and at the Chicago World's Fair," *Canadian Historical Review* 81 (June 2000): 179-81.

14 William Beahen and Stan Horrall, *Red Coats on the Prairies: The North-West Mounted Police, 1886-1900* (Regina: Centax, 1998), 57-58.

15 Historians are divided on the scope and applicability of the pass system. Sarah Carter and Katherine Pettipas argue that the pass system remained in effect until the 1930s, with popular support from white settlers: see Carter, *Lost Harvests,* 151-56, and Pettipas, *Severing the Ties that Bind: Government Repression of Indigenous Religious Ceremonies on the Prairies* (Winnipeg: University of Manitoba Press, 1994), 112-13. Jim Miller, by contrast, argues that the system was rarely enforced in the 1880s and was virtually a dead letter by 1893: see *Skyscrapers Hide the Heavens: A History of Indian-White Relations in Canada,* 3rd ed. (Toronto: University of Toronto Press, 2000), 192. Police incident reports from the Kainai Reserve support Carter's and Pettipas' findings, and elders attest to its use in the 1930s. See Treaty 7 Elders and Tribal Council, with Walter Hildebrandt, Sarah Carter, and Dorothy First Rider, *The True Spirit and Original Intent of Treaty 7* (Montreal and Kingston: McGill-Queen's University Press, 1996), 147; Flora Zaharia and Leo Fox, eds., *Kitomahkita-piiminnooniksi: Stories from Our Elders,* vol. 1 (Edmonton: Donahue, 1995), 110.

16 Carter, *Lost Harvests,* 154-55.

17 Hayter Reed, Commissioner DIA, to Lawrence Herchmer, Commissioner NWMP, 4 February 1891, RG 18, Royal Canadian Mounted Police, Series B-1, vol. 1204, f. 164-891, Library and Archives Canada (LAC).

18 Aside from one case, *R. v. The Rib* (1893), which took place before the SCNWT at Fort Macleod, these were the only sex crime cases (not including incest) tried before the superior courts in the five selected judicial districts that involved Aboriginal victims or perpetrators. In the entire period between 1886 and 1940, there were only three reported cases of Aboriginal men sexually assaulting white women; the courts dismissed one of them for lack of evidence. See, for instance, *R. v. Paul* (1906), SCNWT, Western Assiniboia, R-1286, SAB; *R. v. Plaited Hair* (1921), Supreme Court of Alberta (SCA), Macleod, Acc. 78.235, Provincial Archives of Alberta (PAA).

19 Carter, *Lost Harvests*, 56-57, 159, 193-94, 209.

20 See Louis A. Knafla, "From Oral to Written Memory: The Common Law Tradition in Western Canada," in *Law and Justice in a New Land: Essays in Western Canadian Legal History*, ed. Louis A. Knafla (Toronto: Carswell, 1986), 64-65.

21 Louis Knafla and Richard Klumpenhouwer, *Lords of the Western Bench: A Biographical History of the Supreme and District Courts of Alberta, 1876-1990* (Calgary: Legal Archives Society of Alberta, 1997), 158-59; Thomas Flanagan, "Hugh Richardson," *Dictionary of Canadian Biography Online*, http://www.biographi.ca; Wilbur F. Bowker, "Stipendiary Magistrates and the Supreme Court of the North-West Territories, 1876-1907," *Alberta Law Review* 27 (1988): 262-69.

22 *R. v. Motow* (1889), SCNWT, Western Assiniboia, GR-1286, SAB.

23 "Gopher Tom of File Hills Reserve on Trial for Larceny," "Gopher Tom Says He Was Starving on File Hills Reserve," "Indians Should Be Well-Fed," *Regina Leader*, 6 March 1884. Maureen K. Lux discusses the impact that the peasant farming scheme and the federal government's failure to meet treaty promises had on Aboriginal people's health in the Treaty 4 region in *Medicine That Walks: Disease, Medicine, and Canadian Plains Native People, 1800-1940* (Toronto: University of Toronto Press, 2001), 36, 41, 44.

24 "Yellow Calf Says Indians Starving," "Gov. Dewdney Unjustly Blamed for Uprisings," *Regina Leader*, 6 March 1884, discussed in Carter, *Lost Harvests*, 120-22.

25 "Three Months and Twelve Lashes," *Regina Leader*, 9 July 1889; *Statutes of Canada*, 53 Vict., c. 37, s. 12.

26 *R. v. Evanse* (1890).

27 "A Revolting Crime," *Regina Leader*, 21 October 1890.

28 "Criminal Court – Rape – Exemplary Punishment," *Regina Leader*, 21 October 1890.

29 J.R. Miller, *Shingwauk's Vision: A History of Native Residential Schools* (Toronto: University of Toronto Press, 2000), 252-55; Sarah Carter, "First Nations Women of Prairie Canada in the Early Reserve Years, the 1870s to the 1920s: A Preliminary Inquiry," in *Women of the First Nations: Power, Wisdom, and Strength*, ed. Christine Miller and Patricia Chuchryk (Winnipeg: University of Manitoba Press, 1996), 67.

30 *R. v. Bourassa* (1892), SCNWT, Western Assiniboia, GR-1286, SAB. *Bourassa* was one of the few case files I read that included a full transcript. Its addition perhaps reflected the seriousness with which legal authorities and the public perceived the trial.

31 For in-depth explorations of the emergence of the stereotype of the dangerous and dissolute Aboriginal woman in prairie Canada, see Sarah Carter, "Categories and Terrains of Exclusion: Constructing the 'Indian Woman' in the Early Settlement Era in Western Canada," *Great Plains Quarterly* 13 (Summer 1993): 156-57; and *Capturing Women*, Chapter 5.

32 "An Act to Amend the Criminal Law," 1890, c. 37, s. 3, 7, and 12.

33 *R. v. Bourassa* (1892).

34 "Supreme Court," *Regina Leader*, 11 July 1892.

35 Similar arguments have been made for British Columbia: see Tina Loo, "The Road from Bute Inlet: Crime and Colonial Identity in British Columbia," in Phillips, Loo, and Lewthwaite, *Crime and Criminal Justice*, 112-42; and Hamar Foster, "'The Queen's Law Is Better Than Yours': International Homicide in British Columbia," in ibid., 41-91.

36 See in particular, Daniel Francis, *The Imaginary Indian: The Image of the Indian in Canadian Culture* (Vancouver: Arsenal Pulp Press, 1992); Robert F. Berkhofer Jr., *The White Man's Indian* (New York: Alfred A. Knopf, 1978); and Bruce Trigger, *Natives and Newcomers: Canada's "Heroic Age" Reconsidered* (Montreal and Kingston: McGill-Queen's University Press, 1985), Chapter 1.

37 As Joan Sangster notes, legal historian Martin Chanock distinguishes between custom and customary law. Whereas custom is a set of values and social practices that maintained order in pre-colonial times, customary law is a product of interaction between missionaries, courts, administrators, and Aboriginal peoples in the post-contact period. In North America, legal historian Sidney Harring has likewise argued that when the courts and historians call Aboriginal law customary, they set up a false dichotomy between Indian law and English common law, which is also rooted in custom. Customary law, consequently, is a process that is shaped by the relations of power and hegemony endemic to colonialism. For a discussion of theoretical debates on customary law and the applicability of these debates to Canada, see Joan Sangster, *Regulating Girls and Women: Sexuality, Family, and the Law in Ontario, 1920-1960* (Don Mills, ON: Oxford University Press, 2001), 172-74; Sidney L. Harring, "Indian Law, Sovereignty and State Law," in *A Companion to American Indian History*, ed. Philip J. Deloria and Neal Salisbury (Malden, MA: Blackwell, 2002), 444.

38 Tina Loo, "Savage Mercy: Native Culture and the Modification of Capital Punishment in Nineteenth-Century British Columbia," in *Qualities of Mercy: Justice, Punishment, and Discretion*, ed. Carolyn Strange (Vancouver: UBC Press, 1996), 104-6; Carter, *Capturing Women*, 158. The cultural defence is discussed in Paul J. Magnarella's, "Justice in a Pluralistic Society: The Cultural Defence on Trial," *Journal of Ethnic Studies* 19 (1991): 65-84; and Julia P. Sams, "The Availability of the 'Cultural Defence' as an Excuse in Criminal Behaviour," *Georgia Journal of International and Comparative Law* 16 (1986): 335-54; Kimberlé Crenshaw, "Mapping the Margins: Intersectionality, Identity Politics, and Violence against Women of Color," *Stanford Law Review* 43 (July 1991): 1241-99.

39 For a similar trend in suicide prosecutions, see Lesley Erickson, "Constructed and Contested Truths: Aboriginal Suicide, Law, and Colonialism in the Canadian West(s), 1823-1927," *Canadian Historical Review* 86 (December 2005): 595-618;

40 *R. v. Machekequonabe* (1897), 28 O.R. 309; Robert Seidman, "Witch Murder and Mens Rea," *Modern Law Review* 28 (1965): 46-61, and "Mens Rea and the Reasonable African," *International and Comparative Law Quarterly* 15 (1966): 1135-64; Harring, *White Man's Law*, 217.

41 There is a growing literature, particularly for British Columbia, which reveals that Canadian justice systems continued to take custom and culture into consideration well into the twentieth century. See, for instance, Kenneth Coates and William R. Morrison, "A Drunken Impulse: Aboriginal Justice Confronts Canadian Law," *Western Historical Quarterly* 27, 4 (1996): 452-77.

42 *R. v. Laferty* (1902), SCNWT, Northern Alberta, Acc. 83.1, PAA.

43 Canadian Criminal Code, 1892 (CCC), 55 & 56 Vict., c. 29, s. 176; *R. v. Lafournaise* (1933), Manitoba Court of King's Bench (MCKB), Eastern Manitoba/Winnipeg, GR 180, microfilm, Provincial Archives of Manitoba (PAM).

44 *R. v. Lafontaine* (1910), SCA, Macleod, Acc. 78.235, microfilm, guilty, PAA; incest cases that involved Aboriginal accused included *R. v. Tanner* (1905), MCKB, Eastern Manitoba/Winnipeg, not guilty, and *R. v. Young* (1915), MCKB, Eastern Manitoba/Winnipeg, not guilty, PAM.

45 Harring, *White Man's Law,* 235.

46 Father A. Lacombe to David Mills, Minister of Justice, 8 December 1899, in *R. v. Sabourin* (1899), SCNWT, Edmonton, Acc. 83.1, PAA.

47 *R. v. Jackson* (1920), Department of Justice, Capital Case Files, RG 13, vol. 1509, f. CC147, LAC; "Mysterious Disappearance of Swan River Man Cleared Up by Constable's Grim Find," *Edmonton Journal,* 3 June 1920.

48 W.L. Walsh to the Secretary of State, 30 September 1920, in *R. v. Jackson.*

49 "Mrs. Jackson's Daughter Minutely Describes the Fatal Events at Swan River," *Edmonton Journal,* 28 September 1920, in *R. v. Jackson.*

50 "Convicted of Murdering Her Husband, Mrs. Jackson Is Given Death Sentence," *Edmonton Journal,* 29 September 1920.

51 H.H. Robertson to the Minister of Justice, 3 November 1920, in *R. v. Jackson.*

52 Ibid.

53 CCC, 1892, s. 235.

54 "Full-Blooded Treaty Indian, Zerma Coutereille Admits Guilt of Assisting Mrs. Sadie Jackson," *Edmonton Journal,* 29 September 1920.

55 "Prison Term Is Court Decision against Indian," *Edmonton Journal,* 10 October 1920.

56 RCMP, "K" Division, report to Indian agent, 4 January 1940, Blood Indian Agency Series (BA), DIA, M-1788, f. 183-194, Glenbow Archives (GA); *R. v. Round Nose* (1940), SCA, Macleod, Acc. 78.235, PAA.

57 RCMP, "K" Division, report to Indian agent, 4 January 1940, ibid.

58 Ibid.

59 "Court Hears Story of Blood Indians Drinking Diluted Rubbing Alcohol; Round Nose Murder Trial Proceeds," *Lethbridge Herald,* 12 March 1940; "Round Nose Is Found 'Not Guilty' By Jury; Deliberate an Hour," *Lethbridge Herald,* 13 March 1940.

60 Newspaper clipping, "Indian Acquitted in Murder Case," RG 10, Reel C-14768, vol. 7468, f. 19103-6, LAC.

61 RCMP, "K" Division, Cardston, report to Indian Agent, 29 November 1933, BA, DIA, M-1788, f. 173-77, GA.

62 R.C.S. Hawkins, RCMP, "K" Division, Lethbridge, report to Indian agent, 29 December 1935, ibid.

63 "An Act to Amend and Consolidate the Laws Respecting Indians," *Revised Statutes of Canada* (R.S.C.), 1876, c. 18, s. 3(c) and (e).

64 J.E. Pugh, Cardston, to the Secretary of the Department of Indian Affairs, Ottawa, 24 November 1935, BA, DIA, M-1788, f. 173-77, GA.

65 Hugh A. Dempsey, *Charcoal's World* (Saskatoon: Western Producer Books, 1978), 106, and *Tribal Honours: A History of the Kainai Chieftainship* (Calgary: Kainai Chieftainship, 1997), 11-19, 31.

66 Julia Emberley, "The Bourgeois Family, Aboriginal Women, and Colonial Governance in Canada: A Study in Feminist Historical and Cultural Materialism," *Signs* 27, 1 (2001): 59-85; Sarah Carter, "'Complicated and Clouded': The Federal Administration of Marriage and Divorce among the First Nations of Western Canada, 1887-1906," in *Unsettled Pasts: Reconceiving the West through Women's History,* ed. Sarah Carter, Lesley Erickson, Patricia Roome, and Char Smith (Calgary: University of Calgary Press, 2005), 151-78; and Carter,

"Creating 'Semi-Widows' and 'Supernumerary Wives': Prohibiting Polygamy in Prairie Canada's Aboriginal Communities to 1900," in Pickles and Rutherdale, *Contact Zones,* 131-59; Robin Jarvis Brownlie, "Intimate Surveillance: Indian Affairs, Colonization, and the Regulation of Aboriginal Women's Sexuality," in Pickles and Rutherdale, *Contact Zones,* 160-78; Joan Sangster, "Criminalizing the Colonized: Ontario Native Women Confront the Criminal Justice System, 1920-1960," *Canadian Historical Review* 80 (March 1999): 33; and Sangster, "Domesticating Girls: The Sexual Regulation of Aboriginal and Working-Class Girls in Twentieth-Century Canada," in Pickles and Rutherdale, *Contact Zones,* 179-203.

67 Indian Act, 1876, R.S.C., c. 18, s. 3(a)(c).
68 Sangster, *Regulating Girls and Women,* 183.
69 Indian Act, 1876, R.S.C., c. 18, s. 11, 12, 13.
70 Renisa Mawani provides an excellent analysis of these issues and the legal authorities' response as it played out in British Columbia in "In Between and Out of Place: Racial Hybridity, Liquor, and the Law in Late 19th and Early 20th Century British Columbia," *Canadian Journal of Law and Society* 15, 2 (2000): 9-38. See also Constance Backhouse, *Colour-Coded: A Legal History of Racism in Canada, 1900-1950* (Toronto: University of Toronto Press for the Osgoode Society for Canadian Legal History, 1999), 21-27, 132-72; and James W. St. G. Walker, *"Race," Rights and the Law in the Supreme Court of Canada* (Waterloo, ON: Wilfrid Laurier University Press for the Osgoode Society for Canadian Legal History, 1997).
71 Constance Backhouse, "Nineteenth-Century Canadian Prostitution Law: Reflection of a Discriminatory Society," *Histoire sociale/Social History* 36 (November 1985): 420-21; Indian Act, 1880, 43 Vict., c. 28, s. 95, amended by 47 Vict., c. 27, s. 14 (1884); CCC, 1892, ss. 190, 198.
72 L. Vankoughnet to Department of Justice, RG 13, A-2, vol. 2250, f. 1886-1287, LAC.
73 Macleod and Rollason, "'Restrain the Lawless Savages,'" 168; *R. v. Vital and Flora Ghostkeeper* (1912), SCA, Edmonton Judicial District, PAA; Winnipeg Police Record Books, GR 651, 1886 (M-1210, M-1214), 1894 (M-1125), PAM.
74 Richard Burton Deane, Lethbridge, to Commissioner Herchmer, Regina, 27 August 1888 and 3 December 1888, RG 18, Series B-1, vol. 1123, f. 427-1888, LAC.
75 Deane to Herchmer, 21 and 30 November 1889, Lethbridge Detachment Reports, RG 18, vol. 30, f. 130-89, A-1, LAC.
76 Deane to Herchmer, 12 February 1891, RG 18, Series B-1, vol. 1204, f. 164-891, LAC.
77 S.B. Steele, Macleod, to Herchmer, 7 December 1891, RG 18, vol. 3863, Reel C-10152, 83757, LAC.
78 Deane to Herchmer, July 1889, Lethbridge Detachment Reports, RG 18, vol. 30, f. 130-89, A-1, LAC.
79 Indian Act, 1880, 43 Vict., c. 28, s. 90.
80 John Leslie and Ron Macguire, "The Historical Development of the Indian Act," 2nd ed. (Ottawa: Treaties and Historical Research Branch, DIAND, 1979); Indian Act, 1876, R.S.C., c. 18, s. 83.
81 Deane to Herchmer, 8 December 1888, RG 18, Series B-1, vol. 1123, f. 427-1888, LAC.
82 Deane, report to Herchmer, 31 October 1893, RG 18, Series A-1, vol. 74, f. 73-93, LAC.
83 R.N. Wilson, Agent, Peigan Agency, 2 March 1891, to NWMP, and Officer Primrose to NWMP Commissioner, 5 March 1903, RG 18, vol. 255, f. 403-03, LAC.

84 Homi Bhabha, "Of Mimicry and Man: The Ambivalence of Colonial Discourse," in *Tensions of Empire: Colonial Discourse in a Bourgeois World*, ed. Frederick Cooper and Ann Laura Stoler (Berkeley: University of California Press, 1997), 152-60.
85 H.W. Gibbon-Stocken, St. Barnabas Mission, Sarcee Reserve, to Hayter Reed, DIA, 1 May 1895, RG 10, Reel C-8532, vol. 6808, f. 470-2-3, p. 3, LAC.
86 "Jus Summum Saepe Summa Malitia Est," *Macleod Gazette*, 19 April 1906, in *R. v. Mary Murphy* (1906), BA, DIA, M-1788, f. 13-14, GA.
87 P.C.H. Primrose, Macleod, to A. Bowen Perry, Commissioner, NWMP, Regina, 11 June 1904; Perry to Primrose, 13 June 1905; Perry to Pedley, 31 August 1905, RG 18, Series A-1, vol. 302, f. 658-05, LAC.
88 David Laird to R.N. Wilson, 15 February 1901, BA, DIA, M-1788, f. 11-15, GA.
89 R.H. Fahey, Kingston Penitentiary, to R.N. Wilson, Blood Agency, 15 February 1905, ibid.
90 *R. v. Mah Hong and Quong How* (1927), SCA, Macleod, Acc. 78.235, PAA.
91 RCMP, "K" Division, Lethbridge, 16 June 1929, BA, DIA, M-1788, f. 142-144, GA.
92 *Connolly v. Woolrich* (1867), 11 Lower Can. Jur., 197. The case is discussed in Constance Backhouse, *Petticoats and Prejudice: Women and Law in Nineteenth-Century Canada* (Toronto: Women's Press for the Osgoode Society for Canadian Legal History, 1991), Chapter 1; and Sarah Carter, *The Importance of Being Monogamous: Marriage and Nation Building in Western Canada to 1915* (Edmonton: University of Alberta Press/Athabasca University Press, 2008), 134-38. In *Capturing Women*, Carter likewise discusses the process by which mixed marriages according to the custom of the country were invalidated in the late nineteenth century. In the 1886 case *Jones v. Fraser*, for instance, the judge ruled that cohabitation between a white man and Aboriginal woman did not give rise to the presumption that they had consented to be married "in our sense of marriage" (191).
93 Indian Act, 1894, *Statutes of Canada*, 47 & 48 Vict., c. 32, cl. 4.
94 Sangster, *Regulating Girls and Women*, 176-80; Roderick Graham Martin, "The Common Law and the Justices of the Supreme Court of the North-West Territories, 1887-1907" (master's thesis, University of Calgary, 1997), 100-4; Backhouse, *Petticoats and Prejudice*, 15-26; Carter, *The Importance of Being Monogamous*, 222-23.
95 Sangster, *Regulating Girls and Women*, 172-74.
96 Mike Mountain Horse, *My People the Bloods*, ed. Hugh Dempsey (Calgary: Glenbow-Alberta Institute and Blood Tribal Council, 1979), 75-76; Beverly Hungry Wolf, *The Ways of My Grandmothers* (New York: Quill, 1982), 26-31. On free marriages, see Carter, *The Importance of Being Monogamous*, 109-10.
97 Sabine Lang, *Men as Women, Women as Men: Changing Gender in Native American Cultures* (Austin: University of Texas Press, 1998), xiv-xv.
98 Carter, *Capturing Women*, 165, and *The Importance of Being Monogamous*, 111-12.
99 Carter, *The Importance of Being Monogamous*, 112.
100 John H. Provinse, "The Underlying Sanctions of Plains Indian Culture," in *Social Anthropology of the North American Tribes*, ed. Frederick Eggan (1937; repr., Chicago: University of Chicago Press, 1955), 343.
101 Ibid., 352, 362.
102 James Wilson, Agent, Blood Reserve, Macleod, to Secretary, Department of Indian Affairs, 23 July 1898, RG 10, Black Series, Reel C-10188, vol. 3559, f. 74, pt. 19, LAC.
103 A.E. Forget, Commissioner DIA, to J. Wilson, 18 August 1898, ibid.
104 J. Wilson to A.E. Forget, 13 March 1899, ibid.

105 Blackfoot Agency, Gleichen, to J. Wilson, 18 June 1900, Incoming Correspondence, Blood Reserve, RG 10, Series A, Reel C-14297, vol. 1535 and 1536, LAC.

106 J.A. Markel, Agent, Blackfoot Reserve, to J. Wilson, 18 June 1902, ibid.

107 Joseph Hicks to R.N. Wilson, Macleod, 22 August 1905, RCMP, BA, DIA, M-1788, f. 58, GA.

108 J.N. Wilson to Secretary, DIA, 4 June 1909, ibid.

109 Ibid.; Carter discusses a similar case from Saskatchewan in *The Importance of Being Monogamous*, 242-43.

110 Correspondence Regarding Indian Marriage and Divorce Law, RG 10, Reel C-8538, vol. 6816, f. 486-2-8, LAC.

111 Report to Indian agent, 16 June 1933, BA, DIA, RCMP, M-1788, f. 173-177, GA. Other investigated cases of domestic violence included Bullshield (1908); Many Feathers (1909); White Hat (1909); Strangling Wolf (1933); Chief Moon (1933); Bruised Head (1934); Red Crane (1934); Shanting (1934); Black Sheep (1935); First Charger (1936); Creighton (1939); Steel (1940); Good Rider (1940); Big Head (1940); Young Pine (1940).

112 Pamela Scully makes this observation in "Rape, Race, and Colonial Culture: The Sexual Politics of Identity in the Nineteenth-Century Cape Colony, South Africa," *American Historical Review* 100 (April 1995): 335-59.

113 Sherene Razack, "What Is to Be Gained by Looking White People in the Eye? Culture, Race, and Gender in Cases of Sexual Violence," in *Criminology at the Crossroads: Feminist Readings in Crime and Justice*, ed. Kathleen Daly and Lisa Maher (Oxford: Oxford University Press, 1998), 231-37; Teressa Nahanee, "Sexual Assault and Inuit Females: A Comment on Cultural Bias," in *Confronting Sexual Assault: A Decade of Legal and Social Change*, ed. Julian Roberts and Renate Mohr (Toronto: University of Toronto Press, 1994), 192-204; Margo Nightingale, "Judicial Attitudes and Differential Treatment: Native Women in Sexual Assault Cases," *Ottawa Law Review* 23, 1 (1991): 71-98; Barman, "Taming Aboriginal Sexuality," 237-38; Angela Davis, *Women, Race, and Class* (New York: Random House, 1981), 182.

114 *R. v. Cardinal* (1909), SCA, Edmonton, Acc. 83.1, indecent assault, not guilty; and *R. v. Câpot* (1912), SCA, Edmonton, Acc. 83.1, indecent assault, not guilty; *R. v. The Rib* (1893), SCNWT, Southern Alberta, Acc. 78.235, rape, not guilty; *R. v. Plaited Hair* (1921), SCA, Macleod, Acc. 78.235, attempted rape, discharged; and *R. v. Strikes with a Gun and David* (1937), SCA, Macleod, Acc. 78.235, microfilm, rape, dismissed, PAA. *R. v. Robillard* (1898), SCNWT, Western Assiniboia, R-1286, unlawful carnal knowledge of a sixteen-year-old, guilty, one month in Regina jail; *R. v. Lenoire* (1919-20), Saskatchewan Court of King's Bench (SCKB), Regina, R-1287, rape, found guilty of indecent assault, nine months in Regina jail, SAB. *R. v. Flat Foot* (1931), MCKB, Dauphin, GR 540, indecent assault, pleaded guilty, thirty days in jail, PAM. For cases that ended with harsh sentences, see *R. v. Ross* (1900) and *R. v. Flammond* (1912), MCKB, Eastern Manitoba/Winnipeg, GR 180, microfilm, PAM.

115 *R. v. Strikes with a Gun and David* (1937).

116 "Assault Case," *Lethbridge Herald*, 22 March 1938.

117 *R. v. Strikes with a Gun and David* (1937).

118 See, for instance, *Redcrow, Lost Star, and Tallman* (1900), rape, dismissed; *Daly and Black White Man* (1901), rape, dismissed; *Veille* (1933), indecent assault, guilty; *Badman* (1933), indecent assault, guilty, BA, DIA, M-1788, f. 14, 15, 173, 177, 194, GA.

119 R.C.S. Hawkins, RCMP, "K" Division, Lethbridge, report to the Indian agent, 22 September 1934, BA, DIA, M-1788, f. 183-94, GA.
120 Lauren Benton, "Colonial Law and Cultural Difference: Jurisdictional Politics and the Formation of the Colonial State," *Comparative Studies in Society and History* 41, 3 (1999): 564.
121 Carter, "Creating 'Semi-Widows' and 'Supernumerary Wives,'" 131-59.

CHAPTER 3: THE MOST PUBLIC OF PRIVATE WOMEN

1 "Commissioners Take Drastic Measures," *Manitoba Daily Free Press*, 5 January 1904; "Thomas Street Resorts Closed," *Manitoba Daily Free Press*, 11 January 1904.
2 *Winnipeg Tribune*, 9 January 1904.
3 See, for instance, Susan J. Johnston, "Twice Slain: Female Sex-Trade Workers and Suicide in British Columbia, 1870-1920," *Journal of the Canadian Historical Association* 5 (1994): 147-66. The literature on prostitution and the movements for moral and social reform is vast and growing. For an excellent, in-depth review, see Timothy J. Gilfoyle, "Prostitutes in History: From Parables of Pornography to Metaphors of Modernity," *American Historical Review* 104 (February 1999): 117-41. The following selected studies delineate the symbolic and discursive meanings attached to prostitution in distinct colonial and national contexts: Philippa Levine, *Prostitution, Race, and Politics: Policing Venereal Disease in the British Empire* (New York: Routledge, 2003); Bronwyn Dalley, "'Fresh Attraction': White Slavery and Feminism in New Zealand, 1885-1918," *Women's History Review* 9, 3 (2000): 585-606; Paula Bartley, *Prostitution: Prevention and Reform in England, 1860-1914* (London: Routledge, 2000); Trevor Fisher, *Prostitution and the Victorians* (Gloucestershire, UK: Sutton Publishing, 1997); Keith Shear, "'Not Welfare or Uplift Work': White Women, Masculinity, and Policing in South Africa," *Gender and History* 8, 3 (1996): 393-415; Judith Walkowitz, *City of Dreadful Delight: Narratives of Sexual Danger in Late-Victorian London* (Chicago: University of Chicago Press, 1992), and *Prostitution and Victorian Society: Women, Class, and the State* (Cambridge: Cambridge University Press, 1980); Mariana Valverde, *The Age of Light, Soap, and Water: Moral Reform in English Canada, 1885-1925* (Toronto: McClelland and Stewart, 1991), 77-103; Donna J. Guy, *Sex and Danger in Buenos Aires: Prostitution, Family, and Nation in Argentina* (Lincoln: University of Nebraska Press, 1991); Alain Corbin, *Women for Hire: Prostitution and Sexuality in France after 1850*, trans. Alan Sheridan (Cambridge: Cambridge University Press, 1990); Elizabeth B. van Heyningen, "The Social Evil in the Cape Colony, 1868-1902: Prostitution and the Contagious Diseases Act," *Journal of South African Studies* 10, 2 (1984): 170-97; Mark Connelly, *The Response to Prostitution in the Progressive Era* (Chapel Hill: University of North Carolina Press, 1980).
4 Philippa Levine, "The White Slave Trade and the British Empire," in *Criminal Justice History*, vol. 17, *Crime, Gender, and Sexuality in Criminal Prosecutions*, ed. Louis A. Knafla (Westport, CT: Greenwood Press, 2002), 133.
5 Ralph Connor, *Black Rock: A Tale of the Selkirks* (Toronto: Westminster Company, 1898); Frederick Phillip Grove, *Settlers of the Marsh* (1925; repr., Toronto: McClelland and Stewart, 1989). Lindsey McMaster explores literary representations of prostitution and the white slave trade in western Canada in *Working Girls in the West: Representations of Wage-Earning Women* (Vancouver: UBC Press, 2008), Chapter 3.

6 Reverend J.B. Silcox, "Poets Who Sing of Ruined Womanhood," Silcox Papers, MS 353, file 3, Rare Books and Special Collections Division, McGill University Library.

7 Sherene Razack, "Race, Space, and Prostitution: The Making of a Bourgeois Subject," *Canadian Journal of Women and the Law* 10, 2 (1998): 339.

8 Susan Wood, "God's Doormats: Women in Canadian Prairie Fiction," *Journal of Popular Culture* 14, 2 (1980): 350-59. Northrop Frye viewed the pioneer woman as a metaphor for Canadian femininity: see Alan Hunt, *Governing Morals: A Social History of Moral Regulation* (Cambridge: Cambridge University Press, 1999), 85; and Elizabeth Thompson, *The Pioneer Woman: A Canadian Character* (Montreal and Kingston: McGill-Queen's University Press, 1991).

9 Cecily Devereux, "'And Let Them Wash Me from the Clanging World': *Hugh and Ion*, 'The Last Best West,' and Purity Discourse in 1885," *Journal of Canadian Studies* 32 (Summer 1997): 100-15; Valverde, *The Age of Light, Soap, and Water*, 77-79; Andrée Lévesque, "Éteindre le 'Red Light': Les reformateurs et la prostitution – Montréal, 1865-1925," *Urban History Review* 17, 3 (1989): 191-201; Lori Rotenberg, "The Wayward Worker: Toronto's Prostitute at the Turn of the Century," in *Women at Work: Ontario, 1850-1930*, ed. Janice Acton, Penny Goldsmith, and Bonnie Shepard (Toronto: Canadian Women's Educational Press, 1974), 33-69; Deborah Nilsen, "The 'Social Evil': Prostitution in Vancouver, 1900-1920," in *In Her Own Right: Selected Essays in Women's History*, ed. Barbara Latham and Cathy Kess (Victoria: Camosun College, 1980), 205-28.

10 Gilfoyle, "Prostitutes in History," 137-40. On prostitution on the Canadian Prairies, see, in particular, Alan Artibise, *Winnipeg: A Social History of Urban Growth* (Montreal and Kingston: McGill-Queen's University Press, 1975); Joy Cooper, "Red Lights in Winnipeg," *Transactions*, Manitoba Historical and Scientific Society (16 February 1971): 67-74; John McLaren, "White Slavers: The Reform of Canada's Prostitution Laws and Patterns of Enforcement, 1900-1920," *Criminal Justice History* 8 (1987): 53-119; Judy Bedford, "Prostitution in Calgary, 1905-1914," *Alberta History* 29 (1981): 1-11; David Bright, "The Cop, the Chief, the Hooker, and Her Life," *Alberta History* 45 (1997): 16-26; S.W. Horrall, "The (Royal) North-West Mounted Police and Prostitution on the Canadian Prairies," *Prairie Forum* 10 (Spring 1985): 105-27. Rhonda L. Hinther's "The Oldest Profession in Winnipeg: The Culture of Prostitution in the Point Douglas Segregated District, 1909-1912," *Manitoba History* 41 (Spring/Summer 2001): 2-13; and Christine Anne Macfarlane's "'Unfortunate Women of My Class': Prostitution in Winnipeg" (master's thesis, University of Manitoba and University of Winnipeg, 2002), which switch the analytic focus to prostitutes themselves, are recent exceptions.

11 Gilfoyle, "Prostitutes in History," 127; Walkowitz, *City of Dreadful Delight*, 21, 41; Mary P. Ryan, *Women in Public: Between Banners and Ballots, 1825-1880* (Baltimore: Johns Hopkins University Press, 1992), 95-128.

12 For similar perspectives, see Pippa Holloway, "Regulation and the Nation: Comparative Perspectives on Prostitution and Public Policy," *Journal of Women's History* 15, 1 (2003): 202; Ruth Rosen, "Go West Young Woman? Prostitution on the Frontier," *Reviews in American History* 14 (March 1986): 91; Ann-Louise Shapiro, *Breaking the Codes: Female Criminality in Fin-de-Siècle Paris* (Stanford: Stanford University Press, 1996).

13 Madeleine Blair [pseud.], *Madeleine: An Autobiography* (1919; repr., New York: Persea Books, 1986), 249-54.

14 Ibid., 249.

15 Ibid., x.

16 Ibid., 322-23. The legal battle over this publication, *John Sumner v. Ben B. Lindsey,* involved Denver juvenile court judge Ben Lindsey, a liberal judicial activist who championed compassionate juvenile justice and progressive thinking about family life. For other rare, early-twentieth-century personal accounts of prostitution, see Josie Wasburn, *The Underworld Sewer: A Prostitute Reflects on Life in the Trade, 1871-1909* (Lincoln: University of Nebraska Press, 1997); and Ruth Rosen and Sue Davidson, eds., *The Mamie Papers* (Old Westbury, NY: Feminist Press, 1977).

17 Blair, *Madeleine,* 177.

18 Ibid., 180.

19 Corbin, *Women for Hire,* 123-26, 336-38; Gail Hershatter, *Dangerous Pleasures: Prostitution and Modernity in Twentieth-Century Shanghai* (Berkeley: University of California Press, 1997), 65; Gilfoyle, "Prostitutes in History," 135.

20 Corbin, *Women for Hire,* 4-17, 62, 331; Gilfoyle, "Prostitutes in History," 120-21. For studies that trace Parent-Duchâtelet's influence on other national regulatory systems, see Guy, *Sex and Danger,* 13; Luise White, *The Comforts of Home: Prostitution in Colonial Nairobi* (Chicago: University of Chicago Press, 1990), ix, 4-5, 40; Hershatter, *Dangerous Pleasures,* 253, 262-63; Walkowitz, *Prostitution and Victorian Society,* 36-39, 43-46.

21 Holloway, "Regulation and the Nation," 204. See also David J. Pivar, *Purity and Hygiene: Women, Prostitution, and the "American Plan," 1900-1930* (Westport, CT: Greenwood Press, 2002); Katherine Elaine Bliss, *Compromised Positions: Prostitution, Public Health and Gender Politics in Revolutionary Mexico City* (University Park: Pennsylvania State University Press, 2001); Christian Henriot, *Prostitution and Sexuality in Shanghai: A Social History, 1849-1949,* trans. Noël Castelino (Cambridge: Cambridge University Press, 2001); Donna J. Guy, *White Slavery and Mothers Alive or Dead: The Troubled Meeting of Sex, Gender, Public Health and Progress in Latin America* (Lincoln: University of Nebraska Press, 2000); Yvonne Svanström, *Policing Public Women: The Regulation of Prostitution in Stockholm, 1812-1880* (Stockholm: Atlas Akkademi, 2000).

22 Valverde, *The Age of Light, Soap, and Water,* 80-81.

23 James H. Gray, *Red Lights on the Prairies: The Bonanza Years When the Wide-Open Frontier Was a Hooker's Happy Hunting Ground* (1971; repr., Scarborough, ON: New American Library, 1973), 22-23, and *Booze: When Whisky Ruled the West* (Saskatoon: Fifth House, 1995); Adele Perry, *On the Edge of Empire: Gender, Race, and the Making of British Columbia, 1849-1871* (Toronto: University of Toronto Press, 2001), 40-44; Anne M. Butler, *Daughters of Joy, Sisters of Misery: Prostitutes in the American West, 1865-1890* (Chicago: University of Illinois Press, 1987), 1.

24 *Manitoba Free Press,* 12 November 1910. Rhonda Hinther reconstructs the culture of Winnipeg's prostitutes in "The Oldest Profession in Winnipeg."

25 Kay Saunders, "Controlling (Hetero)Sexuality: The Implementation and Operation of Contagious Diseases Legislation in Australia, 1868-1945," in Kirkby, *Sex, Power, and Justice,* 4-5; Miles Ogborn, "Law and Discipline in Nineteenth-Century English State Formation: The *Contagious Diseases Acts* of 1864, 1866, and 1869," *Journal of Historical Sociology* 6, 1 (1993): 35-37.

26 Saunders, "Controlling (Hetero)Sexuality," 7; M.J.D. Roberts, "Feminism and the State in Later Victorian England," *The Historical Journal* 38, 1 (1995): 90-92; Valverde, *The Age of Light, Soap, and Water,* 80.

27 Walkowitz, *City of Dreadful Delight,* 81-120; Valverde, *The Age of Light, Soap, and Water,* 89-92.

28 Hunt, *Governing Morals*, 102; Corbin, *Women for Hire*, 220-34; Gilfoyle, "Prostitutes in History," 122.
29 Roberts, "Feminism and the State," 101-2.
30 Walkowitz, *City of Dreadful Delight*, 83.
31 Ibid., 24.
32 Blair, *Madeleine*, 263.
33 Ibid., 235.
34 Walkowitz, *City of Dreadful Delight*, 83; Mrinalini Sinha, "Gender and Imperialism: Colonial Policy and the Ideology of Moral Imperialism in Late-Nineteenth-Century Bengal," in *Changing Men: New Directions in Research on Men and Masculinity*, ed. M.S. Kimmel (Beverly Hills, CA: Sage, 1987), 217-31; Dagmar Engels, "The Limits of Gender Ideology, Bengali Women, the Colonial State, and the Private Sphere, 1890-1930," *Women's Studies International Forum* 12, 4 (1989): 425-37.
35 Saunders, "Controlling (Hetero)Sexuality," 9-10; Raymond Evans, "Harlots and Helots: Exploitation of the Aboriginal Remnant," in *Race Relations in Colonial Queensland: Exclusion, Exploitation and Extermination*, ed. Raymond Evans, Kay Saunders, and Kathryn Cronin (St. Lucia: University of Queensland Press, 1993), 102-17; Ann McGrath, "'Black Velvet': Aboriginal Women and Their Relations with White Men in the Northern Territory, 1910-40," in *So Much Hard Work: Women and Prostitution in Australian History*, ed. Kay Daniels (Melbourne: Fontana/Collins, 1984), 232.
36 Carolyn Strange, *Toronto's Girl Problem: The Perils and Pleasures of the City, 1880-1920* (Toronto: University of Toronto Press, 1995), 96-100; Valverde, *The Age of Light, Soap, and Water*, Chapter 4.
37 Ramsay Cook, *The Regenerators: Social Criticism in Late Victorian English Canada* (Toronto: University of Toronto Press, 1985); Richard Allen, *The Social Passion: Religion and Social Reform in Canada, 1914-1928* (Toronto: University of Toronto Press, 1971), 3-17. Although I trace how social purity and reform advocates enhanced the regulation of female sexuality through the criminal justice system, I do not discount the idea that advocates of reform and moral purity were motivated by evangelicalism, as Sharon Ann Cook argues in "'Do not ... do anything that you cannot unblushingly tell your mother': Gender and Social Purity in Canada," *Histoire sociale/Social History* 30 (November 1997): 215-39.
38 Howard Palmer, *Patterns of Prejudice: A History of Nativism in Alberta* (Toronto: McClelland and Stewart, 1982), 40; Devereux, "'And Let Them Wash Me,'" 100-15.
39 James G. Snell, "'The White Life for Two': The Defence of Marriage and Sexual Morality in Canada, 1890-1914," in *Canadian Family History: Selected Readings*, ed. Bettina Bradbury (Toronto: Copp Clark Pitman, 1992), 388-89.
40 Artibise, *Winnipeg*, 251-53; Mélanie Méthot, "Social Thinkers, Social Actors in Winnipeg and Montreal at the Turn of the Century" (PhD diss., University of Calgary, 2001), 197, 235, 248.
41 *Winnipeg Daily Times*, 9 April 1883.
42 Quoted in Méthot, "Social Thinkers, Social Actors," 97.
43 Rev. Frederic B. Du Val, *The Problem of Social Vice in Winnipeg: Being a Reply to a Pamphlet Entitled "The Attitude of the Church to the Social Evil": Together with a Brief Examination of the Question in the Light of Physiology, Law and Morality* (Winnipeg: Moral and Social Reform Committee, 1904), microfilm 2763, Peel's Prairie Provinces, University of Alberta, Edmonton.
44 Testimony of James Shearer, Robson Royal Commission on Social Vice, Winnipeg, 1911, Manitoba Legislative Library (hereafter referred to as "Robson Commission").

45 Mary Spongeberg, *Feminizing Venereal Disease: The Body of the Prostitute in Nineteenth-Century Medical Discourse* (New York: New York University Press, 1997), 6.

46 Cited in Patricia Anne Roome, "Henrietta Muir Edwards: The Journey of a Canadian Feminist" (PhD diss., Simon Fraser University, 1996), 142.

47 For a full formulation of the concept of separate spheres as a bourgeois ideology, see Linda Kerber, "Separate Spheres, Female Worlds, Woman's Place: The Rhetoric of Women's History," *Journal of American History* 75, 1 (1988): 9-39; Carol Lee Bacchi, *Liberation Deferred? The Ideas of the English-Canadian Suffragists, 1877-1918* (Toronto: University of Toronto Press, 1983), 7; Veronica Strong-Boag, "'Ever a Crusader': Nellie McClung, First-Wave Feminist," in *Rethinking Canada: The Promise of Women's History*, 3rd ed., ed. Veronica Strong-Boag and Anita Clair Fellman (Toronto: Oxford University Press, 1997), 272-75.

48 Quoted in Roome, "Henrietta Muir Edwards," 230; Valverde, *The Age of Light, Soap, and Water*, 93-95.

49 Bacchi, *Liberation Differed?* 114; *Manitoba Free Press*, 7 October 1916.

50 Strange, *Toronto's Girl Problem*, 90-92.

51 Cited in Méthot, "Social Thinkers, Social Actors," 198.

52 Janice Newton, "From Wage Slave to White Slave: The Prostitution Controversy and the Early Canadian Left," in *Beyond the Vote: Canadian Women and Politics*, ed. Linda Kealey and Joan Sangster (Toronto: University of Toronto Press, 1989), 221-27.

53 Macfarlane discusses and quotes the attitudes of religious leaders toward prostitutes' clients in "'Unfortunate Women of My Class,'" 140-63.

54 Testimony of Adjutant McElhany, Salvation Army, Robson Commission, 3-15, 411-12; Gray, *Red Lights on the Prairie*, 69-73; Mariana Valverde and S. Craig Wilson, "John George Shearer," *Dictionary of Canadian Biography Online*, http://www.biographi.ca.

55 Valverde, *The Age of Light, Soap, and Water*, 77-103.

56 John McLaren, "The Canadian Magistracy and the Anti-White Slavery Campaign," in *Canadian Perspectives on Law and Society: Issues in Legal History*, ed. W. Wesley Pue and Barry Wright (Ottawa: Carelton University Press, 1988), 320.

57 Canadian Criminal Code, 1892 (CCC), 55 & 56 Vict., c. 29, s. 207; CCC, *Revised Statutes of Canada* (R.S.C.), 1906, c. 146, s. 238; Joan Sangster, *Regulating Girls and Women: Sexuality, Family, and the Law in Ontario, 1920-1960* (Don Mills, ON: Oxford University Press, 2001), 93; Constance Backhouse, "Nineteenth-Century Canadian Prostitution Law: Reflection of a Discriminatory Society," *Histoire sociale/Social History* 36 (November 1985): 388.

58 CCC, 1892, s. 198; CCC, R.S.C., 1907, c. 8, s. 2.

59 CCC, 1892, c. 29, s. 185(a), (h); McLaren, "The Canadian Magistracy," 331.

60 CCC, R.S.C., 1913, c. 13, s. 9; CCC, R.S.C., 1915, c. 12, ss. 5, 7; E. Nick Larson, "Canadian Prostitution Control between 1914 and 1970: An Exercise in Chauvinist Reasoning," *Canadian Journal of Law and Society* 7 (Fall 1992): 137-56.

61 Although reported cases indicate that the higher courts often focused on laws dealing with procuring and living off the avails of prostitution in the 1920s and 1930s, and that the courts had turned to punishing males involved in prostitution, Joan Sangster argues that the onus continued to fall on the female prostitute in the interwar period. For the historiographical debate on these issues see Sangster, *Regulating Girls and Women*, 93-97.

62 Horrall, "The (Royal) North-West Mounted Police and Prostitution on the Canadian Prairies," 106.

63 Artibise, *Winnipeg*, 248.

64 Testimony of Chief John McRae, 24 November 1910, Robson Commission, 53.
65 Testimony of Magistrate Thomas Mayne Daly, Robson Commission, 337; McLaren, "The Canadian Magistracy," 338-39.
66 Hunt, *Governing Morals,* 103.
67 Sangster, *Regulating Girls and Women,* 87; Dorothy Chunn, "'Just Plain Everyday Housekeeping on a Grand Scale': Feminists, Family Courts, and the Welfare State in British Columbia, 1928-1945," in *Law, Society, and the State: Essays in Legal History,* ed. Louis A. Knafla and Susan W.S. Binnie (Toronto: University of Toronto Press, 1994), 379-403; and Chunn, *From Punishment to Doing Good: Family Courts and Socialized Justice in Ontario, 1880-1940* (Toronto: University of Toronto Press, 1992).
68 McLaren, "The Canadian Magistracy," 344-45.
69 Emily Murphy, "A Straight Talk on Courts," *Maclean's,* 1 October 1920, 27.
70 Angus McLaren, *Our Own Master Race: Eugenics in Canada, 1885-1945* (Toronto: McClelland and Stewart, 1990).
71 Ibid., 40. See also Strange, *Toronto's Girl Problem,* 16.
72 McLaren, *Our Own Master Race,* 32-40.
73 Nellie L. McClung, *Painted Fires* (Toronto: Thomas Allen, 1925); and Emily Murphy, *The Black Candle* (Toronto: Thomas Allen, 1922).
74 Strange, *Toronto's Girl Problem,* 115.
75 Sangster, *Regulating Girls and Women,* 101-2.
76 Official statistics for Canada reveal that female offenders accounted for 10.2 percent of all indictable offences in 1888 but only 5.7 percent ten years later: D. Owen Carrigan, *Crime and Punishment in Canada: A History* (Toronto: McClelland and Stewart, 1994), 260-61.
77 In his study of female crime in Halifax, Nova Scotia, legal historian Jim Phillips found that women constituted 15 percent of all offenders between 1750 and 1800: "Women, Crime, and Criminal Justice in Early Halifax, 1750-1800," in Phillips, Loo, and Lewthwaite, *Crime and Criminal Justice,* 174-206. By contrast, in Montreal's Court of King's Bench, women accounted for 5.4 percent of all convictions between 1812 and 1862: F. Murray Greenwood and Beverley Boissery, *Uncertain Justice: Canadian Women and Capital Punishment, 1754-1953* (Toronto: Dundern Press, 2000), 17.
78 Legal historian John McLaren has demonstrated that national prosecution rates rose throughout the moral reform era and peaked during the First World War, with the number of arrests not coming close to those rates again for decades: McLaren, "White Slavers," 53-119, and "Chasing the Social Evil: Moral Fervour and the Evolution of Canada's Prostitution Laws, 1867-1917," *Canadian Journal of Law and Society* 1 (1986): 125-65. His findings are supported by historian Carolyn Strange's analysis of prosecutorial trends in Toronto. However, Strange found that the Toronto courts were more willing to punish men: *Toronto's Girl Problem,* 146.
79 Robert Hutchinson, *City of Winnipeg Police Force: A Century of Service* (Winnipeg: City of Winnipeg Police, 1974), 19.
80 City of Winnipeg Police Court, Record Books (WPC), case nos. 3727, 3960, 4023, 4192, 4204, 4565, GR 651, M-1196, Provincial Archives of Manitoba (PAM). Macfarlane explores Trottier's career as an occasional prostitute and her confrontations with the law in depth in "'Unfortunate Women of My Class,'" 28-39.
81 Testimony of Minnie Woods, Robson Commission, 374-79.
82 WPC, case nos. 34334 and 36578, GR 651, M-1220, PAM.

83 Edmonton Police Court, I and II August, 14 September, 9 and 24 November, 31 December 1909, and 31 March 1910, Provincial Archives of Alberta (PAA). Edmonton police court records are filed with the Supreme Court of Alberta (SCA), Edmonton, Acc. 83.1, PAA.

84 Blair, *Madeleine*, 214.

85 Gray, *Red Lights on the Prairies*, 52.

86 WPC, 18 January, 8 March, 2 May, 3 July, 2 August, 17 September, 11 October, 3 November 1902, GR 651, microfilm, PAM.

87 WPC, 1886, GR 651, microfilm, PAM; Criminal Register, County Criminal Court, Eastern Manitoba/Winnipeg, case no. 307, GR 3636, M-1196, PAM.

88 WPC, 1894, 1902, and 1910, GR 651, microfilm, PAM.

89 *R. v. Herzer* (1913), SCA, Edmonton, Acc. 83.1, PAA; *R. v. Roberts* (1922), Saskatchewan Court of King's Bench (SCKB), Regina, R-1287, Saskatchewan Archives Board (SAB).

90 Elizabeth's Langdon's analysis of female crime in the Calgary Police Court, however, revealed startlingly different results: vagrancy charges accounted for 21.7 percent of the court's business in 1939: "Female Crime in Calgary, 1914-1941," in *Law and Justice in a New Land: Essays in Western Canadian Legal History,* ed. Louis A. Knafla (Toronto: Carswell, 1986), 310.

91 Sangster, *Regulating Girls and Women*, 92; Helen Boritch, "The Making of Toronto the Good: The Organization of Policing and the Production of Arrests, 1859-1955" (PhD diss., University of Toronto, 1985); Greg Marquis, "Vancouver Vice: The Police and the Negotiation of Morality, 1904-1935," in *Essays in the History of Canadian Law,* vol. 6, *British Columbia and the Yukon,* ed. Hamar Foster and John McLaren (Toronto: University of Toronto Press for the Osgoode Society for Canadian Legal History, 1995), 242-73.

92 Gray, *Red Lights on the Prairies,* 59-61; Roy St. George Stubbs, "The First Juvenile Court Judge: The Honourable Thomas Mayne Daly, KC," *Papers of the Historical and Scientific Society of Manitoba,* ser. 3, nos. 34-35 (1977-78): 63-64; testimony of McRae, 21, and Daly, 337, Robson Commission.

93 *R. v. Lebansky* (1917), MCKB, Eastern Manitoba/Winnipeg, GR 180, microfilm, PAM.

94 Testimony of McRae, Robson Commission, 35.

95 Langdon discusses the evolution of the law of evidence in prostitution cases in "Female Crime in Calgary," 299-300.

96 Testimony of McRae, 35-37, and Daly, 342-50, Robson Commission.

97 Testimony of Daly, Robson Commission, 343; CCC, R.S.C., 1906, c. 146.

98 *R. v. Moore* (1912), SCA, Edmonton, Acc. 83.1, PAA.

99 Testimony of Amy Morris, Robson Commission, 138.

100 Testimony of Daly, Robson Commission, 343.

101 *R. v. Langston,* SCA, Edmonton, box 104, no. 1249, PAA.

102 Sangster, *Regulating Girls and Women,* 102-3.

103 Macfarlane, "'Unfortunate Women of My Class,'" 119-20.

104 WPC, case nos. 37295 and 38792, 1910, GR 651, microfilm, PAM; *R. v. Rowe* (1911), Manitoba Court of King's Bench (MCKB), Eastern Manitoba/Winnipeg, GR 180, microfilm, PAM; testimony of Daly, Robson Commission, 344.

105 Tamara Myers and Carolyn Strange explore similar patterns of regulation and resistance in "Retorts, Runaways, and Riots: Patterns of Resistance in Canadian Reform Schools for Girls, 1920-1960," *Journal of Social History* 34, 3 (2001): 69-98. See also Tamara Myers, *Caught: Montreal's Modern Girls and the Law, 1869-1945* (Toronto: University of Toronto Press, 2006), Chapter 7.

106 "An Act for the Prevention of Venereal Disease," *Statutes of the Province of Alberta*, c. 50, s. 3.
107 Edmonton Police Court, Supreme Court of Alberta, Edmonton, Acc. 83.1, 1919-1940; box 104, case nos. 1157-1164, 1240, 1241, 1247a, 1249, 1251, 1267, 1273, 1275, 1278, 1313, PAA.
108 Susan Edwards, *Female Sexuality and the Law* (Oxford: Martin Robertson, 1981), 50-51.

CHAPTER 4: THE FARMER, THE PIONEER WOMAN, AND THE HIRED HAND

An earlier version of this chapter was published as "'A Very Garden of the Lord'? Hired Hands, Farm Women, and Sex Crime Prosecutions on the Prairies, 1914-1929," *Journal of the Canadian Historical Association* 12 (2001): 115-36. The article presented the findings of a slightly smaller sample of sex crime cases (391 cases), and conviction rates reflected the outcomes of only those cases that went to trial.

  1 *R. v. Gowland* (1907), Department of Justice, Capital Case Files, RG 13, vol. 1452, f. 389, Library and Archives Canada (LAC); "Gowland to Hang for Brutal Murder," *Manitoba Free Press*, 24 October 1907.
  2 Quoted in W.J.C. Cherwinski, "Wooden Horses and Rubber Cows: Training British Agricultural Labour for the Canadian Prairies, 1890-1930," *Historical Papers* 15, 1 (1980): 139; Cecilia Danysk, *Hired Hands: Labour and the Development of Prairie Agriculture, 1880-1930* (Toronto: McClelland and Stewart, 1994), 59. See also Joy Parr, *Labouring Children: British Immigrant Apprentices to Canada, 1869 to 1924* (Montreal and Kingston: McGill-Queen's University Press, 1980).
  3 Quoted in Tom Mitchell, "'Blood with the Taint of Cain': Immigrant Labouring Children, Manitoba Politics, and the Execution of Emily Hilda Blake," *Journal of Canadian Studies* 28 (Winter 1993-94): 56-57, 60.
  4 Kenneth Bagnell, *The Little Immigrants: The Orphans Who Came to Canada* (Toronto: Macmillan, 1980), 169.
  5 James S. Woodsworth, *Strangers within Our Gates: The Problem of the Immigrant* (1909; repr., Toronto: University of Toronto Press, 1977), 46. By contrast, my investigation of Winnipeg Police Court registers revealed that Canadian-born men and women were more likely than English immigrants to face a magistrate for a summary offence. In 1910, 18 percent of convicted offenders were English, whereas 22 percent were Canadian. Woodsworth himself provides these statistics in *My Neighbour: Urban Ills and Urban Reform, 1911* (Toronto: University of Toronto Press, 1972), 132-34.
  6 *R. v. Gowland* (1907); "Gowland Murder Trial on To-Day," *Manitoba Free Press*, 23 October 1907.
  7 Report and Notes of the Honourable Mr. Phippen to the Governor General of Canada, 26 November 1907, and F.H. Phippen to the Secretary of State, Department of Justice, 5 November 1907, in *R. v. Gowland* (1907).
  8 C.W. Finch to A.B. Aylesworth, Minister of Justice, Ottawa, 30 October 1907, ibid.; "Condemned Man Sends Message ... Writes Pathetic Letter to Sister," *Manitoba Free Press*, 13 December 1907; "Gowland Paid Crime's Penalty," *Manitoba Free Press*, 14 December 1907.
  9 Cecilia Danysk, "'A Bachelor's Paradise': Homesteaders, Hired Hands, and the Construction of Masculinity, 1880-1930," in *Making Western Canada: Essays on European Colonization and Settlement*, ed. Catherine Cavanaugh and Jeremy Mouat (Toronto: Garamond Press, 1996), 168.

10 Winfield S. Hall, "Sex Instruction for the Country Boy," *Rural Manhood* 1 (April 1910);
    D. Vandercock, "Rural Delinquency," *Rural Manhood* 4 (May 1913), 151. Quoted in Danysk,
    "'A Bachelor's Paradise,'" 72.
11 Quoted in W.J.C. Cherwinski, "In Search of Jake Trumper: The Farm Hand and the Prairie
    Farm Family," in *Building beyond the Homestead: Rural History on the Prairies,* ed. David
    C. Jones and Ian MacPherson (Calgary: University of Calgary Press, 1985), 114.
12 Homestead entries on the Prairies peaked in 1911, when the number of men engaged in
    farming – estimated at 43,000 in 1891 – reached 279,000. See Danysk, *Hired Hands,* 49.
    See also Pamela Scully, "Criminality and Conflict in Rural Stellenbasch, South Africa,
    1870-1900," *Journal of African History* 39 (1989): 289-300; Jeremy C. Martens, "Settler
    Homes, Manhood, and 'Houseboys': An Analysis of Natal's Rape Scare of 1886," *Journal
    of South African Studies* 28, 2 (2002): 379-400; S. Dagut, "Gender, Colonial 'Women's
    History' and the Construction of Social Distance: Middle-Class British Women in Later
    Nineteenth-Century South Africa," *Journal of South African Studies* 26, 3 (2000): 555-72;
    Susan Sessions Rugh, "Civilizing the Countryside: Class, Gender, and Crime in Nineteenth-
    Century Rural Illinois," *Agricultural History* 76, 1 (2002): 58-81.
13 Dirk Hoerder, "How the Intimate Lives of Subaltern Men, Women, and Children Confound
    the Nation's Master Narratives," *Journal of American History* 88 (December 2001): http://
    www.historycooperative.org, para. 12.
14 See, for instance, Angus McLaren's, *Trials of Masculinity: Policing Sexual Boundaries, 1870-
    1930* (Chicago: University of Chicago Press, 1997), 2-3.
15 David C. Jones, "'There Is Some Power about the Land': The Western Agrarian Press and
    Country Life Ideology," in *The Prairie West: Historical Readings,* 2nd ed., ed. R. Douglas
    Francis and Howard Palmer (Edmonton: Pica Pica Press, 1995), 457.
16 "Indecent Assault," *Manitoba Morning Free Press,* 14 November 1895.
17 *R. v. Henault* (1895), Manitoba Court of King's Bench (MCKB), Eastern Manitoba/
    Winnipeg, GR 180, microfilm, Provincial Archives of Manitoba (PAM).
18 Mary E. Crawford, ed., *Legal Status of Women in Manitoba* (Winnipeg: Political Equality
    League of Manitoba, 1913), 37.
19 *Morning Leader,* 2 October 1911, 9 November 1921.
20 Estelle B. Freedman, "'Uncontrolled Desires': The Response to the Sexual Psychopath,
    1920-1960," *Journal of American History* 74, 1 (1987): 83-106; Elise Chenier, "The Criminal
    Sexual Psychopath in Canada: Sex, Psychiatry, and the Law at Mid-Century," *Canadian
    Bulletin of Medical History* 20, 1 (2003): 78; Stephen Robertson, "Separating the Men from
    the Boys: Masculinity, Psychosexual Development, and Sex Crime in the United States,
    1930-1960s," *Journal of the History of Medicine and Allied Sciences* 56, 1 (2001): 6-8; Sandy
    Ramos, "'A Most Detestable Crime': Gender Identities and Sexual Violence in the District
    of Montreal, 1803-1843," *Journal of the Canadian Historical Association* 12 (2001): 28.
21 Constance Backhouse, "A Measure of Women's Credibility: The Doctrine of Corroboration
    in Sexual Assault Trials in Early Twentieth-Century Canada and Australia," *York Occasional
    Working Papers in Law and Society* 1 (2002): 1-2.
22 Canadian Criminal Code, 1892 (CCC), 55 & 56 Vict., c. 29, s. 266.
23 Ibid., s. 268.
24 "An Act to Amend the Criminal Code," *Revised Statutes of Canada* (R.S.C.), 1920, 10 &
    11 Geo. V, c. 43, s. 7, and 1921, 11 & 12 Geo. V., c. 25, s. 4.
25 Seymour F. Harris, *Principles of Criminal Law,* 6th ed. (London: Stevens and Haynes,
    1892), 181; and William Oldnell Russel, "Rape," in *Russel on Crimes: A Treatise on Crimes*

and Misdemeanours, 6th ed. (London: Stevens and Sons, 1896). Historian Terry Chapman argues correctly that, contrary to the Canadian criminal law's definition of rape, the criminal courts and the public adhered to an eighteenth-century English common law definition, represented by Hale and Blackstone, as "unlawful carnal knowledge of a woman by force and against her will": "Sex Crimes in Western Canada, 1890-1920" (PhD diss., University of Alberta, 1984), 77.

26 CCC, 1892, s. 269; Backhouse, "A Measure of Women's Credibility," 17; "Drastic Changes Have Been Made to the Criminal Code," *Edmonton Journal*, 30 September 1920. After 1890, corroboration was needed only if the complainant was too young to swear an oath.

27 CCC, 1892, s. 269.

28 James G. Snell, "'The White Life for Two': The Defence of Marriage and Sexual Morality in Canada, 1890-1914," in *Canadian Family History: Selected Readings*, ed. Bettina Bradbury (Toronto: Copp Clark Pitman, 1992), 387.

29 "An Act to Punish Seduction and Like Offences, and to Make Further Provision for the Protection of Women and Girls," *Statutes of Canada*, 1886, 49 Vict., c. 52. See Constance Backhouse, *Petticoats and Prejudice: Women and Law in Nineteenth-Century Canada* (Toronto: Women's Press for the Osgoode Society for Canadian Legal History, 1991), 69-77; and Karen Dubinsky, "'Maidenly Girls and Designing Women'? The Crime of Seduction in Turn-of-the-Century Ontario," in *Gender Conflicts: New Essays in Women's History*, ed. Franca Iacovetta and Mariana Valverde (Toronto: University of Toronto Press, 1993), 28-40, for an in-depth study of the various ways that Canadian academics have interpreted the seduction laws. In the fifty cases studied by Dubinsky, juries typically acquitted the accused. In 20 percent of the cases, guilty verdicts resulted because the accused's status as a stranger to the complainant's family, friends, and neighbours enhanced the complainant's credibility.

30 CCC, 1892, ss. 181-84.

31 Backhouse, *Petticoats and Prejudice*, 87. See also Chapman, "Sex Crimes in Western Canada," 77; Karen Dubinsky, "Sex and Shame: Some Thoughts on the Social and Historical Meaning of Rape," in *Rethinking Canada: The Promise of Women's History*, 4th ed., ed. by Veronica Strong-Boag, Mona Gleason, and Adele Perry (Oxford: Oxford University Press, 2002), 164-73; Catherine MacKinnon, "Feminist Approaches to Sexual Assault in Canada and the United States: A Brief Retrospective," in *Challenging Times: The Women's Movement in Canada and the United States*, ed. Constance Backhouse and David H. Flaherty (Montreal and Kingston: McGill-Queen's University Press, 1992), 191-92.

32 Constance Backhouse, "'Her Protests Were Unavailing': Australian Legal Understandings of Rape, Consent, and Sexuality in the 'Roaring Twenties,'" *Journal of Australian Studies* 64 (2000): 15.

33 Backhouse, "A Measure of Women's Credibility," 4.

34 C.S. Greaves, "On Rape," an Appendix to Henri Elzéar Taschereau's *The Criminal Statute Law of the Dominion of Canada*, 2nd ed. (Toronto: Carswell and Co. Law Publishers, 1888), 1085, 1092.

35 "Convicted of Rape," *Manitoba Morning Free Press*, 9 November 1894.

36 Susan Brownmiller, *Against Our Will* (New York: Bantam, 1975).

37 Lorene Clark and Debra Lewis, *Rape: The Price of Coercive Sexuality* (Toronto: Women's Press, 1977), 124.

38 For a critical analysis of the academic treatment of sexual violence, see Dubinsky, "Sex and Shame," and her full-length study *Improper Advances: Rape and Heterosexual Conflict in*

Ontario, 1880-1929 (Chicago: University of Chicago Press, 1993). Studies that tend to interpret sexual violence and its prosecution as being grounded in the patriarchal structure of Canadian society include the following: Constance Backhouse, *Carnal Crimes: Sexual Assault Law in Canada, 1900-1975* (Toronto: Irwin Law for the Osgoode Society for Legal History, 2008); *Petticoats and Prejudice;* "Nineteenth-Century Judicial Attitudes toward Child Custody, Rape, and Prostitution," in *Equality and Judicial Neutrality,* ed. Sheilah L. Martin and Kathleen E. Mahoney (Calgary: Carswell, 1987), 271-81; and "Nineteenth-Century Canadian Rape Law, 1800-1892," in *Essays in the History of Canadian Law,* vol. 2, ed. David Flaherty (Toronto: University of Toronto Press for the Osgoode Society for Canadian Legal History, 1983), 200-47. Also Graham Parker, "The Legal Regulation of Sexual Activity and the Protection of Females," *Osgoode Hall Law Journal* 21 (June 1983): 187-224; Terry Chapman, "Sex Crimes in the West, 1890-1920," *Alberta History* 35 (Autumn 1987): 6-21; and Chapman's dissertation, "Sex Crimes in Western Canada, 1890-1920."

39   Carolyn Strange, "Patriarchy Modified: The Criminal Prosecution of Rape in York County, Ontario, 1880-1930," in Phillips, Loo, and Lewthwaite, *Crime and Criminal Justice,* 209. Karen Dubinsky and Adam Givertz adopt a similar approach in "'It Was Only a Matter of Passion': Masculinity and Sexual Danger," in *Gendered Pasts: Historical Essays in Femininity and Masculinity in Canada,* ed. Kathryn McPherson, Cecilia Morgan, and Nancy Forestall (Oxford: Oxford University Press, 1999), 65-79. In her study *Women's Silence, Men's Violence: Sexual Assault in England, 1770-1845* (London: Pandora, 1987), English historian Anne Clark argues that rape laws operated to force middle-class Puritan values on working-class women *and* men.

40   Dubinsky, *Improper Advances,* 63.

41   Dorothy Chunn, "Sex and Citizenship: (Hetero)Sexual Offences, Law and 'White' Settler Society in British Columbia, 1885-1940," in *Contesting Canadian Citizenship: Historical Readings,* ed. Robert Adamoski, Dorothy Chunn, and Robert Menzies (Peterborough, ON: Broadview Press, 2002), 379. Conviction rates vary depending upon the sources used by the historian, the chronological framework, and the socio-economic context of the region. In early Halifax, Jim Phillips found an average conviction rate of 28 percent in all sex crime prosecutions between 1750 and 1800: "Women, Crime, and Criminal Justice in Early Halifax, 1750-1800," in Phillips, Loo, and Lewthwaite, *Crime and Criminal Justice,* 174-206. Ramos, who treats all cases of sexual violence together, found that in Montreal between 1803 and 1845, only 26 out of 111 charges of sexual violence (2.3 percent) resulted in conviction: "'A Most Detestable Crime,'" 29. In their study of sexual violence in half the counties and districts of Ontario between 1885 and 1929, Dubinsky and Givertz found that 51 percent of 725 men were convicted between 1880 and 1929: "'It Was Only a Matter of Passion,'" 66. Constance Backhouse found that an average of 21.5 percent of prosecuted rapes resulted in conviction in mid- to late-nineteenth-century Ontario: "Nineteenth-Century Canadian Rape Law," 222. Similarly, in her study of rape trials in York County, Strange found a conviction rate of 7 percent in the 1890s and 33 percent in the early 1900s. The average conviction rate for rape in the period was 20 percent, and 37 percent on lesser charges: "Patriarchy Modified," 210, 215.

42   *R. v. Sheel* (1914), Supreme Court of Saskatchewan (SCS), Regina, R-1287, Saskatchewan Archives Board (SAB); *R. v. Daignault* (1931), MCKB, Eastern Manitoba/Winnipeg, GR 180, microfilm, PAM.

43   *R. v. Daignault* (1920), ibid. Other exceptions in Manitoba include *R. v. Bruce* (1907), five years' imprisonment for rape, no preliminary hearing in file; *R. v. Neyedley* (1930), a Polish

farmer convicted on two counts of rape and indecent assault and sentenced concurrently to four and two years in Manitoba Penitentiary; *R. v. Belanger* (1930), four years for rape; *R. Martagnan* (1933), four years and twenty lashes for rape. Exceptions in Saskatchewan include *R. v. Kolb* (1910), SCS, Regina, R-1286, two years and hard labour, SAB. Kolb, a German farmer, had previously been found guilty of incest. Exceptions in Alberta include *R. v. Bumber* (1907), Supreme Court of Alberta (SCA), Edmonton, Acc. 83.1, five years for rape, Provincial Archives of Alberta (PAA); *R. v. Hapke* (1913), SCA, Wetaskiwin, Acc. 81.198, microfilm, seven years in Edmonton Penitentiary on two counts of rape, served concurrently, PAA.

44 John McLaren, "Chasing the Social Evil: Moral Fervour and the Evolution of Canada's Prostitution Laws, 1867-1917," *Canadian Journal of Law and Society* 1 (1986): 150.

45 *Morning Leader*, 17 September 1924.

46 Only twenty farmhands stood accused of sexual offences in the thirty-year period before 1916, while a mere six faced prosecution or juries during the Depression. Both Dubinsky and Strange noted that complainants had an easier time convincing the courts of their veracity in the 1910s.

47 Danysk, "'A Bachelor's Paradise,'" 157-58, and *Hired Hands*, 50-52.

48 Dominion Bureau of Statistics, *The Prairie Provinces in Their Relation to the National Economy of Canada: A Statistical Study of Their Social and Economic Condition in the Twentieth Century* (Ottawa: Government of Canada, 1934), 30-31. Also see Chapter 5, "Class, Culture, and Community," in Danysk, *Hired Hands*; Cherwinski, "In Search of Jake Trumper," 124, and "Wooden Horses and Rubber Cows," 133-54.

49 Manitoba Department of Agriculture, *Annual Report*, 1920, 12, quoted in Danysk, "'A Bachelor's Paradise,'" 168. In 1921, paid workers constituted 18 percent of the agricultural labour force, while in 1931 they had increased to 20 percent: Danysk, *Hired Hands*, 178; *Census of Canada*, 1921, vol. 4, Table 4, 242-45, 270-71, 292-93; *Census of Canada*, 1931, vol. 7, Table 40, 134-35, 146-47, 167-77.

50 "Do You Want Your Daughter to Marry a Farmer?" *Grain Grower's Guide*, 8 March 1922, 15. The contest is discussed in Danysk, "'A Bachelor's Paradise,'" 173, and Mary Kinnear has studied the survey in some depth in "'Do You Want Your Daughter to Marry a Farmer?' Women's Work on the Farm, 1922," in *Canadian Papers in Rural History*, vol. 6, ed. Donald H. Akenson (Gananoque, ON: Langdale Press, 1988), 137-53. Kinnear, however, noted that some women did answer no.

51 Jones, "'There is Some Power about the Land,'" 466-67; Danysk, "'A Bachelor's Paradise,'" 171-72; Strange, "Patriarchy Modified," 232.

52 Danysk, "'A Bachelor's Paradise,'" 166-73.

53 Rugh, "Civilizing the Countryside," 58-81.

54 Ian MacPherson and John Herd Thompson, "The Business of Agriculture: Prairie Farmers and the Adoption of 'Business Methods,' 1880-1950," in *The Prairie West: Historical Readings*, 2nd ed., ed. R. Douglas Francis and Howard Palmer (Edmonton: Pica Pica Press, 1995), 483-86.

55 David Laycock, *Populism and Democratic Thought in the Canadian Prairies, 1910-1945* (Toronto: University of Toronto Press, 1990); Paul Sharp, *The Agrarian Revolt in Western Canada: A Survey Showing American Parallels* (Minneapolis: University of Minnesota Press, 1949); Richard Allen, "The Social Gospel as the Religion of the Agrarian Revolt," in *The Prairie West: Historical Readings*, 2nd ed., ed. R. Douglas Francis and Howard Palmer (Edmonton: Pica Pica Press, 1995), 561-72.

56 Danysk, *Hired Hands,* 135-41; Sheila McManus, "Gender(ed) Tensions in the Work and Politics of Alberta Farm Women, 1905-29," in *Telling Tales: Essays in Western Women's History,* ed. Catherine A. Cavanaugh and Randi R. Warne (Vancouver: UBC Press, 2000), 123-46; Bradford James Rennie, *The Rise of Agrarian Democracy: The United Farmers and Farm Women of Alberta, 1909-1921* (Toronto: University of Toronto Press, 2000); Cheryle Jahn, "Class, Gender and Agrarian Socialism: The United Farm Women of Saskatchewan, 1926-1931," *Prairie Forum* 19, 2 (1994): 189-204.

57 Allen, "The Social Gospel as the Religion of the Agrarian Revolt," 563.

58 This composite portrait was pieced together from case files, depositions, Canadian statistical records, and newspaper articles.

59 Dubinsky and Givertz, "'It Was Only a Matter of Passion,'" 66.

60 *R. v. Kozma* (1917), Saskatchewan Court of King's Bench (SCKB), Regina, R-1287, SAB.

61 "Joe Kozma Acquitted on a Serious Charge," *Morning Leader,* 19 September 1917.

62 *R. v. Kozma* (1917), preliminary hearing, 7 August 1917.

63 Ibid., deposition of Charles Dunnell, Constable, Saskatchewan Provincial Police.

64 *R. v. Sachatski* (1911), preliminary hearing, 25 October 1911, SCA, Edmonton, Acc. 83.1, PAA.

65 *R. v. Gebhardt* (1922-23), SCKB, Regina, R-1287, SAB.

66 "An Act Respecting Witnesses and Evidence," R.S.C., 1906, 56 Vict., c. 31, s. 16. Terry Chapman addresses the issue of child testimony in sex crime cases at length in "'Inquiring Minds Want to Know': The Handling of Children in Sex Assault Cases in the Canadian West, 1890-1920," in *Dimensions of Childhood: Essays on the History of Children and Youth in Canada,* ed. Russell Smandych, Gordon Dodds, and Alvin Esau (Winnipeg: University of Manitoba Press, 1991), 183-204.

67 *R. v. Gebhardt* (1923), preliminary hearing before J.C. Marlin, Saskatchewan Provincial Police Court, 24 July 1923.

68 *R. v. Connelly* (1911); *R. v. Wysk* (1911); *R. v. Kowalika* (1911); *R. v. Paul* (1911) and retrial (1913), SCA, Edmonton, Acc. 83.1, PAA. W.J. Tremeear, *The Criminal Code and the Law of Criminal Evidence in Canada* (Toronto: Canada Law Book Company, 1908), 301.

69 *Edmonton Bulletin,* 19 May 1911.

70 *R. v. Connelly* (1911).

71 Ibid.

72 *R. v. Kowalika* (1911).

73 *R. v. Paul* (1911).

74 The 18 May 1911 decision of the Supreme Court of Alberta *en banc* is contained within Paul's case file.

75 CCC, 1892, s. 266. In the five judicial districts examined, only one other accused received a similarly harsh sentence. In February 1917, the Winnipeg Court of King's Bench sentenced Marvin Suggitt to fifteen years for the rape of Florence Lillian Stuart: *R. v. Suggit* (1917), MCKB, Eastern Manitoba/Winnipeg, GR 180, microfilm, PAM. I discuss the case further in Chapter 5.

76 "Paul Convicted," *Edmonton Journal,* 19 May 1911.

77 "Two Prisoners Sentenced in the Supreme Court Today," *Edmonton Journal,* 23 May 1911.

78 *R. v. Hryciuk* (1915), MCKB, Eastern Manitoba/Winnipeg, GR 180, microfilm, PAM.

79 McLaren, *The Trials of Masculinity,* and Gail Bederman, *Manliness and Civilization: A Cultural History of Gender and Race in the United States, 1880-1917* (Chicago: University of Chicago Press, 1995). For developments in different regional contexts, see Ramos, "'A Most Detestable Crime,'" 33; and Dubinsky and Givertz, "'It Was Only a Matter of Passion,'" 71-72.

80 *R. v. Coghlan* (1923), SCKB, Regina, R-1287, SAB.
81 Ibid., deposition of O.E. Rothwell, M.D.
82 Ibid.
83 *R. v. Bowie* (1918), SCA, Wetaskiwin, Acc. 81.198, microfilm, PAA.
84 *R. v. Fabian* (1927), SCKB, Regina, R-1287, SAB.
85 *R. v. Molynyk* (1917) and *R. v. Rudnicki* (1919), MCKB, Eastern Manitoba/Winnipeg, GR 180, microfilm, PAM; *R. v. Couch* (1926), MCKB, Dauphin, GR 540, PAM; *R. v. Schwanke* (1919) and *R. v. Musha* (1925), SCA, Westaskiwin, Acc. 81.198, microfilm, PAA; *R. v. Lyttle* (1925), *R. v. Leitner* (1928-29), *R. v. Lorreg* (1916), *R. v. Reeb* (1926), SCKB, Regina, R-1286, SAB.
86 For a general discussion of the overrepresentation of Ukrainian Canadians in prairie criminal prosecutions, see Gregory Robinson, "Rougher Than Any Other Nationality? Ukrainian Canadians and Crime in Alberta, 1915-1929," in *Age of Contention: Readings in Canadian Social History, 1900-1945,* ed. Jeffrey Keshen (Toronto: Harcourt Brace Canada, 1997), 214-30.
87 Frances Swyripa, "Negotiating Sex and Gender in the Ukrainian Bloc Settlement," *Prairie Forum* 20 (Fall 1995): 156, 163.
88 Ibid., 159-164. See also Dubinsky, "'Maidenly Girls and Designing Women,'" 48.
89 R.S.C., 1906, c. 146, s. 315.
90 *R. v. Lorreg* (1916), SCS, Regina, R-1286, SAB.
91 Ibid.
92 *R. v. Rudnicki* (1919).
93 Ibid.
94 Rugh, "Civilizing the Countryside," 62.
95 Emily Murphy, *Janey Canuck in the West* (1910; repr., Toronto: University of Toronto Press, 1975), 138.

CHAPTER 5: FOR FAMILY, NATION, AND EMPIRE

1 Studies that explore the problematization of young women and girls in Canada's interwar urban spaces include Tamara Myers, *Caught: Montreal's Modern Girls and the Law, 1869-1945* (Toronto: University of Toronto Press, 2006), particularly 64-70; and Joan Sangster, *Regulating Girls and Women: Sexuality, Family, and the Law in Ontario, 1920-1960* (Don Mills, ON: Oxford University Press, 2001).
2 Nellie McClung, *The Stream Runs Fast: My Own Story* (Toronto: Thomas Allen, 1945), 237.
3 Marilyn Barber, "The Servant Problem in Manitoba, 1896-1930," in *First Days, Fighting Days: Women in Manitoba History,* ed. Mary Kinnear (Regina: Canadian Plains Research Center, 1987), 108-9.
4 Randi R. Warne, *Literature as Pulpit: The Christian Social Activism of Nellie L. McClung* (Waterloo, ON: Wilfrid Laurier University Press, 1993), 2.
5 Ibid., 56.
6 Nellie McClung, *Painted Fires* (Toronto: Thomas Allen, 1925), 21.
7 Diana Pedersen, "Providing a Woman's Conscience: The YWCA, Female Evangelicalism, and the Girl in the City, 1870-1930," in *Canadian Women: A Reader,* ed. Wendy Mitchinson et al. (Toronto: Harcourt Brace Canada, 1996), 204; Margaret Prang, "'The Girl God Would Have Me Be': The Canadian Girls in Training, 1915-1939," *Canadian Historical*

Review 66, 2 (1985): 154-84; Veronica Strong-Boag, *The New Day Recalled: Lives of Girls and Women in English Canada, 1919-1939* (Markham, ON: Penguin, 1988), 29-30.

8 McClung, *Painted Fires*, 54.

9 Ibid., 68.

10 Ibid., 69.

11 Ibid., 75.

12 Lisa Jacobson, "Revitalizing the American Home: Children's Leisure and the Revitalization of Play, 1920-1940," *Journal of Social History* 30 (Spring 1997): 581; Steven Mintz and Susan Kellog, *Domestic Revolutions: A Social History of American Family Life* (New York: Free Press, 1988), xx, 107-32; Paul Fass, *The Damned and the Beautiful: American Youth in the 1920s* (New York: Oxford University Press, 1977), 89-118.

13 Cynthia Comacchio, "Dancing to Perdition: Adolescence and Leisure in Interwar English Canada," *Journal of Canadian Studies* 32 (Fall 1997): 5; and Carolyn Strange, *Toronto's Girl Problem: The Perils and Pleasures of the City, 1880-1920* (Toronto: University of Toronto Press, 1995), 127.

14 Michel Foucault, *History of Sexuality*, vol. 1 (New York: Random House, 1978), 27-30; Philippe Ariès, *Centuries of Childhood* (New York: Alfred A. Knopf, 1962), 119.

15 Stephen Robertson, "Separating the Men from the Boys: Masculinity, Psychosexual Development, and Sex Crime in the United States, 1930-1960s," *Journal of the History of Medicine and Allied Sciences* 56, 1 (2001): 8-10; and Cynthia Comacchio, *The Dominion of Youth: Adolescence and the Making of Modern Canada, 1920-1950* (Waterloo, ON: Wilfrid Laurier University Press, 2006), 20.

16 Comacchio, "Dancing to Perdition," 4-35.

17 Susan Houston, "'The Waifs and Strays' of a Late Victorian City: Juvenile Delinquency in Toronto," in *Childhood and Family in Canadian History*, ed. Joy Parr (Toronto: McClelland and Stewart, 1982), 134; Neil Sutherland, *Children in English-Canadian Society: Framing the Twentieth-Century Consensus* (Toronto: University of Toronto Press, 1976), 128-32; Strange, *Toronto's Girl Problem*, 131-32.

18 *The Canadian Annual Review*, 1922, 407, quoted in D. Owen Carrigan, *Juvenile Delinquency in Canada: A History* (Concord: Irwin Publishing, 1998), 104.

19 "The Criminal Code Amendment Act," *Statutes of Canada*, 1920, c. 43, s. 300(2); Constance Backhouse, "A Measure of Women's Credibility: The Doctrine of Corroboration in Sexual Assault Trials in Early Twentieth-Century Canada and Australia," *York Occasional Working Papers in Law and Society* 1 (2002): 17.

20 Robertson, "Separating the Men from the Boys," 8-10; Comacchio, "Dancing to Perdition," 5-35; Alexandra M. Lord, "Models of Masculinity: Sex Education, the United States Public Health Service, and the YMCA, 1919-1924," *Journal of the History of Medicine and Allied Sciences* 58, 2 (2003): 123-52.

21 Rebecca Coulter, "The Working Young of Edmonton, 1921-1931," in *Childhood and Family in Canadian History*, ed. Joy Parr (Toronto: McClelland and Stewart, 1982), 144-46; Alan Artibise, *Winnipeg: An Illustrated History* (Toronto: James Lorimer, 1977), 199; J. William Brennan, *Regina: An Illustrated History* (Toronto: James Lorimer, 1989), 190.

22 Coulter, "The Working Young of Edmonton," 148-55.

23 Linda Kealey, "Women and Labour during World War I: Women Workers and the Minimum Wage in Manitoba," in *First Days, Fighting Days: Women in Manitoba History*, ed. Mary Kinnear (Regina: Canadian Plains Research Center, 1987), 78-79.

24 Emily Murphy, *The Black Candle* (Toronto: Thomas Allen, 1922).

25 W. Peter Ward, *White Canada Forever: Popular Attitudes and Public Policy toward Orientals in British Columbia,* 2nd ed. (Montreal and Kingston: McGill-Queen's University Press, 1990), Part 1, "Sinophobia Ascendant"; James W. St. G. Walker, "A Case for Morality: The Quong Wing Files," in Iacovetta and Mitchinson, *On the Case,* 204-26, and *"Race," Rights and the Law in the Supreme Court of Canada* (Waterloo, ON: Wilfrid Laurier University Press for the Osgoode Society for Canadian Legal History, 1997); Constance Backhouse, *Colour-Coded: A Legal History of Racism in Canada, 1900-1950* (Toronto: University of Toronto Press for the Osgoode Society for Canadian Legal History, 1999), 132-72; Madge Pon, "Like a Chinese Puzzle: The Construction of Chinese Masculinity in *Jack Canuck,*" in *Gender and History in Canada,* ed. Joy Parr and Mark Rosenfeld (Toronto: Copp Clark, 1996), 80-100; John McLaren, "Race and the Criminal Justice System in British Columbia, 1892-1920: Constructing Chinese Crimes," in *Essays in the History of Canadian Law,* vol. 8, *In Honour of R.C.B. Risk,* ed. G. Blaine Baker and Jim Phillips (Toronto: University of Toronto Press for the Osgoode Society for Canadian Legal History, 1999), 398-442; Terry Chapman, "The Anti-Drug Crusade in Western Canada, 1885-1925," in *Law and Society in Canada in Historical Perspective,* ed. David Bercuson and Louis A. Knafla (Calgary: University of Calgary Press, 1979), 89-115; Kay J. Anderson, *Vancouver's Chinatown: Racial Discourse in Canada, 1875-1980* (Montreal and Kingston: McGill-Queen's University Press, 1991).

26 Daniel Malleck, "'Its Baneful Influences Are Too Well Known': Debates over Drug Use in Canada, 1867-1908," *Canadian Bulletin of Medical History* 14, 2 (1997): 263-88; Diana L. Ahmad, "Opium Smoking, Anti-Chinese Attitudes, and the American Medical Community, 1850-1890," *American Nineteenth-Century History* 1, 2 (2000): 53-68. For a rare example of an examination of drug law enforcement outside urban Canada, see Yvan Prkachin, "'Chinks Pay Heavily for Hitting the Pipe': The Perception and Enforcement of Canada's New Drug Laws in Rural and Northern British Columbia, 1908-30," *BC Studies* 153 (Spring 2007): 73-105.

27 Chapman, "The Anti-Drug Crusade in Western Canada," 91-102.

28 Ibid., 103.

29 Edmonton Police Court, Acc. 83.1, Provincial Archives of Alberta (PAA).

30 *R. v. Sherwood* (1924), Manitoba Court of King's Bench (MCKB), Eastern Manitoba/ Winnipeg, GR-180, microfilm, Provincial Archives of Manitoba (PAM).

31 *R. v. Dolly and William Lazaruk* (1929), MCKB, Eastern Manitoba/Winnipeg, GR-180, microfilm, PAM.

32 *R. v. Scott, Turner, and Cunningham* (1929), ibid.

33 *R. v. Sam, Shung, Gim Goon, and Ross* (1931), ibid.

34 *R. v. Russell and Maud Dumas* (1914), ibid.

35 Ibid.

36 Angus McLaren and Arlene Tigar McLaren, *The Bedroom and the State: The Changing Practices and Politics of Contraception and Abortion in Canada, 1880-1980* (Toronto: McClelland and Stewart, 1986), 9.

37 Canadian Criminal Code, 1892 (CCC), 55 & 56 Vict., c. 29, ss. 272 and 273.

38 Ibid., s. 179(c) and s. 274.

39 McLaren and McLaren, *The Bedroom and the State,* 10-11.

40 Constance Backhouse, *Petticoats and Prejudice: Women and Law in Nineteenth-Century Canada* (Toronto: Women's Press for the Osgoode Society for Canadian Legal History, 1991), 151-52; and Mariana Valverde, "'When the Mother of the Race is Free': Race,

Reproduction, and Sexuality in First-Wave Feminism," in *Gender Conflicts: New Essays in Women's History*, ed. Franca Iacovetta and Mariana Valverde (Toronto: University of Toronto Press, 1993), 15-19.

41 Backhouse, *Petticoats and Prejudice*, 149.

42 Brennan, *Regina*, 113; Artibise, *Winnipeg*, 130.

43 McLaren and McLaren, *The Bedroom and the State*, 65-68.

44 Leslie J. Reagan, "'About to Meet Her Maker': Women, Doctors, Dying Declarations, and the State's Investigation of Abortion, Chicago, 1867-1940," *Journal of American History* 77 (March 1991): 1245; Susan Klausen, "Doctors and Dying Declarations: The Role of the State in Abortion Regulation in British Columbia, 1917-1937," *Canadian Bulletin of Medical History* 13 (1996): 53-81; Cynthia R. Comacchio, *"Nations Are Built of Babies": Saving Ontario's Mothers and Children, 1900-1940* (Montreal and Kingston: McGill-Queen's University Press, 1993).

45 William Beahen, "Abortion and Infanticide in Western Canada, 1874 to 1916: A Criminal Case Study," *Historical Studies* 53 (1986): 56.

46 Ibid., 57; Strange, *Toronto's Girl Problem*, 71.

47 *R. v. Hay* (1920-21), Saskatchewan Court of King's Bench (SCKB), Regina, R-1287, Saskatchewan Archives Board (SAB).

48 *R. v. Bundy* (1920-21), ibid.

49 *R. v. Hughes* (1921), ibid.

50 *R. v. Beauman* (1921) and *R. v. Swift* (1920-21), ibid.

51 *R. v. Lycka* (1935-39), Supreme Court of Alberta (SCA), Macleod, Acc. 78.235, microfilm, PAA.

52 *R. v. Miller* (1932), MCKB, Winnipeg, GR 180, microfilm, PAM.

53 Deposition of Frederick Todd Cadman, Coroner, 30 December 1921, *R. v. Holden* (1922), MCKB, Eastern Manitoba/Winnipeg, GR 180, microfilm, PAM.

54 *R. v. Holden* (1922), *R. v. Walton* (1922), and *R. v. Canning* (1922), ibid.

55 Constance Backhouse, "Prosecution of Abortions under Canadian Law, 1900-1950," in Phillips, Loo, and Lewthwaite, *Crime and Criminal Justice*, 252-92.

56 See *R. v. Moore* (1914), Supreme Court of Saskatchewan (SCS), Regina, R-1286, stay of process, SAB; *R. v. Dumas* (1914), MCKB, Eastern Manitoba/Winnipeg, GR 180, microfilm, acquitted and (1915), convicted, PAM; *R. v. York* (1936), SCA, Wetaskiwin, Acc. 81.198, microfilm, acquitted, PAA.

57 For prosecution patterns in Ontario, see Carolyn Strange, "Patriarchy Modified: The Criminal Prosecution of Rape in York County, Ontario, 1880-1930," in Phillips, Loo, and Lewthwaite, *Crime and Criminal Justice*, 218.

58 See, for instance, Sangster, *Regulating Girls and Women*, Chapter 5, "'Out of Control': Girls in Conflict with the Law"; Myers, *Caught*, 251-52; and Dorothy Chunn, *From Punishment to Doing Good: Family Courts and Socialized Justice in Ontario, 1880-1940* (Toronto: University of Toronto Press, 1992).

59 McClung, *Painted Fires*, 81.

60 Ibid., 82-88.

61 For an examination of the reality behind the stereotypes, see Varpu Lindström-Best, "'I Won't Be a Slave!' – Finnish Domestics in Canada, 1911-1930," in *Looking into My Sister's Eyes: An Exploration in Women's History*, ed. Jean Burnet (Toronto: Multicultural History Society of Ontario, 1986), 33-54, and *Defiant Sisters: A Social History of Finnish Immigrant Women in Canada* (Toronto: Multicultural History Society of Ontario, 1988).

62 Constance Backhouse discusses the wave of conservatism and repression that swept through the Australian criminal courts in the 1920s in "'Her Protests Were Unavailing': Australian Legal Understandings of Rape, Consent, and Sexuality in the 'Roaring Twenties,'" *Journal of Australian Studies* 64 (2000): 14-33.

63 Strange, *Toronto's Girl Problem*, 152. See also Karen Dubinsky, *Improper Advances: Rape and Heterosexual Conflict in Ontario, 1880-1929* (Chicago: University of Chicago Press, 1993), 37; and Strange, "Patriarchy Modified," 207-51.

64 *R. v. Suggitt* (1919), MCKB, Eastern Manitoba/Winnipeg, GR 180, microfilm, PAM.

65 Preliminary hearing, Winnipeg Police Court, 7 February 1919, ibid.

66 Ibid.

67 "The Criminal Code Amendment Act," *Statutes of Canada*, 1920, c. 43, s. 300(2); Backhouse, "A Measure of Women's Credibility," 17.

68 Backhouse, "A Measure of Women's Credibility," 18.

69 *R. v. Manos* (1926), SCKB, Regina, R-1287, SAB.

70 Ibid.

71 "Manos Freed, But Judge Admonishes: Regina Café Proprietor Warned Not to Entertain Flappers in Future," *Morning Leader*, 6 February 1926.

72 *R. v. MacDonald* (1926), SCKB, Regina, R-1287, SAB.

73 Ibid.

74 Ibid.

75 "M'Donald Goes Free, But Judge Castigates Him," *Morning Leader*, 9 February 1926.

76 Ibid.

77 Ibid.

78 *R. v. Mulligan* (1923-24), SCKB, Regina, R-1287, SAB.

79 Ibid.

80 Ibid.

81 Case nos. 3469-72 and 3494 (Sawka, Lakoski, Lakoski, Dworanoski, Fright, and Dyck), Criminal Register, MCKB, Eastern Manitoba/Winnipeg, 1886-1940, GR 3636, M-1196, PAM.

82 *R. v. Sawka, Lakoski, Lakoski, Dworanoski, Fright* (1938), MCKB, Eastern Manitoba/Winnipeg, GR 180, microfilm, PAM.

83 Ibid.

84 *R. v. Dyck* (1928), MCKB, Eastern Manitoba/Winnipeg, GR 180, microfilm, PAM.

85 Ibid.

86 "Add Lash to Rape Sentences," *Winnipeg Free Press*, 26 February 1938. On the same day, Peter Lakoski, Joe Dworanoski, and Joe Lakoski were sentenced by Justice Adamson to between three and six years for shop breaking and burglary. Their prison terms were to start after the sentences for rape had been served.

87 Case nos. 3514-19 (Kissick, Pawluk, Kissick, Smerek, Masick, Dzunka), Criminal Register, MCKB, Eastern Manitoba/Winnipeg, GR 3636, M-1196, PAM. In this case, the defendants understood that the accused in Kulik's case had been caught only because the complainant had known them previously. The complainant, Jennie Pearl, went for dates on two occasions with Peter Kissick; on one date, an alleged rape occurred, but Pearl made no complaint. On the second date, five other men, unknown to the complainant, joined Kissick and Pearl in the car. They proceeded to the country and, according to Kissick, raped her.

88 *R. v. O'Reilly* (1928), SCKB, Regina, R-1287, SAB.

89 Quoted in Sandy Ramos, "'A Most Detestable Crime': Gender Identities and Sexual Violence in the District of Montreal, 1803-1843," *Journal of the Canadian Historical Association* 12 (2001): 46. For other studies that explore the medical jurisprudence of rape, see James C. Mohr, *Doctors and the Law: Medical Jurisprudence in Nineteenth-Century America* (Baltimore: Johns Hopkins University Press, 1993); Stephen Robertson, "Signs, Marks, and Private Parts: Doctors, Legal Discourses, and Evidence of Rape in the United States, 1823-1930," *Journal of the History of Sexuality* 8, 3 (1998): 345-88.

90 *R. v. O'Reilly* (1928).

91 Strange, *Toronto's Girl Problem*, 65, and "Patriarchy Modified," 225.

92 Deborah Gorham and Judith Walkowitz explore the regulatory impulse that underpinned changes to statutory rape provisions in England: Gorham, "The 'Maiden Tribute to Modern Babylon' Re-Examined: Child Prostitution and the Idea of Childhood in Late Victorian England," *Victorian Studies* 21 (Spring 1978): 353-79; and Walkowitz, *Prostitution and Victorian Society: Women, Class, and the State* (Cambridge: Cambridge University Press, 1980).

93 See Reagan, "'About to Meet Her Maker,'" 1244, and *When Abortion Was a Crime: Women, Medicine, and the Law in the United States, 1867-1973* (Berkeley: University of California Press, 1997).

94 John D'Emilio and Estelle Freedman, *Intimate Matters: A History of Sexuality in America* (New York: Harper and Row, 1988), 229.

95 Stephen Robertson, "Age of Consent Law and the Making of Modern Childhood in New York City, 1886-1921," *Journal of Social History* 35, 4 (2002): 781-98.

CHAPTER 6: THE MIGHT OF A GOOD STRONG HAND

1 *R. v. Oswald* (1924), Supreme Court of Alberta (SCA), Macleod, Acc. 78.235, microfilm, Provincial Archives of Alberta (PAA).

2 "Coleman Husband Gashes Wife Fifty Times with Knife and Makes Escape," *Lethbridge Herald*, 4 September 1923.

3 Ibid.

4 *R. v. Oswald* (1924).

5 Dorothy Chunn, "Secrets and Lies: The Criminalization of Incest and the (Re)Formation of the 'Private' in British Columbia, 1890-1940," in *Regulating Lives: Historical Essays on the State, Society, the Individual, and the Law*, ed. John McLaren, Robert Menzies, and Dorothy Chunn (Vancouver: UBC Press, 2002), 121; see also Joan Sangster, *Regulating Girls and Women: Sexuality, Family, and the Law in Ontario, 1920-1960* (Don Mills, ON: Oxford University Press, 2001), 32.

6 Lawrence Stone, "Interpersonal Violence in English Society, 1300-1980," *Past and Present* no. 101 (1983): 22-33.

7 See, for instance, Terry Chapman, "'Til Death Do Us Part': Wife Beating in Alberta, 1905-1920," *Alberta History* 36 (Autumn 1988): 13-22.

8 Linda Gordon, *Heroes of Their Own Lives: The Politics and History of Family Violence – Boston, 1880-1960* (Champaign: University of Illinois Press, 1988); A. James Hammerton, *Cruelty and Companionship: Conflict in Nineteenth-Century Married Life* (London: Routledge, 1992); Kathryn Harvey, "To Love, Honour and Obey: Wife-Battering in Working-Class Montreal, 1869-1879," in *Age of Transition: Readings in Canadian Social*

History, 1800-1900, ed. Norman Knowles (Toronto: Harcourt Brace Canada, 1998), 227-42; Harvey, "Amazons and Victims: Wife-Abuse in Working-Class Montréal, 1869-1879," *Journal of the Canadian Historical Association* 2 (1991): 131-48; Bernadine Dodge, "Let the Record Show: Women and Law in the United Counties of Durham and Northumberland, 1845-1895," *Ontario History* 92, 2 (2000): 127-45; Judith Fingard, "The Prevention of Cruelty: Marriage Breakdown and the Rights of Wives in Nova Scotia, 1880-1900," in *Separate Spheres: Women's Worlds in the 19th-Century Maritimes*, ed. Janet Guildford and Suzanne Morton (Fredericton: Acadiensis Press, 1994), 211-32; Annalee Gölz, "'If a Man's Wife Does Not Obey Him, What Can He Do?' Marital Breakdown and Wife Abuse in Late Nineteenth-Century and Early Twentieth-Century Ontario," in *Law, Society, and the State: Essays in Modern Legal History*, ed. Louis A. Knafla and Susan W.S. Binnie (Toronto: University of Toronto Press, 1995), 324-50; Gölz, "Murder Most Foul: Spousal Homicides in Ontario, 1870-1915," in Robb and Erber, *Disorder in the Court*, 164-85; Annalee E. Lepp, "Dis/membering the Family: Marital Breakdown, Domestic Conflict, and Family Violence in Ontario, 1830-1920" (PhD diss., Queen's University, 2001). Joan Sangster studies both wife assault and incest in *Regulating Girls and Women*, Chapters 2 and 3, and incest in "Masking and Unmasking the Sexual Abuse of Children: Perceptions of Violence against Children in 'The Badlands' of Ontario, 1916-1930," *Journal of Family History* 25, 4 (2000): 504-26. See also Lorna McLean, "'Deserving' Wives and 'Drunken' Husbands: Wife Beating, Marital Conduct, and the Law in Ontario, 1850-1910," *Histoire sociale/Social History* 35, 69 (2002): 59-81.

9 According to Gölz, 42 percent of the seventy men tried for spousal murder in Ontario between 1870 and 1915 were moderately well-off or well-to-do farmers or members of the middle or professional classes. The vast majority were white and of Anglo-Celtic heritage. Fifty were convicted: seventeen were hanged, nine had their death sentences commuted, and twenty-four were found guilty of manslaughter: "Murder Most Foul," 166-68.

10 Sangster, *Regulating Girls and Women*, 34-35; Karen Dubinsky, *Improper Advances: Rape and Heterosexual Conflict in Ontario, 1880-1929* (Chicago: University of Chicago Press, 1993), 152-54.

11 William M. Baker, ed., *Pioneer Policing in Southern Alberta: Deane of the Mounties, 1888-1914* (Calgary: Historical Society of Alberta, 1993), 72-73.

12 Gölz, "'If a Man's Wife Does Not Obey Him,'" 324.

13 Ibid.

14 James G. Snell, "'The White Life for Two': The Defence of Marriage and Sexual Morality in Canada, 1890-1914," in *Canadian Family History: Selected Readings*, ed. Bettina Bradbury (Toronto: Copp Clark Pitman, 1992), 389-90.

15 Linda Silver Dranoff, *Women in Canadian Life: Law* (Toronto: Fitzhenry and Whiteside, 1977), 26-27.

16 "An Act to Amend the Criminal Code," *Revised Statutes of Canada*, 1913, 3 & 4 Geo. V, c. 13, s. 4; Snell, "'The White Life for Two,'" 391.

17 Gölz, "If a Man's Wife Does Not Obey Him," 335.

18 Chapman, "'Til Death Do Us Part,'" 13-14; Annalee Gölz, "Uncovering and Reconstructing Family Violence: Ontario Criminal Case Files," in Iacovetta and Mitchinson, *On the Case*, 291.

19 Canadian Criminal Code, 1892 (CCC), 55 & 56 Vict., c. 29, s. 176.

20 Sangster, *Regulating Girls and Women*, 21-22. See also Vicki Bell, *Interrogating Incest: Feminism, Foucault and the Law* (London: Routledge, 1993). American historian Danielle

Moon argues that progressive reformers and politicians needed to construct the image of a pure girl, subject to the debauch of lustful men, in order to legitimize demands for incest legislation. They did so by combining the idea of judicial patriarchy with female superiority or victimization: "Unnatural Fathers and Vixen Daughters: A Case of Incest, San Diego, California, 1894," *Journal of the West* 39, 4 (2000): 8-16.

21 Harvey, "Amazons and Victims," 133; Gordon, *Heroes of Their Own Lives*; Louise A. Jackson, "'Singing Birds as Well as Soap Suds': The Salvation Army's Work with Sexually Abused Girls in Edwardian England," *Gender and History* 12, 1 (2000): 107-26; Carol Bauer and Lawrence Ritt, "Wife-Abuse, Late-Victorian English Feminists, and the Legacy of Frances Power Cobb," *International Journal of Women's Studies* 6, 3 (1983): 195-207; Jerome Nadelhaft, "Alcohol and Wife Abuse in Antebellum Male Temperance Literature," *Canadian Review of American Studies* 25, 1 (1995): 15-43.

22 Harvey discusses temperance advocacy and the meanings that were attached to wife abuse in Montreal in "Amazons and Victims," 134-36; for the Maritimes, see Fingard, "The Prevention of Cruelty," 212-16; for Ontario, see Wendy Mitchinson, "The WCTU: 'For God, Home, and Native Land': A Study in Nineteenth-Century Feminism," in *A Not Unreasonable Claim: Women and Reform in Canada, 1880-1920s*, ed. Linda Kealey (Toronto: Women's Press, 1979), 155; and Sharon Ann Cook, *Through Sunshine and Shadow: The Woman's Christian Temperance Union, Evangelicalism and Reform in Ontario, 1874-1939* (Montreal and Kingston: McGill-Queen's University Press, 1995), 86.

23 Catherine C. Cole and Ann Milovic, "Education, Community Service, and Social Life: The Alberta Women's Institutes and Rural Families, 1909-1945," in *Standing on New Ground: Women in Alberta*, ed. Catherine A. Cavanaugh and Randi R. Warne (Edmonton: University of Alberta Press, 1993), 19-32.

24 Nellie McClung, *The Stream Runs Fast: My Own Story* (Toronto: Thomas Allen, 1945), 59, 62.

25 Ibid.

26 Carolyn Strange and Tina Loo, *Making Good: Law and Moral Regulation in Canada, 1867-1939* (Toronto: University of Toronto Press, 1997), Chapter 3.

27 John Herd Thompson, *Harvests of War: The Prairie West, 1914-1918* (Toronto: McClelland and Stewart, 1983), 97-101, and *Forging the Prairie West: The Illustrated History of Canada* (Toronto: Oxford University Press, 1998), 95-97. Carol Lee Bacchi discusses the class and race biases that divided members of the suffrage movement in "Divided Allegiances: The Response of Farm and Labour Women to Suffrage," in *A Not Unreasonable Claim: Women and Reform in Canada, 1880-1920s*, ed. Linda Kealey (Toronto: Women's Press, 1979), 89-107. Mariana Valverde likewise explores these issues in reference to the temperance movement in *The Age of Light, Soap, and Water: Moral Reform in English Canada, 1885-1925* (Toronto: McClelland and Stewart, 1991), 58-61.

28 Sangster, *Regulating Girls and Women*, 49-50.

29 *R. v. Singer* (1903), Supreme Court of the North-West Territories (SCNWT), Northern Alberta, Acc. 83.1, PAA.

30 Academics tend to fall on opposing sides of the debate about whether urbanization increased instances of interpersonal violence in Western industrializing nations. Those who argue that violence increased as geographic mobility freed people from communal constraints include Lawrence Friedman, *Crime and Punishment in American History* (New York: Basic Books, 1993), 194; and Wesley G. Skogan, "Social Change and the Future of Violent Crime," in *Violence in America: The History of Crime*, ed. Ted Robert Gurr (Newbury Park, CA:

Sage Publications, 1989), 235-50. Historians who argue that rural areas were crime ridden and prone to forms of ritual violence, particularly when issues of honour and bravery were at stake, include Pieter Spierenburg, "Long-Term Trends in Homicide: Theoretical Reflections and Dutch Evidence, Fifteenth to Twentieth Centuries," in *The Civilization of Crime: Violence in Town and Country since the Middle Ages,* ed. Eric A. Johnson and Eric H. Monkkonen (Urbana: University of Illinois Press, 1996), 63-105; and Eric H. Monkkonen, *The Dangerous Class: Crime and Poverty in Columbus, Ohio, 1860-1885* (Cambridge, MA: Harvard University Press, 1975).

31 Winnipeg's population jumped dramatically between 1901 and 1911 – from 42,340 to 136,036 individuals: Alan Artibise, *Winnipeg: An Illustrated History* (Toronto: James Lorimer, 1977), 202; Robert Hutchinson, *City of Winnipeg Police Force: A Century of Service* (Winnipeg: Winnipeg City Police, 1974), 35.

32 For similar trends in Ontario and Quebec magistrates' courts, see Sangster, *Regulating Girls and Women,* 54-55; and Harvey, "To Love, Honour and Obey," 236-37.

33 *R. v. Goddelin* (1915), Manitoba Court of King's Bench (MCKB), Eastern Manitoba/ Winnipeg, GR-180, microfilm, Provincial Archives of Manitoba (PAM).

34 Sangster, *Regulating Girls and Women,* 55.

35 City of Winnipeg Police Court, Record Books, 1910, GR 651, microfilm, PAM.

36 *R. v. Webb* (1888), Department of Justice, Capital Case Files, RG 13, vol. 1425, f. 231A, Library and Archives Canada (LAC).

37 See Martin J. Wiener, "The Sad Story of George Hall: Adultery, Murder, and the Politics of Mercy in Mid-Victorian England," *Social History* 24, 2 (1999): 182.

38 Ibid.

39 This assessment also holds true for cases of wife battery in the superior courts: farmers, farm labourers, and ranchers made up the majority of accused. In Winnipeg, the most urban judicial district, the accused included a chauffeur, a brakeman, a carpenter, and a peddler.

40 Wiener, "The Sad Story of George Hall," 193.

41 *R v. Zbyhley* (1909), Department of Justice, Capital Case Files, RG 13, vol. 1456, f. 421A, LAC; "Mundare Ruthenian Faces Murder Charge," *Edmonton Journal,* 19 October 1909.

42 *R v. Ireland* (1914), Department of Justice, Capital Case Files, RG 13, vol. 1467, f. 526A, LAC; "Wife Murderer Will Be Hanged," *Morning Leader,* 23 October 1914; "Appeal for Mercy Made by Jurymen," *Leader-Post,* 23 October 1914.

43 *R. v. Poets* (1934), Department of Justice, Capital Case Files, RG 13, vol. 1595, f. CC428, LAC.

44 *R. v. Paulsen* (1916), ibid., vol. 1505 (1-3), f. 566A/CC135, LAC; *R. v. Gougeon* (1937), ibid., vol. 1613, f. CC480, LAC; *R. v. Anderson* (1913-14), ibid., vol. 1463 (1-2), f. 491A, LAC; *R. v. Ireland* (1914); *R. v. Neigel* (1917), ibid., vol. 1488, f. 599A/CC66, LAC; *R. v. Schmidt* (1927), ibid., vol. 1544, f. CC263, LAC; *R. v. Spellman* (1912), Supreme Court of Saskatchewan (SCS), Regina, R-1286, Saskatchewan Archives Board (SAB); *R. v. Hart* (1915), SCA, Macleod, Acc. 78.235, microfilm, PAA; *R. v. Baird* (1919), Alberta, District Criminal Court, Westaskiwin, Acc. 81.198, microfilm, PAA.

45 *R. v. Paulsen* (1916); "Insanity Will Be the Plea of Marius Paulsen," *Edmonton Journal,* 21 January 1916.

46 Usup Saloman to the Minister of Justice, 15 January 1912, in *R. v. Saloman* (1902), Department of Justice, Capital Case Files, RG 13, vol. 1496, f. 335A/CC94, LAC.

47 R. Ross Sutherland, Winnipeg, to Secretary of State, Canada, 7 May 1902, ibid.

48 Michael Owen, "'Lighting the Pathways for New Canadians': Methodist and United WMS Missions in Eastern Alberta, 1904-1940," in *Standing on New Ground: Women in Alberta*, ed. Catherine A. Cavanaugh and Randi R. Warne, 1-19 (Edmonton: University of Alberta Press, 1993), 2; Frances Swyripa, *Wedded to the Cause: Ukrainian Canadian Women and Ethnic Identity, 1891-1991* (Toronto: University of Toronto Press, 1993), 21-23.

49 *R. v. Hawryliuk* (1935), Department of Justice, Capital Case Files, RG 13, vol. 1598, f. CC436, LAC.

50 *R. v. Bodz* (1929), MCKB (Speedy), Dauphin, GR 540, PAM.

51 *R. v. Bodz* (1931), Department of Justice, Capital Case Files, RG 13, vol. 1573, f. CC362, LAC.

52 Trial transcript, and J.E. Adamson to the Secretary of State, Canada, 4 December 1931, ibid.

53 Report, Sergeant G.A. Renton, Dauphin Division, Manitoba Provincial Police, to the Minister of Justice, 19 December 1931, ibid.

54 R. Ross Sutherland to the Secretary of State, Canada, 7 May 1902.

55 *R. v. Hawryliuk* (1935).

56 *R. v. Neigel* (1917); "Adam Neigel Found Guilty of Murder: After Four Hours Deliberation," *Medicine Hat Weekly News*, 29 November 1917.

57 Ann-Louise Shapiro, "'Stories More Terrifying than the Truth Itself': Narratives of Female Criminality in *Fin de Siècle* Paris," in *Gender and Crime in Modern Europe*, ed. Margaret L. Arnot and Cornelie Usborne (London: University College London Press, 1999), 207.

58 *R. v. Neigel* (1917).

59 *R. v. Zbyhley* (1909).

60 The ethnic breakdown is as follows: Commutations – Ukrainian 2, French Canadian 2, Norwegian 1, Canadian 1, Belgian 1; Hanged – Ukrainian 7, German 2, Aboriginal 2, American 1, British 2, Swedish 1. Jean R. Burnet and Howard Palmer, *"Coming Canadians": An Introduction to a History of Canada's Peoples* (Toronto: McClelland and Stewart, 1988), 34-35; John C. Lehr, "Peopling the Prairies with Ukrainians," in *Immigration in Canada: Historical Perspectives*, ed. Gerald Tulchinsky (Toronto: Copp Clark Longman, 1994), 177-202. For a discussion of the overrepresentation of Ukrainians, see Gregory Robinson, "Rougher Than Any Other Nationality? Ukrainian Canadians and Crime in Alberta, 1915-1929," in *Age of Contention: Readings in Canadian Social History, 1900-1945*, ed. Jeffrey Keshen (Toronto: Harcourt Brace Canada, 1997), 214-30.

61 *R. v. Hart* (1915), SCA, Macleod, Acc. 78.235, microfilm, PAA.

62 "Henrika Zbihley Pleads Guilty," *Edmonton Journal*, 19 October 1909.

63 Rev. P.F. Beaton, Medicine Hat, to the Minister of Justice, Ottawa, 2 March 1918, in *R. v. Neigel* (1917).

64 Ibid.

65 Sangster, *Regulating Girls and Women*, 26.

66 Strange, "Patriarchy Modified: The Criminal Prosecution of Rape in York County, Ontario, 1880-1930," in Phillips, Loo, and Lethwaite, *Crime and Criminal Justice*, 229-30.

67 Chunn, "Secrets and Lies," 124.

68 This analysis was based on the records of the following judicial districts and courts: Winnipeg, county and assize; Regina, district and assize; Battleford, district and assize; Dauphin, assize; Macleod, assize; Wetaskiwin, assize; Edmonton, assize.

69 See Strange, "Patriarchy Modified," 230-31; Dubinsky, *Improper Advances*, 129-31; Chunn, "Secrets and Lies," 124, 127.

70 In her study of appeals of incest convictions in Ontario, Joan Sangster found that the courts often required proof of the emission of seed, or even pregnancy, in order to prove that cohabitation had actually occurred. She also discovered that the courts had trouble believing that non-consensual incest had taken place if the victim was over the age of sixteen. The phenomenon of mother blaming has been examined by a number of historians: Sangster, *Regulating Girls and Women*, 41-44; Dubinsky, *Improper Advances*, 60-61; Janet Liebman Jacobs, "Reassessing Mother Blame in Incest," *Signs* 15, 3 (1990): 499-515.

71 *R. v. Breen* (1903), SCNWT, Western Assiniboia, R-1286, SAB.

72 *R. v. Hebert* (1905), MCKB, Eastern Manitoba/Winnipeg, GR 180, microfilm, PAM.

73 *R. v. Barret* (1910), SCA, Edmonton, Acc. 83.1, PAA.

74 *R. v. Sutherland* (1904), SCNWT, Western Assiniboia, R-1286, SAB.

75 *R. v. Smith* (1918), SCKB, Regina, R-1287, SAB.

76 Dubinsky, *Improper Advances*, 59; Gordon, *Heroes of Their Own Lives*, 96.

77 *R. v. Spence* (1916), MCKB, Eastern Manitoba/Winnipeg, GR 180, microfilm, PAM.

78 *R. v. Spencer* (1913), SCA, Edmonton, Acc. 83.1, PAA.

79 *R. v. Holtz* (1928), SCA, Wetaskiwin, Acc. 81.198, microfilm, PAA.

80 Chunn, "Secrets and Lies," 126, 131.

81 A.K. Dysart to the Minister of Justice, 10 April 1922, in *R. v. Grover* (1922), Department of Justice, Capital Case Files, RG 13, vol. 1517 (1, 2, and 3), f. 686A/CC178, LAC.

82 Cecil St. John to T.A. Crerar, Ottawa, 24 April 1922, ibid.

83 M.F. Gallagher to T.A. Crerar, Ottawa, 12 May 1922, ibid.

84 Sangster, *Regulating Girls and Women*, 30-35.

85 *R. v. Russell* (1929), SCA, Macleod, Acc. 78.235, microfilm, PAA.

86 Michèle Barrett, *Women's Oppression Today: Problems in Marxist Feminist Analysis* (London: Verso, 1980).

87 Sangster, *Regulating Girls and Women*, 83.

88 Annalee Gölz shows that the wife's culpability in her own death was a central component in wife murder trials in Ontario in "Uncovering and Reconstructing Family Violence," 305.

CHAPTER 7: SHE IS TO BE PITIED, NOT PUNISHED

1 "Rev. C.F. Potter Claims Sex Does Enter into Jennie Hawkes Case," *Edmonton Journal*, 15 November 1915.

2 Ibid.

3 C.H.S. Jayewardene, *The Penalty of Death: The Canadian Experiment* (Toronto: Lexington, 1977), 1-2. A major governmental inquiry on capital punishment in Canada did, however, occur in 1937. Parliamentarians reasserted their faith in British precedent and in the ability of Canadian officials to administer punishment fairly and firmly. See Carolyn Strange, "The Undercurrents of Penal Culture: Punishment and the Body in Mid-Twentieth-Century Canada," *Law and History Review* 19 (Summer 2001): http://www.historycooperative.org/journals/lhr/19.2/strange.html, para. 1.

4 Margaret L. Arnot and Cornelie Usborne, "Why Gender and Crime? Aspects of an International Debate," in *Gender and Crime in Modern Europe*, ed. Margaret L. Arnot and Cornelie Usborne (London: University College London Press, 1999), 26-27.

5 For a discussion of this question and responses in the United States, see Carolyn Strange, "Murder and Meanings in US Historiography," *Feminist Studies* 25 (Fall 1999): 685.

6 Over the past decade, a number of historians have explored the impact of first-wave feminism on attitudes toward the murderess through microhistorical examinations of individual
cases. In Canada, see Carolyn Strange, "Wounded Womanhood and Dead Men: Chivalry
and the Trials of Clara Ford and Carrie Davies," in *Gender Conflicts: New Essays in Women's
History,* ed. Franca Iacovetta and Mariana Valverde (Toronto: University of Toronto Press,
1993), 149-48; and Karen Dubinsky and Franca Iacovetta, "Murder, Womanly Virtue, and
Motherhood: The Case of Angelina Napolitano, 1911-1922," *Canadian Historical Review*
72 (December 1991): 505-31. Annalee Gölz has quantitatively explored the trend toward
gendered justice as it occurred in ninety cases of spousal murder that came before the
Ontario superior courts between 1870 and 1915: "Murder Most Foul: Spousal Homicides
in Ontario, 1870-1915," in Robb and Erber, *Disorder in the Court,* 164-85. For international
cases, see Paul T. Hieller, "To Encourage the Preservation and Sanctity of the Marriage
Relation: Victorian Attitudes in Arizona Territory and the Murder Prosecution of Frank
C. Kibbey," *Journal of Arizona History* 42, 3 (2001): 249-76, which explores a case much
like that of Jenny Hawkes; and Sarah Beebe Fryer, "Morality Plays at the Courthouse: The
Celebrated Murder Trials of Anna George and Francine Hughes," *Proteus* 13, 1 (1996):
33-38.

7 See the works in note 6 and Elizabeth F. Moulds, "Chivalry and Paternalism: Disparities
of Treatment in the Criminal Justice System," *Western Political Quarterly* 31 (1978): 418.

8 F. Murray Greenwood and Beverley Boissery, *Uncertain Justice: Canadian Women and
Capital Punishment, 1754-1953* (Toronto: Dundurn Press, 2000); Strange, "Wounded
Womanhood and Dead Men," 151; Dubinsky and Iacovetta, "Murder, Womanly Virtue,
and Motherhood," 505-31; Jill Newton Ainsley, "'Some Mysterious Agency': Women,
Violent Crime, and the Insanity Acquittal in the Victorian Courtroom," *Canadian Journal
of History* 25 (2000): 37-55. Much of the debate regarding chivalry and criminal justice
found its roots in criminological explanations of female under-representation in crime.
While Otto Pollak argued that women failed to appear in criminal statistics because of the
devious nature of their crimes and deferential treatment by legal authorities, Meda Chesney-
Lind argued that deferential treatment constituted harassment intended to keep women
in their place: Otto Pollak, *The Criminality of Women* (New York: A.S. Barnes, 1961); Meda
Chesney-Lind, "Chivalry Re-Examined: Women and the Criminal Justice System," in
Women, Crime, and the Criminal Justice System, ed. Lee H. Bowker (Lexington: D.C.
Heath, 1978), 171-94, and "Women and Crime: The Female Offender," *Signs* 12, 1 (1986):
78-96; Moulds, "Chivalry and Paternalism," 416-30.

9 See, for instance, *R. v. Wright* (1919) and *R. v. Gioia* (1922), Supreme Court of the North-
West Territories (SCNWT) and Supreme Court of Alberta (SCA), Southern Alberta and
Macleod, Acc. 78.235, Provincial Archives of Alberta (PAA); *R. v. Mogush* (1913), *R. v. Butler*
(1913), *R. v. Davis* (1913), SCNWT and SCA, Northern Alberta and Edmonton, Acc. 83.1,
PAA; *R. v. Fechteass* (1889), *R. v. Smelan* (1913), *R. v. Mason and Beggs* (1914), *R. v. Kadeniuk*
(1924), *R. v. Odokychuk* (1933), *R. v. Yakimovich* (1933), *R. v. Rykunyk* (1939), Manitoba
Court of King's Bench (MCKB), Eastern Manitoba/Winnipeg, GR 180, Provincial Archives
of Manitoba (PAM). Punishment in these cases ranged anywhere from the one-year suspended sentence given to Katherine Rykunyk, who pleaded guilty to the accidental death
of her lover's child during a divorce and custody battle, to a twelve-year imprisonment for
Mrs. Dean Davis, who was found guilty of manslaughter in the death of her lover, Sydney
Pallant. In some cases, such as Alice Butler's, there seemed to be no doubt in anyone's mind
that the cause of death was purely accidental: in her case, a gun accidentally fired.

10 *R. v. Semple* (1912), *R. v. Warwick* (1913), *R. v. Gore* (1913-14), *R. v. Hines and Allen* (1922), *R. v. Solomon* (1928), *R. v. Peterson* (1930), Supreme Court of Saskatchewan (SCS) and Saskatchewan Court of King's Bench (SCKB), Regina, R-1286 and R-1287, Saskatchewan Archives Board (SAB).

11 *R. v. Solomon* (1928); "Mrs. Solomon Says Husband Cruel to Her," *Morning Leader,* 12 September 1928.

12 Canadian Criminal Code, 1892 (CCC), 55 & 56 Vict., c. 29, s. 242, *Revised Statues of Canada,* 1906.

13 Ibid., c. 28, s. 234. The maximum punishment for conspiracy to murder was fourteen years' imprisonment.

14 "Question of Admissibility of Evidence Will Be Decided By Chief Justice Today in the Famous Warwick Murder Case," *Morning Leader,* 3 February 1913.

15 *Morning Leader,* 1, 3, 4 February 1913.

16 Evidence presented at the preliminary hearing, Regina, 2, 3, and 8 January 1913 by C.H. King, RNWMP sergeant, and Ian Brown, Moose Jaw coroner, in *R. v. Warwick* (1913), SCS, Regina, R-1286, SAB.

17 "Not Guilty Is Verdict in Warwick Case," *Morning Leader,* 5 February 1913.

18 Ibid.

19 "Mrs. Dean Davis Is Sentenced to Twelve Years," *Edmonton Journal,* 29 October 1913.

20 *R. v. Davis* (1913), SCA, Edmonton, Acc. 83.1, PAA.

21 CCC, 1892, s. 219; William Beahen, "Abortion and Infanticide in Western Canada, 1874-1916: A Criminal Case Study," *Historical Studies* 53 (1986): 63. Beahen, who bases his analysis on NWMP records, found thirty-nine cases of infanticide in the period studied.

22 CCC, 1892, s. 240.

23 The evolution of Canada's criminal laws pertaining to cases of child murder – and their English precedents – is discussed in detail in Backhouse, "Desperate Women and Compassionate Courts: Infanticide in Nineteenth-Century Canada," *University of Toronto Law Journal* 34 (1984): 448-56; and in Kirsten Kramar's *Unwilling Mothers, Unwanted Babies: Infanticide in Canada* (Vancouver: UBC Press, 2005), see Chapter 1, "Regulating Infanticide through Concealment of Birth," in particular.

24 *R. v. Hammond* (1913), Department of Justice, Capital Case Files, RG 13, vol. 1483, f. 490A/CC44, Library and Archives Canada (LAC).

25 Backhouse, "Desperate Women and Compassionate Courts," 457.

26 *R. v. Duryba* (1932), District Criminal Court (DCC), Regina, unprocessed record series, thirty days in Battleford Jail, SAB. Similar cases include *R. v. Williams* (1933), DCC, Regina, unprocessed record series, SAB; *R. v. Walters* (1907), SCA, Macleod, Acc. 78235, microfilm, suspended, PAA; *R. v. Boucher* (1908), SCA, Edmonton, Acc. 83.1, suspended, PAA; *R.v. Neepin* (1927), MCKB, Dauphin, GR 540, two years suspended, PAM; and *R. v. Fadak* (1930), MCKB, Dauphin, GR 540, two years suspended, PAM.

27 Kramar, *Unwilling Mothers, Unwanted Babies,* 5.

28 *R. v. Arischuk* (1905), MCKB, Eastern Manitoba/Winnipeg, GR 180, microfilm, PAM.

29 "Found Guilty of Manslaughter," *Manitoba Free Press,* 3 November 1905.

30 H.Y. Macdonald to the Secretary of State, Canada, 30 September 1940, in *R. v. Rubletz* (1940), Department of Justice, Capital Case Files, RG 13, vol. 1627 (1-3), f. CC552, LAC.

31 Greenwood and Boissery explore the impact of jury nullification in Rubletz's case in *Uncertain Justice,* 205-8.

32 In her exploration of how considerations of environmental conditions influenced assessments of criminality, Kimberley White shows that the public's response to Rubletz's case
revealed a deep-seated belief that one's character or constitution could be weakened by
exposure to an unhealthy environment and that the future health of the nation was at stake.
See White, *Negotiating Responsibility: Law, Murder, and States of Mind* (Vancouver: UBC
Press, 2008), 69-71.

33 Cecil G. Schmidt, Saskatoon, to the Minister of Justice, Ottawa, 10 October 1940, in *R. v.
Rubletz* (1940).

34 Quoted in Greenwood and Boissery, *Uncertain Justice*, 197.

35 Newspaper clippings, *Leader Post*, 18 October 1940, in *R. v. Rubletz* (1940). A number of
historians have noted that modernity was accompanied by more lenient attitudes toward
infanticide as reformers drew attention to the plight of single, working-class women:
Constance Backhouse, "Desperate Women and Compassionate Courts," 447-78; Marie-
Aimée Cliche, "L'infanticide dans la région de Québec, 1660-1969," *Revue d'histoire de
l'Amérique française* 44, 1 (1990): 31-59; Janet L. McShane Galley, "'I Did It to Hide My
Shame': Community Responses to Suspicious Infant Death in Middlesex, Ontario, 1850-
1900" (master's thesis, University of Western Ontario, 1998); Peter C. Hoffer and N.E.H.
Hull, *Murdering Mothers: Infanticide in England and New England, 1558-1803* (New York:
New York University Press, 1981); R. Sauer, "Infanticide and Abortion in Nineteenth-
Century Britain," *Population Studies* 32 (March 1978): 81-93; Margaret L. Arnot, "Gender
in Focus: Infanticide in England, 1840-1880" (PhD diss., University of Essex, 1994).

36 Newspaper clippings, *Leader Post*, 18 October 1940, in *R. v. Rubletz* (1940).

37 Mrs. E. Eaton, Regina, to Minister of Justice, Ottawa, 24 October 1940; Stanley H.
Morrison, Lafleche, to Minister of Justice, Ottawa, 24 October 1940, in *R. v. Rubletz* (1940).

38 "Prairies Relieved as Girl-Mother Escapes Execution," *Montreal Standard*, 22 February
1941, in *R. v. Rubletz* (1940).

39 Judith A. Osborne, "The Crime of Infanticide: Throwing the Baby Out with the Bathwater,"
Canadian Journal of Family and Law 6, 1 (1987): 47-59. Kirsten Kramar argues that the
infanticide provision was a pragmatic solution to the problem of securing conviction rather
than an attempt to regulate heterosexuality and reproduction: *Unwilling Mothers, Unwanted
Babies*, 3.

40 G.P. Owen Fenwick to the Remission Branch, 26 October 1915, in *R. v. Hawkes* (1915), Department of Justice, Capital Case Files, RG 13, vol. 1479-80, vol. 2699, f. 560A/CC33, LAC.

41 In the period studied, these were the only women in Canada to whom the prerogative of
mercy was not extended.

42 This analysis is based on Lorraine Gadoury and Antonio Lechasseur, "Persons Sentenced
to Death in Canada, 1867-1976: An Inventory of Case Files in the Fonds of the Department
of Justice (RG 13)" (Ottawa: National Archives of Canada, 1994); and Carolyn Strange,
"The Lottery of Death: Capital Punishment, 1867-1976," *Manitoba Law Journal* 23 (1996):
607.

43 Jayewardene, *The Penalty of Death*, 98.

44 Ezzat A. Fattah, "The Canadian Public and the Death Penalty: A Study of Social Attitude"
(PhD diss., Simon Fraser University, 1976), 1-2.

45 *R. v. Christensen* (1923), Department of Justice, Capital Case Files, RG 13, vol. 1524, f. 704A/
CC197, LAC. Christensen's original conviction was appealed on the grounds that her
husband's dying declaration should have been declared inadmissible.

46 *R. v. Shulman* (1919), Department of Justice, Capital Case Files, RG 13, vol. 1499, f. 618A/
    CC102, LAC; *R. v. Hawkes* (1915).

47 *R. v. Jackson* (1920), ibid., vol. 1509, f. CC147, LAC; *R. v. Tratch* (1924), ibid., vol. 1528, f.
    722A/CC216, LAC; *R. v. Dranchuk* (1934), ibid., vol. 1592, f. CC418, LAC.

48 Catherine Cavanaugh, "The Limitations of the Pioneering Partnership: The Alberta Cam-
    paign for Homestead Dower, 1909-1925," in *Making Western Canada: Essays on European
    Colonization and Settlement*, ed. Catherine Cavanaugh and Jeremy Mouat (Toronto:
    Garamond Press, 1996), 198-201.

49 This position is put forward in Carol Lee Bacchi, *Liberation Deferred? The Ideas of the
    English-Canadian Suffragists, 1877-1918* (Toronto: University of Toronto Press, 1982); Mariana
    Valverde, *The Age of Light, Soap, and Water: Moral Reform in English Canada, 1885-1925*
    (Toronto: McClelland and Stewart, 1991), and "'When the Mother of the Race Is Free':
    Race, Reproduction, and Sexuality in First-Wave Feminism," in *Gender Conflicts: New
    Essays in Women's History*, ed. Franca Iacovetta and Mariana Valverde (Toronto: University
    of Toronto Press, 1993), 3-26.

50 See Veronica Strong-Boag, "'Ever a Crusader': Nellie McClung, First-Wave Feminist," in
    Rethinking Canada: The Promise of Women's History, 3rd ed., ed. Veronica Strong-Boag
    and Anita Clair Fellman (Toronto: Oxford University Press, 1997), 271-84. Margaret E.
    McCallum supports Strong-Boag's argument in "Prairie Women and the Struggle for a
    Dower Law, 1905-1920," in *Historical Perspectives on Law and Society in Canada*, ed. Tina
    Loo and Lorna R. McLean, 306-20 (Toronto: Copp Clark Longman, 1994).

51 W.C. Ives to Secretary of State, Canada, 4 December 1915, in *R. v. Hawkes* (1915); *Edmonton
    Journal*, 6 and 7 October 1915. F. Murray Greenwood and Beverley Boissery deal with the
    Hawkes case in Chapter 9 of *Uncertain Justice*, 181-95. They argue that she was a woman
    wronged by Canadian society and the criminal justice system because the largely American
    jury did not understand that a murder conviction would result in a death sentence.

52 Chief of Remission Branch to Acting Solicitor-General, Canada, 29 July 1920, in *R. v.
    Hawkes* (1915).

53 Greenwood and Boissery, *Uncertain Justice*, 181-91.

54 "Local Council Executive Deals with the Case of Jennie Hawkes," *Edmonton Journal*, 9
    November 1915.

55 "Appeal for Jennie Hawkes Not Made Because She Is a Woman," *Edmonton Journal*, 13
    November 1915.

56 Cavanaugh, "The Limitations of the Pioneering Partnership," 196 and note 56.

57 E.J. Keerley, Mount Royal College, to the Duke of Connaught, Ottawa, 13 November
    1915, in *R. v. Hawkes* (1915).

58 Ibid.

59 Hendrik Hartog, "Lawyering, Husbands' Rights, and 'The Unwritten Law' in Nineteenth-
    Century America," *Journal of American History* 84, 1 (1997): 67-96; Gordon Morris Bakken,
    "The Limits of Patriarchy: Women's Rights and 'Unwritten Law' in the West: 1997
    Presidential Address," *Historian* 60 (1998): 702-16. In 1881 in California, Lastencia Abarta
    was found not guilty of killing Francisco Foster, who had seduced her and refused to marry
    her. In an 1890 case, Katie Cook was found not guilty of shooting her husband, a known
    violator of servant girls and adolescents.

60 *R. v. Shulman* (1919).

61 Referred to in G.P. Owen Fenwick to the Remission Branch, 26 October 1915, in *R. v.
    Hawkes* (1915).

62 William Carlos Ives to the Minister of Justice, 4 December 1915, in *R. v. Hawkes* (1915). Sifton's letter is referenced in this correspondence.
63 "Mrs. Hawkes Here; Will Serve Time in Kingston Penitentiary," *Edmonton Journal*, 12 December 1915.
64 *R. v. Dranchuk* (1934); "Anxious to Have Sentence Commuted," *Calgary Herald*, 2 October 1935.
65 "Women and the Law," *Calgary Albertan*, 25 October 1934.
66 "Male Protests," *Calgary Albertan*, 25 October 1934.
67 Ibid.
68 See Strong-Boag, *The New Day Recalled: Lives of Girls and Women in English Canada, 1919-1939* (Markham, ON: Penguin, 1988), 7-40; Alison Prentice, Paula Bourne, Gail Cuthbert Brandt, Beth Light, Wendy Mitchinson, and Naomi Black, *Canadian Women: A History*, 2nd ed. (Toronto: Harcourt Brace Canada, 1996), 249-51.
69 Prentice et al., *Canadian Women*, 264-65. See also Theresa Healy, "Engendering Resistance: Women Respond to Relief in Saskatoon, 1930-1932," in *"Other Voices": Historical Essays on Saskatchewan Women*, ed. David De Brou and Aileen Moffatt (Regina: Canadian Plains Research Center, 1995), 94-115.
70 *R. v. Jackson* (1920).
71 Nellie McClung to C.J. Doherty, Minister of Justice, 13 November 1920, ibid.
72 Louise C. McKinney, Legislative Assembly of Alberta, to Minister of Justice, 29 November 1920, ibid.
73 J.F.L. Embury, SCKB, Saskatchewan, to Secretary of State, Ottawa, 18 February 1924, in *R. v. Tratch* (1924); "Tratch Woman Must Hang for Poison Crime," *Morning Leader*, 7 February 1924.
74 J. Harvey Hearn, Saskatoon, to Wallace Stewart, House of Commons, Ottawa, 25 April 1924, in *R. v. Tratch* (1924).
75 John Kidman, Canadian Prisoners' Welfare Association, Montreal, to the Minister of Justice, 15 May 1924, ibid.
76 Catherine Tratch to Ernest Lapointe, Minister of Justice, 9 March 1929, ibid.
77 Printed in full in "Should Not Hang Women," *Lethbridge Herald*, 30 September 1923.
78 Dorothy A. Anderson to the Minister of Justice, 7 February 1923, in *R. v. Lassandro* (1922), Department of Justice, Capital Case Files, RG 13, vol. 1523-24, LAC.
79 Tom Mitchell has re-created Blake's trial and the public reaction to it in "'Blood with the Taint of Cain': Immigrant Labouring Children, Manitoba Politics, and the Execution of Emily Hilda Blake," *Journal of Canadian Studies* 28 (Winter 1993-94): 49-71. See also a more in-depth and multifaceted treatment in Reinhold Kramer and Tom Mitchell, *Walk Towards the Gallows: The Tragedy of Hilda Blake, Hanged 1899* (Don Mills, ON: Oxford University Press, 2002).
80 Mitchell, "'Blood with the Taint of Cain,'" 60.
81 Tom Mitchell argues that, in addition to Blake's social origins as a working-class British orphan, Liberal misfortunes in Manitoba contributed to the executive decision to execute Blake.
82 Lassandro's background has been re-created and told imaginatively in M.A. Macpherson's *Outlaws of the Canadian West* (Edmonton: Lone Pine, 1999), 196-97, and in the opera *Filumena*.
83 William Walsh, Calgary, to Secretary of State, Ottawa, 4 December 1922, in *R. v. Lassandro* (1922); "Mrs. Lassandro's Startling Confession of Murder," *Morning Albertan*, 1 May 1923; "Women Slayer Gives New Light on Crime," *Lethbridge Herald*, 1 May 1923.

84 James S. Woodsworth, *Strangers within Our Gates: The Problem of the Immigrant* (1909; repr., Toronto: University of Toronto Press, 1972), 135.

85 Petition from the Canadian Prisoners' Welfare Association, Montreal, to the Minister of Justice and Governor General of Canada, 15 February 1923, in *R. v. Lassandro* (1922).

86 Dr. Moore, Cross Creek, New Brunswick, telegram to the Minister of Justice, 17 February 1923, ibid.

87 J.W.D. Turner, Edmonton, to Lomer Gouin, Minister of Justice, 12 December 1922, ibid.

88 Emily Murphy, Edmonton, to W.L.M. King, Prime Minister, Canada, 2 February 1923, ibid.

89 W.L. Walsh, Calgary, Memorandum to Secretary of State, Canada, 4 December 1922, ibid.

90 "Crime in the City," *Montreal Gazette,* 1 May 1922.

91 "La Dopier Inpiccaqione in Alberta, e la Proibizione," *La Tribuna Canadiana,* 5 June 1923. Clipping enclosed in Cortland Starnes, Commissioner RCMP, to Minister of Justice, 1923, in *R. v. Lassandro* (1922).

92 Martin Wiener, "The Sad Story of George Hall: Adultery, Murder, and the Politics of Mercy in Mid-Victorian England," *Social History* 24, 2 (1999): 174-95.

93 Marilyn Francis, "Monstrous Mothers, Monstrous Societies: Infanticide and the Rule of Law in Restoration and Eighteenth-Century England," *Eighteenth-Century Life* 21, 2 (1997): 134.

CONCLUSION

1 Steven Maynard, "The Maple Leaf (Gardens) Forever: Sex, Canadian Historians, and National History," *Journal of Canadian Studies* 36, 2 (2001): 90.

2 See John C. Weaver, *The Great Land Rush and the Making of the Modern World: 1650-1900* (Montreal and Kingston: McGill-Queen's University Press, 2003); and Royden Loewen's discussion of the book in "Beyond the Monolith of Modernity: New Trends in Immigrant and Ethnic History," *Agricultural History* 81 (Spring 2007): 204-27.

3 Ian McKay, "The Liberal Order Framework: A Prospectus for a Reconnaissance of Canadian History," *Canadian Historical Review* 81, 4 (December 2000): 621.

4 Catherine Cavanaugh, "'No Place for a Woman': Engendering Western Canadian Settlement," *Western Historical Quarterly* 28 (Winter 1997): 493-518; Sarah Carter, *The Importance of Being Monogamous: Marriage and Nation Building in Western Canada to 1915* (Edmonton: University of Alberta Press/Athabasca University Press, 2008), 283; Ruth W. Sandwell, "The Limits of Liberalism: The Liberal Reconnaissance and the History of the Family in Canada," *Canadian Historical Review* 84 (2003): 423-50; Joan Sangster, "Archiving Feminist Histories: Women, the 'Nation' and Metanarratives in Canadian Historical Writing," *Women's Studies International Forum* 29 (2006): 255-64.

5 Sheila McManus, *The Line Which Separates: Race, Gender, and the Making of the Alberta-Montana Border* (Lincoln: University of Nebraska Press, 2005), 83.

6 Elizabeth Jameson and Jeremy Mouat, "Telling Differences: The Forty-Ninth Parallel and Historiographies of the West and Nation," *Pacific Historical Review* 75, 2 (2006): 136; Myron C. Noonkester, "The Third British Empire: Transplanting the English Shire to Wales, Scotland, Ireland, and America," *Journal of British Studies* 36, 3 (1997): 257.

7 "Criminal Court – Rape – Exemplary Punishment" and "A Revolting Crime," *Regina Leader,* 21 October 1890.

8 Carolyn Strange, "Introduction," in *Qualities of Mercy: Justice, Punishment, and Discretion*, ed. Carolyn Strange (Vancouver: UBC Press, 1996), 3-20.

9 Jennifer Henderson, *Settler Feminism and Race Making in Canada* (Toronto: University of Toronto Press, 2003), 4, emphasis in original.

10 Jill Newton Ainsley, "'Some Mysterious Agency': Women, Violent, Crime, and the Insanity Acquittal in the Victorian Courtroom," *Canadian Journal of History* 25 (April 2000): 37-38.

Bibliography

ARCHIVAL SOURCES

Glenbow Archives (GA), Calgary

Blood Indian Agency Series, Department of Indian Affairs fonds, M-1788
Department of the Interior, Map of Land Registration and Judicial Districts, 1917

Library and Archives Canada (LAC), Ottawa

Department of Indian Affairs, RG 10
Department of the Interior, RG 15
Department of Justice, Capital Case Files, RG 13
Royal Canadian Mounted Police fonds, RG 18

Manitoba Legislative Library, Winnipeg

Robson Royal Commission on Social Vice, Winnipeg, 1911

McGill University Library, Rare Books and Special Collections Division, Montreal

Silcox Papers

Provincial Archives of Alberta (PAA), Edmonton

Supreme Court of Alberta (SCA), Criminal Case Files, Wetaskiwin Judicial District, 1914-38, Acc. 81.198, microfilm
Supreme Court of the North-West Territories (SCNWT), Criminal Case Files, Northern Alberta Judicial District, 1886-1907, Supreme Court of Alberta, Edmonton Judicial District, 1907-40, Acc. 83.1
Supreme Court of the North-West Territories (SCNWT), Criminal Case Files, Southern Alberta Judicial District, 1886-1907, Supreme Court of Alberta, Macleod Judicial District, 1907-40, Acc. 78.235, microfilm

Provincial Archives of Manitoba (PAM), Winnipeg

City of Winnipeg Police Court, Record Books, 1886-1916, GR 651, M-1210-20
City of Winnipeg Police Court, Record Books, 1917-1940, GR 513
County Criminal Court, Criminal Case Files, 1886-1940, Eastern Manitoba/Winnipeg Judicial District, GR 273
Criminal Register, County Criminal Court, 1886-1940, Eastern Manitoba/Winnipeg Judicial District, GR 2412
Criminal Register, Manitoba Court of King's Bench (MCKB) and County Criminal Court, Eastern Manitoba/Winnipeg Judicial District, 1886-1940, GR 3636, M-1196
Criminal Register, Manitoba Court of King's Bench (MCKB), Dauphin Judicial District, 1917-1940, GR 4576, L-4-15
Manitoba Court of King's Bench (MCKB), Criminal Case Files, 1886-1940, Eastern Manitoba/Winnipeg Judicial District, GR 180, M-1314-1594
Manitoba Court of King's Bench (MCKB), Criminal Case Files, 1917-40, Dauphin Judicial District, GR 540

Saskatchewan Archives Board (SAB), Regina

Docket Books, Supreme Court of Saskatchewan (SCS) and Saskatchewan Court of King's Bench (SCKB), Battleford District, 1908-38
Docket Books, Saskatchewan District Court, Battleford District, 1908-40
Saskatchewan Court of King's Bench (SCKB), Criminal Case Files, 1917-31, Regina District, R-1287
Saskatchewan District Court, Criminal Case Files, 1923-40, Regina District, unprocessed series
Supreme Court of the North-West Territories (SCNWT) and Supreme Court of Saskatchewan (SCS), Criminal Cases Files, 1887-1917, District of Western Assiniboia and Regina, R-1286

Newspapers and Journals

Calgary Herald (and Examiner)
Calgary/Morning Albertan
Canadian Police Bulletin
Edmonton Bulletin
Edmonton Journal
Globe and Mail
Grain Grower's Guide
Lethbridge Herald
Macleod Gazette
Manitoba/Winnipeg Free Press
Medicine Hat Weekly News
Regina Leader/Morning Leader
Star Phoenix
Vancouver Sun
Winnipeg Tribune

OTHER SOURCES

Adler, Jeffrey S. "'We've Got a Right to Fight, We're Married': Domestic Homicide in Chicago, 1875-1920." *Journal of Interdisciplinary History* 34 (Summer 2003): 27-48.

Ahmad, Diana L. "Opium Smoking, Anti-Chinese Attitudes, and the American Medical Community, 1850-1890." *American Nineteenth-Century History* 1, 2 (2000): 53-68.

Ainsley, Jill Newton. "'Some Mysterious Agency': Women, Violent Crime, and the Insanity Acquittal in the Victorian Courtroom." *Canadian Journal of History* 25 (April 2000): 37-55.

Alberta Legal History Project. *Specimen File Selections and Analysis with Index*. Calgary: Alberta Law Foundation, 1984.

Allen, Richard. "The Social Gospel as the Religion of the Agrarian Revolt." In *The Prairie West: Historical Readings*, 2nd ed., edited by R. Douglas Francis and Howard Palmer, 561-72. Edmonton: Pica Pica Press, 1995.

–. *The Social Passion: Religion and Social Reform in Canada, 1914-1928*. Toronto: University of Toronto Press, 1971.

Anderson, Benedict. *Imagined Communities: Reflections on the Origin and Spread of Nationalism*. London: Verso, 1991.

Anderson, Kay J. *Vancouver's Chinatown: Racial Discourse in Canada, 1875-1980*. Montreal and Kingston: McGill-Queen's University Press, 1995.

Angus, Albert. "Saskatchewan Justice on Trial: The Pamela George Case." *Saskatchewan Indian* 27 (April 1997): 5, 23.

Ariès, Philippe. *Centuries of Childhood*. New York: Alfred A. Knopf, 1962.

Arnot, Margaret L. "Gender in Focus: Infanticide in England, 1840-1880." PhD diss., University of Essex, 1994.

Arnot, Margaret L., and Cornelie Usborne. "Why Gender and Crime? Aspects of an International Debate." In *Gender and Crime in Modern Europe*, edited by Margaret L. Arnot and Cornelie Usborne, 1-29. London: University College London Press, 1999.

Artibise, Alan. *Winnipeg: A Social History of Urban Growth*. Montreal and Kingston: McGill-Queen's University Press, 1975.

–. *Winnipeg: An Illustrated History*. Toronto: James Lorimer, 1977.

Asher, Brad. *Beyond the Reservation: Indians, Settlers, and the Law in Washington Territory, 1853-1889*. Norman: University of Oklahoma Press, 1999.

Bacchi, Carol Lee. "Divided Allegiances: The Response of Farm and Labour Women to Suffrage." In *A Not Unreasonable Claim: Women and Reform in Canada, 1880-1920s*, edited by Linda Kealey, 89-107. Toronto: Women's Press, 1979.

–. *Liberation Deferred? The Ideas of the English-Canadian Suffragists, 1877-1918*. Toronto: University of Toronto Press, 1982.

Backhouse, Constance. *Carnal Crimes: Sexual Assault Law in Canada, 1900-1975*. Toronto: Irwin Law for the Osgoode Society for Canadian Legal History, 2008.

–. *Colour-Coded: A Legal History of Racism in Canada, 1900-1950*. Toronto: University of Toronto Press for the Osgoode Society for Canadian Legal History, 1999.

–. "Desperate Women and Compassionate Courts: Infanticide in Nineteenth-Century Canada." *University of Toronto Law Journal* 34 (1984): 447-78.

–. "'Her Protests Were Unavailing': Australian Legal Understandings of Rape, Consent, and Sexuality in the 'Roaring Twenties.'" *Journal of Australian Studies* 64 (2000): 14-33.

—. "A Measure of Women's Credibility: The Doctrine of Corroboration in Sexual Assault Trials in Early Twentieth-Century Canada and Australia." *York Occasional Working Papers in Law and Society* 1 (2002): 1-32.

—. "Nineteenth-Century Canadian Prostitution Law: Reflection of a Discriminatory Society." *Histoire sociale/Social History* 36 (November 1985): 387-423.

—. "Nineteenth-Century Canadian Rape Law, 1800-1892." In *Essays in the History of Canadian Law*, vol. 2, edited by David Flaherty, 200-47. Toronto: University of Toronto Press for the Osgoode Society for Canadian Legal History, 1983.

—. "Nineteenth-Century Judicial Attitudes toward Child Custody, Rape, and Prostitution." In *Equality and Judicial Neutrality*, edited by Sheilah L. Martin and Kathleen E. Mahoney, 271-81. Calgary: Carswell, 1987.

—. *Petticoats and Prejudice: Women and Law in Nineteenth-Century Canada*. Toronto: Women's Press for the Osgoode Society for Canadian Legal History, 1991.

—. "Prosecution of Abortions under Canadian Law, 1900-1950." In Phillips, Loo, and Lewthwaite, *Crime and Criminal Justice*, 252-92.

Bagnell, Kenneth. *The Little Immigrants: The Orphans Who Came to Canada*. Toronto: Macmillan, 1980.

Baker, H. Robert. "Creating Order in the Wilderness: Transplanting the English Law to Rupert's Land, 1835-51." *Law and History Review* 17 (Summer 1999): 209-46.

Baker, William M., ed. *Pioneer Policing in Southern Alberta: Deane of the Mounties, 1888-1914*. Calgary: Historical Society of Alberta, 1993.

Bakken, Gordon Morris. "The Limits of Patriarchy: Women's Rights and 'Unwritten Law' in the West: 1997 Presidential Address." *Historian* 60 (1998): 702-16.

Barber, Marilyn. "The Servant Problem in Manitoba, 1896-1930." In *First Days, Fighting Days: Women in Manitoba History*, edited by Mary Kinnear, 100-19. Regina: Canadian Plains Research Center, 1987.

Barman, Jean. "Taming Aboriginal Sexuality: Gender, Power, and Race in British Columbia, 1850-1900." *BC Studies* 115/116 (Autumn/Winter 1997/1998): 237-66.

Barrett, Michèle. *Women's Oppression Today: Problems in Marxist Feminist Analysis*. London: Verso, 1980.

Bartley, Paula. *Prostitution: Prevention and Reform in England, 1860-1914*. London: Routledge, 2000.

Bauer, Carol, and Lawrence Ritt. "Wife-Abuse, Late-Victorian English Feminists, and the Legacy of Frances Power Cobb." *International Journal of Women's Studies* 6, 3 (1983): 195-207.

Beahen, William. "Abortion and Infanticide in Western Canada, 1874 to 1916: A Criminal Case Study." *Historical Studies* 53 (1986): 53-70.

Beahen, William, and Stan Horrall. *Red Coats on the Prairies: The North-West Mounted Police, 1886-1900*. Regina: Centax, 1998.

Bederman, Gail. *Manliness and Civilization: A Cultural History of Gender and Race in the United States, 1880-1917*. Chicago: University of Chicago Press, 1995.

Bedford, Judy. "Prostitution in Calgary, 1905-1914." *Alberta History* 29 (1981): 1-11.

Bell, Vicki. *Interrogating Incest: Feminism, Foucault and the Law*. London: Routledge, 1993.

Benton, Lauren. "Colonial Law and Cultural Difference: Jurisdictional Politics and the Formation of the Colonial State." *Comparative Studies in Society and History* 41, 3 (1999): 563-88.

Berkhofer, Robert F., Jr. *The White Man's Indian*. New York: Alfred A. Knopf, 1978.

Bhabha, Homi. "Of Mimicry and Man: The Ambivalence of Colonial Discourse." In *Tensions of Empire: Colonial Discourse in a Bourgeois World*, edited by Frederick Cooper and Ann Laura Stoler, 152-60. Berkeley: University of California Press, 1997.

Bingaman, Sandra Estlin. "The Trials of Poundmaker and Big Bear, 1885." *Saskatchewan History* 28, 3 (1975): 81-102.

Blair, Madeleine [pseud.]. *Madeleine: An Autobiography*. 1919. Reprint, New York: Persea Books, 1986.

Bliss, Katherine Elaine. *Compromised Positions: Prostitution, Public Health and Gender Politics in Revolutionary Mexico City*. University Park: Pennsylvania State University Press, 2001.

Boritch, Helen. "The Making of Toronto the Good: The Organization of Policing and the Production of Arrests, 1859-1955." PhD diss., University of Toronto, 1985.

Bourgeault, Ron. "Pamela George: A Victim of History and Economic Racism." *Canadian Dimension* 31 (May-June 1997): 41-43.

Bowker, Wilbur F. *A Consolidation of Fifty Years of Legal Writings, 1938-1988*. Edited by Marjorie Bowker. Edmonton: University of Alberta Press, 1989.

–. "Stipendiary Magistrates and the Supreme Court of the North-West Territories, 1876-1907." *Alberta Law Review* 27 (1988): 245-86.

Bradbury, Bettina. "Colonial Comparisons: Rethinking Marriage, Civilization, and Nation in Nineteenth-Century White Settler Societies." In Buckner and Francis, *Rediscovering the British World*, 135-58.

Brennan, J. William. *Regina: An Illustrated History*. Toronto: James Lorimer, 1989.

Bright, David. "The Cop, the Chief, the Hooker, and Her Life." *Alberta History* 45 (1997): 16-26.

–. "'Go Home. Straighten Up. Live Decent Lives': Female Vagrancy and Social Respectability in Alberta." *Prairie Forum* 28 (Fall 2003): 161-72.

–. "Sexual Assaults in Calgary, Alberta, between the Wars." In *Criminal Justice History*. Vol. 19, *Violent Crime in North America*, edited by Louis A. Knafla, 105-30. Westport, CT: Greenwood Press, 2003.

Brown, Kathleen. *Good Wives, Nasty Wenches, and Anxious Patriarchs: Gender, Race, and Power in Colonial Virginia*. Chapel Hill: University of North Carolina Press, 1996.

Brownlie, Robin Jarvis. "Intimate Surveillance: Indian Affairs, Colonization, and the Regulation of Aboriginal Women's Sexuality." In Pickles and Rutherdale, *Contact Zones*, 160-78.

Brownlie, Robin, and Mary-Ellen Kelm. "Desperately Seeking Absolution: Native Agency as Colonialist Alibi." *Canadian Historical Review* 75 (December 1994): 543-57.

Brownmiller, Susan. *Against Our Will*. New York: Bantam, 1975.

Buckner, Phillip A., ed. *Canada and the British Empire*. Oxford: Oxford University Press, 2008.

Buckner, Phillip A., and R. Douglas Francis, eds. *Canada and the British World*. Vancouver: UBC Press, 2006.

–, eds. *Rediscovering the British World*. Calgary: University of Calgary Press, 2005.

Burnet, Jean R., and Howard Palmer. *"Coming Canadians": An Introduction to a History of Canada's Peoples*. Toronto: McClelland and Stewart, 1988.

Butler, Anne M. *Daughters of Joy, Sisters of Misery: Prostitutes in the American West, 1865-90*. Chicago: University of Illinois Press, 1987.

Canadian Council on Social Development. "Social Challenges: The Well-Being of Aboriginal People." Crime Prevention through Social Development. http://www.ccsd .ca/cpsd/ccsd/c_ab.htm.

Carey, David, ed. *Carey's Manitoba Reports.* Calgary: Carswell, 1918.

Carrigan, D. Owen. *Crime and Punishment in Canada: A History.* Toronto: McClelland and Stewart, 1994.

–. *Juvenile Delinquency in Canada: A History.* Concord, ON: Irwin Publishing, 1998.

Carroll, Mark M. *Homesteads Ungovernable: Families, Sex, Race, and the Law in Frontier Texas, 1823-1860.* Austin: University of Texas Press, 2001.

Carter, Sarah. *Aboriginal People and Colonizers of Western Canada to 1900.* Toronto: University of Toronto Press, 1999.

–. *Capturing Women: The Manipulation of Cultural Imagery in Canada's Prairie West.* Montreal and Kingston: McGill-Queen's University Press, 1997.

–. "Categories and Terrains of Exclusion: Constructing the 'Indian Woman' in the Early Settlement Era in Western Canada." *Great Plains Quarterly* 13 (Summer 1993): 147-61.

–. "'Complicated and Clouded': The Federal Administration of Marriage and Divorce among the First Nations of Western Canada, 1887-1906." In *Unsettled Pasts: Reconceiving the West through Women's History,* edited by Sarah Carter, Lesley Erickson, Patricia Roome, and Char Smith, 151-78. Calgary: University of Calgary Press, 2005.

–. "Creating 'Semi-Widows' and 'Supernumerary Wives': Prohibiting Polygamy in Prairie Canada's Aboriginal Communities to 1900." In Pickles and Rutherdale, *Contact Zones,* 131-59.

–. "First Nations Women of Prairie Canada in the Early Reserve Years, the 1870s to the 1920s: A Preliminary Inquiry." In *Women of the First Nations: Power, Wisdom, and Strength,* edited by Christine Miller and Patricia Chuchryk, 51-76. Winnipeg: University of Manitoba Press, 1996.

–. *The Importance of Being Monogamous: Marriage and Nation Building in Western Canada to 1915.* Edmonton: University of Alberta Press/Athabasca University Press, 2008.

–. *Lost Harvests: Prairie Indian Reserve Farmers and Government Policy.* Montreal and Kingston: McGill-Queen's University Press, 1990.

Cavanaugh, Catherine. "The Limitations of the Pioneering Partnership: The Alberta Campaign for Homestead Dower, 1909-1925." In *Making Western Canada: Essays on European Colonization and Settlement,* edited by Catherine Cavanaugh and Jeremy Mouat, 186-214. Toronto: Garamond Press, 1996.

–. "'No Place for a Woman': Engendering Western Canadian Settlement." *Western Historical Quarterly* 28 (Winter 1997): 493-518.

Chambers, Lori. *Married Women and Property Law in Victorian Ontario.* Toronto: University of Toronto Press for the Osgoode Society for Canadian Legal History, 1997.

Chanock, Martin. *Law, Custom, and Social Order: The Colonial Experience in Malawi and Zambia.* Cambridge: Cambridge University Press, 1985.

–. *The Making of South African Legal Culture, 1902-1936: Fear, Favour, and Prejudice.* Cambridge: Cambridge University Press, 2001.

Chapman, Terry. "The Anti-Drug Crusade in Western Canada, 1885-1925." In *Law and Society in Canada in Historical Perspective,* edited by David Bercuson and Louis A. Knafla, 89-115. Calgary: University of Calgary Press, 1979.

–. "'Inquiring Minds Want to Know': The Handling of Children in Sex Assault Cases in the Canadian West, 1890-1920." In *Dimensions of Childhood: Essays on the History of Children and Youth in Canada*, edited by Russell Smandych, Gordon Dodds, and Alvin Esau, 183-204. Winnipeg: University of Manitoba Press, 1991.

–. "Sex Crimes in the West, 1890-1920." *Alberta History* 35 (Autumn 1987): 6-21.

–. "Sex Crimes in Western Canada, 1890-1920." PhD diss., University of Alberta, 1984.

–. "'Til Death Do Us Part': Wife Beating in Alberta, 1905-1920." *Alberta History* 36 (Autumn 1988): 13-22.

Chenier, Elise. "The Criminal Sexual Psychopath in Canada: Sex, Psychiatry, and the Law at Mid-Century." *Canadian Bulletin of Medical History* 20, 1 (2003): 75-101.

Cherwinski, W.J.C. "In Search of Jake Trumper: The Farm Hand and the Prairie Farm Family." In *Building beyond the Homestead: Rural History on the Prairies*, edited by David C. Jones and Ian MacPherson, 111-34. Calgary: University of Calgary Press, 1985.

–. "Wooden Horses and Rubber Cows: Training British Agricultural Labour for the Canadian Prairies, 1890-1930." *Historical Papers* 15, 1 (1980): 133-54.

Chesney-Lind, Meda. "Chivalry Re-Examined: Women and the Criminal Justice System." In *Women, Crime, and the Criminal Justice System*, edited by Lee H. Bowker, 171-94. Lexington: D.C. Heath, 1978.

–. "Women and Crime: The Female Offender." *Signs* 12, 1 (1986): 78-96.

Christie, Nancy. *Engendering the State: Family, Work, and Welfare in Canada*. Toronto: University of Toronto Press, 2000.

Chunn, Dorothy. *From Punishment to Doing Good: Family Courts and Socialized Justice in Ontario, 1880-1940*. Toronto: University of Toronto Press, 1992.

–. "'Just Plain Everyday Housekeeping on a Grand Scale': Feminists, Family Courts, and the Welfare State in British Columbia, 1928-1945." In *Law, Society, and the State: Essays in Legal History*, edited by Louis A. Knafla and Susan W.S. Binnie, 379-403. Toronto: University of Toronto Press, 1994.

–. "Secrets and Lies: The Criminalization of Incest and the (Re)Formation of the 'Private' in British Columbia, 1890-1940." In *Regulating Lives: Historical Essays on the State, Society, the Individual, and the Law*, edited by John McLaren, Robert Menzies, and Dorothy Chunn, 120-44. Vancouver: UBC Press, 2002.

–. "Sex and Citizenship: (Hetero)Sexual Offences, Law, and 'White' Settler Society in British Columbia, 1885-1940." In *Contesting Canadian Citizenship: Historical Readings*, edited by Robert Adamoski, Dorothy Chunn, and Robert Menzies, 359-84. Peterborough, ON: Broadview Press, 2002.

Clancy-Smith, Julie Ann, and Frances Gouda, eds. *Domesticating the Empire: Race, Gender, and Family in French and Dutch Colonialism*. Charlottesville: University of Virginia Press, 1998.

Clark, Anne. *Women's Silence, Men's Violence: Sexual Assault in England, 1770-1845*. London: Pandora, 1987.

Clark, Lorene, and Debra Lewis. *Rape: The Price of Coercive Sexuality*. Toronto: Women's Press, 1977.

Clarkson, Christopher A. *Domestic Reforms: Political Visions and Family Regulation in British Columbia*. Vancouver: UBC Press, 2008.

–. "Property Law and Family Regulation in Pacific British North America, 1862-1873." *Histoire sociale/Social History* 30 (November 1997): 386-418.

Cleverdon, Catherine. *The Woman Suffrage Movement in Canada*. 1950. Reprint, Toronto: University of Toronto Press, 1974.

Cliche, Marie-Aimée. "L'infanticide dans la région de Québec, 1660-1969." *Revue d'histoire de l'Amérique Française* 44, 1 (1990): 31-59.

Coates, Kenneth, and William R. Morrison. "A Drunken Impulse: Aboriginal Justice Confronts Canadian Law." *Western Historical Quarterly* 27, 4 (1996): 452-77.

–. *Strange Things Done: Murder in Yukon Territory*. Montreal and Kingston: McGill-Queen's University Press, 2004.

Cohen, Anthony. *The Symbolic Construction of Community*. New York: Tavistock, 1985.

Cole, Catherine C., and Ann Milovic. "Education, Community Service, and Social Life: The Alberta Women's Institutes and Rural Families, 1909-1945." In *Standing on New Ground: Women in Alberta*, edited by Catherine A. Cavanaugh and Randi R. Warne, 19-32. Edmonton: University of Alberta Press, 1993.

Cole, Douglas, and J.R. Miller. "Desperately Seeking Absolution: Responses and a Reply," *Canadian Historical Review* 76 (December 1995): 628-43.

Comacchio, Cynthia. "Dancing to Perdition: Adolescence and Leisure in Interwar English Canada." *Journal of Canadian Studies* 32 (Fall 1997): 5-35.

–. *The Dominion of Youth: Adolescence and the Making of Modern Canada, 1920-1950*. Waterloo, ON: Wilfrid Laurier University Press, 2006.

–. *"Nations are Built of Babies": Saving Ontario's Mothers and Children, 1900-1940*. Montreal and Kingston: McGill-Queen's University Press, 1993.

Comaroff, John L. "Colonialism, Culture, and the Law: A Foreword." *Law and Social Inquiry* 26 (Spring 2001): 305-14.

–. "Foreword." In Lazarus-Black and Hirsch, *Contested States*, ix-xiii.

Comaroff, John L., and Jean Comaroff. *Ethnography and the Historical Imagination*. Boulder, CO: Westview Press, 1992.

–. *Of Revelation and Revolution: Christianity, Colonialism, and Consciousness in South Africa*. Vol. 1. Chicago: University of Chicago Press, 1991.

Connell, Robert W. *Masculinities*. Berkeley: University of California Press, 1995.

–. "Masculinities, Change, and Conflict in Global Society: Thinking about the Future of Men's Studies." *Journal of Men's Studies* 11 (2003): 249-66.

Connelly, Mark. *The Response to Prostitution in the Progressive Era*. Chapel Hill: University of North Carolina Press, 1980.

Connor, Ralph. *Black Rock: A Tale of the Selkirks*. Toronto: Westminster Company, 1898.

Constant, Jean-François, and Michele Ducharme, eds. *Liberalism and Hegemony: Debating the Canadian Revolution*. Toronto: University of Toronto Press, 2009.

Cook, Ramsay. *The Regenerators: Social Criticism in Late Victorian English Canada*. Toronto: University of Toronto Press, 1985.

Cook, Sharon Ann. "'Do not ... do anything that you cannot unblushingly tell your mother': Gender and Social Purity in Canada." *Histoire sociale/Social History* 30 (November 1997): 215-39.

–. *Through Sunshine and Shadow: The Woman's Christian Temperance Union, Evangelicalism and Reform in Ontario, 1874-1939*. Montreal and Kingston: McGill-Queen's University Press, 1995.

Cooper, Joy. "Red Lights in Winnipeg." *Transactions*, Manitoba Historical and Scientific Society (16 February 1971): 67-74.

Corbin, Alain. *Women for Hire: Prostitution and Sexuality in France after 1850.* Translated by Alan Sheridan. Cambridge: Cambridge University Press, 1990.

Cott, Nancy F. *Public Vows: A History of Marriage and the Nation.* Cambridge, MA: Harvard University Press, 2000.

Coulter, Rebecca. "The Working Young of Edmonton, 1921-1931." In *Childhood and Family in Canadian History,* edited by Joy Parr, 144-59. Toronto: McClelland and Stewart, 1982.

Crawford, Mary E., ed. *Legal Status of Women in Manitoba.* Winnipeg: Political Equality League of Manitoba, 1913.

Crenshaw, Kimberlé. "Mapping the Margins: Intersectionality, Identity Politics, and Violence against Women of Color." *Stanford Law Review* 43 (July 1991): 1241-99.

Curtis, Bruce. "Surveying the Social: Techniques, Practices, Power." *Histoire sociale/ Social History* 35, 69 (May 2002): 83-108.

Dagut, S. "Gender, Colonial 'Women's History' and the Construction of Social Distance: Middle-Class British Women in Later Nineteenth-Century South Africa." *Journal of South African Studies* 26, 3 (2000): 555-72.

Dalley, Bronwyn. "'Fresh Attraction': White Slavery and Feminism in New Zealand, 1885-1918." *Women's History Review* 9, 3 (2000): 585-606.

Daly, T. Mayne. *Canadian Criminal Procedure as the Same Relates to Preliminary Hearings, Summary Convictions and Summary Trials.* 2nd ed. Revised by George Patterson. Toronto: Carswell, 1915.

Danysk, Cecilia. "'A Bachelor's Paradise': Homesteaders, Hired Hands, and the Construction of Masculinity, 1880-1930." In *Making Western Canada: Essays on European Colonization and Settlement,* edited by Catherine Cavanaugh and Jeremy Mouat, 154-85. Toronto: Garamond Press, 1996.

–. *Hired Hands: Labour and the Development of Prairie Agriculture, 1880-1930.* Toronto: McClelland and Stewart, 1994.

Daunton, Martin, and Bernhard Rieger. *Meanings of Modernity: Britain and the Late-Victorian Era to World War II.* Oxford: Oxford University Press, 2001.

Davidoff, Leonore. "Gender and the 'Great Divide': Public and Private in British Gender History." *Journal of Women's History* 15 (Spring 2003): 11-27.

–. "Regarding Some 'Old' Husbands' Tales: Public and Private in Feminist History." In *Feminism, the Public and the Private,* edited by Joan B. Landes, 164-94. Oxford: Oxford University Press, 1998.

Davidoff, Leonore, and Catherine Hall. *Family Fortunes: Men and Women of the English Middle Class, 1780-1850.* New York: Random House, 1987.

Davie, Neil. "Criminal Man Revisited? Continuity and Change in British Criminology, c. 1865-1918." *Journal of Victorian Culture* 8 (Spring 2003): 1-32.

Davin, Anna. "Imperialism and Motherhood." *History Workshop Journal* 5 (Spring 1978): 9-65.

Davin, Nicholas Flood, ed. *Homes for Millions: The Great Canadian North-West; Its Resources Fully Described.* Ottawa: n.p., 1891.

Davis, Angela. *Women, Race, and Class.* New York: Random House, 1981.

Davis, Natalie Zemon. *Fiction in the Archives: Pardon Tales and Their Tellers in Sixteenth-Century France.* Stanford: Stanford University Press, 1987.

–. "The Shapes of Social History." *Storia della storiografia* 17 (1990): 28-34.

Dawson, C.A., and Eva R. Younge. *Pioneering in the Prairie Provinces: The Social Side of the Settlement Process.* Toronto: Macmillan, 1940.

Dawson, Michael. "'That Nice Red Coat Goes to My Head Like Champagne': Gender, Antimodernism, and the Mountie Image, 1880-1960." *Journal of Canadian Studies* 32 (1997): 119-39.

Dean, Carolyn J. *The Frail Social Body: Pornography, Homosexuality, and Other Fantasies in Interwar France.* Berkeley: University of California Press, 2000.

D'Emilio, John, and Estelle Freedman. *Intimate Matters: A History of Sexuality in America.* New York: Harper and Row, 1988.

Dempsey, Hugh A. *Charcoal's World.* Saskatoon: Western Producer Books, 1978.

–. *Tribal Honours: A History of the Kainai Chieftainship.* Calgary: Kainai Chieftainship, 1997.

Devereux, Cecily. "'And Let Them Wash Me from the Clanging World': *Hugh and Ion,* 'The Last Best West,' and Purity Discourse in 1885." *Journal of Canadian Studies* 32 (Summer 1997): 100-15.

Dierks, Konstantin. "Men's History, Gender History, or Cultural History?" *Gender and History* 14 (April 2002): 147-51.

Ditz, Toby L. "The New Men's History and the Peculiar Absence of Gendered Power: Some Remedies from Early American Gender History." *Gender and History* 16 (April 2004): 1-35.

Dixon, Robert. *Writing the Colonial Adventure: Race, Gender, and Nation in Anglo-Australian Popular Fiction, 1875-1914.* Cambridge: Cambridge University Press, 1995.

Dodge, Bernadine. "Let the Record Show: Women and Law in the United Counties of Durham and Northumberland, 1845-1895." *Ontario History* 92, 2 (2000): 127-45.

Dominion Bureau of Statistics. *The Prairie Provinces in Their Relation to the National Economy of Canada: A Statistical Study of Their Social and Economic Condition in the Twentieth Century.* Ottawa: Government of Canada, 1934.

Dranoff, Linda Silver. *Women in Canadian Life: Law.* Toronto: Fitzhenry and Whiteside, 1977.

Du Val, Frederic B. *The Problem of Social Vice in Winnipeg: Being a Reply to a Pamphlet Entitled "The Attitude of the Church to the Social Evil": Together with a Brief Examination of the Question in the Light of Physiology, Law and Morality.* Winnipeg: Moral and Social Reform Committee, 1904. Microfilm 2763, Peel's Prairie Provinces, University of Alberta, Edmonton.

Dubinsky, Karen. *Improper Advances: Rape and Heterosexual Conflict in Ontario, 1880-1929.* Chicago: University of Chicago Press, 1993.

–. "'Maidenly Girls and Designing Women'? The Crime of Seduction in Turn-of-the-Century Ontario." In *Gender Conflicts: New Essays in Women's History,* edited by Franca Iacovetta and Mariana Valverde, 28-66. Toronto: University of Toronto Press, 1993.

–. "Sex and Shame: Some Thoughts on the Social and Historical Meaning of Rape." In *Rethinking Canada: The Promise of Women's History,* 4th ed., edited by Veronica Strong-Boag, Mona Gleason, and Adele Perry, 164-73. Don Mills, ON: Oxford University Press, 2002.

–. "Telling Stories about Dead People." In Iacovetta and Mitchinson, *On the Case,* 359-66.

Dubinsky, Karen, and Adam Givertz. "'It Was Only a Matter of Passion': Masculinity and Sexual Danger." In *Gendered Pasts: Historical Essays in Femininity and Masculinity in Canada,* edited by Kathryn McPherson, Cecilia Morgan, and Nancy Forestall, 65-79. Oxford: Oxford University Press, 1999.

Dubinksy, Karen, and Franca Iacovetta. "Murder, Womanly Virtue, and Motherhood: The Case of Angelina Napolitano, 1911-1922." *Canadian Historical Review* 72 (December 1991): 505-31.

Dudas, Jeffrey R. "Law and the American Frontier." *Law and Social Inquiry* 29 (Fall 2004): 860-61.

Duran, Bonnie. "Indigenous versus Colonial Discourse: Alcohol and American Indian Identity." In *Dressing in Feathers: The Construction of the Indian in American Popular Culture,* edited by S. Elizabeth Bird, 111-28. Boulder, CO: Westview Press, 1996.

Edwards, Susan. *Female Sexuality and the Law.* Oxford: Martin Robertson, 1981.

Elofson, Warren B. "Law and Disorder on the Ranching Frontiers of Montana and Alberta/ Assiniboia, 1870-1914." *Journal of the West* 42, 1 (2003): 40-51.

Emberley, Julia. "The Bourgeois Family, Aboriginal Women, and Colonial Governance in Canada: A Study in Feminist Historical and Cultural Materialism." *Signs* 27, 1 (2001): 59-85.

Engels, Dagmar. "The Limits of Gender Ideology, Bengali Women, the Colonial State, and the Private Sphere, 1890-1930." *Women's Studies International Forum* 12, 4 (1989): 425-37.

Engle, Sally Merry. *Colonizing Hawai'i: The Cultural Power of Law.* Princeton, NJ: Princeton University Press, 2000.

—. "Courts as Performances: Domestic Violence Hearings in a Hawai'i Family Court." In Lazarus-Black and Hirsch, *Contested States,* 35-58.

—. "From Law and Colonialism to Law and Globalization." *Law and Social Inquiry* 28 (Spring 2003): 569-90.

—. "Hegemony and Culture in Historical Anthropology: A Review Essay on Jean and John L. Comaroff's *Of Revelation and Revolution.*" *American Historical Review* 108 (April 2003): 460-70.

Erickson, Lesley. "Constructed and Contested Truths: Aboriginal Suicide, Law, and Colonialism in the Canadian West(s), 1823-1927." *Canadian Historical Review* 86 (December 2005): 595-618.

—. "Murdered Women and Mythic Villains: The Criminal Case and the Imaginary Criminal in the Canadian West, 1886-1930." In *People and Place: Historical Influences on Legal Culture,* edited by Jonathan Swainger and Constance Backhouse, 95-119. Vancouver: UBC Press, 2003.

—. "'A Very Garden of the Lord'? Hired Hands, Farm Women, and Sex Crime Prosecutions on the Prairies, 1914-1929." *Journal of the Canadian Historical Association* 12 (2001): 115-36.

Etherington, Norman. "Natal's Black Rape Scare of the 1870s." *Journal of South African Studies* 15, 1 (1988): 36-53.

Evans, Raymond. "Harlots and Helots: Exploitation of the Aboriginal Remnant." In *Race Relations in Colonial Queensland: Exclusion, Exploitation and Extermination,* edited by Raymond Evans, Kay Saunders, and Kathryn Cronin, 102-17. St. Lucia: University of Queensland Press, 1993.

Fanon, Frantz. *Wretched of the Earth.* Translated by Constance Farrington. New York: Grove Weidenfeld, 1963.

Fass, Paul. *The Damned and the Beautiful: American Youth in the 1920s.* New York: Oxford University Press, 1977.

Fattah, Ezzat A. "The Canadian Public and the Death Penalty: A Study of Social Attitude." PhD diss., Simon Fraser University, 1976.

Fingard, Judith. "The Prevention of Cruelty: Marriage Breakdown and the Rights of Wives in Nova Scotia, 1880-1900." In *Separate Spheres: Women's Worlds in the 19th-Century Maritimes,* edited by Janet Guildford and Suzanne Morton, 211-32. Fredericton: Acadiensis Press, 1994.

Fisher, Trevor. *Prostitution and the Victorians.* Gloucestershire, UK: Sutton Publishing, 1997.

Fitzgerald, Michele. *A Research Guide to Court Records in the Provincial Archives of Manitoba.* Winnipeg: Legal Research Institute, 1994.

Fitzpatrick, Peter, and Eve Darian-Smith, eds. *Laws of the Postcolonial.* Ann Arbor: University of Michigan Press, 1999.

Foster, Hamar. "Long-Distance Justice: The Criminal Jurisdiction of Canadian Courts West of the Canadas, 1763-1859." *American Journal of Legal History* 34 (1990): 1-48.

—. "'The Queen's Law Is Better Than Yours': International Homicide in British Columbia." In Phillips, Loo, and Lewthwaite, *Crime and Criminal Justice,* 41-91.

Foucault, Michel. *History of Sexuality.* Vol. 1. New York: Random House, 1978.

Francis, Daniel. *The Imaginary Indian: The Image of the Indian in Canadian Culture.* Vancouver: Arsenal Pulp Press, 1992.

Francis, Marilyn. "Monstrous Mothers, Monstrous Societies: Infanticide and the Rule of Law in Restoration and Eighteenth-Century England." *Eighteenth-Century Life* 21, 2 (1997): 133-56.

Francis, R. Douglas. *Images of the West: Changing Perceptions of the Prairies, 1690-1960.* Saskatoon: Western Producer Prairie Books, 1989.

Francis, R. Douglas, and Chris Kitzan, eds. *The Prairie West as Promised Land.* Calgary: University of Calgary Press, 2007.

Freedman, Estelle B. "'Uncontrolled Desires': The Response to the Sexual Psychopath, 1920-1960." *Journal of American History* 74, 1 (1987): 83-106.

Friedman, Lawrence. *Crime and Punishment in American History.* New York: Basic Books, 1993.

Friesen, Gerald. *The Canadian Prairies: A History.* Toronto: University of Toronto Press, 1984.

—. "Critical History in Western Canada, 1900-2000." In *The West and Beyond: New Perspectives on an Imagined Region,* edited by Alvin Finkel, Sarah Carter, and Peter Fontina, 3-12. Edmonton: Athabasca University Press, 2010.

—. "Defining the Prairies: Or, Why the Prairies Don't Exist." In *Toward Defining the Prairies: Region, Culture, and History,* edited by Robert Wardhaugh, 13-28. Winnipeg: University of Manitoba Press, 2001.

Fryer, Sarah Beebe. "Morality Plays at the Courthouse: The Celebrated Murder Trials of Anna George and Francine Hughes." *Proteus* 13, 1 (1996): 33-38.

Furniss, Elizabeth. *The Burden of History: Colonialism and Frontier Myth in a Rural Canadian Community.* Vancouver: UBC Press, 2000.

Gadoury, Lorraine, and Antonio Lechasseur. "Persons Sentenced to Death in Canada, 1867-1976: An Inventory of Case Files in the Fonds of the Department of Justice (RG 13)." Ottawa: National Archives of Canada, 1994.

Galley, Janet L. McShane. "'I Did It to Hide My Shame': Community Responses to Suspicious Infant Death in Middlesex, Ontario, 1850-1900." Master's thesis, University of Western Ontario, 1998.

Geertz, Clifford. *Local Knowledge: Further Essays in Interpretive Anthropology.* New York: Basic Books, 2000.

Gikandi, Simon. *Maps of Englishness: Writing Identity in the Culture of Colonialism.* New York: Columbia University Press, 1996.

Gilfoyle, Timothy J. "Prostitutes in History: From Parables of Pornography to Metaphors of Modernity." *American Historical Review* 104 (February 1999): 117-41.

Gilman, Sander. *Difference and Pathology: Stereotypes of Sexuality, Race, and Madness.* Ithaca, NY: Cornell University Press, 1995.

Golder, Hilary, and Diane Kirkby. "Mrs. Mayne and Her Boxing Kangaroo: A Married Woman Tests Her Property Rights in Colonial New South Wales." *Law and History Review* 21, 3 (2003): 585-604.

Gölz, Annalee. "'If a Man's Wife Does Not Obey Him, What Can He Do?' Marital Breakdown and Wife Abuse in Late Nineteenth-Century and Early Twentieth-Century Ontario." In *Law, Society, and the State: Essays in Modern Legal History*, edited by Louis A. Knafla and Susan W.S. Binnie, 323-50. Toronto: University of Toronto Press, 1995.

–. "Murder Most Foul: Spousal Homicides in Ontario, 1870-1915." In Robb and Erber, *Disorder in the Court*, 164-85.

–. "Uncovering and Reconstructing Family Violence: Ontario Criminal Case Files." In Iacovetta and Mitchinson, *On the Case*, 289-311.

Gordon, Linda. *Heroes of Their Own Lives: The Politics and History of Family Violence – Boston, 1880-1960.* Champaign: University of Illinois Press, 1988.

Gorham, Deborah. "The 'Maiden Tribute to Modern Babylon' Re-Examined: Child Prostitution and the Idea of Childhood in Late Victorian England." *Victorian Studies* 21 (Spring 1978): 353-79.

Gouglas, Sean, and John C. Weaver. "A Postcolonial Understanding of Law and Society: Exploring Criminal Trials in Colonial Queensland." *Australian Journal of Legal History* 7 (2003): 231-53.

Govier, Katherine. *Between Men.* Markham, ON: Penguin Books Canada, 1987.

Gray, James H. *Booze: When Whisky Ruled the West.* Saskatoon: Fifth House, 1995.

–. *Red Lights on the Prairies: The Bonanza Years When the Wide-Open Frontier Was a Hooker's Happy Hunting Ground.* 1971. Reprint, Scarborough, ON: New American Library, 1973.

Graybill, Andrew R. *Policing the Great Plains: Rangers, Mounties, and the North American Frontier, 1875-1920.* Lincoln: University of Nebraska Press, 2007.

–. "Rangers, Mounties, and the Subjugation of Indigenous Peoples, 1870-1885." *Great Plains Quarterly* 24 (Spring 2004): 83-100.

Greaves, C.S. "On Rape." An appendix to Henri Elzéar Taschereau, *The Criminal Statute Law of the Dominion of Canada.* 2nd ed. Toronto: Carswell and Co. Law Publishers, 1888.

Greenwood, F. Murray, and Beverley Boissery. *Uncertain Justice: Canadian Women and Capital Punishment, 1754-1953.* Toronto: Dundurn Press, 2000.

Grove, Frederick Phillip. *Settlers of the Marsh.* 1925. Reprint, Toronto: McClelland and Stewart, 1989.

Guy, Donna J. *Sex and Danger in Buenos Aires: Prostitution, Family, and Nation in Argentina.* Lincoln: University of Nebraska Press, 1991.

–. *White Slavery and Mothers Alive or Dead: The Troubled Meeting of Sex, Gender, Public Health and Progress in Latin America.* Lincoln: University of Nebraska Press, 2000.

Hall, Catherine. "Introduction: Thinking the Postcolonial, Thinking the Empire." In *Cultures of Empire: A Reader; Colonizers in Britain and the Empire in the Nineteenth and Twentieth Centuries*, edited by Catherine Hall, 1-35. New York: Routledge, 2000.

Hall, Stuart. *The Multicultural Question*. Milton Keynes, UK: Pavis Centre for Social and Cultural Research, 2001.

Hamilton, A.C., C.M. Sinclair, and Gerald Friesen. "'Justice Systems' and Manitoba's Aboriginal People: An Historical Survey." In *River Road: Essays in Manitoba and Prairie History*, edited by Gerald Friesen, 49-78. Winnipeg: University of Manitoba Press, 1996.

Hammerton, A. James. *Cruelty and Companionship: Conflict in Nineteenth-Century Married Life*. London: Routledge, 1992.

Hanson, Carter F. "'Working in the West': The Canadian Prairie as Playground in Late-Victorian Literature." *American Review of Canadian Studies* 31 (Winter 2001): 657-77.

Harring, Sidney L. "Indian Law, Sovereignty and State Law." In *A Companion to American Indian History*, edited by Philip J. Deloria and Neal Salisbury, 441-59. Malden, MA: Blackwell, 2002.

–. *White Man's Law: Native People in Nineteenth-Century Canadian Jurisprudence*. Toronto: University of Toronto Press for the Osgoode Society for Canadian Legal History, 1998.

Harris, Douglas. *Fish, Law, and Colonialism: The Legal Capture of Salmon in British Columbia*. Toronto: University of Toronto Press, 2001.

Harris, Seymour F. *Principles of Criminal Law*. 6th ed. London: Stevens and Haynes, 1892.

Hartog, Hendrik. "Lawyering, Husbands' Rights, and 'The Unwritten Law' in Nineteenth-Century America." *Journal of American History* 84, 1 (1997): 67-96.

Harvey, Kathryn. "Amazons and Victims: Wife-Abuse in Working-Class Montréal, 1869-1879." *Journal of the Canadian Historical Association* 2 (1991): 131-48.

–. "To Love, Honour and Obey: Wife-Battering in Working-Class Montreal, 1869-1879." In *Age of Transition: Readings in Canadian Social History, 1800-1900*, edited by Norman Knowles, 227-42. Toronto: Harcourt Brace Canada, 1998.

Hay, Douglas. "Property, Authority, and the Criminal Law." In *Albion's Fatal Tree: Crime and Society in Eighteenth-Century England*, edited by Douglas Hay, Peter Linbaugh, John G. Rule, and E.P. Thompson, 17-63. New York: Pantheon, 1975.

Healy, Theresa. "Engendering Resistance: Women Respond to Relief in Saskatoon, 1930-1932." In *"Other Voices": Historical Essays on Saskatchewan Women*, edited by David De Brou and Aileen Moffatt, 94-115. Regina: Canadian Plains Research Center, 1995.

Henderson, Jennifer. *Settler Feminism and Race Making in Canada*. Toronto: University of Toronto Press, 2003.

Henriot, Christian. *Prostitution and Sexuality in Shanghai: A Social History, 1849-1949*. Translated by Noël Castelino. Cambridge: Cambridge University Press, 2001.

Hershatter, Gail. *Dangerous Pleasures: Prostitution and Modernity in Twentieth-Century Shanghai*. Berkeley: University of California Press, 1997.

Hewitt, Steve. "The Masculine Mountie: The Royal Canadian Mounted Police as a Male Institution, 1914-1939." *Journal of the Canadian Historical Association* 7 (1996): 153-74.

Hieller, Paul T. "To Encourage the Preservation and Sanctity of the Marriage Relation: Victorian Attitudes in Arizona Territory and the Murder Prosecution of Frank C. Kibbey." *Journal of Arizona History* 42, 3 (2001): 249-76.

Higham, Carol L., and Bob Thacker, eds. *One West, Two Myths: A Comparative Reader*. Calgary: University of Calgary Press, 2004.

Hildebrandt, Walter. *Views from Fort Battleford: Constructed Visions of an Anglo-Canadian West*. Regina: Canadian Plains Research Center, 1994.

Hinther, Rhonda L. "The Oldest Profession in Winnipeg: The Culture of Prostitution in the Point Douglas Segregated District, 1909-1912." *Manitoba History* 41 (Spring/Summer 2001): 2-13.

Hirsch, Susan F., and Mindie Lazarus-Black. "Performance and Paradox: Exploring Law's Role in Hegemony and Resistance." In Lazarus-Black and Hirsch, *Contested States*, 1-31.

Hoerder, Dirk. "How the Intimate Lives of Subaltern Men, Women, and Children Confound the Nation's Master Narratives." *Journal of American History* 88 (December 2001): http://www.historycooperative.org.

Hoffer, Peter C., and N.E.H. Hull. *Murdering Mothers: Infanticide in England and New England, 1558-1803*. New York: New York University Press, 1981.

Hogeveen, B. "An Intrusive and Corrective Government: Political Rationalities and the Governance of Plains Aboriginals, 1870-1890." In *Governable Places: Readings on Governmentality and Crime Control*, edited by Russell Smandych, 287-312. Aldershot, UK: Dartmouth Publishing, 1999.

Holloway, Pippa. "Regulation and the Nation: Comparative Perspectives on Prostitution and Public Policy." *Journal of Women's History* 15, 1 (2003): 202-21.

Horrall, S.W. "The (Royal) North-West Mounted Police and Prostitution on the Canadian Prairies." *Prairie Forum* 10 (Spring 1985): 105-27.

Houston, Susan. "'The Waifs and Strays' of a Late Victorian City: Juvenile Delinquency in Toronto." In *Childhood and Family in Canadian History*, edited by Joy Parr, 129-42. Toronto: McClelland and Stewart, 1982.

Hungry Wolf, Beverly. *The Ways of My Grandmothers*. New York: Quill, 1982.

Hunt, Alan. *Governing Morals: A Social History of Moral Regulation*. Cambridge: Cambridge University Press, 1999.

Hurtado, Albert. *Intimate Frontiers: Sex, Gender, and Culture in Old California*. Albuquerque: University of New Mexico Press, 1999.

Hutchinson, Robert. *City of Winnipeg Police Force: A Century of Service*. Winnipeg: City of Winnipeg Police, 1974.

Iacovetta, Franca, and Wendy Mitchinson, eds. *On the Case: Explorations in Social History*. Toronto: University of Toronto Press, 1998.

–. "Social History and Case File Research." In Iacovetta and Mitchinson, *On the Case*, 3-21.

Inglis, Amirah. *"Not a White Woman Safe": Sexual Anxiety and Politics in Port Moresby, 1920-1934*. Canberra: Australian National University Press, 1974.

Jackel, Susan, ed. *A Flannel Shirt and Liberty: British Emigrant Gentlewomen in the Canadian West, 1880-1914*. Vancouver: UBC Press, 1982.

Jackson, Louise A. "'Singing Birds as Well as Soap Suds': The Salvation Army's Work with Sexually Abused Girls in Edwardian England." *Gender and History* 12, 1 (2000): 107-26.

Jacobs, Janet Liebman. "Reassessing Mother Blame in Incest." *Signs* 15, 3 (1990): 499-515.

Jacobson, Lisa. "Revitalizing the American Home: Children's Leisure and the Revitalization of Play, 1920-1940." *Journal of Social History* 30 (Spring 1997): 581-96.

Jahn, Cheryle. "Class, Gender and Agrarian Socialism: The United Farm Women of Saskatchewan, 1926-1931." *Prairie Forum* 19, 2 (1994): 189-204.

Jameson, Elizabeth, and Jeremy Mouat. "Telling Differences: The Forty-Ninth Parallel and Historiographies of the West and Nation." *Pacific Historical Review* 75, 2 (2006): 183-230.

Jayewardene, C.H.S. *The Penalty of Death: The Canadian Experiment*. Toronto: Lexington, 1977.

Jennings, John N. "The Northwest Mounted Police and Indian Policy, 1874-1896." PhD diss., University of Toronto, 1979.

Johnston, Susan J. "Twice Slain: Female Sex-Trade Workers and Suicide in British Columbia, 1870-1920." *Journal of the Canadian Historical Association* 5 (1994): 147-66.

Jones, David C. "'There Is Some Power about the Land': The Western Agrarian Press and Country Life Ideology." In *The Prairie West: Historical Readings*, 2nd ed., edited by R. Douglas Francis and Howard Palmer, 455-74. Edmonton: Pica Pica Press, 1995.

Kann, Mark E. *The Republic of Men: The American Founders, Gendered Language, and Patriarchal Politics*. New York: New York University Press, 1998.

Katerberg, William H. "A Northern Vision: Frontiers and the West in the Canadian and American Imagination." *American Review of Canadian Studies* 33 (Winter 2003): 543-63.

Kealey, Linda. "Women and Labour during World War I: Women Workers and the Minimum Wage in Manitoba." In *First Days, Fighting Days: Women in Manitoba History*, edited by Mary Kinnear, 76-99. Regina: Canadian Plains Research Center, 1987.

Kerber, Linda. "Separate Spheres, Female Worlds, Woman's Place: The Rhetoric of Women's History." *Journal of American History* 75, 1 (1988): 9-39.

Kermoal, Nathalie. "Les rôles et les souffrances des femmes métisses lors de la Résistance de 1870 et de la Rébellion de 1885." *Prairie Forum* 19 (Fall 1994): 153-68.

Kinnear, Mary. "'Do You Want Your Daughter to Marry a Farmer?' Women's Work on the Farm, 1922." In *Canadian Papers in Rural History*, vol. 6, edited by Donald H. Akenson, 137-53. Ganonoque, ON: Langdale Press, 1988.

Kirkby, Diane, ed. *Sex, Power, and Justice: Historical Perspectives on Law in Australia*. Melbourne: Oxford University Press, 1995.

Kirkby, Diane, and Catherine Coleborne, eds. *Law, History, Colonialism: The Reach of Empire*. Manchester, UK: Manchester University Press, 2001.

Klassen, Henry C. "Lawyers, Finance, and Economic Development in Southwestern Alberta, 1884 to 1920." In *Beyond the Law: Lawyers and Business in Canada, 1830-1930*, edited by Carol Wilton, 298-319. Toronto: Butterworths Canada for the Osgoode Society for Canadian Legal History, 1990.

Klausen, Susan. "Doctors and Dying Declarations: The Role of the State in Abortion Regulation in British Columbia, 1917-1937." *Canadian Bulletin of Medical History* 13 (1996): 53-81.

Knafla, Louis A. "From Oral to Written Memory: The Common Law Tradition in Western Canada." In *Law and Justice in a New Land: Essays in Western Canadian Legal History*, edited by Louis A. Knafla, 31-77. Toronto: Carswell, 1986.

–. "Introduction: Laws and Societies in the Anglo-Canadian North-West Frontier and Prairie Provinces, 1670-1940." In *Laws and Societies in the Canadian Prairie West, 1670-1940*, edited by Louis A. Knafla, 1-55. Vancouver: UBC Press, 2005.

–. "Violence on the Western Canadian Frontier: A Historical Perspective." In *Violence in Canada: Sociopolitical Perspectives*, 2nd ed., edited by Jeffrey Ian Ross, 10-39. Somerset, NJ: Transaction Publishers, 2004.

Knafla, Louis A., and Susan W.S. Binnie, "Beyond the State: Law and Legal Pluralism in the Making of Modern Societies." In *Law, Society, and the State: Essays in Modern Legal History*, edited by Louis A. Knafla and Susan W.S. Binnie, 3-35. Toronto: University of Toronto Press, 1995.

Knafla, Louis A., and Richard Klumpenhouwer. *Lords of the Western Bench: A Biographical History of the Supreme and District Courts of Alberta, 1876-1990*. Calgary: Legal Archives Society of Alberta, 1997.

Knowles, Valerie. *Strangers at Our Gates: Canadian Immigration and Immigration Policy, 1540-1997*. Rev. ed. Toronto: Dundurn Press, 1997.

Kramar, Kirsten. *Unwilling Mothers, Unwanted Babies: Infanticide in Canada*. Vancouver: UBC Press, 2005.

Kramer, Reinhold, and Tom Mitchell. *Walk Towards the Gallows: The Tragedy of Hilda Blake, Hanged 1899*. Don Mills, ON: Oxford University Press, 2002.

Kushner, Howard I. "The Persistence of the Frontier Thesis: Gender, Myth, and Self-Destruction." In "Reinterpreting the American Experience: Women, Gender, and American Studies." Special issue, Part 1, *Canadian Review of American Studies* 23 (1992): 53-82.

Lang, Sabine. *Men as Women, Women as Men: Changing Gender in Native American Cultures*. Austin: University of Texas Press, 1998.

Langdon, M. Elizabeth. "Female Crime in Calgary, 1914-1941." In *Law and Justice in a New Land: Essays in Western Canadian Legal History*, edited by Louis A. Knafla, 293-312. Toronto: Carswell, 1986.

Larson, E. Nick. "Canadian Prostitution Control between 1914 and 1970: An Exercise in Chauvinist Reasoning." *Canadian Journal of Law and Society* 7 (Fall 1992): 137-56.

Laycock, David. *Populism and Democratic Thought in the Canadian Prairies, 1910-1945*. Toronto: University of Toronto Press, 1990.

Lazarus-Black, Mindie, and Susan F. Hirsch, eds. *Contested States: Law, Hegemony and Resistance*. New York: Routledge, 1994.

Leger-Anderson, Ann. "Canadian Prairie Women's History: An Uncertain Enterprise." *Journal of the West* 37 (January 1998): 47-59.

Lehr, John C. "Peopling the Prairies with Ukrainians." In *Immigration in Canada: Historical Perspectives*, edited by Gerald Tulchinsky, 177-202. Toronto: Copp Clark Longman, 1994.

Lepp, Annalee E. "Dis/membering the Family: Marital Breakdown, Domestic Conflict, and Family Violence in Ontario, 1830-1920." PhD diss., Queen's University, 2001.

Leslie, John, and Ron Macguire. "The Historical Development of the Indian Act." 2nd ed. Ottawa: Treaties and Historical Research Branch, Department of Indian Affairs and Northern Development, 1979.

Lévesque, Andrée. "Éteindre le 'Red Light': Les reformateurs et la prostitution – Montréal, 1865-1925." *Urban History Review* 17, 3 (1989): 191-201.

Levine, Philippa. *Prostitution, Race, and Politics: Policing Venereal Disease in the British Empire*. New York: Routledge, 2003.

–. "The White Slave Trade and the British Empire." In *Criminal Justice History*. Vol. 17, *Crime, Gender, and Sexuality in Criminal Prosecutions*, edited by Louis A. Knafla, 133-46. Westport, CT: Greenwood Press, 2002.

Lindström-Best, Varpu. *Defiant Sisters: A Social History of Finnish Immigrant Women in Canada*. Toronto: Multicultural History Society of Ontario, 1988.

–. "'I Won't Be a Slave!' – Finnish Domestics in Canada, 1911-1930." In *Looking into My Sister's Eyes: An Exploration in Women's History*, edited by Jean Burnet, 33-54. Toronto: Multicultural History Society of Ontario, 1986.

Loewen, Royden. "Beyond the Monolith of Modernity: New Trends in Immigrant and Ethnic History." *Agricultural History* 81 (Spring 2007): 204-27.

Loo, Tina. *Making Law, Order, and Authority in British Columbia, 1821-1871.* Toronto: University of Toronto Press, 1994.

—. "Of Moose and Men: Hunting for Masculinities in British Columbia, 1880-1939." *Western Historical Quarterly* 32, 3 (2001): 296-319.

—. "The Road from Bute Inlet: Crime and Colonial Identity in British Columbia." In Phillips, Loo, and Lewthwaite, *Crime and Criminal Justice*, 112-42.

—. "Savage Mercy: Native Culture and the Modification of Capital Punishment in Nineteenth-Century British Columbia." In *Qualities of Mercy: Justice, Punishment, and Discretion*, edited by Carolyn Strange, 104-29. Vancouver: UBC Press, 1996.

Lord, Alexandra M. "Models of Masculinity: Sex Education, the United States Public Health Service, and the YMCA, 1919-1924." *Journal of the History of Medicine and Allied Sciences* 58, 2 (2003): 123-52.

Lutz, John. "Relating to the Country: The Lekwammen and the Extension of European Settlement." In *Beyond the City Limits: Rural History in British Columbia*, edited by Ruth Sandwell, 17-32. Vancouver: UBC Press, 1999.

Lux, Maureen K. *Medicine That Walks: Disease, Medicine, and Canadian Plains Native People, 1800-1940.* Toronto: University of Toronto Press, 2001.

MacDonald, Robert H. *Sons of the Empire: The Frontier and the Boy Scout Movement, 1890-1918.* Toronto: University of Toronto Press, 1993.

Macfarlane, Christine Anne. "'Unfortunate Women of My Class': Prostitution in Winnipeg." Master's thesis, University of Manitoba and University of Winnipeg, 2002.

MacKinnon, Catherine. "Feminism, Marxism, Method, and the State: Toward a Feminist Jurisprudence." *Signs* 8, 4 (1983): 635-58.

—. "Feminist Approaches to Sexual Assault in Canada and the United States: A Brief Retrospective." In *Challenging Times: The Women's Movement in Canada and the United States*, edited by Constance Backhouse and David H. Flaherty, 186-92. Montreal and Kingston: McGill-Queen's University Press, 1992.

Macleod, R.C. *The North-West Mounted Police and Law Enforcement, 1873-1905.* Toronto: University of Toronto Press, 1976.

Macleod, R.C., and Heather Rollason. "'Restrain the Lawless Savages': Native Defendants in the Criminal Courts of the North-West Territories, 1878-1885." *Journal of Historical Sociology* 10 (June 1997): 157-83.

MacPherson, Ian, and John Herd Thompson. "The Business of Agriculture: Prairie Farmers and the Adoption of 'Business Methods,' 1880-1950." In *The Prairie West: Historical Readings*, 2nd ed., edited by R. Douglas Francis and Howard Palmer, 475-96. Edmonton: Pica Pica Press, 1995.

Macpherson, M.A. *Outlaws of the Canadian West.* Edmonton: Lone Pine Publishing, 1999.

Magnarella, Paul J. "Justice in a Pluralistic Society: The Cultural Defence on Trial." *Journal of Ethnic Studies* 19 (1991): 65-84.

Malleck, Daniel. "'Its Baneful Influences Are Too Well Known': Debates over Drug Use in Canada, 1867-1908." *Canadian Bulletin of Medical History* 14, 2 (1997): 263-88.

Marquis, Greg. "Vancouver Vice: The Police and the Negotiation of Morality, 1904-1935." In *Essays in the History of Canadian Law.* Vol. 6, *British Columbia and the Yukon*, edited by Hamar Foster and John McLaren, 242-73. Toronto: University of Toronto Press for the Osgoode Society for Canadian Legal History, 1995.

Martens, Jeremy C. "Settler Homes, Manhood and 'Houseboys': An Analysis of Natal's Rape Scare of 1886." *Journal of South African Studies* 28, 2 (2002): 379-400.

Martin, Roderick Graham. "The Common Law and the Justices of the Supreme Court of the North-West Territories, 1887-1907." Master's thesis, University of Calgary, 1997.

Mawani, Renisa. *Colonial Proximities: Crossracial Encounters and Juridical Truths in British Columbia, 1871-1921*. Vancouver: UBC Press, 2009.

–. "In Between and Out of Place: Racial Hybridity, Liquor, and the Law in Late 19th and Early 20th Century British Columbia." *Canadian Journal of Law and Society* 15, 2 (2000): 9-38.

Maynard, Steven. "The Maple Leaf (Gardens) Forever: Sex, Canadian Historians, and National History." *Journal of Canadian Studies* 36, 2 (2001): 70-105.

McCallum, Margaret E. "Prairie Women and the Struggle for a Dower Law, 1905-1920." In *Historical Perspectives on Law and Society in Canada*, edited by Tina Loo and Lorna R. McLean, 306-20. Toronto: Copp Clark Longman, 1994.

McClintock, Anne. *Imperial Leather: Race, Gender, and Sexuality in the Colonial Contest*. New York: Routledge, 1995.

McClung, J.W. *Law West of the Bay*. Calgary: Legal Archives Society of Alberta, 1998.

McClung, Nellie L. *Painted Fires*. Toronto: Thomas Allen, 1925.

–. *The Stream Runs Fast: My Own Story*. Toronto: Thomas Allen, 1945.

McCulloch, Jock. *Black Peril, White Virtue: Sexual Crime in Southern Rhodesia, 1902-1935*. Bloomington: Indiana University Press, 2000.

McGrath, Ann. "'Black Velvet': Aboriginal Women and Their Relations with White Men in the Northern Territory, 1910-40." In *So Much Hard Work: Women and Prostitution in Australian History*, edited by Kay Daniels, 233-97. Melbourne: Fontana/Collins, 1984.

McGrath, Ann, and Winona Stevenson. "Gender, Race, and Policy: Aboriginal Women and the State in Canada and Australia." *Labour/Le Travail* 38 (Fall 1996): 37-53.

McKay, Ian. "The Liberal Order Framework: A Prospectus for a Reconnaissance of Canadian History." *Canadian Historical Review* 81, 4 (December 2000): 617-45.

McLaren, Angus. *Our Own Master Race: Eugenics in Canada, 1885-1945*. Toronto: McClelland and Stewart, 1990.

–. *Trials of Masculinity: Policing Sexual Boundaries, 1870-1930*. Chicago: University of Chicago Press, 1997.

McLaren, Angus, and Arlene Tigar McLaren. *The Bedroom and the State: The Changing Practices and Politics of Contraception and Abortion in Canada, 1880-1980*. Toronto: McClelland and Stewart, 1986.

McLaren, John. "The Canadian Magistracy and the Anti-White Slavery Campaign." In *Canadian Perspectives on Law and Society: Issues in Legal History*, edited by W. Wesley Pue and Barry Wright, 329-53. Ottawa: Carleton University Press, 1998.

–. "Chasing the Social Evil: Moral Fervour and the Evolution of Canada's Prostitution Laws, 1867-1917." *Canadian Journal of Law and Society* 1 (1986): 125-65.

–. "Race and the Criminal Justice System in British Columbia, 1892-1920: Constructing Chinese Crimes." In *Essays in the History of Canadian Law*. Vol. 8, *In Honour of R.C.B. Risk*, edited by G. Blaine Baker and Jim Phillips, 398-442. Toronto: University of Toronto Press for the Osgoode Society for Canadian Legal History, 1999.

–. "White Slavers: The Reform of Canada's Prostitution Laws and Patterns of Enforcement, 1900-1920." *Criminal Justice History* 8 (1987): 53-119.

McLaren, John, A.R. Buck, and Nancy E. Wright, eds. *Despotic Dominion: Property Rights in British Settler Societies*. Vancouver: UBC Press, 2004.

McLaren, John, Hamar Foster, and Chet Orloff, eds. *Law for the Elephant, Law for the Beaver: Essays in the Legal History of the North American West.* Regina: Canadian Plains Research Center, 1992.

McLean, Lorna. "'Deserving' Wives and 'Drunken' Husbands: Wife Beating, Marital Conduct, and the Law in Ontario, 1850-1910." *Histoire sociale/Social History* 35, 69 (2002): 59-81.

McManus, Sheila. "Gender(ed) Tensions in the Work and Politics of Alberta Farm Women, 1905-29." In *Telling Tales: Essays in Western Women's History,* edited by Catherine A. Cavanaugh and Randi R. Warne, 123-46. Vancouver: UBC Press, 2000.

–. *The Line Which Separates: Race, Gender, and the Making of the Alberta-Montana Border.* Lincoln: University of Nebraska Press, 2005.

McMaster, Lindsey. *Working Girls in the West: Representations of Wage-Earning Women.* Vancouver: UBC Press, 2008.

McPherson, Kathryn. "Was the 'Frontier' Good for Women? Historical Approaches to Women and Agricultural Settlement in the Prairie West, 1870-1925." *Atlantis* 25, 1 (2000): 75-86.

Méthot, Mélanie. "Social Thinkers, Social Actors in Winnipeg and Montreal at the Turn of the Century." PhD diss., University of Calgary, 2001.

Miller, J.R. "Owen Glendower, Hotspur, and Canadian Indian Policy." In *Sweet Promises: A Reader on Indian-White Relations in Canada,* edited by J.R. Miller, 323-52. Toronto: University of Toronto Press, 1991.

–. *Shingwauk's Vision: A History of Native Residential Schools.* Toronto: University of Toronto Press, 2000.

–. *Skyscrapers Hide the Heavens: A History of Indian-White Relations in Canada.* 3rd ed. Toronto: University of Toronto Press, 2000.

Mintz, Steven, and Susan Kellog. *Domestic Revolutions: A Social History of American Family Life.* New York: Free Press, 1988.

Mitchell, Tom. "'Blood with the Taint of Cain': Immigrant Labouring Children, Manitoba Politics, and the Execution of Emily Hilda Blake." *Journal of Canadian Studies* 28 (Winter 1993-94): 49-71.

Mitchinson, Wendy. "The WCTU: 'For God, Home, and Native Land': A Study in Nineteenth-Century Feminism." In *A Not Unreasonable Claim: Women and Reform in Canada, 1880-1920s,* edited by Linda Kealey, 151-67. Toronto: Women's Press, 1979.

Mohr, James C. *Doctors and the Law: Medical Jurisprudence in Nineteenth-Century America.* Baltimore: Johns Hopkins University Press, 1993.

Monkkonen, Eric H. *The Dangerous Class: Crime and Poverty in Columbus, Ohio, 1860-1885.* Cambridge, MA: Harvard University Press, 1975.

Moon, Danielle. "Unnatural Fathers and Vixen Daughters: A Case of Incest, San Diego, California, 1894." *Journal of the West* 39, 4 (2000): 8-16.

Moore, Erin P. *Gender, Law, and Resistance in India.* Tucson: University of Arizona Press, 1998.

Mosse, George L. *The Image of Man: The Creation of Modern Masculinity.* New York: Oxford University Press, 1996.

Moulds, Elizabeth F. "Chivalry and Paternalism: Disparities of Treatment in the Criminal Justice System." *Western Political Quarterly* 31 (1978): 416-30.

Mountain Horse, Mike. *My People the Bloods.* Edited by Hugh Dempsey. Calgary: Glenbow-Alberta Institute and Blood Tribal Council, 1979.

Muir, Edward, and Guido Ruggiero, eds. *Microhistory and the Lost Peoples of Europe.* Translated by Eren Branch. Baltimore: Johns Hopkins University Press, 1991.

Murphy, Emily. *The Black Candle.* Toronto: Thomas Allen, 1922.

–. *Janey Canuck in the West.* 1910. Reprint, Toronto: University of Toronto Press, 1975.

–. "A Straight Talk on Courts." *Maclean's,* 1 October 1920, 9-10, 27, 58.

Myers, Tamara. *Caught: Montreal's Modern Girls and the Law, 1869-1945.* Toronto: University of Toronto Press, 2006.

Myers, Tamara, and Carolyn Strange. "Retorts, Runaways, and Riots: Patterns of Resistance in Canadian Reform Schools for Girls, 1920-1960." *Journal of Social History* 34, 3 (2001): 69-98.

Nadelhaft, Jerome. "Alcohol and Wife Abuse in Antebellum Male Temperance Literature." *Canadian Review of American Studies* 25, 1 (1995): 15-43.

Nagel, Joane. "Masculinity and Nationalism: Gender and Sexuality in the Making of Nations." *Ethnic and Racial Studies* 21 (March 1998): 242-69.

Nahanee, Teressa. "Sexual Assault and Inuit Females: A Comment on Cultural Bias." In *Confronting Sexual Assault: A Decade of Legal and Social Change,* edited by Julian Roberts and Renate Mohr, 192-204. Toronto: University of Toronto Press, 1994.

Newton, Janice. "From Wage Slave to White Slave: The Prostitution Controversy and the Early Canadian Left." In *Beyond the Vote: Canadian Women and Politics,* edited by Linda Kealey and Joan Sangster, 217-39. Toronto: University of Toronto Press, 1989.

Nightingale, Margo. "Judicial Attitudes and Differential Treatment: Native Women in Sexual Assault Cases." *Ottawa Law Review* 23, 1 (1991): 71-98.

Nilsen, Deborah. "The 'Social Evil': Prostitution in Vancouver, 1900-1920." In *In Her Own Right: Selected Essays in Women's History,* edited by Barbara Latham and Cathy Kess, 205-28. Victoria: Camosun College, 1980.

Noonkester, Myron C. "The Third British Empire: Transplanting the English Shire to Wales, Scotland, Ireland, and America." *Journal of British Studies* 36, 3 (1997): 251-84.

Ogborn, Miles. "Law and Discipline in Nineteenth-Century English State Formation: The *Contagious Diseases Acts* of 1864, 1866, and 1869." *Journal of Historical Sociology* 6, 1 (1993): 28-54.

Osborne, Judith A. "The Crime of Infanticide: Throwing the Baby Out with the Bathwater." *Canadian Journal of Family and Law* 6, 1 (1987): 47-59.

Owen, Michael. "'Lighting the Pathways for New Canadians': Methodist and United WMS Missions in Eastern Alberta, 1904-1940." In *Standing on New Ground: Women in Alberta,* edited by Catherine A. Cavanaugh and Randi R. Warne, 1-19. Edmonton: University of Alberta Press, 1993.

Owram, Douglas. "*On the Case: Explorations in Social History*: A Roundtable Discussion." *Canadian Historical Review* 81 (June 2000): 266-92.

–. *Promise of Eden: The Canadian Expansionist Movement and the Idea of the West, 1856-1900.* Toronto: University of Toronto Press, 1992.

Palmer, Bryan D. "Foucault and the Historians: The Case of *On the Case*." *Literary Review of Canada* (Summer 1999): 11-17.

Palmer, Howard. *Patterns of Prejudice: A History of Nativism in Alberta.* Toronto: McClelland and Stewart, 1982.

–. "Reluctant Hosts: Anglo-Canadian Views of Multi-Culturalism in the Twentieth Century." In *Immigration in Canada: Historical Perspectives,* edited by Gerald Tulchinsky, 297-333. Toronto: Copp Clark Longman, 1994.

Parker, Graham. "The Legal Regulation of Sexual Activity and the Protection of Females." *Osgoode Hall Law Journal* 21 (June 1983): 187-224.

Parr, Joy. *Labouring Children: British Immigrant Apprentices to Canada, 1869 to 1924.* Montreal and Kingston: McGill-Queen's University Press, 1980.

Pascoe, Peggy. "Western Women at the Cultural Crossroads." In *Trails: Towards a New Western History,* edited by Patricia Nelson Limerick, Clyde A. Milner II, and Charles E. Rankin, 40-58. Lawrence: University of Kansas Press, 1991.

Paxton, Nancy L. *Writing under the Raj: Gender, Race, and Rape in the British Colonial Imagination, 1830-1947.* New Brunswick, NJ: Rutgers University Press, 1999.

Pedersen, Diana. "Providing a Woman's Conscience: The YWCA, Female Evangelicalism, and the Girl in the City, 1870-1930." In *Canadian Women: A Reader,* edited by Wendy Mitchinson et al., 194-210. Toronto: Harcourt Brace Canada, 1996.

Peers, Douglas M. "Is Humpty Dumpty Back Together Again? The Revival of Imperial History and the *Oxford History of the British Empire.*" *Journal of World History* 13 (Fall 2002): 451-67.

Perry, Adele. "The Autocracy of Love and the Legitimacy of Empire: Intimacy, Power, and Scandal in Nineteenth-Century Metlakahtlah." *Gender and History* 16, 2 (2004): 261-88.

–. *On the Edge of Empire: Gender, Race, and the Making of British Columbia, 1849-1871.* Toronto: University of Toronto Press, 2001.

Peterson del Mar, David. *Beaten Down: A History of Interpersonal Violence in the West.* Seattle: University of Washington Press, 2002.

Pettipas, Katherine. *Severing the Ties that Bind: Government Repression of Indigenous Religious Ceremonies on the Prairies.* Winnipeg: University of Manitoba Press, 1994.

Phillips, Jim. "Crime and Punishment in the Dominion of the North: Canada from New France to the Present." In *Crime History and Histories of Crime,* edited by Clive Emsley and Louis A. Knafla, 163-99. Westport, CT: Greenwood Press, 1996.

–. "The History of Canadian Criminal Justice, 1750-1920." In *Criminology: A Reader's Guide,* edited by Jane Gladstone, Richard Ericson, and Clifford Shearing, 65-124. Toronto: Centre of Criminology, University of Toronto, 1991.

–. "Women, Crime, and Criminal Justice in Early Halifax, 1750-1800." In Phillips, Loo, and Lewthwaite, *Crime and Criminal Justice,* 174-206.

Phillips, Jim, Tina Loo, and Susan Lewthwaite, eds. *Crime and Criminal Justice: Essays in the History of Canadian Law.* Toronto: University of Toronto Press for the Osgoode Society for Canadian Legal History, 1994.

Pickles, Katie, and Myra Rutherdale, eds. *Contact Zones: Aboriginal and Settler Women in Canada's Colonial Past.* Vancouver: UBC Press, 2005.

Pierson, Ruth Roach, and Nupur Chaudhuri, eds. *Nation, Empire, Colony: Historicizing Gender and Race.* Bloomington: Indiana University Press, 1998.

Pivar, David J. *Purity and Hygiene: Women, Prostitution, and the "American Plan," 1900-1930.* Westport, CT: Greenwood Press, 2002.

Pollak, Otto. *The Criminality of Women.* New York: A.S. Barnes, 1961.

Pon, Madge. "Like a Chinese Puzzle: The Construction of Chinese Masculinity in *Jack Canuck.*" In *Gender and History in Canada,* edited by Joy Parr and Mark Rosenfeld, 80-100. Toronto: Copp Clark, 1996.

Ponting, J. Rick, and Roger Gibbins. *Out of Irrelevance: A Socio-Political Introduction to Indian Affairs in Canada.* Toronto: Butterworths, 1980.

Prang, Margaret. "'The Girl God Would Have Me Be': The Canadian Girls in Training, 1915-1939." *Canadian Historical Review* 66, 2 (1985): 154-84.

Pratt, Mary Louise. *Imperial Eyes: Travel Writing and Transculturation.* New York: Routledge, 1992.

Prentice, Alison, Paula Bourne, Gail Cuthbert Brandt, Beth Light, Wendy Mitchinson, and Naomi Black. *Canadian Women: A History.* 2nd ed. Toronto: Harcourt Brace Canada, 1996.

Prkachin, Yvan. "'Chinks Pay Heavily for Hitting the Pipe': The Perception and Enforcement of Canada's New Drug Laws in Rural and Northern British Columbia, 1908-30." *BC Studies* 153 (Spring 2007): 73-105.

Provinse, John H. "The Underlying Sanctions of Plains Indian Culture." In *Social Anthropology of the North American Tribes*, edited by Frederick Eggan, 341-63. 1937. Reprint, Chicago: University of Chicago Press, 1955.

Pue, W. Wesley. "Planting Legal Culture in Colonial Soil: Legal Professionalism in the Lands of the Beaver and Kangaroo." In *Shaping Nations: Constitutionalism and Society in Australia and Canada,* edited by Linda Cardinal and David Headon, 91-115. Ottawa: University of Ottawa Press, 2002.

Quintero, Gilbert. "Making the Indian: Colonial Knowledge, Alcohol, and Native Americans." *American Indian Culture and Research Journal* 25, 4 (2001): 57-71.

Raibmon, Paige. "Theatres of Contact: The Kwakwaka'wakw Meet Colonialism in British Columbia and at the Chicago World's Fair." *Canadian Historical Review* 81 (June 2000): 157-90.

Ramey, Jessie. "The Bloody Blonde and the Marble Woman: Gender and Power in the Case of Ruth Snyder." *Journal of Social History* 37, 3 (2004): 625-40.

Ramos, Sandy. "'A Most Detestable Crime': Gender Identities and Sexual Violence in the District of Montreal, 1803-1843." *Journal of the Canadian Historical Association* 12 (2001): 27-48.

Ray, Arthur J., Jim Miller, and Frank Tough. *Bounty and Benevolence: A History of Saskatchewan Treaties.* Montreal and Kingston: McGill-Queen's University Press, 2000.

Razack, Sherene. "Gendered Racial Violence and Spatialized Justice: The Murder of Pamela George." In *Race, Space, and the Law: Unmapping a White Settler Society,* edited by Sherene Razack, 121-56. Toronto: Between the Lines, 2002.

—. "Race, Space, and Prostitution: The Making of a Bourgeois Subject." *Canadian Journal of Women and the Law* 10, 2 (1998): 338-78.

—. "What Is to Be Gained by Looking White People in the Eye? Culture, Race, and Gender in Cases of Sexual Violence." In *Criminology at the Crossroads: Feminist Readings in Crime and Justice,* edited by Kathleen Daly and Lisa Maher, 225-45. Oxford: Oxford University Press, 1998.

Read, Frederick. "Early History of the Manitoba Courts." *Manitoba Bar News* 10 (October 1987): 451-55, 467-71, 482-84.

Reagan, Leslie J. "'About to Meet Her Maker': Women, Doctors, Dying Declarations, and the State's Investigation of Abortion, Chicago, 1867-1940." *Journal of American History* 77 (March 1991): 1240-64.

—. *When Abortion Was a Crime: Women, Medicine, and the Law in the United States, 1867-1973.* Berkeley: University of California Press, 1997.

Reid, John Phillip. *Patterns of Vengeance: Crosscultural Homicide in the North American Fur Trade.* Pasadena, CA: North Judicial Circuit Historical Society, 1999.

–. *Policing the Elephant: Crime, Punishment, and Social Behaviour on the Overland Trail.* San Marino, CA: Huntington Library, 1997.

Rennie, Bradford James. *The Rise of Agrarian Democracy: The United Farmers and Farm Women of Alberta, 1909-1921.* Toronto: University of Toronto Press, 2000.

Robb, George, and Nancy Erber, eds. *Disorder in the Court: Trials and Sexual Conflict at the Turn of the Century.* New York: New York University Press, 1999.

Roberts, M.J.D. "Feminism and the State in Later Victorian England." *The Historical Journal* 38, 1 (1995): 85-110.

Roberts, Marie-Louise. *Civilization without Sexes: Reconstructing Gender in Postwar France, 1917-1927.* Chicago: University of Chicago Press, 1994.

Robertson, Stephen. "Age of Consent Law and the Making of Modern Childhood in New York City, 1886-1921." *Journal of Social History* 35, 4 (2002): 781-98.

–. "Separating the Men from the Boys: Masculinity, Psychosexual Development, and Sex Crime in the United States, 1930-1960s." *Journal of the History of Medicine and Allied Sciences* 56, 1 (2001): 3-35.

–. "Signs, Marks, and Private Parts: Doctors, Legal Discourses, and Evidence of Rape in the United States, 1823-1930." *Journal of the History of Sexuality* 8, 3 (1998): 345-88.

Robinson, Gregory. "Rougher Than Any Other Nationality? Ukrainian Canadians and Crime in Alberta, 1915-1929." In *Age of Contention: Readings in Canadian Social History, 1900-1945,* edited by Jeffrey Keshen, 214-30. Toronto: Harcourt Brace Canada, 1997.

Rollings-Magnusson, Sandra. "Hidden Homesteaders: Women, the State, and Patriarchy in the Saskatchewan Wheat Economy, 1870-1930." *Prairie Forum* 24, 2 (1999): 171-83.

Roome, Patricia Anne. "Henrietta Muir Edwards: The Journey of a Canadian Feminist." PhD diss., Simon Fraser University, 1996.

Rosen, Ruth. "Go West Young Woman? Prostitution on the Frontier." *Reviews in American History* 14 (March 1986): 91-96.

Rosen, Ruth, and Sue Davidson, eds. *The Mamie Papers.* Old Westbury, NY: Feminist Press, 1977.

Rotenberg, Lori. "The Wayward Worker: Toronto's Prostitute at the Turn of the Century." In *Women at Work: Ontario, 1850-1930,* edited by Janice Acton, Penny Goldsmith, and Bonnie Shepard, 33-69. Toronto: Canadian Women's Educational Press, 1974.

Rotundo, Anthony. *American Manhood: Transformations in Masculinity from the Revolution to the Modern Era.* New York: Basic Books, 1993.

Rugh, Susan Sessions. "Civilizing the Countryside: Class, Gender, and Crime in Nineteenth-Century Rural Illinois." *Agricultural History* 76, 1 (2002): 58-81.

Russel, William Oldnell. "Rape." In *Russel on Crimes: A Treatise on Crimes and Misdemeanours.* 6th ed. London: Stevens and Sons, 1896.

Russell, Peter H. *The Judiciary in Canada: The Third Branch of Government.* Toronto: McGraw-Hill Ryerson, 1987.

Rutherdale, Myra. *Women and the White Man's God: Gender and Race in the Canadian Mission Field.* Vancouver: UBC Press, 2002.

Ryan, Mary P. *Women in Public: Between Banners and Ballots, 1825-1880.* Baltimore: Johns Hopkins University Press, 1992.

Sams, Julia P. "The Availability of the 'Cultural Defence' as an Excuse in Criminal Behaviour." *Georgia Journal of International and Comparative Law* 16 (1986): 335-54.

Sandwell, Ruth W. "The Limits of Liberalism: The Liberal Reconnaissance and the History of the Family in Canada." *Canadian Historical Review* 84 (September 2003): 423-50.

Sangster, Joan. "Archiving Feminist Histories: Women, the 'Nation' and Metanarratives in Canadian Historical Writing." *Women's Studies International Forum* 29 (2006): 255-64.

–. "Criminalizing the Colonized: Ontario Native Women Confront the Criminal Justice System, 1920-1960." *Canadian Historical Review* 80 (March 1999): 32-60.

–. "Domesticating Girls: The Sexual Regulation of Aboriginal and Working-Class Girls in Twentieth-Century Canada." In Pickles and Rutherdale, *Contact Zones,* 179-203.

–. *Girl Trouble: Female Delinquency in English Canada.* Toronto: Between the Lines, 2002.

–. "Masking and Unmasking the Sexual Abuse of Children: Perceptions of Violence against Children in 'The Badlands' of Ontario, 1916-1930." *Journal of Family History* 25, 4 (2000): 504-26.

–. "'Pardon Tales' from Magistrate's Courts: Women, Crime, and the Court in Peterborough County, 1920-50." *Canadian Historical Review* 74 (June 1993): 505-31.

–. *Regulating Girls and Women: Sexuality, Family, and the Law in Ontario, 1920-1960.* Don Mills, ON: Oxford University Press, 2001.

Sauer, R. "Infanticide and Abortion in Nineteenth-Century Britain." *Population Studies* 32 (March 1978): 81-93.

Saunders, Kay. "Controlling (Hetero)Sexuality: The Implementation and Operation of Contagious Diseases Legislation in Australia, 1868-1945." In Kirkby, *Sex, Power, and Justice,* 2-18.

Scully, Pamela. "Criminality and Conflict in Rural Stellenbasch, South Africa, 1870-1900." *Journal of African History* 39 (1989): 289-300.

–. "Rape, Race, and Colonial Culture: The Sexual Politics of Identity in the Nineteenth-Century Cape Colony, South Africa." *American Historical Review* 100 (April 1995): 335-59.

Seidman, Robert. "Mens Rea and the Reasonable African." *International and Comparative Law Quarterly* 15 (1966): 1135-64.

–. "Witch Murder and Mens Rea." *Modern Law Review* 28 (1965): 46-61.

Shapiro, Ann-Louise. *Breaking the Codes: Female Criminality in Fin-de-Siècle Paris.* Stanford: Stanford University Press, 1996.

–. "'Stories More Terrifying than the Truth Itself': Narratives of Female Criminality in *Fin de Siècle* Paris." In *Gender and Crime in Modern Europe,* edited by Margaret L. Arnot and Cornelie Usborne, 204-21. London: University College London Press, 1999.

Sharp, Paul. *The Agrarian Revolt in Western Canada: A Survey Showing American Parallels.* Minneapolis: University of Minnesota Press, 1949.

Sharpe, Jenny. "The Unspeakable Limits of Rape: Colonial Violence and Counter-Insurgency." *Genders* 10 (Spring 1991): 25-46.

Shear, Keith. "'Not Welfare or Uplift Work': White Women, Masculinity, and Policing in South Africa." *Gender and History* 8, 3 (1996): 393-415.

Simmons, Christina. *Making Marriage Modern: Women's Sexuality from the Progressive Era to World War II.* Oxford: Oxford University Press, 2009.

Singha, Radhika. *A Despotism of Law: Crime and Justice in Early Colonial India.* Oxford: Oxford University Press, 1998.

Sinha, Mrinalini. *Colonial Masculinity: The "Manly Englishman" and the "Effeminate Bengali" in the Late Nineteenth Century.* Manchester, UK: Manchester University Press, 1995.

–. "Gender and Imperialism: Colonial Policy and the Ideology of Moral Imperialism in Late-Nineteenth-Century Bengal." In *Changing Men: New Directions in Research on Men and Masculinity*, edited by M.S. Kimmel, 217-31. Beverly Hills, CA: Sage, 1987.

Skogan, Wesley G. "Social Change and the Future of Violent Crime." In *Violence in America: The History of Crime*, edited by Ted Robert Gurr, 235-50. Newbury Park, CA: Sage Publications, 1989.

Smith, Donald. "Bloody Murder Almost Became Miscarriage of Justice." *Calgary Herald Sunday Magazine*, 23 July 1989.

Smith, Erica. "'Gentlemen, This Is No Ordinary Trial': Sexual Narratives in the Trial of the Reverend Corbett, Red River, 1863." In *Reading beyond Words: Contexts for Native History*, edited by Jennifer S.H. Brown and Elizabeth Vibert, 364-80. Peterborough, ON: Broadview Press, 1996.

Smith, Keith D. *Liberalism, Surveillance, and Resistance: Indigenous Communities in Western Canada, 1877-1927.* Edmonton: Athabasca University Press, 2009.

Snell, James G. "'The White Life for Two': The Defence of Marriage and Sexual Morality in Canada, 1890-1914." In *Canadian Family History: Selected Readings*, edited by Bettina Bradbury, 381-96. Toronto: Copp Clark Pitman, 1992.

Spierenburg, Pieter. "Long-Term Trends in Homicide: Theoretical Reflections and Dutch Evidence, Fifteenth to Twentieth Centuries." In *The Civilization of Crime: Violence in Town and Country since the Middle Ages*, edited by Eric A. Johnson and Eric H. Monk-konen, 63-105. Urbana: University of Illinois Press, 1996.

Spurr, David. *The Rhetoric of Empire: Colonial Discourse in Journalism, Travel Writing, and Imperial Administration.* Durham, NC: Duke University Press, 1993.

Spongeberg, Mary. *Feminizing Venereal Disease: The Body of the Prostitute in Nineteenth-Century Medical Discourse.* New York: New York University Press, 1997.

Stasiulis, Daiva, and Radha Jhappan. "The Fractious Politics of a Settler Society: Canada." In *Unsettling Settler Societies: Articulations of Gender, Race, Ethnicity, and Class*, edited by Daiva Stasiulis and Nira Yuval-Davis, 95-131. London: Sage Publications, 1995.

Stasiulis, Daiva, and Nira Yuval-Davis. "Introduction: Beyond Dichotomies – Gender, Race, Ethnicity, and Class in Settler Societies." In *Unsettling Settler Societies: Articulations of Gender, Race, Ethnicity, and Class*, edited by Daiva Stasiulis and Nira Yuval-Davis, 1-38. London: Sage Publications, 1995.

Stoler, Ann Laura. "Tense and Tender Ties: The Politics of Comparison in North American History and (Post) Colonial Studies." *Journal of American History* 88 (December 2001): 829-65.

Stone, Lawrence. "Interpersonal Violence in English Society, 1300-1980." *Past and Present* no. 101 (1983): 22-33.

Strange, Carolyn. "Discretionary Justice: Political Culture and the Death Penalty in New South Wales and Ontario, 1890-1920." In *Qualities of Mercy: Justice, Punishment, and Discretion*, edited by Carolyn Strange, 130-65. Vancouver: UBC Press, 1996.

–. "Introduction." In *Qualities of Mercy: Justice, Punishment, and Discretion*, edited by Carolyn Strange, 3-20. Vancouver: UBC Press, 1996.

–. "The Lottery of Death: Capital Punishment, 1867-1976." *Manitoba Law Journal* 23 (1996): 594-619.

–. "Murder and Meanings in US Historiography." *Feminist Studies* 25 (Fall 1999): 679-90.

–. "Patriarchy Modified: The Criminal Prosecution of Rape in York County, Ontario, 1880-1930." In Phillips, Loo, and Lewthwaite, *Crime and Criminal Justice,* 207-51.

–. "Stories of Their Lives: The Historian and the Capital Case File." In Iacovetta and Mitchinson, *On the Case,* 25-48.

–. *Toronto's Girl Problem: The Perils and Pleasures of the City, 1880-1920.* Toronto: University of Toronto Press, 1995.

–. "The Undercurrents of Penal Culture: Punishment and the Body in Mid-Twentieth-Century Canada." *Law and History Review* 19 (Summer 2001): http://www.history cooperative.org/journals/lhr/19.2/strange.html.

–. "Wounded Womanhood and Dead Men: Chivalry and the Trials of Clara Ford and Carrie Davies." In *Gender Conflicts: New Essays in Women's History,* edited by Franca Iacovetta and Mariana Valverde, 149-88. Toronto: University of Toronto Press, 1993.

Strange, Carolyn, and Tina Loo. *Making Good: Law and Moral Regulation in Canada, 1867-1939.* Toronto: University of Toronto Press, 1997.

Strong-Boag, Veronica. "'Ever a Crusader': Nellie McClung, First-Wave Feminist." In *Rethinking Canada: The Promise of Women's History,* 3rd ed., edited by Veronica Strong-Boag and Anita Clair Fellman, 271-84. Toronto: Oxford University Press, 1997.

–. *The New Day Recalled: Lives of Girls and Women in English Canada, 1919-1939.* Markham, ON: Penguin Books, 1988.

Stubbs, Roy St. George. "The First Juvenile Court Judge: The Honourable Thomas Mayne Daly, KC." *Papers of the Historical and Scientific Society of Manitoba* ser. 3, nos. 34-35 (1977-78): 49-66.

Sutherland, Neil. *Children in English-Canadian Society: Framing the Twentieth-Century Consensus.* Toronto: University of Toronto Press, 1976.

Svanström, Yvonne. *Policing Public Women: The Regulation of Prostitution in Stockholm, 1812-1880.* Stockholm: Atlas Akkademi, 2000.

Swainger, Jonathan. "Advisors to the Crown and the Prerogative of Mercy." Chapter 4 in *The Canadian Department of Justice and the Completion of Confederation, 1867-78.* Vancouver: UBC Press, 2000.

–, ed. *Alberta Supreme Court at 100: History and Authority.* Edmonton: University of Alberta Press for the Osgoode Society for Canadian Legal History, 2007.

–. "Creating the Peace: Crimes and Community Identity in Northeastern British Columbia, 1930-1950." In *Criminal Justice History.* Vol. 19, *Violent Crime in North America,* edited by Louis A. Knafla, 131-54. Westport, CT: Greenwood Press, 2003.

–. "A Distant Edge of Authority: Capital Punishment and the Prerogative of Mercy in British Columbia, 1872-1880." In *Essays in the History of Canadian Law.* Vol. 6, *British Columbia and the Yukon,* edited by Hamar Foster and John McLaren, 204-41. Toronto: University of Toronto Press for the Osgoode Society for Canadian Legal History, 1995.

–. "Ideology, Social Capital, and Entrepreneurship." In *Beyond the Law: Lawyers and Business in Canada, 1830-1930,* edited by Carol Wilton, 377-402. Toronto: Butterworths Canada for the Osgoode Society for Canadian Legal History, 1990.

Swyripa, Frances. "Negotiating Sex and Gender in the Ukrainian Bloc Settlement." *Prairie Forum* 20 (Fall 1995): 149-74.

–. *Wedded to the Cause: Ukrainian Canadian Women and Ethnic Identity, 1891-1991.* Toronto: University of Toronto Press, 1993.

Thomas, Nicholas. *Colonialism's Culture: Anthropology, Travel, and Government.* Princeton, NJ: Princeton University Press, 1994.

Thompson, Elizabeth. *The Pioneer Woman: A Canadian Character*. Montreal and Kingston: McGill-Queen's University Press, 1991.

Thompson, John Herd. *Forging the Prairie West: The Illustrated History of Canada*. Toronto: Oxford University Press, 1998.

–. *Harvests of War: The Prairie West, 1914-1918*. Toronto: McClelland and Stewart, 1983.

Treaty 7 Elders and Tribal Council, with Walter Hildebrandt, Sarah Carter, and Dorothy First Rider. *The True Spirit and Original Intent of Treaty 7*. Montreal and Kingston: McGill-Queen's University Press, 1996.

Tremeear, W.J. *The Criminal Code and the Law of Criminal Evidence in Canada*. Toronto: Canada Law Book Company, 1908.

Trexler, Richard C. *Sex and Conquest: Gendered Violence, Political Order and the European Conquest of the Americas*. Ithaca, NY: Cornell University Press, 1995.

Trigger, Bruce. *Natives and Newcomers: Canada's "Heroic Age" Reconsidered*. Montreal and Kingston: McGill-Queen's University Press, 1985.

Usborne, Cornelie. *The Politics of the Body in Weimar Germany: Women's Reproductive Rights and Duties*. Ann Arbor: University of Michigan Press, 1992.

Valverde, Mariana. *The Age of Light, Soap, and Water: Moral Reform in English Canada, 1885-1925*. Toronto: McClelland and Stewart, 1991.

–. "'When the Mother of the Race is Free': Race, Reproduction, and Sexuality in First-Wave Feminism." In *Gender Conflicts: New Essays in Women's History*, edited by Franca Iacovetta and Mariana Valverde, 3-26. Toronto: University of Toronto Press, 1993.

van Heyningen, Elizabeth B. "The Social Evil in the Cape Colony, 1868-1902: Prostitution and the Contagious Diseases Act." *Journal of South African Studies* 10, 2 (1984): 170-97.

Van Kirk, Sylvia. *"Many Tender Ties": Women in Fur-Trade Society, 1670-1870*. 1980. Reprint, Winnipeg: Watson and Dwyer, 1991.

Vibert, Elizabeth. *Traders' Tales: Narratives of Cultural Encounters in the Columbia Plateau, 1807-1846*. Norman: University of Oklahoma Press, 1997.

Wagner, Martin. *A Sociology of Modernity: Liberty and Discipline*. London: Routledge, 1994.

Waiser, Bill. "Introduction: Place, Process, and the New Prairie Realities." *Canadian Historical Review* 84 (December 2003): 509-17.

Waiser, Bill, and Blair Stonechild. *Loyal Till Death: Indians and the North-West Rebellion*. Calgary: Fifth House, 1997.

Waite, Robert. "Violent Crime on the Western Frontier: The Experience of the Idaho Territory, 1863-1890." In *Criminal Justice History*. Vol. 19, *Violent Crime in North America*, edited by Louis A. Knafla, 53-74. Westport, CT: Greenwood Press, 2003.

Walker, Garthine. *Crime, Gender, and Social Order in Early Modern England*. Cambridge: Cambridge University Press, 2003.

Walker, James W. St. G. "The Case for Morality: The Quong Wing Files." In Iacovetta and Mitchinson, *On the Case*, 204-26.

–. *"Race," Rights and the Law in the Supreme Court of Canada*. Waterloo, ON: Wilfrid Laurier University Press for the Osgoode Society for Canadian Legal History, 1997.

Walkowitz, Judith. *City of Dreadful Delight: Narratives of Sexual Danger in Late-Victorian London*. Chicago: University of Chicago Press, 1992.

–. *Prostitution and Victorian Society: Women, Class, and the State*. Cambridge: Cambridge University Press, 1980.

Ward, W. Peter. *White Canada Forever: Popular Attitudes and Public Policy toward Orientals in British Columbia*. 2nd ed. Montreal and Kingston: McGill-Queen's University Press, 1990.

Ware, Vron. *Beyond the Pale: White Women, Racism, and History*. London: Verso, 1992.

Warne, Randi R. *Literature as Pulpit: The Christian Social Activism of Nellie L. McClung*. Waterloo, ON: Wilfrid Laurier University Press, 1993.

Wasburn, Josie. *The Underworld Sewer: A Prostitute Reflects on Life in the Trade, 1871-1909*. Lincoln: University of Nebraska Press, 1997.

Weaver, John C. *The Great Land Rush and the Making of the Modern World, 1650-1900*. Montreal and Kingston: McGill-Queen's University Press, 2003.

White, Kimberley. *Negotiating Responsibility: Law, Murder, and States of Mind*. Vancouver: UBC Press, 2008.

White, Luise. *The Comforts of Home: Prostitution in Colonial Nairobi*. Chicago: University of Chicago Press, 1990.

White, Pamela. "Restructuring the Domestic Sphere: Prairie Indian Women on Reserves – Image, Ideology, and State Policy, 1880-1930." PhD diss., McGill University, 1987.

Wiener, Martin J. *Men of Blood: Violence, Manliness, and Criminal Justice in Victorian England*. New York: Cambridge University Press, 2004.

–. *Reconstructing the Criminal: Culture, Law, and Policy in England, 1830-1914*. Cambridge: Cambridge University Press, 1990.

–. "The Sad Story of George Hall: Adultery, Murder, and the Politics of Mercy in Mid-Victorian England." *Social History* 24, 2 (1999): 174-95.

Willie, Richard A. *"These Legal Gentlemen": Lawyers in Manitoba: 1839-1900*. Winnipeg: Legal Research Institute, 1994.

Windholz, Anne M. "An Emigrant and a Gentleman: Imperial Masculinity, British Magazines, and the Colony That Got Away." *Victorian Studies* 42 (Summer 1999/2000): 631-58.

Wood, Susan. "God's Doormats: Women in Canadian Prairie Fiction." *Journal of Popular Culture* 14, 2 (1980): 350-59.

Woodsworth, James S. *My Neighbour: Urban Ills and Urban Reform, 1911*. Toronto: University of Toronto Press, 1972.

–. *Strangers within Our Gates: The Problem of the Immigrant*. 1909. Reprint, Toronto: University of Toronto Press, 1972.

Zaharia, Flora, and Leo Fox, eds. *Kitomahkitapiiminnooniksi: Stories from Our Elders*. Vol. 1. Edmonton: Donahue, 1995.

Index

NOTES: "(i)" after a page number indicates an illustration or map; "(t)," a table. "DIA" stands for Department of Indian Affairs

Aboriginal law, 45, 55, 68-70
Aboriginal men: depiction of Aboriginal masculinity, 232-33; grounds for divorce, 69; influence of negative stereotyping on white juries, 53, 76; legal defences and negative images of, 12, 53-54, 57-58, 76, 232; legal defences of ignorance, drunkenness, or culture, 53-54, 76, 232; mixed-blood men characterized as bad, 62
Aboriginal people: after Riel Rebellion, 20-21, 47; crime rate (1878-85), 45; culture vs liberal economic order, 37; defences used in court, 53, 54, 55, 73, 76, 232; dismantling of tribal system, 20-21; government efforts to disband and assimilate, 36-38; intrusive role of Indian agents re domestic violence, 72-73; justice system discriminatory, 2, 232, 238; murder trials (Aboriginal parties only), 53, 55, 58-59; pass system, 47, 64, 76, 254n15; perception of, courts' influence on, 12; sexual violence (within Aboriginal communities), 73-75, 123-24.

See also Aboriginal men; Aboriginal women; Indian Act
Aboriginal women: accusations of promiscuity from sexual offenders, 52, 53, 54, 76, 235-36; arrest and conviction patterns for prostitution, 103; effect of prison, 66-67; grounds for divorce, 69; liquor laws to control, 59-60, 62, 63-67, 76; mixed-blood women characterized as bad, 62; prostitution offences a special category of crime, 62-63, 76; race as mitigating circumstance in crimes by and against women, 52; rape linked to colonial conquest, 44-45; sexual assault complaints ignored due to negative stereotyping, 12, 45, 67, 73-75, 77, 232; statutory subordination, 37-38, 59-63; stereotyped as dangerous and dissolute, 17, 52, 53, 63, 76, 232; trespassing laws to control, 59-60, 62
abortion: courts' treatment of accomplices, 157-58; criminalization of, 152-54, 159, 172; in novel *Painted Fires*, 144, 145; prosecution and convictions patterns,

109; for equal treatment of male and female murderers, 216, 226; fears about miscegenation and female delinquency, 99; first female magistrate in British Empire, 97, 98(i); idyllic view of the West, 141; opinion re birth control, 153-54; on testing prostitutes for venereal disease, 110-11; view of female offenders, 98-99; for woman suffrage within cult of domesticity, 91

Murray, Anna C., 212

My People the Bloods (Mountain Horse and Hungry Wolf), 68-69

Nagey, Annie, 130-31

Nahanee, Teressa, 73

nation building: definition, 243n7; family as foundation of freedom in liberal order, 22-25, 230, 237; hierarchies of difference and national identity, 13; settlement of the West as cornerstone, 18, 230; sexual relations between colonized and colonizer prohibited, 19

National Committee for the Suppression of the White Slave Traffic, 95

National Council of Women in Canada, 92-93, 97, 112, 178

national identity, 13

National Ladies Association, 86

National Policy, 20, 128-29

nativism, 39-40

Neigel, Adam, 191, 192-93

New Imperialism, 20

newspapers' coverage of sex crimes, 120-21

Noonkester, Myron, 33

North West Mounted Police (NWMP): difficulty in regulating Aboriginal prostitution, 63-64; epitome of normative British Canadian masculinity, 29, 30(i), 31(i); increase in manpower after Riel Rebellion, 47; legal records involving Aboriginal peoples, 6-7; myth re role in ensuring peacefulness of West, 2-3, 12, 31; portrayal as moral icon, 32; purported purpose, 31; reaction to complaints about Indian agent, 66

North-West Territories, 4, 5(i), 6, 33-35. *See also* Alberta; Saskatchewan

Northwest Rebellion, 20-21

Noseda, Bertha. *See Motow* case

Nye, Alfred, 107

Oleskiw, Theodore, 221-22

Oliver, Frank, 38-39, 115

On Prostitution in the City of Paris (Parent-Duchâtelet), 84

On the Case: Explorations in Social History (Iacovetta and Mitchinson), 7

Opium and Drug Act, 150, 172

O'Reilly, Frank, 169-71

Osborne, Judith, 212

Oswald, Tammy, 174-75

Owram, Doug, 4

Painted Fires (McClung): city as site of potential moral ruin, 143-46; critique of carceral regime for women, 160; fears for moral decline and national malaise, 99, 144; narrative of narcoticism, 149-50; portrayal of male-dominated judicial system, 143-44, 145-46; portrayal of youth's sexual and moral delinquency, 146; stereotyping of working-class and immigrant girls, 160-61; trials of young immigrant girl in the city, 143-46

Pall Mall Gazette, 86

Parent-Duchâtelet, Alexandre Jean-Baptiste, 84

Pascoe, Peggy, 2, 12

paternalism, 3

patriarchy: companionate marriage and, 24; legitimation by hegemonic masculinity, 26; monogamous heterosexuality and patriarchal dominance imposed, 19, 68, 76-77, 233; murderesses viewed as symbol of unjust patriarchal legal system, 202-3; state intervention required if patriarch abused power, 175, 181, 200

Paul, Carl, 133-34

Paulsen, Marius, 187

Pearl, Jennie, 169

Pedley, Frank, 66, 71

PUBLICATIONS OF THE OSGOODE SOCIETY
FOR CANADIAN LEGAL HISTORY

2011   ROBERT J. SHARPE, *The Lazier Murder: Prince Edward County, 1884*
       PHILIP GIRARD, *Lawyers and Legal Culture in British North America: Beamish Murdoch of Halifax*
       JOHN MCLAREN, *Dewigged, Bothered and Bewildered: British Colonial Judges on Trial*
       LESLEY ERICKSON, *Westward Bound: Sex, Violence, the Law, and the Making of a Settler Society*

2010   JUDY FUDGE and ERIC TUCKER, eds., *Work on Trial: Canadian Labour Law Struggles*
       CHRISTOPHER MOORE, *The British Columbia Court of Appeal: The First Hundred Years*
       FREDERICK VAUGHAN, *Viscount Haldane: The Wicked Step-father of the Canadian Constitution*
       BARRINGTON WALKER, *Race on Trial: Black Defendants in Ontario's Criminal Courts, 1850-1950*

2009   WILLIAM KAPLAN, *Canadian Maverick: The Life and Times of Ivan C. Rand*
       R. BLAKE BROWN, *A Trying Question: The Jury in Nineteenth-Century Canada*
       BARRY WRIGHT AND SUSAN BINNIE, eds., *Canadian State Trials, Volume III: Political Trials and Security Measures, 1840-1914*
       ROBERT J. SHARPE, *The Last Day, the Last Hour: The Currie Libel Trial*

2008   CONSTANCE BACKHOUSE, *Carnal Crimes: Sexual Assault Law in Canada, 1900-1975*
       JIM PHILLIPS, R. ROY MCMURTRY, and JOHN SAYWELL, eds., *Essays in the History of Canadian Law, Vol. X: A Tribute to Peter N. Oliver*
       GREGORY TAYLOR, *The Law of the Land: Canada's Receptions of the Torrens System*
       HAMAR FOSTER, BENJAMIN BERGER, and A.R. BUCK, eds., *The Grand Experiment: Law and Legal Culture in British Settler Societies*

2007   ROBERT J. SHARPE and PATRICIA MCMAHON, *The Persons Case: The Origins and Legacy of the Fight for Legal Personhood*
LORI CHAMBERS, *Misconceptions: Unmarried Motherhood and the Ontario Children of Unmarried Parents Act, 1921-1969*
JONATHAN SWAINGER, ed., *The Alberta Supreme Court at 100: History and Authority*
MARTIN FRIEDLAND, *My Life in Crime and Other Academic Adventures*

2006   DONALD FYSON, *Magistrates, Police and People: Everyday Criminal Justice in Quebec and Lower Canada, 1764-1837*
DALE BRAWN, *The Court of Queen's Bench of Manitoba 1870-1950: A Biographical History*
R.C.B. RISK, *A History of Canadian Legal Thought: Collected Essays,* edited and introduced by G. Blaine Baker and Jim Phillips

2005   PHILIP GIRARD, *Bora Laskin: Bringing Law to Life*
CHRISTOPHER ENGLISH, ed., *Essays in the History of Canadian Law, Vol. IX: Two Islands, Newfoundland and Prince Edward Island*
FRED KAUFMAN, *Searching for Justice: An Autobiography*

2004   JOHN D. HONSBERGER, *Osgoode Hall: An Illustrated History*
FREDERICK VAUGHAN, *Aggressive in Pursuit: The Life of Justice Emmett Hall*
CONSTANCE BACKHOUSE and NANCY BACKHOUSE, *The Heiress vs the Establishment: Mrs. Campbell's Campaign for Legal Justice*
PHILIP GIRARD, JIM PHILLIPS, and BARRY CAHILL, eds., *The Supreme Court of Nova Scotia, 1754-2004: From Imperial Bastion to Provincial Oracle*

2003   ROBERT J. SHARPE and KENT ROACH, *Brian Dickson: A Judge's Journey*
GEORGE FINLAYSON, *John J. Robinette: Peerless Mentor*
PETER OLIVER, *The Conventional Man: The Diaries of Ontario Chief Justice Robert A. Harrison, 1856-1878*
JERRY BANNISTER, *The Rule of the Admirals: Law, Custom and Naval Government in Newfoundland, 1699-1832*

2002   JOHN T. SAYWELL, *The Law Makers: Judicial Power and the Shaping of Canadian Federalism*
DAVID MURRAY, *Colonial Justice: Justice, Morality and Crime in the Niagara District, 1791-1849*

F. MURRAY GREENWOOD and BARRY WRIGHT, eds., *Canadian State Trials, Volume II: Rebellion and Invasion in the Canadas, 1837-1839*
PATRICK BRODE, *Courted and Abandoned: Seduction in Canadian Law*

2001   ELLEN ANDERSON, *Judging Bertha Wilson: Law as Large as Life*
JUDY FUDGE and ERIC TUCKER, *Labour Before the Law: Collective Action in Canada, 1900-1948*
LAUREL SEFTON MACDOWELL, *Renegade Lawyer: The Life of J.L. Cohen*

2000   BARRY CAHILL, "*The Thousandth Man*": *A Biography of James McGregor Stewart*
A.B. MCKILLOP, *The Spinster and the Prophet: Florence Deeks, H.G. Wells, and the Mystery of the Purloined Past*
BEVERLEY BOISSERY and F. MURRAY GREENWOOD, *Uncertain Justice: Canadian Women and Capital Punishment*
BRUCE ZIFF, *Unforeseen Legacies: Reuben Wells Leonard and the Leonard Foundation Trust*

1999   CONSTANCE BACKHOUSE, *Colour-Coded: A Legal History of Racism in Canada, 1900-1950*
G. BLAINE BAKER and JIM PHILLIPS, eds., *Essays in the History of Canadian Law, Vol. VIII: In Honour of R.C.B. Risk*
RICHARD W. POUND, *Chief Justice W.R. Jackett: By the Law of the Land*
DAVID VANEK, *Fulfilment: Memoirs of a Criminal Court Judge*

1998   SIDNEY HARRING, *White Man's Law: Native People in Nineteenth-Century Canadian Jurisprudence*
PETER OLIVER, "*Terror to Evil-Doers*": *Prisons and Punishments in Nineteenth-Century Ontario*

1997   JAMES W. ST. G. WALKER, "*Race,*" *Rights and the Law in the Supreme Court of Canada: Historical Case Studies*
LORI CHAMBERS, *Married Women and Property Law in Victorian Ontario*
PATRICK BRODE, *Casual Slaughters and Accidental Judgments: Canadian War Crimes and Prosecutions, 1944-1948*
IAN BUSHNELL, *The Federal Court of Canada: A History, 1875-1992*

1996   CAROL WILTON, ed., *Essays in the History of Canadian Law, Vol. VII: Inside the Law – Canadian Law Firms in Historical Perspective*

WILLIAM KAPLAN, *Bad Judgment: The Case of Mr. Justice Leo A. Landreville*

F. MURRAY GREENWOOD and BARRY WRIGHT, eds., *Canadian State Trials, Volume I: Law, Politics and Security Measures, 1608-1837*

1995 DAVID WILLIAMS, *Just Lawyers: Seven Portraits*

HAMAR FOSTER and JOHN MCLAREN, eds., *Essays in the History of Canadian Law, Vol. VI: British Columbia and the Yukon*

W.H. MORROW, ed., *Northern Justice: The Memoirs of Mr. Justice William G. Morrow*

BEVERLEY BOISSERY, *A Deep Sense of Wrong: The Treason, Trials and Transportation to New South Wales of Lower Canadian Rebels after the 1838 Rebellion*

1994 PATRICK BOYER, *A Passion for Justice: The Legacy of James Chalmers McRuer*

CHARLES PULLEN, *The Life and Times of Arthur Maloney: The Last of the Tribunes*

JIM PHILLIPS, TINA LOO, and SUSAN LEWTHWAITE, eds., *Essays in the History of Canadian Law, Vol. V: Crime and Criminal Justice*

BRIAN YOUNG, *The Politics of Codification: The Lower Canadian Civil Code of 1866*

1993 GREG MARQUIS, *Policing Canada's Century: A History of the Canadian Association of Chiefs of Police*

F. MURRAY GREENWOOD, *Legacies of Fear: Law and Politics in Quebec in the Era of the French Revolution*

1992 BRENDAN O'BRIEN, *Speedy Justice: The Tragic Last Voyage of His Majesty's Vessel Speedy*

ROBERT FRASER, ed., *Provincial Justice: Upper Canadian Legal Portraits from the Dictionary of Canadian Biography*

1991 CONSTANCE BACKHOUSE, *Petticoats and Prejudice: Women and Law in Nineteenth-Century Canada*

1990 PHILIP GIRARD and JIM PHILLIPS, eds., *Essays in the History of Canadian Law, Vol. III: Nova Scotia*

CAROL WILTON, ed., *Essays in the History of Canadian Law, Vol. IV: Beyond the Law – Lawyers and Business in Canada 1830-1930*

1989   DESMOND BROWN, *The Genesis of the Canadian Criminal Code of 1892*
       PATRICK BRODE, *The Odyssey of John Anderson*

1988   ROBERT J. SHARPE, *The Last Day, the Last Hour: The Currie Libel Trial*
       JOHN D. ARNUP, *Middleton: The Beloved Judge*

1987   C. IAN KYER and JEROME BICKENBACH, *The Fiercest Debate: Cecil A.
       Wright, the Benchers and Legal Education in Ontario, 1923-1957*

1986   PAUL ROMNEY, *Mr. Attorney: The Attorney General for Ontario in Court,
       Cabinet and Legislature, 1791-1899*
       MARTIN FRIEDLAND, *The Case of Valentine Shortis: A True Story of
       Crime and Politics in Canada*

1985   JAMES SNELL and FREDERICK VAUGHAN, *The Supreme Court of Canada:
       History of the Institution*

1984   PATRICK BRODE, *Sir John Beverley Robinson: Bone and Sinew of the
       Compact*
       DAVID WILLIAMS, *Duff: A Life in the Law*

1983   DAVID H. FLAHERTY, ed., *Essays in the History of Canadian Law, Vol. II*

1982   MARION MACRAE and ANTHONY ADAMSON, *Cornerstones of Order:
       Courthouses and Town Halls of Ontario, 1784-1914*

1981   DAVID H. FLAHERTY, ed., *Essays in the History of Canadian Law, Vol. I*

LAW AND
SOCIETY

KIMBERLEY BROOKS, ed., *Justice Bertha Wilson: One Woman's Difference*

WAYNE V. MCINTOSH and CYNTHIA L. CATES, *Multi-Party Litigation: The Strategic Context*

RENISA MAWANI, *Colonial Proximities: Crossracial Encounters and Juridical Truths in British Columbia, 1871-1921*

JAMES B. KELLY and CHRISTOPHER P. MANFREDI, eds., *Contested Constitutionalism: Reflections on the Canadian Charter of Rights and Freedoms*

2008 CATHERINE E. BELL and ROBERT K. PATERSON, eds., *Protection of First Nations Cultural Heritage: Laws, Policy, and Reform*

RICHARD J. MOON, ed., *Law and Religious Pluralism in Canada*

CATHERINE E. BELL and VAL NAPOLEON, eds., *First Nations Cultural Heritage and Law: Case Studies, Voices, and Perspectives*

DOUGLAS C. HARRIS, *Landing Native Fisheries: Indian Reserves and Fishing Rights in British Columbia, 1849-1925*

PEGGY J. BLAIR, *Lament for a First Nation: The Williams Treaties of Southern Ontario*

2007 LORI G. BEAMAN, *Defining Harm: Religious Freedom and the Limits of the Law*

STEPHEN TIERNEY, ed., *Multiculturalism and the Canadian Constitution*

JULIE MACFARLANE, *The New Lawyer: How Settlement Is Transforming the Practice of Law*

KIMBERLEY WHITE, *Negotiating Responsibility: Law, Murder, and States of Mind*

DAWN MOORE, *Criminal Artefacts: Governing Drugs and Users*

HAMAR FOSTER, HEATHER RAVEN, and JEREMY WEBBER, eds., *Let Right Be Done: Aboriginal Title, the* Calder *Case, and the Future of Indigenous Rights*

DOROTHY E. CHUNN, SUSAN B. BOYD, and HESTER LESSARD, eds., *Reaction and Resistance: Feminism, Law, and Social Change*

MARGOT YOUNG, SUSAN B. BOYD, GWEN BRODSKY, and SHELAGH DAY, eds., *Poverty: Rights, Social Citizenship, and Legal Activism*

ROSANNA L. LANGER, *Defining Rights and Wrongs: Bureaucracy, Human Rights, and Public Accountability*

C.L. OSTBERG and MATTHEW E. WETSTEIN, *Attitudinal Decision Making in the Supreme Court of Canada*

CHRIS CLARKSON, *Domestic Reforms: Political Visions and Family Regulation in British Columbia, 1862-1940*

2006   JEAN MCKENZIE LEIPER, *Bar Codes: Women in the Legal Profession*
       GERALD BAIER, *Courts and Federalism: Judicial Doctrine in the United States, Australia, and Canada*
       AVIGAIL EISENBERG, ed., *Diversity and Equality: The Changing Framework of Freedom in Canada*

2005   RANDY K. LIPPERT, *Sanctuary, Sovereignty, Sacrifice: Canadian Sanctuary Incidents, Power, and Law*
       JAMES B. KELLY, *Governing with the Charter: Legislative and Judicial Activism and Framers' Intent*
       DIANNE POTHIER and RICHARD DEVLIN, eds., *Critical Disability Theory: Essays in Philosophy, Politics, Policy, and Law*
       SUSAN G. DRUMMOND, *Mapping Marriage Law in Spanish Gitano Communities*
       LOUIS A. KNAFLA and JONATHAN SWAINGER, eds., *Laws and Societies in the Canadian Prairie West, 1670-1940*
       IKECHI MGBEOJI, *Global Biopiracy: Patents, Plants, and Indigenous Knowledge*
       FLORIAN SAUVAGEAU, DAVID SCHNEIDERMAN, and DAVID TARAS, with RUTH KLINKHAMMER and PIERRE TRUDEL, *The Last Word: Media Coverage of the Supreme Court of Canada*
       GERALD KERNERMAN, *Multicultural Nationalism: Civilizing Difference, Constituting Community*
       PAMELA A. JORDAN, *Defending Rights in Russia: Lawyers, the State, and Legal Reform in the Post-Soviet Era*
       ANNA PRATT, *Securing Borders: Detention and Deportation in Canada*
       KIRSTEN JOHNSON KRAMAR, *Unwilling Mothers, Unwanted Babies: Infanticide in Canada*
       W.A. BOGART, *Good Government? Good Citizens? Courts, Politics, and Markets in a Changing Canada*
       CATHERINE DAUVERGNE, *Humanitarianism, Identity, and Nation: Migration Laws in Canada and Australia*
       MICHAEL LEE ROSS, *First Nations Sacred Sites in Canada's Courts*
       ANDREW WOOLFORD, *Between Justice and Certainty: Treaty Making in British Columbia*

2004   JOHN MCLAREN, ANDREW BUCK, and NANCY WRIGHT, eds., *Despotic Dominion: Property Rights in British Settler Societies*
       GEORGES CAMPEAU, *From UI to EI: Waging War on the Welfare State*

ALVIN J. ESAU, *The Courts and the Colonies: The Litigation of Hutterite Church Disputes*

CHRISTOPHER N. KENDALL, *Gay Male Pornography: An Issue of Sex Discrimination*

ROY B. FLEMMING, *Tournament of Appeals: Granting Judicial Review in Canada*

CONSTANCE BACKHOUSE and NANCY L. BACKHOUSE, *The Heiress vs the Establishment: Mrs. Campbell's Campaign for Legal Justice*

CHRISTOPHER P. MANFREDI, *Feminist Activism in the Supreme Court: Legal Mobilization and the Women's Legal Education and Action Fund*

ANNALISE ACORN, *Compulsory Compassion: A Critique of Restorative Justice*

2003   JONATHAN SWAINGER and CONSTANCE BACKHOUSE, eds., *People and Place: Historical Influences on Legal Culture*

JIM PHILLIPS and ROSEMARY GARTNER, *Murdering Holiness: The Trials of Franz Creffield and George Mitchell*

DAVID R. BOYD, *Unnatural Law: Rethinking Canadian Environmental Law and Policy*

IKECHI MGBEOJI, *Collective Insecurity: The Liberian Crisis, Unilateralism, and Global Order*

2002   REBECCA JOHNSON, *Taxing Choices: The Intersection of Class, Gender, Parenthood, and the Law*

JOHN MCLAREN, ROBERT MENZIES, and DOROTHY E. CHUNN, eds., *Regulating Lives: Historical Essays on the State, Society, the Individual, and the Law*

2001   JOAN BROCKMAN, *Gender in the Legal Profession: Fitting or Breaking the Mould*